To Mom - On Her 60TH -
Happy Birthday.
Happy Cooking.
Happy Eating

ura e Courtney
Dec. 21, 1985

Original Pen and Ink Illustrations
By
Polly Samuelson

COVER: QUEEN ANNE'S LACE
HALF TITLE PAGE: MOUNTAIN LAUREL
CONNECTICUT STATE FLOWER

Wild Iris

Wood Geranium

Moccasin Orchid (Lady's Slipper)

Eastern Columbine

Milkweed Pods

Longspur Violet

Dog Tooth Violet

Black-eyed Susan

Thistle

Jack-in-the Pulpit

Our Special Blend

a cookbook

Additional Copies may be obtained from:
OUR SPECIAL BLEND
226 Mill Hill Avenue
Bridgeport, Connecticut 06610
$13.95 per copy
$1.50 postage & handling

Make checks payable to The Rehabilitation Center of Eastern Fairfield County. Order blanks have been provided for your convenience in the back of this book. Share them with your friends or use them for your next gift order.

For wholesale or quantity buying, contact the above address.

Copyright © 1984 by
The Easter Seal Rehabilitation Center
of Eastern Fairfield County, Inc.
226 Mill Hill Avenue
Bridgeport, Connecticut 06610

Library of Congress Catalog Number 83-73727
ISBN Number 0-9613209-0-7

PRINTED IN U.S. BY HART GRAPHICS
8000 SHOAL CREEK BLVD.
AUSTIN, TEXAS 78758
NAN MULVANEY

Table of Contents

A MESSAGE FROM CRAIG CLAIBORNE, THE NEW YORK TIMES

*OUR SPECIAL BLEND is published for you by
The Auxiliary, The Rehabilitation Center
of Eastern Fairfield County, Connecticut, a
member of the Easter Seal Society.*

*All proceeds realized from the sale of this
book go to the "Rehab Center" to enable it
to continue its work with the physically
handicapped people of all ages and walks of
life from the surrounding communities it
serves.*

*I sincerely believe in the work they are
doing. Their efforts toward improving the
daily lives of handicapped individuals are
to be commended.*

Craig Claiborne

"I would be happy for you to use one of my favorite recipes, a Hazelnut Cheesecake. I think it is one of the best ever printed in The New York Times.*"*

Hazelnut Cheesecake

Bake: 300° 2 hr
Stand: 4 hr
Pan: 8x3 round (NOT a springform)

PREPARE NUTS: Because of the importance of the oven temperature for baking the cheesecake, the nuts must be toasted well in advance.

1½	cups	**hazelnuts,** shelled, toasted, hulled (almonds blanched, toasted, can also be used)	Preheat oven to 400°. Place nuts on a baking sheet or in a skillet. Bake, stirring often to brown evenly. When nicely browned, remove and cool. Cool oven also.

PREPARE PAN:

⅓	cup	**graham cracker crumbs** **butter**	Butter bottom and sides of pan well; shake crumbs around bottom and sides until well coated. Shake out excess; set pan aside.

PREPARE CHEESECAKE: When ready to make cheesecake, preheat oven to 300°. Place nuts in container of blender or food processor and blend to the desired texture (crunchy cake – coarse/fine; smooth cake – almost pastelike). Set aside.

2	lb	**cream cheese,** room temp	Place in bowl of electric mixer. Beat at low speed, increasing to high as the ingredients blend. Continue beating until smooth.
½	cup	**heavy cream**	
4		**eggs**	
1¾	cups	**sugar**	
1	tsp	**vanilla extract**	
		reserved nuts	Blend in thoroughly; pour and scrape batter into prepared pan and shake gently to level.

TO BAKE: Set pan inside a slightly wider pan. Pour ½" boiling water into larger pan. (Do not let edge of cheesecake pan touch the larger pan.) Place in oven. Bake (2hr). Turn off oven, let cake set in oven (1hr) longer. Lift cake out of water bath, place on rack. Let stand at least (2hr). To unmold, place a round cake plate over, turn both upside down. Serve lukewarm or at room temperature.

Craig Claiborne, The New York Times

About Our MicroScan Technique

...... The **MicroScan** technique which is a special feature of **OUR SPECIAL BLEND,** enables you to determine, at a glance, all ingredients and equipment needed, plus the approximate amount of time required to prepare each recipe. It also presents the ingredients in the order in which they are to be used. So, first you scan to quickly determine your cooking needs then you are ready to blend your masterpiece using our brief directions – all adding up to a real timesaver for today's busy culinary artist.

About Our Symbol

 ...... You will find our own symbol scattered throughout your book. It indicates added information about cooking in general or special hints for preparing the recipe at hand.

A Message From the Editor

...... Whether you whet your appetite with the beautiful illustrations or by preparing one of the carefully selected recipes using the **MicroScan** technique, we hope you will enjoy our book as much as we have enjoyed compiling it for you.

Now, encourage others to share your joy of accomplishment by giving **OUR SPECIAL BLEND** to family and friends. Remember – all proceeds go to help handicapped individuals so they too can create their own masterpieces in their kitchens and in their lives.

A Message To

...... Ken Thoman, Phyllis Aiello, Pat Braun, Teresa Carey, Barbara Clark, Judy Perkins, Monique Pouget, Wes Sager, Mary Telford ...... and many many more, too numerous to mention individually ...... a million thank you's for all your help.

Louise Thoman, Editor

Appetizers & Beverages

To encourage you to "join" our family via food, we have published here, menus and recipes representative of many of the diverse people of our area. You will find these menus on the reverse sides of all divider pages.

FRENCH
Soupe a l'Oignon
Bass – Beurre Blanc ou Rouge
Green Bean Bundles
Broiled Tomato Halves
Grand Marnier Soufflé

PUERTO RICAN
Caldo Gallego (Spanish Stew)
Almojabanas (Crullers)
Salad
Bien me Sabe or Mango Preserves
with Native Cheese
Coffee

ITALIAN
The Best Pasta Yet with Mom's
Spaghetti Sauce
Minestrone (Soup)
Bracciole di Manzo (Beef)
Broccoli al Limone
Tortoni or Spumoni

CUBAN
Black Bean Soup
Chicken Fricassee
Rice
Tomatoes, Green Peppers on Lettuce
Bed
Summer Lemon Layers or Fresh Fruit

A Super Mexican Nacho

Serve hot with corn chips for dipping

Serves: 10 or more
Bake: 400° 20-25 min
Pans: skillet (med); 11x7

1	lb	**ground beef,** lean
1	med	**onion,** chopped
1	tsp	**margarine**

Brown in skillet; drain fat.

	drops	**Tabasco sauce**
		salt to taste

Add to above; set aside.

1	can	**refried beans** (lg)
		reserved beef mix
1	can	**green chilies,** chopped (4oz)
3	cups	**Monterey Jack, Colby, OR cheddar cheese,** shredded

Layer in baking dish ending with cheese.

1	cup	**taco sauce**

Drizzle over cheese. Bake uncovered.

	chopped green onions; black olives, sliced; **avocado dip** OR **sour cream**

Garnish with any or all. Serve hot.

Christine Powers, Wallingford, Vt

Holiday Pie Snack

Serve hot with assorted crackers

Serves: 8-10
Bake: 350° 15 min
Pan: pie plate (9")

16	oz	**cream cheese,** room temp
4	Tbsp	**milk**

Combine in medium bowl and beat well.

1	jar	**chipped dried beef,** minced (5oz)
3	Tbsp	**green peppers,** chopped
2	Tbsp	**instant onion**
½	tsp	**pepper,** white
1	cup	**sour cream**

Add to above and mix well; pour into baking dish.

½	cup	**walnuts,** chopped

Sprinkle over top. Bake until hot.

Janet Ross, Trumbull

 PEPPER grows on a tropical vine bearing clusters that contain the round peppercorns. Black pepper uses the whole peppercorn. White pepper uses only the white inner kernel. Cayenne, paprika and tabasco are the products of capsicum which is more like our red and green peppers.

Sausage Rolls
(British)

Tasty

Yield: 20-25
Bake: 425° 20-25 min
Pan: baking sheet

PASTRY

1	cup	**flour**	}	Sift together.
	pinch	**salt**		

¾	cup	**margarine**	Cut into flour.
7	Tbsp	**water**, cold	Add to above mixing gently until a smooth elastic dough is formed.

(Add a few drops of water if needed.) Turn onto floured surface; knead briskly (5min). Sprinkle with flour; cover with damp cloth and let rest (10min). Roll out thinly; cut into pieces (2½x3).

1	lb	**sausage meat**, skinned	Cut into the same number of pieces as pastry strips.
		flour	Coat each piece of sausage; place in center of pastry strip. Starting with

shorter end, wrap pastry around sausage; dampen one side and seal. Leave ends open. Make 3 diagonal cuts across top of each roll.

1		**egg** (or milk)	Brush over crust; place on ungreased baking sheet. Bake; serve hot.

Margaret Lindsay, Trumbull

Marge's Hanky Panky

A tasty hot spread

Yield: 40 pieces
Bake: 350° 15 min
Pans: skillet (lg); cookie sheet

½	lb	**pork sausage**, sweet	}	Crumble into small pieces. Brown in skillet; drain well.
½	lb	**ground beef**, lean		

1	lb	**Velveeta cheese**, diced	}	Combine; add to above and blend well. (Garlic powder can be substituted if served on Triscuits.)
4	Tbsp	**taco sauce**		
1	tsp	**oregano**		
1	tsp	**garlic salt**		

1	loaf	**party rye bread**	Spread mixture on bread; place on cookie sheet. Bake until top bubbles.

Serve immediately. (Mixture can be frozen before spreading on bread.) Broil (2min) for a more brown appearance.

Alberta Kinne, Trumbull

Ch'un Chuan
(Chinese)

Spring rolls

Yield: 20 rolls
Marinate: 1 hr
Stovetop: 10 min
Pan: wok

½	lb	pork cutlet	Cut into string-size strips.
1½	tsp	soy sauce	
1	tsp	cornstarch	Combine; add pork and marinate.
1	tsp	cooking wine	
5	Tbsp	vegetable oil	On high heat, stir/fry pork (30sec); remove meat and drain well. Leave oil in pan.
½	lb	cabbage, shredded	
4		Chinese black mushrooms, shredded	Soak mushrooms until soft; pat dry. Add to wok and stir/fry quickly.
1		bamboo shoot, shredded	
1	Tbsp	soy sauce	
1	tsp	salt	Add to above; cover and cook (2min).
½	cup	chicken broth	
¼	cup	scallions, shredded reserved pork	Add to above and stir/fry (30sec).
1	Tbsp	cornstarch	Combine; add to above and cook until thickened. Remove from heat.
1	Tbsp	water, cold	
20		egg roll skins	Place 2 Tbsp of above mixture on each skin; roll into egg roll shape.
1	Tbsp	flour	Mix into paste; seal loose flap of rolls with paste.
1½	tsp	water, cold	
6	cups	oil	Deep fry in oil (375°) until golden (approx 5 rolls at a time). Remove; drain well and serve hot with a mixture of soy sauce and brown vinegar or duck sauce.

Mabel Yu, Trumbull

Chicken Livers in Wine

A special treat!

Serves: 8-10
Stovetop: 15-20 min
Pans: skillet (lg); chafing dish

1	lb	chicken livers	Wash; section.
½	cup	flour	
½	tsp	pepper	Combine; coat livers.
¾	tsp	salt	
¼	cup	vegetable oil	Heat; sauté livers until browned.
½	cup	wine, dry white	Add to above; cover tightly and simmer (15min). Remove to chafing dish; serve hot.
1	Tbsp	Worcestershire sauce	

Dorothy Noreiks, Stratford

Chicken Liver and Sausage Pâté

A pretty mold for any festive occasion

Serves: 20-24
Stovetop: 10-15 min
Blender or processor
Chill: 8-10 hr
Pan: loaf (7x5)

			Butter pan; line bottom and sides with wax paper.
1	lb	**chicken livers**	Rinse in cold water; pat dry. Set aside.
½	lb	**Italian sweet sausage**	Remove skin; cut in pieces. Sauté until fats are rendered but meat is not browned; remove and set aside.
		reserved livers	Add to skillet, sauté until pink but not browned; reserve.
¼	cup	**onion,** chopped	Puree in blender at low speed.
1	Tbsp	**bourbon**	
⅓	cup	**heavy cream** (divided)	Increase speed to medium; add livers one quarter at a time, alternating with 3 Tbsp cream. When smooth, remove half to large bowl.
		reserved livers (divided)	
		reserved sausage	To remaining mixture in blender, add sausage one third at a time, alternating with 2 Tbsp cream. Blend well.
½	tsp	**salt**	Add; blend 15 seconds. Pour contents into liver mixture in bowl; mix together well. Pour into prepared pan and refrigerate (8-10hr). Unmold and frost (2hr) before serving.
⅛	tsp	**nutmeg**	

FROSTING

16	oz	**cream cheese,** softened	Whip until smooth; frost loaf then refrigerate. Decorate as desired.
2	Tbsp	**butter,** softened	
¼	cup	**parsley,** chopped	

Jan McNaughton, Fairfield

NUTMEG is the only fruit to produce two spices (mace). When fruit ripens the husk splits and exposes the aril known as mace. This is outside the hard inner shell that holds the nutmeg. These pits are dried over slow fires for several weeks until the kernels rattle within. The shells are cracked and the kernels are then sold whole or ground.

Oeufs Aux Escargots
(French)

Elegant party fare

Serves: 4
Bake: 350° 8 min
Pan: skillet (med); 11x7

4		**eggs,** hard cooked	Cut each in half, lengthwise. Reserve whites; chop yolks and set aside.
1	can	**snails** (24), drained, diced	Sauté a few minutes in skillet.
2	Tbsp	**butter**	
4-6	drops	**lemon juice**	Sprinkle over snails.
2		**scallions,** minced	Add to above; mix well.
4	oz	**white wine** reserved egg yolks	
		reserved egg whites	Arrange on baking dish; fill with snail mixture and cover with Mornay sauce (see Index).
		paprika	Garnish. Bake.

Franceen Fugr-Dila, Fairfield

Clams Casino

Delicious

Serves: 2
Bake: 350° 15 min
Broil: 2-3 min

12		**clams**	Scrub shells; open but leave flesh in shells.
½	cup	**butter**	Blend well; top each clam with 1 tsp of mixture.
1	Tbsp	**garlic,** minced	
1	Tbsp	**pimiento,** minced	
3	Tbsp	**parsley,** chopped	
1	Tbsp	**Muenster cheese,** grated	
	dash	**white wine**	
1	Tbsp	**lemon juice**	
¼	lb	**bacon slices,** (1" squares)	Place one square on each clam. Bake then broil until golden.
		parsley **lemon wedges**	Garnish each clam.

Uwe Moeller, Chef
Hawley Manor Inn, Newtown

Hot Clam Dip

Can also be frozen

Serves: 12
Bake: 350° 20 min
Pans: 2 saucepans (sm);
    casserole (1qt)

2	cans	**clams**, minced (6½oz,ea)	Place in small saucepan; simmer (15min)
1	tsp	**lemon juice**	
½	cup	**butter**	In separate saucepan, melt butter. Sauté remainder of ingredients until soft. Combine with above; spoon into casserole.
1	med	**onion**, chopped	
1	clove	**garlic**, minced	
½		**green pepper**, chopped	
1	tsp	**parsley**	
1	tsp	**oregano**	
	dash	each:**Tabasco, cayenne pepper**	
½	cup	**Italian bread crumbs**	
8	oz	**Velveeta cheese,** crumbled	Sprinkle over top. Bake. Serve warm. To freeze, do not bake. When ready, bake while still frozen (45min).
	dash	**paprika**	
2	Tbsp	**Parmesan cheese**	

Carol Longo, Hamden

Perky Stuffed Clams

Great peppy flavor

Yield: 6 lg shells
Bake: 350° 15 min
Pans: skillet (med); shells

4	Tbsp	**butter**	Sauté until tender.
½	cup	each:**onions, celery,** minced	
¼	cup	**green pepper**, minced	
2	Tbsp	**flour**	Stir into above and mix well.
1	Tbsp	**Parmesan cheese,** grated	
¼	tsp	**salt**	
	dash	**pepper, Worcestershire sauce** and **hot pepper sauce**	
½	cup	**ritz cracker crumbs** (reserve ¼cup)	Add one quarter cup to above; mix well.
1	can	**minced clams,** undrained (7½oz)	Add and stir while cooking until thick and bubbly. Spoon into individual shells or spread in buttered casserole (8x12).
		reserved cracker crumbs	Combine and sprinkle over stuffing. Bake just until heated through.
1	Tbsp	**butter**, melted	

Florence Bolcer, Trumbull

Crab Dip

Serve warm on crackers or party rye

Serves: 6-8
Bake: 375° 15 min
Pan: casserole (sm)

8	oz	**cream cheese,** softened	Blend in medium bowl.
1	Tbsp	**milk**	
1	can	**crabmeat** (6½oz)	Add to above; mix and spread in casserole.
2	Tbsp	**onion,** chopped	
½	tsp	**horseradish**	
¼	tsp	each: **salt, pepper**	
		almonds, slivered (optional)	Sprinkle on top. Bake.

Joan Bendtsen, Stratford

Jazzland Crabmeat Balls

Creole joy in every bite

Yield: 2 doz
Broil: 10 min
Pan: cookie sheet

2	cans	**crabmeat** (6½oz,ea)	Drain; flake and place in medium bowl.
1	cup	**bread crumbs,** soft	Add to above and mix well. Shape into walnut-sized balls.
3	Tbsp	**sherry**	
1	Tbsp	**lemon juice**	
1	Tbsp	**onion,** grated	
1	tsp	**dry mustard**	
½	tsp	**salt**	
		pepper to taste	
12	slices	**bacon,** cut in half	Wrap around balls overlapping to allow for shrinkage; secure with toothpicks. Broil until crisp, turning to brown evenly.
		parsley	Garnish. Serve warm.

Hillandale Gourmet Club, Trumbull

 HORSERADISH is also known as German mustard and is known to stimulate the appetite.

Shrimp and Cheese Beignets

Two delicious morsels

Yield: 24 of each
Chill: 30 min to 8 hr
Deep fat: 3 min
Pans: saucepan (2qt); cookie sheet

PUFF PASTRY

½	cup	**butter**	} Place in saucepan over low heat; simmer until butter is melted.
1	cup	**water,** cold	
1	cup	**flour**	} Add to above; stir with wooden spoon until mixture forms a ball of paste and leaves side of pan (3-4min). Remove from heat.
⅛	tsp	**salt**	
4		**eggs**	Add to above, one at a time; mix by hand or mixer until smooth and glossy but pasty.

FOR CHEESE BEIGNETS

4	oz	**sharp cheddar cheese,** grated	} Combine; add to half of puff pastry and mix well. Drop (¾tsp) onto cookie sheet; chill thoroughly.
2	Tbsp	**Parmesan cheese,** grated	
¼	tsp	**salt**	

FOR SHRIMP BEIGNETS

1	lb	**shrimp,** cooked, minced	} Combine; add to remaining half of puff pastry and mix well. Drop (¾tsp) onto cookie sheet; chill thoroughly.
1	Tbsp	**scallions,** minced	
1	Tbsp	**parsley,** chopped	
1	tsp	**soy sauce**	

When ready to prepare, heat oil in kettle (400°). Slide six beignets at a time into hot fat; remove when puffed and brown (3-4min). Drain on paper towels. Serve immediately.

Barbara Clark, Westport

Sweet and Sour Meatballs

Always a good hot appetizer

Serves: 8-10
Bake: see recipe
Pans: 7x11 with rack

1½	lb	**ground beef**	} Mix thoroughly; shape into 1" balls. Place on ovenproof rack, over pan. Bake: 375° (15-20min). Remove to baking dish and discard fats.
2		**eggs**	
1	lg	**onion,** minced	
2	cups	**bread crumbs,** dry	
		salt, pepper to taste	
1	btl	**chili sauce** (12oz)	} Combine and pour over meatballs. Bake: 350° (5-10min) until glazed.
1	jar	**currant jelly** (10oz)	

Michelle Murray, Stratford

Shrimp Mold

Something special!

Serves: 8-10
Chill: 2-3 hr
Pan: mold, greased (6-8cup)

1	Tbsp	**gelatin**	} Soak in water; set aside.
¼	cup	**water**	
½	can	**tomato soup**	} In small saucepan, heat until smooth; add gelatin. Cool.
4½	oz	**cream cheese**	
½	cup	**mayonnaise**	} Add to above; pour into greased mold. Chill well. If using fish mold, place a slice of olive in eye. Serve with favorite crackers.
¾	cup	**celery, onions,** mixed, diced	
2	cans	**shrimp,** drained, (4½oz,ea)	
1-2	tsp	**horseradish** (optional)	Can be added for a delicious tang.

Eileen Buckley, Weston

Asparagus in Shrimp Sauce

Deliciously different

Serves: 6-8
Marinate: 30-60 min
Pan: 13x9 (nonmetal)

2	lb	**asparagus,** fresh, trimmed, cleaned	} Cook until crisp-tender then drain well. Arrange in dish.
	OR		
2	pkg	**asparagus,** frozen (10½oz,ea)	
⅓	cup	**vegetable oil**	} Mix together in small bowl.
⅓	cup	**lemon juice,** fresh	
¼	tsp	**dill,** dried, crushed	
¼	tsp	**mustard,** dry	
½	tsp	**salt**	
¼	tsp	**pepper,** fresh ground	
8	oz	**shrimp,** tiny Alaska (frozen or canned)	Thaw and drain; add to marinade and mix. Pour over asparagus; marinate, occasionally spooning liquid over asparagus. Arrange on serving platter.
		parsley sprigs, fresh **lemon slices**	} Garnish.

Doris Hadad, Trumbull

 ASPARAGUS is rich in minerals and vitamins A & B.

Herring in Mustard Sauce
(Swedish)

Serves: 6-8
Chill: 1-2 hr

Also served as a vegetable sauce over new boiled potatoes

Have all ingredients at room temperature.

2	jars	**herring** (6oz,ea)	Drain; arrange on serving dish.
3	Tbsp	**brown mustard**	
1	Tbsp	**sugar**	In small bowl, stir until blended.
1½	Tbsp	**white vinegar**	
½	cup	**vegetable oil**	While beating, add a little at a time to above mixture.
2	Tbsp	**onions,** chopped	Add to above mixture; pour over herring. Refrigerate.
1	bunch	**dill,** fresh, chopped	

Kerstin Nilson, Trumbull

Chopped Herring Salad
(Jewish)

Serves: 6
Chill: 8-12 hr

1	jar	**herring filets,** marinated in wine, drained (8oz)	
1		**egg,** hard cooked	Combine and grind or chop fine.
1	lg	**apple,** peeled, cored	
1	slice	**white bread,** crust trimmed	
2	Tbsp	**wine,** sweet	Add to above; mix well and chill. Serve on crackers or party slices.

Gail Cohen, Trumbull

 DILL is a member of the parsley family. It is served to stimulate appetite.

Salmon Party Ball

Serve with cherry tomatoes and crackers

Serves: 8-10
Chill: 3-4 hr

1	can	**salmon** (16oz)	Drain; remove skin and bones; flake.
8	oz	**cream cheese,** softened	
1	Tbsp	**lemon juice**	
2	tsp	**onion,** grated	Combine with above; mix thoroughly.
2	tsp	**horseradish,** prepared	Chill several hours; shape into a ball.
¼	tsp	**salt**	
¼	tsp	**liquid smoke** (optional)	
½	cup	**pecans,** chopped	Combine; roll ball in mixture. Chill
3	Tbsp	**parsley,** snipped	well.

Theresa Acselrod, Trumbull

Amuse-Gueule au Roquefort

(French)

Delightful miniature cheese balls

Yield: 20 balls
Chill: 1-2 hr

½	lb	**Roquefort** OR **Bleu cheese**	Combine to form a smooth paste.
4	Tbsp	**butter,** softened	
1½	Tbsp	**chives** OR **green onion** tops, minced	
1	Tbsp	**celery,** minced	Beat into above thoroughly. If mixture
	dash	**cayenne pepper**	is too stiff, add more butter in small
		salt to taste	amounts. Roll into balls about ½" in
⅛	tsp	**pepper**	diameter.
1	tsp	**cognac** OR few drops **Worcestershire sauce**	
½	cup	**bread crumbs,** dry	Combine; chill. Roll cheeseballs to
2	Tbsp	**parsley,** minced	coat well and serve pierced with toothpick.

Hillandale Gourmet Club, Trumbull

Artichoke Squares

Delicious served warm or cold

Serves: 18-20
Bake: 350° 30 min
Pans: skillet (sm); 11x7, buttered

2	jars	**marinated artichoke hearts** (6oz,ea)	Drain juice from one jar into skillet. Discard juice from second jar. Chop artichokes; set aside.
⅓	cup	**onion,** minced	Sauté in artichoke liquid until onion is transparent; set aside.
1	clove	**garlic,** minced	
4		**eggs,** well beaten	
¼	cup	**bread crumbs,** dry	
¼	tsp	**salt**	Mix together.
⅛	tsp	each:**pepper, oregano, Tabasco sauce**	
8	oz	**cheddar cheese,** shredded	Add to egg mixture along with artichokes and onion mixture. Turn into prepared pan. Bake; cool in pan. Cut into 1" squares. Reheat: 325° (10-12 min).
2	tsp	**parsley,** minced	

Elaine DeBernardo, Trumbull

Requeson Mexicali

Simple, different

Yield: 1 pt
Chill: 3 hr

16	oz	**cottage cheese**
1-3	tsp	**taco sauce** (to taste)
3	Tbsp	**onion,** minced
¼	tsp	**garlic powder**
1	tsp	**cumin seeds,** crushed

Blend thoroughly. Chill well. Serve with tortilla chips.

Pegge Axline, Fairfield

Dill Cheese Spread

Simply delicious!

Yield: 2 cups

16	oz	**cream cheese,** softened
¼	cup	**mayonnaise**
2	tsp	**Dijon mustard**
2	Tbsp	**fresh dill,** chopped
2	Tbsp	**scallions,** chopped
1	clove	**garlic,** minced

Beat together with mixer or food processor. Spread on your favorite crackers.

Jan Simko, Bridgeport

Cheese Puff Tarts

A great "do ahead"

Yield: 24
Bake: 350° 30 min
Pan: muffin (1¾")

6	Tbsp	**butter**	Cream well.
3	oz	**cream cheese**	

1	cup	**flour**	Work into above; chill (30min) if dough is too soft. Roll into 24 balls. Press one ball over bottom and sides of each muffing cup. Do not go over the top.

1	cup	**Muenster cheese,** grated	Pat into pastry shells.

¼	cup	**mayonnaise**	Stir together; spoon over cheese.
¼	cup	**sour cream**	

		paprika	Garnish. Bake until done. Loosen edges and remove from pans carefully.

Serve hot. Can be prepared ahead as much as 2-3 hours and refrigerated before baking. Spraying muffin cups with non-stick spray makes removal of tarts easier.

Jacqueline Pelletier, Stratford

Mozzarella in Carozza
(Italian)

A delectable "sandwich"

Serves: 6-8
Deep fry: See recipe
Pan: deep fryer

1	lb	**Italian bread,** sliced	Remove crusts; cut into 3" rounds, ½" thick.
1	lb	**Mozzarella cheese** (¼" thick)	Cut into rounds slightly smaller than bread. Form sandwiches by placing cheese between 2 rounds of bread.
		oil for deep frying	Heat (375°).
1	cup	**milk**	Dip sandwich; press edges to seal.
1	cup	**bread crumbs,** fine	Coat all sides of sandwich.
4		**eggs,** beaten	Combine; dip sandwich in mixture. Fry until golden on all sides (3-5min).
3	Tbsp	**milk**	
		tomato sauce, favorite	To serve, heat sauce and spoon over hot sandwich.

Carole Manjoney, Trumbull

Panzarotti

(Italian)

An old family favorite directly from Italy

Serves: 6
Fry: 4-5 min
Pan: skillet (lg)

CRUST

2	cups	**flour**	
½	tsp	**salt**	Combine.
½-1	tsp	**pepper** (to taste)	
2	Tbsp	**shortening**	Cut into above.
1		**egg**	Add to above; mix well. Roll out
1	Tbsp	**water**	dough; cut into six circles (3-4").

FILLING

1	pkg	**Mozzarella cheese,** cubed (12oz)	
½	lb	**Prosciutto,** diced	Mix; divide evenly, placing on half of each pastry circle. Fold over and seal with a fork.
½	cup	**parsley,** chopped	
1		**egg**	
½	tsp	each:**pepper, salt**	
		oil for frying	Fry (375°) until golden brown. Serve warm.

Florence Massey, Trumbull

Armenian Pizzas

Delicious and so simple

Serves: 10-12
Bake: 425° 5-10 min
Pan: cookie sheet

1¼	cups	**cheddar cheese,** grated	
1	cup	**black olives,** chopped	
1	cup	**onion,** grated	
½	tsp	**salt**	Mix together until well blended.
½	tsp	**curry powder**	
2	tsp	**Worcestershire sauce**	
½	cup	**mayonnaise**	
1	pkg	**pita bread,** torn into pieces	Spread above on bread. Bake until crisp.

Bonnie Yarrington, Fairfield

California Sunshine Dip

Just listen to the compliments

Serves: 10-12
Chill: 1-2 hr

1	can	**enchilada bean dip** (10½oz)
½	cup	**guacamole** (see Index)
1	can	**green chilies,** chopped (4oz)
1	can	**black olives,** chopped (6oz)
½	cup	**sour cream** (optional)
½	cup	**tomatoes,** chopped (optional)
3		**eggs,** hard cooked, chopped
1	cup	**sharp cheddar cheese,** shredded
1	pkg	**tortilla chips**

Chill all ingredients well. To serve, layer each in the order given, in a round dish. Serve immediately with tortilla chips for dipping.

For Trevor, a ray of sunshine.

Patti Wirtz, Tustin, Ca

Easy Guacamole Dip

Yield: 2 cups

2		**avocados,** peeled, mashed
½	sm	**tomato,** chopped (drain off liquid)

Blend.

1	sm	**onion,** halved

Mince half of onion; add to mixture above. Squeeze in juice of other half.

¼	tsp	**garlic powder**
1		**lime,** juice of
	drops	**Tabasco sauce** (optional)
1	Tbsp	**mayonnaise**

Add to above; mix well. Place plastic wrap directly on dip sealing well. Chill or serve immediately with corn chips.

Kathy Byrne, Somerville, Ma

 AVOCADO should be purchased only when they have a bright, fresh, appearance and are fairly firm.

Arizona's Black Bean Dip

Deliciously different!

Serves: 10-12
Simmer: 1 hr
Pan: saucepan (2qt)

2	cans	**black bean soup,** undiluted (10¾oz,ea)
1	cup	**onions,** chopped
5		**hot chili peppers,** chopped
5	cloves	**garlic,** skewer each **salt** to taste

Simmer slowly (1hr), stirring occasionally. Remove garlic.

8	oz	**Longhorn cheddar cheese,** grated

Stir into above, heat through. Serve with corn chips.

Linda Neubauer, Weston

Dolmadakia
(Greek)

Delicious stuffed grape leaves

Yield: 24
Pan: skillet (lg)

½	cup	**olive oil**
3	lg	**onions,** chopped
1	clove	**garlic,** minced

Sauté until tender.

1	cup	**rice,** raw
1	tsp	**salt**
½	tsp	**pepper**

Add to above; cook (5min).

2	Tbsp	**dill,** fresh, chopped
¼	cup	**parsley,** fresh, chopped
½	cup	**lemon juice,** fresh
1	cup	**water**

Add; stir and cover. Simmer until liquid is absorbed; remove from heat.

1	jar	**grape leaves** (8oz)

Separate and rinse; place on board, shiny side down. Place 1 tsp rice filling at stem end of leaves, roll up tucking in edges.

½	cup	**olive oil**
1	cup	**water**
½	cup	**lemon juice**

Place in skillet; arrange rolls in this liquid. Put heavy plate over top of rolls. Simmer (25min). Add approx. 1 additional cup water as it is simmering until rice is tender. Cool; serve at room temperature with lemon wedges.

Lemonia Bargas, Trumbull

Tyropitta
(Greek)

Wonderful cheese triangles

Yield: 45-50
Bake: 350° 15-20 min
Pan: cookie sheets

1	pkg	**phyllo dough**	Defrost according to package directions. Keep well covered (plastic wrap, dry towel, etc.) to prevent drying.
1	lb	**butter** melted	Set aside.

8		**eggs,** large, beaten
6	Tbsp	reserved butter
12	oz	**cream cheese,** cubed
1½	lb	**cottage cheese,** creamed
¼	lb	**Feta cheese** (white Greek), crumbled

Combine well; set aside.

Cut each sheet phyllo in half lengthwise.	Brush lightly with butter; fold in half lengthwise.	Brush lightly with butter; add 1 Tbsp cheese mixture.	Fold corner up to the left.	Fold up straight.	Continue folding until a triangle is formed.

Repeat, using all phyllo dough; place on cookie sheets. Bake. Serve warm.

Ollie Crist, Fairfield

Seaweed: Thin Laver
(Korean)

Serves: 1
Broil: 3-4 sec

"This dark purple, paper thin seaweed is sold in packages of 10 sheets. As a side dish, laver is often wrapped around some rice and vegetables. It is another staple of a picnic or lunch box."

4	sheets	**laver**	Pour oil into a saucer; brush over laver, both sides.
1	Tbsp	**dark sesame seed oil**	
		salt to taste	Sprinkle over each sheet. Heat briefly under broiler or on grill (3-4sec).

Laver will be crisp when it has cooled. Stack laver sheets, then cut into quarters. Arrange in a mound and spear with toothpicks.

Gloria Lee, Trumbull

Baked Stuffed Mushrooms

A great crumb stuffing

Serves: 4-6
Bake: 350° 15-20 min
Pans: skillet (sm); 11x7

12	oz	mushrooms, (lg) stems removed	Sprinkle few drops lemon juice on each cap; set aside. Chop stems very fine.
		lemon juice	
2	Tbsp	butter OR margarine	Sauté chopped stems.
¼	cup	bread crumbs	
2	Tbsp	Parmesan cheese, grated	
2	Tbsp	parsley, minced	Combine in bowl; add stems and mix thoroughly. Stuff caps; place in lightly greased baking dish.
	dash	garlic powder	
1	Tbsp	onion, minced	
2	Tbsp	dry vermouth OR dry sherry	
		salt, pepper to taste	
1-2	Tbsp	butter	Dot each with butter. Bake; serve hot.

Odette Renner, Trumbull

Pickled Mushrooms

A nice change

Serves: 10-12
Steam: 10 min
Marinate: 1 hr
Pan: Steamer or rack

1	lb	mushrooms (med)	Wash; steam (10min). Cool; drain and slice.
½	cup	white wine vinegar	
3	Tbsp	olive oil	
1	Tbsp	capers	
1	Tbsp	onion, minced	Combine; marinate mushrooms in brine at least 1 hour. Serve chilled.
1	tsp	garlic, minced	
1	tsp	each: oregano, parsley, basil	
½	tsp	each: salt, pepper	

Joan Bryk, New Canaan

 CANAPES are bite-sized savory foods spread on edible bases and garnished.

Spinach Balls with Mustard Sauce

Prepare ahead – great

Yield: 3-4 doz
Bake: 350° few min
Simmer: 5 min
Pans: cookie sheet; saucepan (1qt)

2	pkg	**spinach**, frozen, chopped (10oz,ea)

Thaw; squeeze dry.

2	cups	**herb stuffing mix**, (crushed)
1	cup	**Parmesan cheese**, grated, packed
½	cup	**scallions**, minced
3		**eggs**, beaten
	dash	**nutmeg**

Combine with spinach; mix well. Shape into balls (1"). Place on ungreased cookie sheet; chill. Bake until golden. Freeze well.

MUSTARD SAUCE

½	cup	**dry mustard**
½	cup	**white vinegar**

Combine.

¼	cup	**sugar**
1		**egg yolk**

Mix in saucepan, add mustard mixture. Cook over low heat, stirring constantly, until thickened. Cover and chill. To serve, spear each ball with a toothpick. Have guests dip into sauce or pour sauce over balls. Serve at room temperature.

Christine Vazzano, Huntington

Apple Fritters

Just a little bit special

Yield: 3½ doz
Deep fry: 3 min

1		**egg**, beaten
1	cup	**milk**
1	cup	**apple**, unpeeled, cored, minced
¼	cup	**sugar**
¼	tsp	**salt**
3	Tbsp	**orange juice**
1	tsp	**orange peel**, grated
½	tsp	**vanilla**

Combine in medium size bowl.

2	cups	**flour**, sifted
3	tsp	**baking powder**

Mix together; fold into above mixture. Stir gently only until flour is moistened.

vegetable oil for deep frying

Drop by rounded teaspoons into deep hot fat (350°). When fritters rise to the surface, turn and fry until golden brown. Drain thoroughly on paper towels.

confectioners' sugar

Roll each fritter and serve hot.

Darlene Nelson, Fairfield

Spanakopitta
(Greek)

A delicate spinach pie

Yield: 35 pieces
Bake: 350° 45-60 min
Pan: 14x12, buttered

4	pkg	**spinach,** frozen, chopped (10oz,ea)	Defrost; squeeze out liquid. Set aside.
16	oz	**cottage cheese**	
8	oz	**Greek Feta cheese,** crumbled	
¼	cup	**onion,** chopped (optional)	Combine; add to spinach. Mix well and set aside.
6	ex lg	**eggs,** beaten	
	dash	**salt**	
¼	cup	**butter,** melted	
2-3	Tbsp	**olive oil** (optional)	
1-1½	pkg	**phyllo dough**	Wrap carefully in plastic wrap and/or towel to prevent drying while it defrosts.
¾	lb	**butter,** melted	Butter pan, bottom and sides (1Tbsp).
		defrosted phyllo (divide in half)	Cover bottom and sides of pan with single layer of leaves; brush lightly with butter. Spread half of leaves, in layers, buttering each well.
		reserved spinach mixture	Spread over phyllo layers.
		remaining 1/2 phyllo leaves	Continue layering and buttering until 4 sheets remain. Use these 4 sheets

to cover top, overlaping pan 1". Tuck in on all four sides. Brush top with remaining butter. Cut into (2x2") pieces with a very sharp knife. Bake until golden.

Ollie Crist, Fairfield

Cranberry Fruit Dip

Use assorted fresh fruit pieces for dipping

Yield: 1¼ cups
Chill: 1-2 hr

8	oz	**yogurt,** vanilla flavored	
½	cup	**cranberry-orange relish**	Blend well; cover and chill.
¼	tsp	**nutmeg**	
¼	tsp	**ginger**	
		apples, pears, bananas, oranges, melon, etc.	Cut into wedges and spears. Serve chilled.

Lillian Thiede, Stratford

Champagne-Fruit Cup

Pretty and delicious

Serves: 6-8
Chill: 1 hr
pitcher (2qt); wine glasses, chilled

1	btl	champagne OR **Rhine wine**	
6	oz	club soda OR **Perrier water**	Chill thoroughly.
1	cup	fresh fruits, your choice (orange or grapefruit sections, lemon slices, strawberries, peach slices, pineapple chunks)	Place in pitcher.
4		maraschino cherries	
4	oz	brandy	Pour over fruit. Refrigerate (1hr) or freeze (½hr).
4	oz	Benedictine	
4	oz	maraschino liqueur	
12-16		ice cubes OR an ice block	When ready to serve, remove pitcher from refrigerator; fill with ice.
		reserved champagne reserved club soda	Add, stir briefly. Serve immediately in chilled wine glasses.

Elaine DeBernardo, Trumbull

Rum Fruit Punch

A punch with "punch"

Serves: 8

		juice of 4 oranges	
		juice of 2 lemons	
1	jar	maraschino cherries (6oz)	
1	can	pineapple, diced (sm)	Mix in punch bowl; let stand (2hr). Add ice when ready to serve.
1½	oz	Cointreau	
2		oranges, sliced	
1		lemon, sliced	
1	btl	dark rum (750ml)	
1	btl	club soda (750ml)	
½	cup	sugar	

Jean Elsasser, Fairfield

Banana Slush Punch

Yield: 8 qt

4	cups	**sugar**	Combine and boil (3min); cool to keep bananas from browning.
6	cups	**water**	
12	oz	**orange juice,** frozen	Combine in large bowl. Add cooled liquid; mix. Freeze in one or two round containers.
2		**lemons,** juice of	
46	oz	**pineapple juice**	
20	oz	**pineapple,** crushed	
5		**bananas,** crushed	
2	btl	**lemon-lime juice** (28oz,ea)	When ready to serve, pour over frozen fruit base; mix gently. Serve while some of the base is still frozen.
40	oz	**ginger ale**	

Marjorie Crump, Trumbull

Hot Spiced Galliano

There won't be a drop left

Yield: 2½ qt
Stovetop: 5 min
Pan: saucepan (4qt)

4	cups	**hot tea**	Combine; simmer (5min). Pour into punchbowl; serve warm. Reheats well.
¼	cup	**sugar**	
5	cups	**orange juice**	
¾	cup	**Galliano liqueur**	
2-3	sticks	**cinnamon**	
		fresh mint, orange slices	Garnish.

Carol Naylor, Trumbull

SUGAR – confectioners' sugar is made by grinding granulated sugar and passing it through meshed screens. Brown sugar is made as sugar but boiled at a lower temp, resulting in retaining more syrup. Place a piece of fresh bread, piece of apple or lettuce leaf in your container of brown sugar to revive if hardened, to keep properly moistened.

Grog à la Jones

Glorious aroma and taste!

Yield: 1 gal
Simmer: 3 hr
Pan: kettle (8qt)

2-3		cinnamon sticks	
10-12		cloves, whole	Tie in cheesecloth bag; place in kettle.
½		ginger nugget	
8-12	oz	raisins	
8-12	oz	almonds	Add to above; simmer at least 3 hr
1		vanilla bean	(do not boil). Serve warm. Doubles
½	lb	sugar cubes	well.
1	gal	Burgundy	
1	btl	vodka (fifth)	

Anne Jones, DeKalb, NY

Wassail

A favorite at Rehab's Xmas party

Yield: 10-12 cups
Stovetop: 15 min
Pan: saucepan (4qt)

6	in	stick cinnamon, broken into pieces	Tie in cheesecloth bag; put into large
½	tsp	cardamon seeds, crushed	saucepan.
4	cups	white grape juice	
4	cups	orange juice	Add; bring to a boil. Cover and sim-
1½	cups	apricot nectar (12oz)	mer (15min). Remove spices.
¼	cup	lemon juice	
2	cups	apricot brandy (1pt)	Stir into above; heat through and serve warm.

Diane Lombardi, Milford

Bruce's Oriental

From an expert!

Yield: 32 oz
Serves: 4

8	oz	blended rye	Pour into blender; blend well. Pour
4	oz	sweet vermouth	over ice cubes in "Old Fashion"
2	oz	orange curaçao	glasses.
2	oz	lime juice	
16	oz	crushed ice	

Bruce McNaughton, Fairfield

Frozen Coconut Daiquiri

Super

Serves: 2
Highball glasses

6	oz	**rum** (medium)
3	oz	**cream of coconut** (canned)
1½	oz	**lime juice**

Pour into blender; turn to high. Add enough ice to make a slush thick enough so straw stands alone. Enjoy!

Bruce McNaughton, Fairfield

Kahlua Frost

Creamy and refreshing!

Serves: 4
Prepare each separately

4	Tbsp	**Kahlua**
¼	cup	**heavy cream,** whipped (divided)

In each 8 oz glass, put 1 Tbsp of each.

2	btl	**club soda** (7oz,ea) (divided)

2 Tbsp in each glass; stir until foamy.

1	pt	**coffee ice cream**

1 large scoop in each glass. Pour soda to fill the glasses. Top each with a dollop of whipped cream.

4		**cinnamon sticks**

One in each glass to be used as stirrers.

Eddy Bernard, Trumbull

Fruit Slush

"My most requested recipe"

Yield: 1 gal
Freeze: 24 hr
Storage container; 6 glasses (8oz)

1	btl	**Vodka** (fifth)
2	cans	**orange juice concentrate,** frozen (12oz,ea)
2	cans	**lemonade concentrate,** frozen (12oz,ea)
2	qt	**7-Up**
2	cups	**cranberry juice**
½	cup	**sugar**

Mix well; freeze for 24 hours. Spoon into glasses. Guests will enjoy "drinking" this one with a spoon.

		mint leaves (optional)

Garnish each serving.

Mary Angela Welsh

Mimosa Cocktail

"Delightful for brunch or lunch"

Serves: 8
Glasses: 8oz

1	qt	**orange juice,** chilled (fresh best)	Each Glass 4oz (½cup)
½	btl	**champagne,** chilled	2oz (¼cup)
1	btl	**Cointreau** OR **TripleSec,** chilled (sm)	1oz (2Tbsp)

Stir gently; serve immediately.

Trina Oswald, New Haven

Coffee Hawaiian

Great luncheon finale

Serves: 4
Blender: glasses (8oz)

2	cups	**coffee,** strong, cold
1	cup	**pineapple juice,** cold
1	pt	**vanilla ice cream,** softened

Beat well in blender. Serve chilled or freeze and serve with a spoon.

Bettie Roberts, Fairfield

Barley Tea
(Bori Cha) Korean

This mild, traditional, Korean tea accompanies almost every meal. It is made by dropping 4 tsp **toasted barley** (found in gourmet section and oriental grocery) into 4 cups **boiling water;** continue boiling vigorously (5min). Strain and serve.

Gloria Lee, Trumbull

Zippy Tomato Juice Toddy

Serves: 10-12

1	btl	**tomato juice (32oz)**
1	can	**chicken broth (13¾oz)**
2	Tbsp	**sugar**
2	Tbsp	**lemon juice**
2-3	tsp	**Worcestershire sauce**
6	drops	**Tabasco sauce**
1	tsp	**celery salt**
1	tsp	**parsley**
1	tsp	**onion powder**
	sprinkle	**dill**
		salt, pepper to taste
1	cup	**water**

Mix well; let set at least 1 hr at room temperature so flavors can blend. Serve hot with celery stalk as stirrer. Keeps refrigerated 2-3 weeks.

Esther Sayles, Bridgeport

Soups

PUERTO RICAN
Vegetable Salad
Arroz Con Pollo (Chicken and Rice)
Pasteles (Plantain Meat Pies)
Bunuelos de Viento or Mango Preserves and Native Cheese
Coffee

MEXICAN
Guacamole and Nachos
Chicken Chamizal
Rice
Pigeon Pea Croquettes
Tossed Green Salad
Fresh Fruit and Snow Caps

SPANISH
Gazpacho
Paella
Green Salad with Oil and Vinegar
Garlic Bread
Pastel de Manzana
Fresh Fruit

ITALIAN BANQUET
Cappeletti Alla Carbonara
Escarole Soup
Tomato-Cucumber Marinade
Garlic Bread
Beef Scaloppine Casalinga
Broccoli Al Limone
Zabaglione Parfait

Southwest Chili, Up North

Serves: 8-10
Stovetop: 2 hr
Pan: Dutch oven

1	lb	**pinto beans**	} Soak overnight.
8	cups	**water**	

1	tsp	**salt**	Add; simmer (1hr) or until beans are almost tender. Drain; set aside.

2	Tbsp	**vegetable oil**	} Sauté until tender.
3	cups	**onion,** chopped	

2	lb	**ground beef**	Add; cook until light brown. Spoon off fat.

2	cans	**tomatoes** (28oz,ea)	
1	can	**tomato paste** (6oz)	
2-3	Tbsp	**chili powder** (to taste)	Add; bring to a boil. Reduce heat, simmer (2hr). Stir occasionally. Serve hot with cornbread.
1	Tbsp	**salt**	
2	tsp	**sugar**	
2	tsp	**cumin** (to taste)	
¼	tsp	**cayenne pepper**	
		reserved beans	

Kay Speck, Trumbull

Chicken Soup
(Hungarian)

An unusual serving style

Serves: 4-6
Stovetop: 1 hr
Pan: kettle (5qt)

1	lb	**chicken parts**	} Bring to a boil; skim to remove sediment.
3	qt	**water,** cold	

2	lg	**carrots,** chopped	
2		**parsley** roots and greens	Prepare vegetables, the size you desire. Add to above; cover and simmer (1hr). Strain; serve broth as consomme or add fine noodles. Serve meat and vegetables in a preheated serving dish.
2	stalks	**celery,** chopped	
1		**tomato,** fresh, chopped	
1	med	**onion,** chopped	
1	Tbsp	**salt** (to taste)	
	pinch	**Spanish saffron**	

Ann Hawie, Stratford

Chick-a-Leekie Soup

"So good, with crusty bread, for lunch"

Serves: 8
Stovetop: 50-60 min
Pan: kettle (4-5qt)

3	lb	**chicken,** cut up
4	cups	**water**
½	cup	each:**carrot, celery,** chopped
¼	cup	**onion,** chopped
2	sprigs	**parsley**
1		**bay leaf**
2	tsp	**salt** (to taste)
¼	tsp	**pepper**

Simmer (30min) or until chicken is tender. Remove chicken, bay leaf and parsley; cool. Remove meat from bones; cut into bite-sized pieces and set aside. Skim excess fat from broth.

1½	cups	**leek,** sliced thin
1	sm	**potato,** cubed
½	cup	**barley**

Add to above; bring to a boil. Simmer, covered (15-20 min) then cool slightly.

reserved chicken

Return to kettle.

2	cups	**cream,** light

Blend in; heat through but do not boil. Serve piping hot.

Lillian Thiede, Stratford

Champagne-Almond Soup

A favorite in Hawaii

Serves: 5-6
Stovetop: 20-25 min
Pan: saucepan (4qt)

1	cup	**chicken,** cooked, diced
½	cup	**almonds,** blanched, chopped
½	tsp	**almond extract**
3	cups	**chicken broth**
1	Tbsp	**onion,** minced

In saucepan, cover and simmer (15min).

3	Tbsp	**flour**
4	Tbsp	**butter,** melted

Blend to a smooth paste using some of the hot broth. Return to broth; bring to a boil stirring continuously. Reduce heat.

1½	cups	**cream,** light
1	cup	**champagne**
		salt, pepper to taste

Add and heat through but DO NOT BOIL.

1	cup	**avocado cubes**
1	Tbsp	**parsley,** fresh, minced

Garnish each serving. Serve hot.

Hillandale Gourmet Club, Trumbull

Hearty Scotch Broth

Delicious with crusty French bread

Serves: 6-8
Soak: 12 hr
Simmer: 2-2½ hr
Pan: saucepan (4qt)

¼	cup	**pearl barley**
1	cup	**water**

Soak barley (12hr).

1½	lb	**lamb** with bones (beef may be substituted)
5	cups	**water**
		reserved barley

Cover; simmer (1½hr).

1	Tbsp	**butter**
2	Tbsp	**Scotch whiskey**
1	cup	**vegetables**, diced (celery, carrot, turnip, onion)

Sauté in small saucepan. Add to above and simmer (15-30min). Remove meat; dice and return to saucepan.

1	Tbsp	**flour**
½	tsp	**salt**
	dash	**pepper**

Blend with small amount of broth. Add to soup along with reserved lamb and heat to blend. Serve piping hot.

Joan Kacin, Trumbull

Hearty Fish Chowder

Serves: 8
Stovetop: 30-40 min
Pan: saucepan (4qt)

2	lb	**fish filet** (haddock, halibut)
3	cups	**water**

Bring to a boil; reduce heat. Cover; simmer (10-15min). Remove fish; flake into bite-sized pieces and set aside. Remove broth and set aside.

1	cup	reserved broth
4	cups	**potatoes**, cubed (½")
1	cup	**onion**, chopped
1	cup	**green pepper**, minced

Simmer in saucepan (15min).

		reserved broth and fish
¾	cup	**tomato**, peeled, diced
1	cup	**half and half**
1¾	tsp	**salt** (to taste)
¼	tsp	**pepper**

Stir into above; heat slowly. Do not boil.

⅓	cup	**cheddar cheese**, shredded (optional)

Garnish each serving. Serve immediately.

Billie McNamara, Milford

 CHOWDER comes from the French word chaudiere which is a large cauldron used to make native stews and soups.

Oriental Noodle Soup

"Delicious - hot rolls and your meal is complete!"

Serves: 4-6
Stovetop: 60-70 min
Pan: saucepan (4qt)

2½	lb	**chicken**, cut-up
1	tsp	**salt**
5½	cups	**water**

Simmer (40min); remove chicken and refrigerate broth. Discard skin; remove meat from bones. Cut into bite-sized pieces. Skim fat from broth. Return chicken to kettle.

2	cans	**mushrooms** with liquid (4oz,ea)
¾	cup	**scallions**, sliced
1½	cups	**carrots**, peeled, diagonal slices
¼	cup	**soy sauce**
1	Tbsp	**sugar**
½	tsp	**ginger**
1	Tbsp	**sherry**, dry

Add to kettle; bring to a boil then reduce heat. Cook until carrots are crisp-tender (15-20min).

4	oz	**vermicelli**

Add; simmer (5min). Serve hot.

Billie McNamara, Milford

Avgolemono
(Greek)

An authentic egg and lemon joy

Serves: 8
Pan: kettle (4qt)

8	cups	**chicken broth**, clear

Bring to a boil.

⅓	cup	**rice**, raw

Add to broth. Cook until tender (15-20min). Turn heat to low.

3		**eggs**

In small bowl, beat with mixer until frothy.

3	Tbsp	**lemon juice**, fresh
1	cup	broth from pot

Combine; add to eggs while mixing constantly. Return this mixture to kettle while stirring constantly to prevent curdling of eggs. Remove from heat and serve.

Lemonia Bargas, Trumbull

 FILÉ *is a powder derived from tender leaves of the sassafras tree. It is essential to Creole cookery.*

Gumbo
(sausage/chicken/shrimp/filé)

The best of New Orleans

Serves: up to 20
Stovetop: 2-3 hr
Pan: heavy gauge kettle (8-10qt)

Amount	Ingredient	Instruction
1 cup	**oil** (vegetable, lard, meat fats, etc.)	Fry over high heat (15min). Remove sausage; set aside.
1½ lb	**sausage** (½" slices), your favorite except Italian with anise.	
1	**chicken** (fryer), skinned, boned (cut 2-3" pcs)	Season meats well. Continuing on high heat, fry until browned (10min). Remove chicken; set aside.
1-2 tsp	**salt**	
1-2 tsp	**cayenne pepper**	
	oil in kettle (1cup)	"Make a roux" (see Index): High heat (5min); Low heat (20-25min). Cook until toasty dark brown.
1 cup	**flour**	
1 tsp	**filé seasoning** (optional)	
1 Tbsp	**brown sugar**	Add to roux; caramelize, stirring constantly: High heat (5min); Low heat (15-20 min).
4 cups	**onion**, diced	Add to kettle all at once; stir well to coat with roux. Cook: High heat (5-10min); Low heat (10-15min).
2 cups	**celery**, diced	
2 cups	**green pepper**, diced	
1 Tbsp	**garlic**, minced	Add during the last minute.
	reserved chicken	Return to kettle.
8 cups	**water** OR **stock**, heated	Add gradually; mix in well.
⅓ cup	**sherry** (optional)	
	reserved sausage	Return to kettle; mix. Adjust seasonings; cook uncovered: High heat (30-35min); Low heat (1hr).
1 cup	**green onions**, diced	Add during last 15 minutes of cooking.
1 cup	**fresh parsley**, chopped	
1 lb	**shrimp** (optional)	Add any or all during the last 10 minutes of cooking.
1 pt	**oysters**, drained (optional)	
4-5 cups	**white rice**, cooked	When finished, juices will have reduced somewhat. To serve, ladle piping hot soup over a mound of rice in bottom of soup dish. Do not mix.

Filé seasoning may be added individually (¼-½ tsp per serving) if desired. (Never add filé to boiling pot as it will become stringy.)

VARIATIONS: Gumbo was created to use anything available in the kitchen – be venturesome. Use ham, duck, turkey, bacon, any meat.

New Orleans School of Cooking, French Quarter, New Orleans, La
Via Claudia McKenna, Trumbull

Lobster Stew

If you ever have leftover lobster!

Serves: 4
Stovetop: 10-15 min
Pan: saucepan (3qt)

3	Tbsp	**butter,** melted
1	Tbsp	**onion,** minced

} Sauté slowly, do not brown.

2-3 cups **lobster pieces,** cooked

Add along with any juices from cutting. Sauté gently (1-2min).

		salt, pepper to taste
½	tsp	**parsley,** minced (optional)

} Add to above.

1	can	**evaporated milk** (13oz)
1	qt	**milk**
6-8		**saltines,** crushed

} Add; stir and heat until piping hot (do not boil). Stir occasionally. Serve hot.

paprika
oyster crackers

} Garnish and serve with crackers.

VARIATION: ½ Cup each carrots, celery, chopped fine, can be added to sauté with the onion.

Esther Sayles, Bridgeport

Oyster Stew

Piping hot, rich and delectable!

Serves: 3-4
Stovetop: 10-15 min
Pan: double boiler

Fill bottom of double boiler with water to just below bottom of bowl; heat (do not boil).

1	pt	**oysters,** fresh, drained (reserve liquid)
3	Tbsp	**butter**
	dash	**onion powder**

} Simmer gently in top of double boiler until juices bubble (3-5min).

		water
		reserved oyster liquid
	dash	**salt, pepper**

} Add water to make 1 cup liquid; add to double boiler and simmer (4-5min).

1	pt	**half and half**
1	cup	**milk**

} Add to above; heat until piping hot (do not boil). Serve with oyster crackers.

Esther Sayles, Bridgeport

Cream of Broccoli

Without cream!

Serves: 4-6
Stovetop: 35-50 min
Pan: saucepan (4qt)

2	pkg	**broccoli,** frozen, chopped (10oz,ea)	Defrost; drain WELL on paper towels.
¼	cup	**onion,** minced	Combine with above, in saucepan; cook (10min). Drain (reserve stock for other dishes); puree vegetables.
1	can	**chicken broth** (13¾oz)	
2	Tbsp	**BUTTER,** melted	In saucepan, add flour to butter; cook (1-2min) stirring.
1	Tbsp	**flour**	
1	qt	**milk**	Add half, slowly; return pureed vegetables to pan and mix well. Add enough of remaining half of milk to obtain the desired consistency.
		salt, pepper, mace to taste	Cook (20min) longer on low heat. Reheats well.

Agnes Swords, Stratford

Blumenkohl Suppe

(German)

Cream of cauliflower soup; "my mother's recipe"

Serves: 6
Stovetop: 40 min
Pan: kettle (6qt)

6	cups	**water**	Bring to a boil.
1	head	**cauliflower**	Divide into small florets; add to boiling water.
1	clove	**garlic,** crushed	Add to above; reduce heat and simmer until tender. Drain broth; reserve. Remove cauliflower; reserve.
1	tsp	**salt**	
4	Tbsp	**butter**	Heat in kettle.
¼	cup	**flour** reserved broth	Add to kettle; mix to form a thin paste. Bring to a boil; simmer (2min).
3		**egg yolks**	Blend; add to above while stirring continuously.
½	cup	**cream,** heavy	
½	tsp	**nutmeg** **pepper** to taste reserved cauliflower	Add to kettle; heat, do not boil.
		fresh chives OR **parsley,** chopped	Garnish each serving.

Gertrud Bargas, Trumbull

Escarole Soup
(Italian)

Excellent

Serves: 6
Stovetop: 30 min
Pan: kettle (6qt)

2	cups	**escarole,** minced
⅔	cup	**carrot,** diced
6		**scallions,** chopped
6	cups	**chicken broth**
½	tsp	**salt**
	dash	**pepper**

Place all ingredients in kettle; bring to a boil. Simmer (30min), stirring occasionally.

Parmesan cheese, grated

Garnish.

Maria De Cesare, Trumbull

Black Bean Soup
(Cuban)

A meal in itself

Serves: 8
Soak: overnight
Stovetop: 3-4 hr
Pan: kettle (6qt)

2	cups	**black turtle beans,** dried

In large kettle, soak in cold water to cover, overnight; drain.

3	qt	**water**
1-2		**bay leaves**
1		**ham bone**

Add to kettle; simmer until beans are soft and liquid is fairly thick. Add liquid if necessary.

1		**grapefruit,** membranes removed

Add pulp to above.

1		**beef bouillon cube**
1	sm	**green pepper,** minced
1	clove	**garlic,** crushed
¼	cup	**sherry,** dry

Add to above; simmer (½hr) longer.

1	cup	**rice,** cooked, buttered
½	cup	**onion,** minced

Let each guest garnish to taste.

Dee Maggiori, Trumbull

VARIATION: Can eliminate sherry and grapefruit and add ½ tsp oregano and ¼ tsp cumin.

Gloria Alvarez, Bridgeport

Pea Soup

Special on a cold winter eve!

Serves: 8
Stovetop: 3 hr
Pan: kettle (6qt)

1		**ham bone** with meat OR 2 cups **ham,** diced
2	qt	**water,** cold
1	lb	**dried split peas**
2		**carrots,** sliced
1	lg	**onion,** chopped
2	stalks	**celery,** chopped
1		**bay leaf**
		salt, pepper to taste

Combine in kettle; cover and simmer (3hr). Remove bone, gristle, bay leaf and peppercorns.

1	can	**hominy** (optional) (16oz)

Add during last 15 minutes of cooking. Serve hot.

Louise Cronan, Trumbull

Lentil Soup

Great on a cold winter night

Serves: 12
Stovetop: 1½ hr
Pans: kettle (8qt); skillet (med)

1	lb	**lentils**
3	qt	**water**
		salt to taste

Simmer in kettle (1hr).

¼	cup	**oil**
2	med	**onions,** chopped
2	stalks	**celery,** chopped
2	cloves	**garlic,** minced
2	Tbsp	**parsley,** minced

Sauté in skillet until lightly browned.

1	can	**Italian tomatoes** (16oz)

Add to skillet; simmer (10min).

2	cups	**spinach,** fresh, chopped
		salt, pepper to taste

Add to kettle along with contents of skillet. Cover and simmer until lentils are tender (1hr).

cheese, grated

Garnish each serving as desired.

Phyllis Aiello, Stratford

Cream of Lettuce Soup

Something different

Serves: 3-4
Stovetop: 15 min
Pan: saucepan (4qt)

1	Tbsp	vegetable oil
1	clove	garlic, minced
1	lg	onion, chopped

Sauté gently (2-3min).

2		carrots, grated
1	sm	head lettuce, chopped
2	cups	chicken broth OR vegetable stock

Add to above; cover and simmer (5min).

1	cup	water
1	tsp	salt (to taste)
2	Tbsp	cornstarch
¼	cup	non-fat dry milk
1	tsp	rosemary

Blend well; add to soup stirring slowly until thickened. Serve hot.

June Bartnett, Monroe

Savory Mushroom Soup

Tastes like oyster!

Yield: 4 cups
Stovetop: 10-15 min
Pan: saucepan (2qt)

4	Tbsp	butter
½	cup	each: celery, onion, minced
⅛	tsp	each: oregano, thyme, crushed

Sauté until onion is golden.

½	lb	mushrooms, fresh

Wash (quarter if large); add to above and sauté briefly.

4½	tsp	flour
1	tsp	salt
		pepper to taste

Add to above; mix well.

2	cups	half and half

Add slowly while stirring. Continue to stir until thickened. (Do not boil). Doubles well.

		parsley, fresh, chopped

Garnish each serving. Serve piping hot.

Lillian Thiede, Stratford

Soupe à l'Oignon

A French Canadian delight!

Serves: 4-6
Simmer: 30 min
Broil: 2-3 min
Pan: saucepan (3qt); ovenproof bowls

2	Tbsp	**butter**	
12	oz	**spanish onions,** sliced thin	Sauté in heavy saucepan (2-3min).
		salt to taste	
		pepper, fresh ground	

2	Tbsp	**flour**	Stir in; continue cooking over medium heat (2min), stirring continuously.

½	cup	**cider** OR **vermouth**	Add to above; bring to a boil and allow to reduce by one half.

1	qt	**beef consommé**	Bring to a boil in separate saucepan. While boiling, pour over onion mixture. Simmer (30min). Pour into individual ovenproof bowls.

6	slices	**French bread** (¼"), toasted	Top each bowl with a slice; sprinkle cheese over top. Broil until melted
4	oz	**Gruyere** OR **Swiss cheese,** grated	and cheese turns golden brown. Serve immediately.

VARIATION: Place a large slice of cheese over top of each bowl, allow cheese to overlap edges. Broil as directed above.

Joy Tait, Monroe

Country Style Potato Soup

A great low-cost meal!

Serves: 6
Stovetop: 30 min
Pan: saucepan (4qt)

2	Tbsp	**butter** OR **margarine**	In saucepan, sauté until tender (5min).
½	cup	**onions,** chopped	

½	cup	**carrots,** minced	
1	cup	**celery,** sliced thin	
3	cups	**potatoes,** cubed	Add to above; cover and simmer until vegetables are tender (15min). Reduce heat.
2	Tbsp	**parsley,** snipped	
1	can	**chicken broth** (13¾oz,ea)	
¾	tsp	**salt, pepper** (to taste)	

3½	cups	**milk**	Stir into above; heat to scalding but do not boil.

¼	cup	**flour**	Blend, then add stirring continuously. Cook until bubbly and slightly thickened. Serve hot.
½	cup	**milk**	

Carol Caputa, Huntington

Minestrone
(Italian)

Vegetable soup, Milan style

Serves: 8-10
Simmer: 2 hr
Pans: kettle (4qt); skillet (lg)

1	cup	**white beans,** dried **water** to cover	In kettle, bring to a boil; turn off stove. Let soak (1hr); drain.
2½	qt	**water**	Pour over beans; bring to a boil and simmer (1½hr).
3	slices	**bacon,** diced	Fry until lightly brown; pour off fat leaving 1 Tbsp.
1	cup	**onions,** sliced thin	Add; sauté (5min).
1		**carrot,** diced	Mix into above; sauté (5min longer), stirring frequently. Add these vegetables to the cooked beans.
1	cup	**potatoes,** diced	
2	cups	**zucchini,** diced	
1	cup	**tomatoes,** peeled, diced	
3	cups	**cabbage,** shredded	
2	tsp	**salt**	Add and simmer (1¼hr).
½	tsp	**pepper**	
1	clove	**garlic,** minced	
½	tsp	**basil**	
¼	cup	**rice,** raw	Stir into soup; cook (20min).
3	Tbsp	**parsley,** minced	
½	cup	**Parmesan cheese,** grated	Stir in just before serving. Garnish with additional cheese.

Marie Caldana, Fairfield

Green Soup
(Portuguese)

Excellent!

Serves: 8
Stovetop: 1hr 15 min
Pans: kettle (6qt); skillet (sm)

6	med	**potatoes,** peeled, quartered	Boil until soft; remove from water (reserve water) and mash. Return to water.
8	cups	**water**	
3	Tbsp	**olive oil**	In skillet, brown lightly on all sides. Add sausage and drippings to kettle.
1	lb	**sausage** (Portuguese or Sweet Italian) sliced	
10	oz	**Swiss chard** OR **spinach,** minced	Add to kettle and simmer (45min). Serve piping hot.
1½	tsp	**salt**	
		pepper to taste	

Mrs. Francisco Goncalves, Bridgeport

Gazpacho

A great summer cold soup

Serves: 8
Blender
Chill: 3-4 hr

1	can	**tomato juice** OR **V8** (46oz) (reserve half)
1	lg	**green onion,** cubed
1	med	**green pepper,** cubed
2	7"	**cucumbers,** peeled, cubed
2-4	cloves	**garlic**

In deep bowl combine vegetables then add half of tomato juice.

½	cup	**bread crumbs**
¼	cup	**olive oil**
2	Tbsp	**lemon juice** OR **vinegar**

Place over top of vegetables. Blend in amounts your blender will accommodate. Repeat until all blended. Add remainder of tomato juice. Mix and chill.

tomatoes, green peppers, cucumbers, onions, diced

Serve in separate dishes for your guests to garnish their soups as they choose.

Patricia Braun, Trumbull

Gazpacho Estromeno

Serves: 4
Chill: 3-4 hr

3	slices	**bread,** well trimmed
1	med	**green pepper,** chopped
2	cloves	**garlic**
1	lg	**egg**
6	Tbsp	**olive oil**
4	Tbsp	**wine vinegar**

Liquefy in blender.

	canned	**chicken broth*** (2-4 cups)

Add; mix well and chill. Serve cold.

*Use fresh broth for a gelled soup.

Patricia Braun, Trumbull

Garlic Soup

Serves: 2

2	cloves	**garlic,** diced
2	Tbsp	**olive oil**

Sauté gently, remove garlic when brown.

2-3	cups	**chicken stock**
2	slices	**old bread**

Soak bread well. Add all to above; simmer (5min) then remove from heat.

2		**eggs**

Poach in soup. Serve hot.

Patricia Braun, Trumbull

Spring Vegetable Soup
(British)

A nice first course for a special meal!

Yield: 2½ qt
Stovetop: 10-15 min
Pans: 2 saucepans (4qt,1qt)

3	Tbsp	**butter**
1	cup	**scallions,** minced
2	cups	**green peas,** fresh
1	head	**lettuce,** cut coarse
1	lb	**spinach,** chopped coarse
½	cup	**parsley,** chopped
1	tsp	**tarragon,** dried
		sorrel leaves (optional)

Sauté (2min) in large kettle.

2	qt	**water,** hot
		salt, pepper to taste

Add to above; cover and simmer until tender, stirring occasionally. Remove vegetables. Remove 1 cup liquid; set aside. Put vegetables into blender (5sec); return to kettle. Bring to a boil, then reduce heat.

3		**egg yolks,** beaten
½	cup	**heavy cream**
		reserved liquid

In small saucepan, combine; cook over low heat, stirring continuously (do not boil). When thickened, stir into soup; mix well. Season to taste. Serve hot.

Margaret Lindsay, Trumbull

"Lifesaver" Soup

For the calorie conscious

Serves: 6
Stovetop: 40 min
Pan: kettle (4qt)

1	can	**green beans,** french cut, undrained (1lb)
2	cups	**cabbage,** chopped fine
3-4	stalks	**celery** OR 1 tsp **celery flakes**
1	tsp	**onion salt** OR **powder**

Purée in blender or processor; pour into kettle.

3	cubes	**beef bouillon**
		water, hot

Add just enough water to dissolve. Add to kettle.

2	Tbsp	**pimiento,** minced
1	can	**tomatoes** (1lb)
18	oz	**water**

Add; simmer (20min), covered. Tastes blend and soup thickens as it sets. Freezes well.

Judy Webster of Thin's Inn, Monroe

Continental Fruit Soup

Gorgeous chilled and served in clear glass dishes!

Serves: 8
Soak: 1 hr
Simmer: 15 min
Chill: 8-10 hr
Pan: kettle (6qt)

½	cup	each: **dried prunes, apricots, seedless raisins**	Soak (1hr).
3	cups	**water,** cold	
1	stick	**cinnamon**	Cover and simmer (15min) or until just tender.
2	med	**apples,** cored, peeled, sliced round	
2	med	**fresh pears,** peeled, sliced	
1	can	**sour red cherries,** unsweetened, undrained (16oz)	Add; bring to a boil.
1	pkg	**cherry-flavored gelatin** (3oz)	Stir until dissolved. Add to fruit; stir gently. Chill overnight. Serve cold.
1	cup	**water,** boiling	
		lemon slices	Garnish.

SUGGESTION: Can add 2-4 Tbsp orange-flavored liqueur or fruit-flavored brandy during last 5 minutes of cooking or when ready to chill. Mix carefully.

Aster Seale, Bridgeport

La Soupe de Fromage

A delightful hot cheese soup

Serves: 6-8
Stovetop: 20-25 min
Pan: saucepan (4qt)

1	med	**onion,** minced	
1	cup	**celery,** minced	Sauté in large saucepan (5min).
¼	cup	**butter**	
¼	cup	**flour**	
½	tsp	**dry mustard**	Blend into above stirring constantly.
1	tsp	**Worcestershire sauce**	
2	cubes	**chicken bouillon**	
2	cups	**water**	Add; mix well. Cover and simmer
1	med	**carrot,** grated fine	(15min).
	dash	**garlic powder** (optional)	
4	cups	**milk**	Add to above; bring to a boil and reduce heat.
1½	cups	**sharp cheddar cheese,** shredded	Add and stir until melted.
		salt, pepper to taste	
		croutons	Garnish and serve at once.

Ester Sealy, Bridgeport

Mulligatawny Soup

Light and refreshing!

Serves: 6
Stovetop: 1 hr
Pan: kettle (4qt)

2	cups	**orange juice**	
6	cups	**water**	
1½	lb	**chicken,** cut into pieces	
1	cup	**celery,** chopped (with leaves)	Combine in kettle; cover and simmer (1hr). Remove chicken; debone and cut into bite-size pieces. Return to broth.
1	cup	**carrot,** sliced	
1	cup	**onion,** chopped	
2		**apples,** pared, diced (reserve half)	
2		**tomatoes,** peeled, diced (reserve half)	
1-1½	Tbsp	**salt** (to taste)	
		reserved apple	
		reserved tomato	Add to soup; cover and simmer
1	tsp	**curry powder**	(30min). Serve hot.
⅓	cup	**rice,** raw	

Darlene Nelson, Fairfield

54   Soups

Salads & Preserves

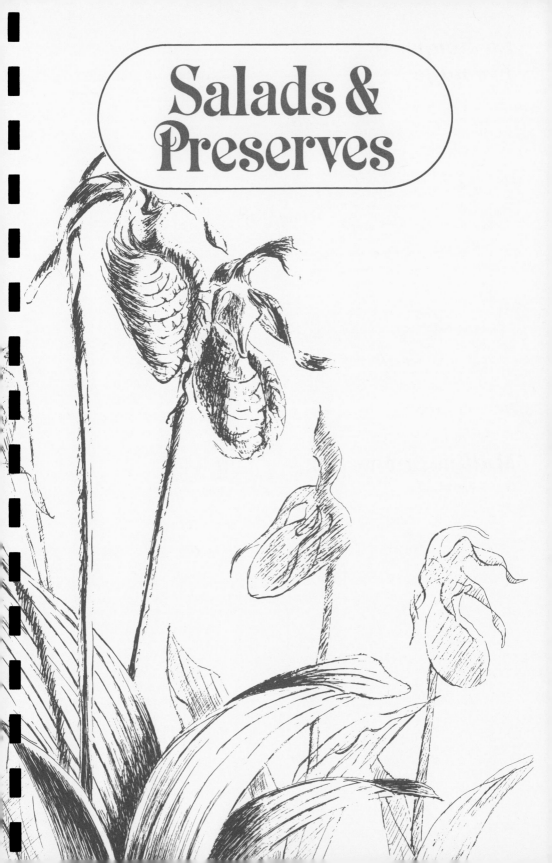

CHINESE
Ch'un Chuan (Spring Rolls)
Ku Lu Jou (Sweet Sour Pork
Kan Shao Hsia Jen (Shrimp with hot
sauce)
Empress Chicken
Steamed Rice
Yin Hsiang Ch'ien Tzu (Eggplant
Szechuan Style)
Seasonal Fresh Fruits

BRITISH
Sausage Rolls
Spring Vegetable Soup
Beefsteak and Kidney Pie
Small New Potatoes with Mint
Baked Leeks
Trifle

INDIAN
Raita (Salad)
Dals (Chick Peas)
Pilau (Rice)
Chapati or Pouri (Bread)

GREEK
Dolmadakia (Stuffed Grape Leaves)
Avgolemono Soup (Soup)
Greek Salad
Roast Leg of Lamb
Pastitsio (Pasta and Cheese)
Broccoli al Limone or Greek Okra
Retsina Dine (Wine)
Baklava

La Ensalada

A great lunch dish!

Serves: 6-8
Stovetop: 10-15 min
Pan: skillet (med)

1	lb	**ground beef**	Brown and drain.
1-2	tsp	**chili powder** OR 1 env **Taco mix**	
1	can	**kidney beans,** washed, drained (15oz)	Add to above; set aside.
½	cup	**onion,** chopped	
1	cup	**cheddar cheese,** extra sharp, grated	Can be added to above while hot or just before serving.
1	med	**iceberg lettuce,** chopped	Add just before serving; toss lightly.
1	btl	**Catalina dressing** (16oz)	
1	cup	**nacho chips,** crushed coarse	
		avocado, cucumber OR **tomato slices** (optional)	Garnish.

Angela Doyle, Trumbull

Corned Beef Salad

"Easy, delicious, always a hit"

Serves: 8-12
Chill: 3-4 hr
Pan: mold (6cup)

1	pkg	**lemon** OR **lime gelatin**	Dissolve then cool.
1	cup	**water,** boiling	
1	cup	**salad dressing**	Beat into above.
1	can	**corned beef,** shredded	Fold into gelatin mixture; chill in greased mold until firm.
2	cups	**celery,** diced	
¼-½	cup	**scallions,** fresh, chopped (optional)	
3		**eggs,** hard cooked, chopped	
½	tsp	**salt**	

Nancy Johnson, Shelton

Chicken Salad

A nice change

Serves: 6
Chill: 2-4 hr

6	cups	**chicken,** cooked, diced
1	can	**pineapple chunks,** drained (15oz)
½	lb	**cherry tomatoes,** halved
½		**cantaloupe,** cubed
1	cup	**sour cream**
1	cup	**mayonnaise**
½	tsp	**lemon juice**
		salt, pepper to taste

Combine; refrigerate at least one hour. Serve on **lettuce** leaves and garnish with **hard cooked eggs,** sliced.

Barbara Daley, Trumbull

Chicken Salad with Curry Dressing

A really unusual and delicious salad

Serves: 6
Chill: 2-4 hr

2	cups	**chicken, turkey, pork** OR **ham,** cooked, diced
6	cups	**mixed greens,** torn
2	cups	**cabbage,** shredded
1	can	**mandarin orange** sections, chilled, drained (11oz)
½	cup	**peanuts,** salted OR unsalted
1	Tbsp	**green onion,** chopped

Arrange in salad bowl.

DRESSING

½	cup	**yogurt,** plain
⅓	cup	**peanut butter,** smooth OR chunky
⅓	cup	**milk**
3	Tbsp	**wine vinegar,** white
1	Tbsp	**sugar** OR equivalent substitute
1	Tbsp	**salad oil**
1-2	tsp	**curry powder**

Combine; drizzle over salad and toss. Serve chilled.

Diane Lombardi, Milford

Curried Chicken-Pâté Mold

Beautiful garnished with fresh fruit

Serves: 8
Stovetop: 1 hr
Chill: 2-24 hr
Pan: Dutch oven (6qt); platter (lg)

¼	cup	butter
1	cup	celery, chopped
1	cup	onion, chopped
½	cup	carrots, chopped
1	cup	apples, unpeeled, chopped
1	Tbsp	parsley, fresh
1	Tbsp	thyme, dried
1		bay leaf
2-4	Tbsp	curry (to taste)

In Dutch oven, sauté over medium heat, stirring (5min).

2	cans	chicken broth (10½oz)
4	lb	whole chicken breasts, boned, skinned, halved
1	tsp	salt
1	cup	water

Add to above; bring to a boil then reduce heat and simmer covered (30min) or until chicken is tender. Remove from heat; cool thoroughly in broth (2hr).

| 4¾ | oz | liver paté (your own, canned or deli) |

On large platter, divide into 8 portions. Place 1 breast on top of each paté; press. Cover and refrigerate.

reserved broth

Remove fat; strain. Remove ½ cup broth; set aside. Bring to a boil, uncovered; reduce to 1½ cups (15min).

		reserved ½ cup broth
1	env	unflavored gelatin
1-2	drops	red food coloring (optional)

Combine; let stand (5min). Add to boiling broth; stir until dissolved. Refrigerate until slightly firm (20min).

chilled breasts and paté

Spoon above over chilled breasts; refrigerate.

		watercress OR parsley
1	pt	strawberries
1	lb	green grapes, small bunches
		pineapple chunks
2	med	bananas, sliced
1	cup	melon balls

Garnish just before serving. Can be prepared, covered, refrigerated the day before then garnished just before serving. So special!

Jan McNaughton, Fairfield

My Own Salad

Bright colors show through clear broth

Serves: 10
Chill: 6-8 hr
Pan: mold (12cup)

3-4	cups	**mixed vegetables** (carrots, radishes, red and green peppers, yellow squash, zucchini, artichoke hearts, cucumbers, cauliflower, broccoli, your choice	Prepare a variety of these colorful vegetables; chop into varied sizes. Put into large bowl; set aside.
1	can	**chicken broth** (10½oz)	Dissolve; let set (5min).
4-6	pkg	**unflavored gelatin***	*4 pkg if used where cool and 6 pkg if to be taken on picnic.
1	can	**chicken broth** (10½oz)	Heat; add gelatin mixture; stir until thoroughly dissolved.
4	cans	**chicken broth** (10½oz,ea) **parsley, basil, chives, watercress,** chopped, to taste	Pour into above; stir well (total of 6 cans used).
5	squirts	**Tabasco sauce**	Pour over vegetables.
6	Tbsp	**sherry**	
2	cups	**chicken,** cooked, diced	Fold in gently; pour into mold and refrigerate until set.
1	pt	**mushrooms,** sliced	Dip mushrooms quickly into lemon water to prevent darkening; pat dry. When ready to serve, place in center of mold.
1	qt	**water**	
1	tsp	**lemon juice**	
		French dressing	Serve with mold.

Bebe Stetson, Southport

GELATIN MOLD – moisten dish on which mold is to be placed so mold can easily be centered after unmolding. INCREASE gelatin during summer or DECREASE liquids. Fruit juices can be used (heated) instead of water. When using FRESH PINEAPPLE in a mold, SCALD both fruit and juice or it will not congeal.

German Potato Salad

Great with any meal

Serves: 12-16
Stovetop: 10-15 min

5	lb	**potatoes,** new	Boil until just tender. Peel; slice ⅛" thick. Cool to room temperature.
		water	

1	cup	**chicken broth**	
½	cup	**vegetable oil**	
¼	cup	**vinegar**	Combine; pour over potatoes. Mix; let
1	lg	**onion,** diced	stand at room temperature 1 hour.
2-3	tsp	**salt**	Mix again. Adjust seasonings to taste.
¼	tsp	**pepper**	
½	tsp	**garlic powder**	

5	strips	**bacon,** cooked, crumbled	
1		**egg,** hard cooked, sliced	Garnish to taste. Chill or serve at room temperature.
2	Tbsp	**parsley** OR **chives**	

Gertrud Bargas, Trumbull

Portuguese Salad

Simple and colorful

Serves: 8
Pans: saucepans (med, sm)

5		**potatoes,** cubed	
5		**carrots,** cubed	
2	cups	**water**	Cook until tender; drain well.
1	tsp	**salt**	

1	pkg	**frozen peas** (10oz)	Cook according to directions; drain well. Arrange vegetables on serving dish.

1	cup	**olive oil**	
3		**egg yolks**	
3	Tbsp	**mustard**	Blend and pour over vegetables. Serve at room temperature.
½	tsp	**salt**	
		pepper to taste	

Mrs. Francisco Goncalves, Bridgeport

German Slaw

Stays crisp for up to two weeks

Serves: 12
Chill: 24 hr
Pan: saucepan (1½qt)

1	med	**green cabbage,** shredded
2		**onions,** sliced thin

} Alternate layers of each in large bowl.

¾	cup	**sugar**

Sprinkle over top.

DRESSING

1	cup	**vinegar**
1	tsp	**celery seed**
1	tsp	**prepared mustard**
1½	tsp	**salt**

} Combine in saucepan, bring to boil.

¾	cup	**salad oil**

Add to above mixture, bring to a boil again. Pour over cabbage while still hot. DO NOT STIR. Cover and refrigerate.

Joan Kacin, Trumbull

Sauerkraut Salad

(Polish)

Use as a relish or in place of coleslaw

Yield: 6 cups
Chill: 8-10 hr

1	can	**sauerkraut,** undrained (lg)
1	med	**onion,** chopped
1	med	**green pepper,** chopped
1	jar	**pimiento,** chopped (4oz)
1¼	cups	**sugar**
¼	cup	**vinegar**

Combine and refrigerate overnight. Great on hot dogs.

Helen Drovy, Trumbull

 ONION – leeks, chives, garlic, shallots, green onions, scallions. Moisture at the neck shows decay inside.

Gazpacho Salad

Serves: 8
Chill: 4 hr

DRESSING

⅔	cup	**salad oil**
⅓	cup	**wine vinegar**
1	clove	**garlic,** crushed
1	Tbsp	**basil,** fresh OR 1 tsp dried
1	tsp	**salt**
½	tsp	**pepper**
½	tsp	**sugar**
½	cup	**scallions,** sliced thin
½	cup	**parsley,** chopped

Combine in sealed container. Chill thoroughly.

SALAD

1	med	**iceberg lettuce**
2	med	**zucchini,** sliced thin
1	med	**green pepper,** strips
1	lg	**cucumber,** sliced
3	med	**tomato,** wedges
4	oz	**mushrooms,** fresh, sliced

Line salad bowl with lettuce; layer vegetables, mushrooms last. To serve, shake dressing well; pour over vegetables. Do not toss.

8	oz	**Swiss cheese,** slivered

Garnish.

Lillian Thiede, Stratford

Layered Garden Surprise

A "do ahead" joy

Serves: 6-8
Chill: 24 hr
Pan: bowl (2½qt)

2	cups	**romaine lettuce**, torn	
½	cup	**parsley**, snipped	
½	cup	**red pepper**, chopped, coarse	
1	cup	**cauliflower** OR **broccoli**, chopped, coarse	Layer vegetables in salad bowl in this order.
2	stalks	**celery**, sliced	
1	lg	**carrot**, julienned	
1	med	**zucchini**, julienned	
1	cup	**peas**, frozen	

½	cup	**mayonnaise**	
½	cup	**sour cream**	
1	Tbsp	**Dijon mustard**	
½	tsp	each **rosemary, basil,** and **oregano**	Combine; spread over peas.
1	tsp	**garlic powder** **pepper** to taste	

1½	cups	**cheddar cheese**, grated	Combine; sprinkle over top. Cover.
½	cup	**scallions**, sliced thin	Chill up to 24 hours.

Susan Lewis, Easton

Stuffed Lettuce

Serves: 4-6
Chill: 4 hr

1	med	**iceberg lettuce**	From stem end, hollow out center, leaving 1" shell.

2-4	oz	**blue cheese**, room temp	In small bowl, beat 2 oz blue cheese with cream cheese until smooth.
3	oz	**cream cheese**, room temp	

2	Tbsp	**mayonnaise**	
1	Tbsp	**half and half**	Stir into above; blend well. Add more
1	Tbsp	**green onion**, chopped	blue cheese, if desired. Fill lettuce
1	Tbsp	**parsley**, fresh, chopped	hollow and chill at least 4 hours.
1	Tbsp	**pimiento**, chopped	

		French dressing (optional)	To serve, cut into wedges.

VARIATION: Can use red cabbage; add chopped walnuts to cheese mixture; serve with additional blue cheese dressing.

Doris Hadad, Trumbull

Spinach Salad
(Korean)

Another way to prepare an old favorite

Serves: 4
Broil and blanch
Pans: kettle (4qt); saucepan (1qt)

1	Tbsp	**sesame seeds**	Toast under broiler.
1	pkg	**spinach,** fresh (10oz)	Wash well; drop into boiling water to blanch (20sec). Drain well; squeeze out excess water. Knead with wooden spoon; cut solid mass into 1½" sections. Place in bowl. Keep warm.
1½	Tbsp	**soy sauce**	
1½	Tbsp	**dark sesame oil**	Combine; toss with warm spinach. Cool or chill. Sprinkle with sesame seeds; serve.
1½	Tbsp	**vinegar**	
1½	tsp	**sugar**	

Gloria Lee, Trumbull

Korean Salad

Delicate and delicious

Serves: 6-8
Pan: salad bowl

1	pkg	**spinach,** fresh (10oz)	Tear into pieces.
1	can	**bean sprouts** (16oz), drained	
1	can	**water chestnuts,** sliced, drained	
2		**eggs,** hard cooked, sliced	Add to above.
6-8	slices	**bacon,** cooked, crumbled	

DRESSING

1	cup	**vegetable oil**	
¼	cup	**cider vinegar**	
½-¾	cup	**sugar**	Combine; mix dressing thoroughly. Pour over salad and toss. Serve immediately.
⅓	cup	**catsup**	
½	tsp	**salt**	
1	sm	**onion,** chopped	
2	tsp	**Worcestershire sauce**	

Gloria Schleicher, Weston

French Dressing

Yield: 2 cups

½	cup	**catsup**
1	tsp	**paprika**
⅔	cup	**sugar**
1	tsp	**celery seed**
1	tsp	**dry mustard**
	pinch	**salt**

Blend well.

½	cup	**cider vinegar**
⅓	cup	**honey**
1	Tbsp	**lemon juice**

Add to above mixture.

1	cup	**salad oil**

Pour into above mixture slowly, while beating. Serve over favorite greens. Processor works well for this.

Diane Lombardi, Milford

Yogurt Dressing

Serve over tomato-cucumber slices

Yield: 1½ cups

½	cup	**mayonnaise**
½	cup	**yogurt**, plain
½	cup	**spaghetti sauce**, meatless

Blend well. Pour over prepared salad or serve separately.

June Bartnett, Monroe

Cucumber Salad
(Hungarian)

Serves: 4
Marinate: 1 hr
Chill: 2-3 hr

6		**cucumbers**, peeled, sliced thin

Place in bowl.

3	Tbsp	**salt**
2	cloves	**garlic**, chopped

Sprinkle over cucumbers; marinate (1hr) then squeeze out excess moisture.

4	Tbsp	**vinegar**
1	cup	**sour cream**
1	tsp	**paprika**

Combine; add to above and mix well. Chill.

Ann Hawie, Stratford

Marinated Mushrooms and Green Beans

"Especially good with fresh spinach and topped with croutons"

Serves: 4-6
Marinate: 2 hr
Pan: saucepan (1½qt)

2	cloves	**garlic,** minced	
½	tsp	**salt**	
¼	tsp	**pepper**	
¼	tsp	**lemon peel,** grated	
¼	cup	**lemon juice**	Combine; mix well. Set aside.
¾	cup	**salad oil**	
1	Tbsp	**parsley,** chopped	
¼	cup	**Parmesan cheese,** grated	
½	lb	**green beans,** fresh, whole	Steam beans until tender, but not soft; plunge into cold water. Drain; dry.
2	cups	**mushrooms,** fresh, sliced	Add to beans. Pour dressing over all; marinate. Combine no more than 3 hours before serving to preserve crispness.
1	Tbsp	**scallions,** sliced	

Charlotte Brittain, Fairfield

Oriental Sprout Salad

A delightful change

Serves: 6-8
Chill: 4-6 hr
Marinate: 4-5 hr

2	lb	**bean sprouts,** fresh	Rinse; remove green seed coverings. Place in colander.
2	qt	**water,** boiling	Pour over sprouts; drain well.
2	Tbsp	**scallions,** chopped	
2	Tbsp	**sesame oil**	
1	Tbsp	**vinegar**	
1		**cayenne pepper,** fresh, chopped	Combine with above and mix well. Chill thoroughly.
3	Tbsp	**soy sauce**	
1	tsp	**sugar**	
1	tsp	**sesame seeds,** toasted	

Valerie Bozzone, Trumbull

Tomato-Cucumber Salad

(Italian)

Serves: 4-6
Marinate: 5-24 hr

1	cup	**tomatoes,** sliced
1¼	cups	**cucumber,** pared, sliced thin
¼	cup	**onion,** sliced thin, separated

Layer in baking dish.

½	cup	**salad oil**
¼	cup	**vinegar**
1	tsp	**basil** OR **dill,** dried, crushed
1	tsp	**tarragon,** dried, crushed
1	tsp	**salt**
⅛	tsp	**pepper**

Mix well; pour over vegetables. Cover and marinate in refrigerator.

lettuce	Line bowl. Drain and reserve marinade. Arrange vegetables over lettuce.
reserved marinade	Pass in sauce dish.

Maria DeCesare, Trumbull

Vegetable Marinade

Great buffet vegetable or appetizer

Serves: 6-8
Marinate: overnight
Pan: saucepan (1qt)

1	cup	**vegetable oil**
1½	cups	**wine vinegar**
2	tsp	**salt**
¾	tsp	**pepper**
4	Tbsp	**sugar**
¼	tsp	**garlic powder**
1	sm	**onion,** chopped fine

Mix in saucepan; bring to a boil and simmer (5min). Cool.

2	cans	**artichoke hearts,** drained (8oz,ea)
1	bunch	**broccoli,** cut into florets
1	med	**cauliflower,** cut into florets
6-12	oz	**mushrooms,** fresh, sliced
1	can	**black olives** (7¾oz)

Combine in large bowl; pour marinade over. Toss; cover then refrigerate overnight. This marinade can also be used over zucchini, carrots, cherry tomatoes–any nice crisp vegetable.

Rosemary Poole, Monroe

Hot Snap Bean Salad
(Pennsylvania Dutch)

Serves: 6
Stovetop: 15-20 min
Pan: skillet (10")

4	slices	**bacon,** cooked crisp, crumbled	Set aside.
2-3	Tbsp	**pan drippings**	
½	cup	**onion,** minced	
⅓-½	cup	**vinegar**	Combine; cook (2min).
2	Tbsp	**sugar**	
½	tsp	**salt**	
½	tsp	**pepper**	
3	cups	**green beans,** fresh, cut, cooked, drained OR 2 cans green beans, drained (16oz,ea)	Add to above mixture, stirring to coat thoroughly; heat through. Top with crumbled bacon.

Hillandale Gourmet Club, Trumbull

Carrot-Peanut Salad
A great source of fiber

Serves: 4
Chill: 3-4 hr

1½	cups	**carrots,** grated	
1½	cups	**celery,** minced	
1	cup	**peanuts**	
½	cup	**raisins**	Combine.
¾	cup	**mayonnaise**	
3	Tbsp	**orange juice**	
4		**lettuce leaves**	Place two orange slices on each lettuce leaf; top with carrot mixture; chill.
1		**orange,** 8 slices	

Gloria Fennell, Trumbull

Eggplant Caviar
(Hungarian)

A great appetizer also!

Bake: 400° 40-45 min
Chill: 3 hr
Pan: pie plate (8or9")

1	med	**eggplant,** chilled
		oil
		salt

Preheat oven; brush plate with oil. Cut eggplant in half lengthwise. Brush with oil; sprinkle with salt. Place cut side up on pie plate. Bake until soft (40-45min). Remove and set aside to cool. Scoop out pulp.

1	med	**onion,** minced
1	lg	**green pepper,** chilled, minced
		reserved eggplant pulp

Mix thoroughly; chop again until fine.

1	tsp	**salt**
½	tsp	**pepper,** fresh ground
3	Tbsp	**vegetable oil**

Blend with above. Correct seasonings; cover and chill about 3 hours.

		lettuce, black olives, radishes, cherry tomatoes

Serve salad on bed of lettuce, garnished to taste or as appetizer with crisp crackers.

Wini Suss, Harrison, NY

Frühlings Salat
(German)

Spring Salad

Serves: 8
Chill: 1-2 hr

8	lg	**tomatoes**

Scoop out pulp, reserve.

1	can	**baby peas** (4oz)
1	jar	**onions,** white pearl (sm)
1	can	**pineapple,** crushed (4oz)
1	can	**mandarin orange** slices (4oz)
1	can	**mushrooms,** diced (4oz)
2		**eggs,** hard cooked, chopped
1	cup	**mayonnaise**
		reserved tomato pulp, chopped

Drain all fruits and vegetables well. Combine carefully. Fill tomato casings; chill well. Serve with French bread. This is also a great luncheon dish.

Monika Kohnen, West Germany

Greek Salad

Serves: 8

1	clove	**garlic**	Lightly crush clove just enough to release oils. Rub bowl; discard garlic.
1	lg	**iceberg lettuce**	Break into bite-size pieces; place in bowl.
1	med	**red onion,** peeled, cut into rings	
1	med	**green pepper,** cut into strips	
1	med	**cucumber,** sliced	
½	cup	**Greek black olives**	Add to salad bowl.
2	med	**tomatoes,** cubed	
5		**anchovy filets,** chopped	
8		**radishes,** sliced	
½	cup	**feta cheese,** crumbled	
		salt, pepper to taste	
¼	cup	**olive oil**	Sprinkle over top; toss and serve.
2	Tbsp	**vinegar**	

Lemonia Bargas, Trumbull

Red-Horse Special Mold

Great with beef or chicken

Chill: 4-5 hr
Mold: 6-8 cup, greased

2	pkg	**lemon flavored gelatin** (3oz,ea)	
2½	cups	**water,** boiling	Dissolve gelatin in water and beet juice; pour into mold and chill until almost jelled.
1	jar	**beets,** shoestring, drained (reserve beets and juice)	
		reserved beets	Stir into mold. Chill thoroughly.
1	jar	**red horseradish** (3oz)	

Mrs. Arthur Lunin, Bridgeport

Creamy Cucumber Mold

A delicious non-sweet salad

Chill: 4-6 hr
Mold: 6 cup, greased

1	pkg	**gelatin, lime** (3oz)
¾	cup	**water,** boiling

Stir until dissolved; chill until partially set.

1	lg	**cucumber,** minced
¼	cup	**onion,** minced
1	cup	**mayonnaise**
1	cup	**cottage cheese,** creamed
1	tsp	**horseradish**
¼	tsp	**salt**

Combine; fold into gelatin then pour into mold. Chill.

Connie Volante, Trumbull

Molded Spinach Salad

Chill: 4-5 hr
Mold: 6 cup, greased

2	pkg	**spinach,** frozen, chopped (10oz,ea)

Thaw; drain thoroughly then set aside.

2	pkg	**lemon flavored gelatin** (3oz,ea)
1	cup	**water,** boiling

Stir until dissolved.

2	cups	**water,** cold

Stir in; mix well.

3	Tbsp	**vinegar**
1	cup	**salad dressing**
⅓	tsp	**salt**

Stir in; chill until slightly thickened and beat until smooth.

		reserved spinach
⅔	cup	**celery,** chopped
¼	cup	**carrots,** shredded (optional)
1½	cups	**cottage cheese**

Add; blend well. Pour into mold; chill until set. Serve topped with mixture of sour cream, dill and a little salad dressing.

Ruth Gilchrist, Wenham, Ma

Zippy Applesauce Mold

Easy and tasty!

Stovetop: 5 min
Chill: 6 hr
Pans: saucepan (sm); mold (6cup), greased

½	cup	**red cinnamon candies**	Cook, stirring frequently until candies melt. Heat to boiling.
1	cup	**water**	
1	pkg	**raspberry flavored gelatin (6oz)**	Place in bowl; pour melted candies over and stir to dissolve.
1	jar	**applesauce (30oz)**	Stir into above; pour into mold. Refrigerate several hours.
2	Tbsp	**vinegar**	
		endive	Garnish.
		orange slices	

Patricia Fox, Stratford

Ambrosia Mold

Also a nice summer refresher

Chill: 6 hr
Pan: ring mold (6-8 cups)

1	pkg	**apricot flavored gelatin (6oz)**	Stir until dissolved.
2	cups	**water,** boiling	
1	can	**unsweetened pine-apple,** crushed, drained (8oz) (reserve juice)	Set pineapple aside.
1½	cups	**water,** cold	Combine; add to gelatin mixture above. Mix well; refrigerate until gelled.
½	cup	**reserved pineapple juice**	
8	oz	**cream cheese,** softened, diced	With mixer, beat into gelled mixture.
8	oz	**whipped topping,** thawed	
		reserved pineapple	Fold in; pour into mold and chill until firm.
		grapes	Fill center with grapes; garnish with coconut.
		coconut, shredded	

Virginia Smith, Bridgeport

Vegetable Crunch Mold

Chill: 4-5 hr
Mold: 8 cup, greased

1	pkg	**gelatin, unflavored**	Combine and stir until gelatin is dissolved.
1	pkg	**orange gelatin (6oz)**	
2	cups	**water,** boiling	
2	cups	**water,** cold	Add; stir in well and chill until slightly thickened.
1	cup	**red apples,** unpeeled, diced	
½	cup	**carrots,** shredded	
½	cup	**carrots,** grated	Add; mix into above.
½	cup	**raisins**	
½	cup	**celery,** chopped	
1	cup	**walnuts,** chopped	
1	cup	**ice cream,** vanilla, softened	Add; mix well and chill until firm (3-4hr).

Sophie Lapinski, Stratford

Ambrosia Salad

Always welcome

Serves: 4
Marinate: 10 min

2		**apples,** peeled	
2		**oranges,** peeled	
1	cup	**pineapple**	Cut into bite size pieces; mix together.
10		**grapes**	
¼	cup	**walnut pieces**	
1	Tbsp	**coconut,** shredded	Stir into fruit; let stand (10min).
1	tsp	**honey**	
		lettuce	Shred lettuce and arrange on plates.
½	cup	**yogurt,** plain	Combine; stir into fruit mixture just before serving. Spoon over lettuce.
¼	cup	**stawberry, raspberry** OR **currant jelly**	

June Bartnett, Monroe

Cranberry Molded Salad

"A great partner for chicken or turkey"

Serves: 8-12
Chill: 6 hr
Pan: mold (4cup)

6	oz	**raspberry** OR **cherry flavored gelatin**	Dissolve gelatin in boiling water. Cool.
2	cups	**water,** boiling	
1	cup	**cranberry sauce,** whole OR jellied	Stir into gelatin mixture; mix well. Pour into mold; chill until set.
1	cup	**sour cream**	

Ann Zowine, Easton

Zesty Grapefruit Crunch Mold

Super with ham

Chill: 4-5 hr
Mold: 3 cup, greased
Pan: saucepan (1qt)

1	can	**grapefruit sections,** unsweetened (1lb) **water**	Drain well (reserve juice to which you add enough water to make 1¼ cups liquid). Set sections aside.
1	env	**unflavored gelatin**	Mix well in saucepan; place over low heat, stirring constantly until gelatin is dissolved. Remove from heat then add remaining grapefruit liquid.
2	Tbsp	**sugar**	
	dash	**salt**	
½	cup	reserved grapefruit liquid	
2	Tbsp	**lemon juice**	Add; stir in then chill until it begins to thicken.
¼	cup	**celery,** diced	Fold into gelatin; pour into mold. Chill until firm.
¼	cup	**apple,** diced	
1	tsp	**crystaline ginger,** chopped reserved grapefruit sections	

Esther Seely, Bridgeport

 GRAPEFRUIT was named because it grows in grape-like clusters.

Festive Peach Bavarian Mold

Cool and refreshing

Serves: 10
Chill: 4 hr
Mold: 4 cup, greased

1	can	**peaches,** drained, chopped	(Reserve ⅓ cup syrup.)
3	oz	**lemon flavored gelatin** ⎫	
1	cup	**water,** boiling ⎬	Stir together until dissolved.
	dash	**salt** ⎭	
		reserved syrup	Add; mix well and chill until slightly thickened.
4	oz	**whipped topping,** thawed (2cups) ⎫	Combine; gradually blend in gelatin mixture.
¼	tsp	**almond extract** ⎭	
		reserved peaches	Fold into above; pour into mold. Chill thoroughly.

Sophie Lapinski, Stratford

Spiced Green Onions

Great with cottage cheese and liver paté

Yield: 2 cups
Chill
Pan: saucepan (1½qt)

1	lb	**scallions** (sliced ¼") ⎫	
1	cup	**seedless white raisins**	
1	cup	**white wine vinegar**	
1	cup	**sugar** ⎬	Place all in saucepan; bring to a boil.
⅛	tsp	**nutmeg**	
⅛	tsp	**cinnamon**	
½	tsp	**paprika** ⎭	
	few	**peppercorns**	Wrap in gauze for easy retrieval. Add to above; simmer until mixture reaches jamlike consistency. Chill and serve cold.

Patricia Braun, Trumbull

The President's Pickles

You haven't lived!

Yield: 4 pt
Soak: overnight
Cook: 5 min
Pan: kettle (6qt)

6	cups	**cucumbers**, unpeeled, sliced
½	cup	**salt**
		water, cold, to cover

Combine; let stand overnight. Drain; rinse with fresh water and drain again.

2	med	**onions**, peeled, sliced thin
2	med	**green peppers**, seeded, chopped

Add to drained cucumbers.

3½	cups	**vinegar**
1	cup	**water**
3½	cups	**sugar**
1	Tbsp	**celery seed**
2	Tbsp	**mustard seed**
1	tsp	**turmeric**

Combine in large kettle; bring to a boil then add vegetables. Bring again to boiling and cook (5min). Seal in sterilized jars.

Edmund S. McLaughlin, Bridgeport,
President, The Rehabilitation Center

Southwestern Tomato Relish

Great with meats, hamburgers, everything!

Yield: 10-12
Stovetop: 2 hr
Pan: kettle (8qt); jars (8oz)

8	lb	**tomatoes**, ripe

Remove stem end; core and peel. Place in saucepan; boil (5min). Drain off juice (use for soups or drink). For thicker relish, drain well.

1	pt	**vinegar**, cider
3	lb	**sugar**

Add to above.

3-5	Tbsp	**stick cinnamon**, broken
1	Tbsp	**cloves**, whole

Tie in cheesecloth; add to tomatoes and simmer slowly (2hr). Remove cheesecloth. Pour immediately into sterilized jars; seal.

Julie Sweeny, Albuquerque, NM

Red Beet Eggs
(Penna Dutch)

A delicious condiment

Serves: 6-8
Marinate: 3 days
Pan: 1 qt jar, tight lid; saucepan (sm)

1	jar	**sliced beets,** drained (16oz) (reserve juice) **water**

Place beets in quart jar. Add water to juice to make 1 cup liquid. Pour into small saucepan.

1	cup	**vinegar**
¼	cup	**sugar**
½	tsp	**salt**
1	stick	**cinnamon**
4		**cloves**

Add to liquid and bring to boil. Pour over beets while hot; cool in jar.

6-8		**eggs,** hard cooked, peeled
1	sm	**onion,** sliced thin

Add to mixture in jar. Cover; refrigerate (3days), inverting jar occasionally to assure even coloring. Cut eggs lengthwise to serve.

Hillandale Gourmet Club, Trumbull

McIntire's Mustard

Microwave Simple!

Yield: 1 pt
Soak: overnight
Microwave: see recipe
Pan: glass bowl

4	oz	**dry mustard**
1	cup	**tarragon vinegar**

In large ceramic or glass bowl, pour vinegar over mustard. DO NOT STIR. Cover; let stand overnight at room temp.

½	cup	**sugar**
1	tsp	**salt**
½	cup	**butter**

Add to mustard; stir. Place in microwave and cook until butter melts.

6		**eggs**

Add, one at a time, beating with wire whisk after each addition. Return to microwave. Cook 1 min at a time until thickening begins around edges. (Mustard is done when still runny in middle, but sides look solid.) Whisk mixture briskly.

1		**lemon, juice of**

Add to above; cool. Place in containers.

Deborah McIntire, Trumbull

Breads

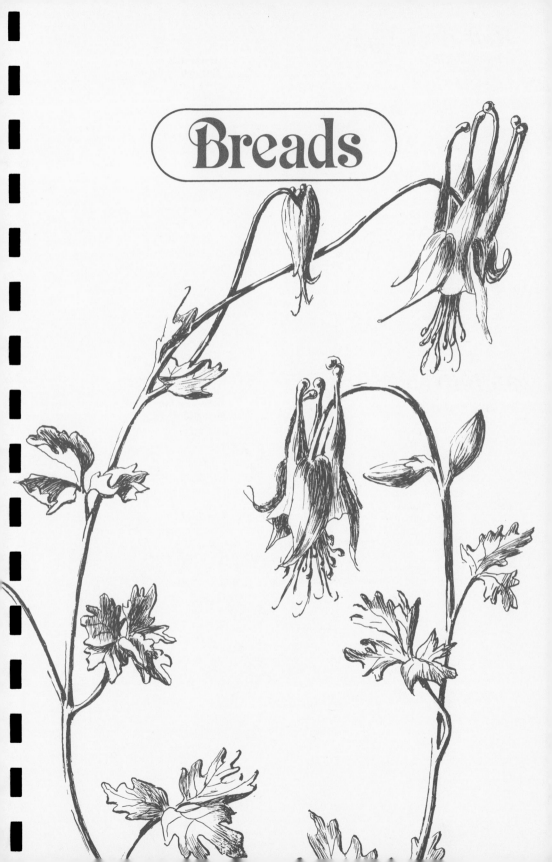

JEWISH
Chopped Herring Salad
Challah
Kugel
Duck with Bing Cherry Sauce
Red Cabbage
Ruggelah

FRENCH
Oeufs aux Escargots
Lettuce with Oil and Vinegar Dressing
Rognon Wisers (Kidney)
Steamed Rice
Mushrooms, Celery, Green Peppers
Fresh Strawberries with Lemon Juice

HUNGARIAN
Hungarian Chicken Soup
Hungarian Cucumber Salad
Chicken or Veal Paprikas
Dumplings
Lekvar Squares

GERMAN
Blumenkohl Suppe
(Cream of Cauliflower Soup)
Kopfsalat (Salad)
Schweinebraten (Pork Loin Roast)
Semmelklosse (Dumplings)
Bohnen und Karotten Gemuise
(Beans and Carrots with Summer
Savory Butter)
Liebesbirnen (Love Pears)

Hints to Help You Become a Great Bread Baker

Working with yeast dough is a fascinating experience. You can watch it rise and feel the warmth of the yeast action before it goes into the oven. It is alive! The following should help you to understand what is happening and why.

Ingredient temperatures and the amount of flour used are the most important factors in bread making. Your breads can really take rough handling. Apply the following guidelines and you will be a successful and happy yeast bread baker.

Be sure to have all ingredients at room temperature.

FLOUR	Measure the total amount of flour into a bowl. Because humidity affects the moisture content of flour, an exact amount can never be given. Add only enough flour to form a dough that can be handled. You may need more flour on humid days.
LIQUIDS	Milk, water, potato or rice water are all interchangeable. Beer is great in breads. DRY MILK POWDER: use ⅓ cup to each cup of water. Add the powder directly to the flour. Heat the water to dissolve the yeast in. So simple and no lumping.
DISSOLVING YEAST	The temperature of the liquid in which yeast is dissolved is CRUCIAL. Too hot will kill the yeast action, too cool delays the action and your bread will be tougher. When DRY yeast is mixed with DRY ingredients, liquid should be 120° to 130°. When DRY yeast is dissolved in liquid, liquid should be 105° to 115°. When using COMPRESSED yeast, liquid should be 95° to 105°.
SOURDOUGH STARTER	These make great, moist breads. Be sure to feed them as regularly as possible. If the liquid turns green, and/or action is sluggish after being fed, discard and start again.
DEHYDRATED POTATO FLAKES	¼ cup added to the batter makes a moist bread.
SUGAR/SALT	Sugar is food for rising and salt controls and holds the rising. A good balance of each of these is needed.
FATS/EGGS	Neither is necessary except in egg breads. They just add to the richness of the dough and make a softer, smoother crumb.
HOW MUCH FLOUR IS ENOUGH	Add flour until dough comes away from sides of the bowl, forms a ball but is still slightly sticky for handling. Dough hooks work well here. They blend and knead thoroughly, cutting down on the kneading time.
KNEADING	This step is very important. It activates the action of the yeast on the gluten in the flour. Knead firmly with the heels of your hands. The firmer and longer you knead, the finer the texture of your bread. When dough is ready, air blisters will appear, dough will be shiny, smooth, elastic and should no longer stick.

RISING OR PROOFING

Grease a large bowl; place dough in; turn to coat well. Cover with plastic wrap to keep humidity level high and warmth in. Preheat oven to lowest temperature; turn oven off. Place bowl of dough in oven over a shallow pan of steaming hot water. This begins the fermentation of the yeast on sugar. The sugar changes into carbon dioxide which lightens the dough and alcohol, which gives the aroma peculiar to yeast breads. Never let rising temp. exceed 85-90° or your bread will have a strong yeasty flavor and rise too quickly, causing large air bubbles. Let rise until doubled. Dough will sometimes fall if allowed to rise higher. This could cause your bread to be dry and coarse. If your dough should fall, knead lightly and let rise again, do not throw out.

PUNCHING OR STIRRING DOWN

This step redistributes yeast cells to a new food supply and encourages continued growth of dough. To do this, punch fist into center of dough, pull edges into center and turn dough over. Batter dough should be stirred with wooden spoon until almost its original size.

SECOND RISING

The only purpose for this rising is a finer texture. It is not needed when using soft grain flours. To prepare dough, punch down; knead lightly (5-6 times) right in bowl. Let rise again until ALMOST doubled.

SHAPING FOR FINAL RISING

Knead lightly, let rest (5-10 min). This rest is important. It allows the dough to relax for easier rolling and shaping. Cut into equal sized pieces. Roll each piece with a rolling pin. This will bring large bubbles in your dough to the surface. Roll into a rectangle (12x9x½). Beginning at narrow end, roll to form a loaf by stretching and rolling tightly. Press down ends to prevent air from seeping into rising dough. Place in prepared pans, seam side down. Cover and let rise again. Bread reaches much of its volume at this time but do not allow dough to reach expected final size before baking, only to ALMOST doubled in size. Dough may fall in the oven because the yeast has no more strength left to support bread while baking if allowed to rise too high.

BRUSHES OR GLAZES

Loaves can be brushed with various ingredients; BUTTER, melted, can be brushed on before baking, toward the end of baking or after bread is removed from the oven. This helps to brown the crust or keep it soft. MILK, can be brushed on toward the end of baking to help brown crust. Return to oven 5-10 minutes. MILK and SUGAR are brushed over pastry sweet-doughs for color. WATER, brushed or sprayed on makes a crisp crust. A hot oven can be sprayed with water to produce steam for a crusty bread. WATER AND SALT (1 tsp to 2 cups water) can be brushed on when loaves are partially baked. EGG WASH (1 egg yolk and 1-2 Tbsp water or milk) can be brushed on before baking or toward end of baking.

OVEN SETTINGS FOR CRUST VARIATIONS

Soft golden crust: remove water; remove risen loaves; preheat oven then bake.

Chewy crust, darker brown: remove water from oven; do not disturb loaves; cold-start oven to designated temperature. Bake the maximum amount of time given in recipe.

Crusty, brown crust: refill pan with hot steamy water. Remove risen loaves. Preheat oven to 500° then turn control to temperature specified in recipe. Paint or spray loaves with water or salted water. Spray hot oven. Place loaves in oven. Bake 10-15 minutes then spray or paint loaves once or twice more. Continue baking according to directions.

BREAD IS DONE

1. When loaf no longer sticks to side of the pan.
2. When it sounds hollow when tapped on top, sides or bottom.

Remove from pans immediately to prevent crust from becoming soggy. Cool on racks. Keep out of drafts to prevent "pruning" and shrinking.

Enjoy the fruits of your labors, you deserve it.

Edith Skoog, Trumbull

Homemade Bread
(Sourdough)

Excellent light family loaf, so versatile

Yield: 3 loaves
Rise: 1½-2 hr
Bake: 350° 45 min
Pans: 3 loaf, greased (9x5)

5-7	cups	**flour,** unbleached	Measure; set aside.
1	cup	**Sourdough Starter III**	In a very large bowl, mix well. (Batter
2	cups	**water** (115°)	should be thick but not firm.) Let set
3	cups	reserved flour	in warm place (75-80°) overnight.
1		**egg,** beaten	
1½-2	tsp	**salt**	Add to above; beat well.
3	Tbsp	**sugar**	
3	Tbsp	**vegetable oil**	
3-5	cups	reserved flour	Add gradually, beating well after each addition. Use only enough flour to

form a medium soft dough. Knead well (10min); cut into 3 pieces. Knead lightly; form into loaves. Place in pans; let rise in warm place until double. Bake; remove from pans immediately. Cool on racks.

VARIATION: Excellent dough for plain rolls or cinnamon rolls with raisins. Bake: 400° 15-20 min.

Louise Thoman, Trumbull

 Add ¼ tsp ginger for each 2 loaves of bread you are mixing. This adds no taste but improves rising.

Sourdough Starter I

Try it – it's fun

Yield: 4-6 cups
Glass storage container (2qt)
Utensils: plastic or wooden (no metal)

1	pkg	**yeast,** dry
2	cups	**water,** warm (115°)

Dissolve yeast in water in storage container.

2	cups	**flour**

Add to above; mix well. Leave uncovered at room temperature. Stir occasionally to redistribute action.

1	cup	**flour**
1	cup	**milk**
¼	cup	**sugar**

24 hours later, add to above, mix well then let set out overnight again. The following morning, cover, store in the refrigerator. Return to room temperature for further feeding or when ready to use. Save at least 1 cup for replenishing but do not increase to over 6 cups. Discard one cup if it needs feeding and you have not used it. Replenish with flour, milk and sugar every 5-8 days or after earlier use; mix well; let set out overnight again then refrigerate until ready to use or replenish again. Sourdough I recipes are best when starter is replenished often keeping the starter "sweet".

Nancy Thoman, New Bern, NC

Sourdough Starter II

Simple and versatile

Yield: 3 cups
Glass container (2qt)

2	cups	**flour**
2	cups	**water** (105-110°)
1	pkg	**yeast,** dry

Put all ingredients in storage container and mix. Let set in warm place overnight, stirring occasionally. Refrigerate. Stir well before using. Feed every 6-7 days or after earlier use. If you do not use between feedings, discard 1 cupful, then replenish. Never allow to go under 1 cup.

Replenish with equal parts of flour and warm water (average 1 cup each). Let stand uncovered overnight, then refrigerate. Never add anything but flour and water to your starter sponge. Never allow it to come into prolonged contact with metal. Use wooden or plastic utensils to stir. Starter sponge should be very active after feeding. If liquid turns green or it seems very lethargic, discard and start over again.

Louise Thoman, Trumbull

 "Hooch" was a specialty of the Hoochinoo Indians and was made from the liquor that rose to the top of the starter hung in a pail above the stove in the camps of Gold Rush days.

Sourdough Starter III
(Potato)

Well worth the effort

Yield: 3 cups
Pans: saucepan (2qt); glass storage
(2qt)

2	cups	**potatoes,** cubed
1	qt	**water**

Cook until soft (5min). Place potatoes and water in blender. Blend until the consistency of mashed potatoes.

2	tsp	**salt**
¼	cup	**sugar**

Add to above; cool to lukewarm (115°).

1	pkg	**yeast,** dry

Sprinkle over potato mixture; stir until dissolved. Pour into glass storage container; let set in warm place (8-10hr) or until fermentation stops. Stir several times. Store covered in refrigerator. Use as starter. When only 1 cup remains, replenish.

To replenish: prepare starter again using remaining cup of starter **instead** of dry yeast. Let set at room temperature overnight. Refrigerate.

Louise Thoman, Trumbull

Toasting Loaf
(Sourdough)

A delicious "sweet" English muffin type bread

Yield: 1 loaf
Rise: 1-1½ hr
Bake: 350° 30-35 min
Pan: loaf, greased (8x4)

2	cups	**flour**
1	Tbsp	**baking powder**
1	tsp	**salt** (to taste)
2	Tbsp	**sugar**

In large bowl, mix well.

2	cups	**Sourdough Starter I** (stir well)
1		**egg**

Add to above; mix well. Turn into loaf pan; allow to rise until doubled. Bake.

Nancy Thoman, New Bern, NC

 LEAVENING AGENTS: Steam or air – these expand upon heating while baking, making foods light (popovers). Baking powder and soda – combine with an agent such as sour milk or buttermilk to form gas. Yeast and bacteria are biological agents. Egg whites hold air and release it during baking.

Cinnamon-Raisin Bread
(Sourdough)

Orange flavored raisins make this bread so tasty

Yield: 2 lg loaves
Soak: 1 hr
Rise: 3½-4 hr
Bake: 375° 50-60 min
Pans: 2 loaf, greased (9x5)

1-2	cups	**raisins**	Soak raisins in juice to cover (1hr). Drain well; reserve liquid. Set raisins aside. Measure 1 cup liquid (add water if short). Heat to lukewarm (115°).
1	cup	**orange juice**	
1	pkg	**yeast**	Add to above; stir until dissolved; set aside.
1½	cups	**Sourdough Starter II**	In large bowl, mix well.
1	cup	**oatmeal,** quick	
3	Tbsp	**instant potato FLAKES** (optional)	
1½-2	tsp	**salt**	
⅓	cup	**sugar**	
3	Tbsp	**shortening**	
		reserved yeast mix	Add to starter mixture.
4	cups	**flour**	Mix; add just enough to form a medium dough. Beat well (8-10min). Turn out onto floured surface; knead well until dough is satiny smooth and elastic, adding flour as needed. Grease a large bowl; roll dough to coat all sides. Cover and allow to rise until double (1½-2hr). Punch down; knead lightly (3-4min). Cut into 2 pieces. On lightly floured surface, roll half of dough into rectangle (½"thick).
1-2	tsp	**cinnamon**	
¼	cup	**brown sugar**	Combine; spread half on dough. Roll tightly; form a loaf. Place in pan. Repeat with other half. Let rise until doubled (1-1½hr). Bake.
¾	cup	**sugar**	
2-3	tsp	**cinnamon**	
		reserved raisins	

Louise Thoman, Trumbull

 BRAN is the ground husk or outer coat of wheat and other grains. It is great fiber food.

French Loaves
(Sourdough)

Stays fresh and moist. Toasts beautifully.

Yield: 2 loaves
Rise: 2 hr
Bake: 375° 30-35 min
Pan: cookie sheet, greased

6-7½	cups	**flour**	Measure; set aside.
1	pkg	**yeast,** dry	Stir until yeast is dissolved; pour into large mixer bowl.
12	oz	**beer** (110°)	
1	cup	**Sourdough Starter III,** room temp	Add to above; blend.
3	Tbsp	**sugar**	
2	Tbsp	**butter,** softened	
2	cups	reserved flour	Combine; add to above. Beat well.
2	tsp	**salt**	
½	tsp	**baking soda**	
2	cups	reserved flour	Add; beat well. Stir in as much of remaining flour as needed to form a firm dough; knead (10-12min). When smooth and elastic, form into a ball; place in greased bowl. Turn to coat all sides. Cover with plastic wrap. Let rise in warm place until doubled (1-1½hr). Punch down; knead and divide into 2 pieces. Let rest (10min). Form into 2 long loaves.
		corn meal	Sprinkle over prepared cookie sheet. Place loaves over. Let rise approx 20-

30 min. Preheat oven to 500°; spray with water to form steam. Place pan of steaming hot water on lower rack. Reduce oven to 375°. Bake until golden.

Louise Thoman, Trumbull

To provide a warm place for rising yeast doughs:
Warm bowl in hot water then dry before greasing.
Set bowl in a deep pan of warm water.

Place dough in bowl then in large plastic bag to retain heat and moisture, this will hasten rising.

Basic White Bread Plus

"A tasty bread, most easy to prepare"

Yield: 2 loaves
Rise: 2½ hr total
Bake: 400° 20 min
Pans: 2 loaf, greased (8x4)

5½-6½ cups	**flour**		Measure; set aside.

2 cups	**water**	Heat to 120-130°. Shortening need not melt completely.
3 Tbsp	**butter, margarine** OR **vegetable shortening**	

3 Tbsp	**sugar**	Combine in large bowl. Add above liquid and beat with electric mixer (3min).
1½ tsp	**salt**	
2 cups	reserved flour	
1 pkg	**yeast,** dry	
⅔ cup	**dry milk powder**	
1	**egg**	

1 cup	reserved flour	Add to above; beat (3min). Work in enough remaining flour to make a stiff dough. Turn out onto lightly floured

surface. Knead (8-10min) until dough is springy and smooth. Place in greased bowl, turning to coat all sides; cover and let rise in warm place until double (1hr). Punch down; let rest on floured surface (10min). Divide in half, shape into loaves and place in pans. Cover; let rise until almost doubled (40-50min). Bake; remove from pans immediately. Cool on racks.

VARIATIONS:
- Substitute an equal amount of honey for sugar; add to liquid while warming.
- Substitute 1½-2 cups rye or whole wheat flour for an equal amount of white flour.
- Add 1 Tbsp crushed herbs to any variation.
- Add 1 Tbsp crushed caraway or dill seeds to rye bread.
- Cinnamon-Raisin Bread: increase sugar to 3½Tbsp, add 2½tsp cinnamon and ½-1 cup raisins directly into pre-kneaded dough.
- Add ¼ cup raw bran or wheat germ to any variation.

Edith Skoog, Trumbull

For plump, juicy raisins in your cakes and breads, rinse thoroughly in hot water, drain very well. Flour lightly just before adding to your batter. This will prevent sinking to the bottom.

KC's High Fiber Loaf Bread

A delicious, light, high protein bread

Yield: 3-4 loaves
Rise: 1 hr 45 min
Bake: 325° 25-30 min
Pans: 3 loaf, greased (9x5) or 4
  1-1½qt casseroles

5-6	cups	**flour,** unbleached	Measure; set aside.
1-2	cups	**whole wheat flour**	Combine; set aside.
1	cup	**dry milk powder**	
3	cups	**water**	Combine; heat to 110°.
4	Tbsp	**margarine**	
2	pkg	**yeast,** dry	Add to water and stir to dissolve;
4	Tbsp	**honey** OR 3Tbsp **sugar**	pour into large bowl.
3		**eggs**	
2-3	tsp	**salt**	
¼	cup	**wheat germ**	
½	cup	**bran cereal**	
½	cup	**oatmeal,** raw	Add; beat in well.
½	cup	**instant potato flakes** (optional)	
2	cups	reserved flour	
		reserved whole wheat flour	
		reserved flour	Add enough flour to form a dough that comes away from the side of the

bowl and can be handled although still slightly sticky. Turn out onto lightly floured surface; knead well (10-12min) adding flour as needed. Place in greased bowl; turn to coat all sides. Cover and let rise in warm place until doubled (1hr). Punch down. Divide into 4 pieces; knead lightly. Let rest (10min). Form into loaves; place in prepared pans. Let rise until almost doubled (45min). Heat oven to 400°, immediately turn to 325°. Bake. Remove from pans immediately and cool on racks.

Louise Thoman, Trumbull

 HONEY gets its color and flavor from the various flowers from which the bees gather their nectar. Foods remain moist longer when honey is used. Substitutions: medium thick honey. If honey is used for half of the sugar, reduce liquids by ¼. If honey is used to replace all of the sugar, reduce liquids by ½. Bake at the lowest temperature possible to save moisture and prevent scorching. Store in a dry but warm place to prevent clouding. If it crystallizes, warm in water not above 140°.

Dilly Bread

"Delicious with fine, light consistency"

Yield: 1 loaf*
Rise: 1½-2 hr
Bake: 40-50 min
Pan: casserole, greased (1½-2qt)

1	pkg	**yeast**	
¼	cup	**water** (115°)	In mixer bowl, mix until dissolved.

1 cup **cottage cheese**, small curd — Heat to lukewarm (115°); add to above.

2	Tbsp	**sugar**
1	Tbsp	**instant minced onion**
1	Tbsp	**butter**
2	tsp	**dill seed**
1	tsp	**salt**
¼	tsp	**baking soda**
1		**egg**, unbeaten
2-2½	cups	**flour**

Combine; add to above. Mix well. Cover; let rise in warm place until double (50-60min). Stir down; pour into casserole and let rise again (30-40min). Bake. Optional: after removing from oven, brush top with butter and sprinkle with salt.

NOTE: *Doubles well. DO NOT DOUBLE YEAST. May be baked in loaf pan; slices well for sandwiches.

Nancy Renner, West Haven

The Best Pizza Dough

Freezes well too, cooked or uncooked

Yield: 3 pizzas
Bake: 450° 15-20 min
Pans: grease with OLIVE OIL

2	cups	**flour**
½	tsp	**sugar**
½	tsp	**salt**

Combine in medium bowl.

1	env	**yeast**, dry
½	cup	**water** (110°)

Mix to dissolve; add to above.

3 Tbsp **olive oil** — Add, along with yeast mixture. Combine quickly (processor best) only until dough comes away from sides of bowl. On lightly floured surface, knead well (just lightly if processor is used). Allow to rise (1-1½hr) until doubled. Press down and divide into 3 or 4 equal pieces. Roll each into a ball and allow to rise (15min). Stretch each to fit bottom of prepared pan. Spread with favorite sauce and toppings. Let set (10min). Bake in hot oven until crust is golden and toppings are hot and bubbly.

Aster Seele, Bridgeport

 ALWAYS prepare pizza pan with OLIVE OIL for that "fried", crispy crust.

John Santilli, Fairfield

Spinach-Pepperoni Bread
(Italian)

"Delicious, with lots of spice"

Yield: 1 loaf
Rise: 1½ hr total
Bake: 350° 35 min
Pan: cookie sheet, greased

1	lb	**pizza dough,** fresh or frozen (see Index)	Prepare or thaw; let rise in warm place (45min).
1	pkg	**spinach,** frozen (10oz)	
1	clove	**garlic,** grated **vegetable oil**	Defrost and drain spinach; sauté.
1		**egg**	
4	Tbsp	**Parmesan cheese**	
1	tsp	**oregano**	Combine; add to spinach mixture. Warm thoroughly (5min).
½	tsp	**salt**	
½	tsp	**pepper**	
1	stick	**pepperoni,** sliced thin (approx ½lb)	Add to above; continue warming (5min). Punch down bread dough. Roll into rectangle (9x12x½); spoon

mixture along center of rectangle (lengthwise). Fold dough overlapping to form a loaf, or roll out (12x15x¼); spread filling to within 1" of edges of dough then roll up as for jelly roll. Seal seam; place on cookie sheet seam side down. Rub with a small amount of vegetable oil; let rise again (45min). Bake; serve warm.

VARIATION: Broccoli may be substituted for spinach. Cut lengthwise up the middle then into small slices and serve as appetizer.

Kathy Miller, Easton

Sweet Bread
(Portuguese)

"Delicious, excellent toasted"

Yield: 4 loaves
Rise: 3 hr total
Bake: 350° 20 min
Pan: cookie sheets

6½	cups	**flour**	Measure; set aside.
2	cups	reserved flour	
¾	cup	**sugar**	Combine in large mixer bowl.
1	tsp	**salt**	
2	pkg	**yeast**, dry	
1	cup	**milk**	
¼	cup	**water**	Heat to 120°; add to flour mixture
¼	cup	**margarine**	and beat (2min) at medium speed.
3		**eggs**	Add to above; beat on high speed
1	cup	reserved flour	(2min).
3½	cups	reserved flour	Add; mix by hand. Turn onto lightly floured surface; knead (5min). Place

in greased bowl; roll dough to coat. Let rise (1½hr). Punch down; divide into 4 pieces. Shape into round loaves. Place 2 on each cookie sheet; let rise (1½hr). Bake 2 at a time on rack high in oven.

Dolores Segala, Trumbull

Cheese Pepper Bread

"Different and so tasty!"

Yield: 2 loaves
Rise: 50 min
Bake: 350° 40 min
Pans: 2 coffee cans (1lb), greased

2⅓	cups	**flour**	Measure then set aside.
1	pkg	**yeast**, dry	In large bowl, stir until dissolved.
¼	cup	**water**, warm (115°)	
1⅓	cups	reserved flour	
2	Tbsp	**sugar**	Add to above; blend with electric
¼	tsp	**baking soda**	mixer (½min) on low speed. Scrape
1	tsp	**salt**	bowl continuously. Beat (2min) on
1	cup	**sour cream**	high speed, scraping occasionally.
1		**egg**	
1	cup	reserved flour	Stir into above; mix thoroughly. Divide in half and place in cans. Let rise
1	cup	**cheddar cheese**, yellow, grated*	in warm place (50min). Dough will not double. Bake until golden; remove
½	tsp	**pepper**	from cans immediately. Cool then slice.

SUBSTITUTION: *Can use ⅓ cup Provolone cheese and ⅔ cup Parmesan cheese instead of cheddar.

Nancy Gray, Trumbull

Challah
(Jewish)

Sabbath bread

Yield: 2 large
Rise: 4 hr total
Bake: 375° 50 min
Pan: large cookie sheet

10	cups	**flour**
2	cakes	**yeast**
¾	cup	**sugar**
1	Tbsp	**salt** (rounded)
¼	cup	**vegetable oil**
12		**egg yolks**
2	cups	**water,** lukewarm (105°)

Mix well, adding enough flour to form a medium dough. Turn out on lightly floured surface; knead (10min) until smooth and elastic. Place in greased bowl; roll to coat well. Cover; let rise (1½hr). Punch down; cover and let rise again until double. Punch down; divide in half. Cut each half in 3 pieces; roll each into a "rope". Dampen ends to hold together; braid. Place on cookie sheet.

1		**egg,** beaten

Brush loaves; let rise on cookie sheet (1 hr).

poppy seeds

Sprinkle over loaves. Bake.

Gail Cohen, Trumbull

Babka
(Polish)

Easter egg bread

Rise: 1½-2 hr
Bake: 350° 30 min
Pan: tube (8"), greased

½	cup	**flour**
¾	cup	**milk,** hot

Combine; stir until smooth and lump free. Set aside to cool slightly.

1		**yeast cake,** crushed
1	tsp	**sugar**
1	Tbsp	**water,** warm (115°)

Combine and add to above; set aside to rise (1hr) until doubled.

2	lg	**egg yolks**
½	tsp	**salt**

Beat until thick; add to risen yeast mixture.

2-2¼	cups	**flour**
2	Tbsp	**butter,** soft
⅓	cup	**sugar**
½	tsp	**vanilla**
¼	cup	**raisins** (optional)

Add; work in by hand until dough no longer sticks. Let rise in warm place until doubled. Punch down and let rise again (45min) until almost doubled. Bake. Frost top with lemon flavored icing allowing it to drip over sides.

Pat McCathron, Trumbull

Panettone
(Italian)

Easter bread

Yield: 1 lg loaf
Rise: 1-1½ hr
Bake: 375° 50 min
Pan: soufflé (9"), greased

3	cups	**flour**	Measure; set aside.
½	cup	**milk,** scalded, cooled	Set aside.
½	cup	**butter**	
¼	cup	**sugar**	Cream well; set aside.
1	tsp	**salt**	
¼	cup	**water,** warm (115°)	In large bowl, stir until dissolved; add
1	pkg	**yeast,** dry	milk and creamed mixture.
2		**eggs,** beaten	Add to above; mix well.
½	tsp	**anise extract** (optional)	
1½	cups	reserved flour	Add gradually beating well after each addition.

Add to above; add enough flour to make a very soft dough. Turn out onto lightly floured surface; knead until smooth and elastic. Place in greased bowl; cover. Let rise in warm place until double (1½hr). Punch down; turn out on lightly floured surface. Let rest (10min); shape into round loaf. Place in pan; cover and let rise until doubled. Bake.

⅓	cup	**raisins,** seedless
¼	cup	**candied fruit,** diced
¼	cup	**almonds,** roasted, diced
1	Tbsp	**lemon peel,** grated
1½	cups	reserved flour

Helen Sorchiotti, Trumbull

Malasadas
(Portuguese)

A light delicious sweet dough, fried. Yum!

Yield: 5 doz
Rise: 1½ hr
Deep fry: 20-30 min total
Pan: kettle (4-6qt)

1	pkg	**yeast**	Stir until dissolved. Let stand while mixing other ingredients.
⅓	cup	**water,** lukewarm (115°)	
1	tsp	**sugar**	

7	cups	**flour**	Measure into large bowl.
⅓	cup	**sugar**	
1	tsp	**salt**	

1⅓	cup	**cream**	Mix then add to dry ingredients.
1⅓	cup	**water,** warm (115°)	

⅓	cup	**butter** OR **margarine,** melted, cooled	Add and mix well. This should form a soft dough. Cover and let rise in a warm place until doubled (1-1½hr).
8		**eggs,** lightly beaten reserved yeast mix	

vegetable oil for frying	Drop by spoonfuls into deep hot oil, frying until light brown. Turn over only once to brown all sides. Remove; drain well on brown paper.
granulated sugar	Roll in sugar; serve. Can be reheated in oven (5min).

Celeste Jardim, Trumbull

 EGGS are a good source of protein, iron, vitamin A, B and D. They act as a "binder" and stabilizer when interacting with other foods when beaten together.

Vanocka
(Czechoslovakian)

A Christmas morning tradition in our family for many generations

Yield: 2 braids
Rise: 2½ hr
Bake: 325° 30-35 min
Pans: cookie sheets, greased

1½	cups	**milk,** scalded	Mix until melted; cool to lukewarm (110°).
1	cup	**butter**	
1	cup	**sugar**	
2	pkg	**yeast,** dry	Stir until dissolved; add to above.
¼	cup	**water,** lukewarm	
2		**eggs**	Add to above; mix well.
8	cups	**flour**	Sift together in large bowl; add liquids. Beat until dough does not stick to side of bowl. (Dough will be stiff.) Place in greased bowl; let rise in warm place until double (2hr).
1	tsp	**salt**	
½	tsp	**mace**	
½	tsp	**lemon rind,** grated	
½	cup	**almonds,** blanched, chopped	Stir into dough; knead on lightly floured surface until shiny. Divide dough in half, then 1st half into 4 pieces and second half into 5 smaller pieces. Roll each piece into a long roll and let all rise in warm place. To form loaf, punch down each roll; braid the 4 large pieces together forming a loaf. Place on greased cookie sheet. Braid 3 of the smaller pieces and place on top of loaf. Twist remaining 2 pieces and place on top. Let rise (approx ½hr).
1	cup	**raisins** (half golden, if desired)	
1	Tbsp	**candied cherries,** halved	
1		**egg yolk**	Mix well and brush loaf. Bake until golden and delicious.
1	tsp	**water**	

Barbara Jelinek, Bayport, NY

Coffee Braid
(Swedish)

Scrumptious warm or cold

Yield: 3 small braids or 24 buns
Rise: 2 hr
Bake: see recipe
Pans: cookie sheets, greased

5	cups	**bread flour**	Mix in large bowl; set aside.
1	tsp	**cardamon,** ground	
1½	cups	**milk,** scalded	
1	cup	**butter** OR **margarine**	Add to hot milk; cool to lukewarm (110°).
½	cup	**sugar**	
1	tsp	**salt**	
1		**egg**	Add to above; beat well.
2	pkg	**yeast**	Stir until dissolved; add to above. Add liquids to flour; knead until smooth. When dough no longer sticks to your hands, it has been worked enough. Sprinkle with flour and cover with towel. Let rise in warm place until double (1hr). Place on floured surface, knead again until pliable. Form into desired shapes. Place on greased baking sheets; cover. Let rise again until double (45min).
¼	cup	**water,** lukewarm	
1		**egg white,** well beaten	Brush over dough.
		sugar	Sprinkle very generously. Bake: 350° 3 small braids (25min); 24 buns (15-20min).

Phyllis Aiello, Stratford

Vinerbrod
(Swedish)

Best right after baking but can be frozen and reheated

Yield: 20 pastries
Rise: 1hr
Bake: 400° 12 min
Pan: cookie sheets, greased

3	cups	**flour**	Place in large bowl; form nest.
1		**egg**	Drop into nest.
2	pkg	**yeast**	Dissolve; add to above.
¼	cup	**water,** warm (115°)	
⅓	cup	**sugar**	Add; stir until mixture becomes dough. Roll out on well floured surface to form rectangle (10x15). When dough is manageable, flour top lightly.
¾	cup	**milk,** room temp	
1	cup	**BUTTER,** softened (no substitutes)	Spread over dough. Fold dough over 3 times starting at narrow end. Roll out again. Repeat, folding and rolling out 3 or 4 times. Roll out. Cut long thin pieces of dough and twist into figure eights.
1		**egg white,** stiffly beaten	Brush with egg white.
½	cup	**sugar**	Dip each in sugar. Place on baking sheets; let rise until double (1hr). Bake until golden. Serve warm.

Phyllis Aiello, Stratford

Hot Cross Buns

A Lenten tradition

Yield: 4 doz
Rise: 2½ hr
Bake: 350° 20-25 min
Pans: 3 8x8, greased

2	cups	**milk,** scalded
1	cup	**sugar**
5	Tbsp	**shortening** (part butter)

Mix in large bowl; cool to lukewarm (105-115°).

1½	cups	**raisins**

Steam over hot water to soften; set aside to cool.

7	cups	**flour**
4	tsp	**salt**
3	tsp	**cinnamon**
¼	tsp	**nutmeg**

Sift together; set aside.

2	pkg	**yeast**
1	tsp	**sugar**
¼	cup	**water**

Mix well to dissolve. Proof (5min) then add to cooled milk mixture.

2-3	cups	reserved flour mix
1		**egg,** beaten

Stir in; beat well.

reserved raisins — Add to above; mix well.

reserved flour mix — Add remaining flour gradually; mix well. Place in greased bowl; cover and let stand in warm, draft-free place until doubled (1½hr). Turn out on well floured surface; divide in thirds, then each third into fourths. Shape rolls; place 16 in each pan and cover. Let rise to top of pan.

1		**egg,** beaten
1	tsp	**water**

Mix; brush top of rolls. Bake. Ice each roll in the form of a cross with Confectioners' Icing (see Index).

Frieda Schmidt, Trumbull

RAISINS are dried grapes, seeded. To plump, rinse well, drain then place over boiling water and steam (5min).

Cinnamon Pecan Rolls

Also delicious as coffeecake!

Yield: 32 rolls
Chill: overnight
Rise: 1 hr
Bake: 350° 25-30 min
Pans: 2 9x9, greased

¾	cup	**milk,** scalded	In large bowl, mix; cool to lukewarm (115°).
½	cup	**sugar**	
2	tsp	**salt**	
½	cup	**margarine**	
2	pkg	**yeast,** dry	When bubbly, add to cooled milk mixture.
½	cup	**water** (115°)	
	pinch	**sugar**	
1		**egg,** beaten	Add; mix well.
2	cups	**flour**	Add; beat well.
2	cups	**flour**	Add; mix well by hand. Cover; refrigerate overnight. Next morning, punch down; divide in half. On floured surface, roll into 2 rectangles (8x16).
2-3	Tbsp	**butter,** melted	Brush over dough.

FILLING

6	Tbsp	**butter** OR **margarine,** melted	Mix; spread half on each rectangle. Roll tightly, starting with long side. Cut into 1" pieces; place in pans, 4 per row. Cover; let rise until doubled. Bake. Frost with Confectioners' Icing (see Index).
6	Tbsp	**flour**	
1	cup	**lt brown sugar,** packed hard	
1½	tsp	**cinnamon**	
1	cup	**pecans,** chopped	

COFFEE RINGS: Form into 2 rings on cookie sheets. Snip deep cuts 1" apart; twist each piece. Can push chopped dates or raisins into cuts. Bake. Drizzle with frosting when cool.

Barbara Gustafson, Lyme

 To soften brown sugar quickly, place package in 250° oven (10min) then roll out lumps with a rolling pin.

Cinnamon Rolls
(Sourdough)

Great after school snack

Yield: 12
Bake: 350° 20 min
Pan: 9x9, greased

ROLLS

1	cup	**flour**	
1	tsp	**baking powder**	} Combine.
¼	tsp	**salt**	

⅓	cup	**margarine**	Cut into above

1	cup	**Sourdough Starter I** (stir well)	Add; mix well. On floured surface, roll into rectangle (¼" thick).

2	Tbsp	**margarine,** softened	Spread over dough carefully.

FILLING

¼	cup	**sugar**	Sprinkle over margarine. Roll, starting with long side; cut into 1" thick pieces. (To cut, use a coarse thread, wrap around dough; cross at top; pull in opposite directions to cut without damage to your rounds.) DO NOT LET DOUGH RISE. Prepare topping or bake as is, then ice. (see Index for Confectioners' Icing)
1	tsp	**cinnamon**	
¼	cup	**nuts,** chopped (optional)	
⅓	cup	**raisins,** chopped; **apples,** chopped OR **blueberries** (optional)	

TOPPING (optional)

½	cup	**brown sugar**	Melt in saucepan, over low heat. Spread over bottom of prepared pan.
¼	cup	**margarine**	
1	Tbsp	**light corn syrup**	

¼-½	cup	**nuts,** chopped OR **coconut** (optional)	Sprinkle over topping if desired. Arrange rolls over all. Bake; invert on serving dish while hot.

Nancy Thoman, New Bern, NC

To make your own coconut milk, moisten shredded coconut in fresh milk with a bit of sugar added. Let set several minutes then strain.

Ice Box Crescents

A no-knead bread that needs only one rising

Yield: 4
Chill: overnight
Bake: 400° 25 min
Pans: cookie sheets, greased

DOUGH

4	cups	**flour**	
2	Tbsp	**sugar**	Sift together.
1	tsp	**salt**	

1	cup	**butter,** cold	Cut into flour mixture until the consistency of coarse meal; set aside.

1	cup	**milk,** cold	Combine to dissolve yeast.
1	pkg	**yeast**	

3		**eggs,** separated (reserve whites)	Beat yolks; add to milk-yeast mixture. Add combined liquids to dry ingredients; mix until well blended. Form into a ball; place in small bowl. Cover tightly; chill overnight.

FILLING

		reserved egg whites	Beat whites until frothy; add sugar, 1 Tbsp at a time, beating well after each addition. Set aside.
1	cup	**sugar**	

1	cup	**walnuts** OR **pecans,** chopped	Set aside.

To prepare crescents, divide chilled dough into 4 parts; roll each on a floured surface as for pie crust (¼"). Spread ¼ filling on each round, sprinkle with nuts. Roll loosely as for jelly roll. Place on cookie sheets, in crescent shapes (2 per sheet). Let rise in warm place until doubled (1-1½hr). Bake one sheet at a time. Do not allow to brown too early. Frost with Confectioners' Icing when almost at room temperature.

VARIATION: Cut dough into 6" squares then cut each square into 2 triangles. Place approximately 1-2 tsp filling on each triangle. Roll starting with the wide edge of the triangle. Curve into a crescent. Bake: 375° (15-18min). Can use any variety of fruit or nut filling.

Mary Telford, Trumbull

SHORTENING for biscuits should be very cold and cut in well. Liquid should be chilled and add only the smallest amount needed. Liquid should be added slowly. This will make your biscuits light. Pat or roll gently.

Beer Bread

Try it you'll like it

Yield: 1 loaf
Bake: 375° 50-60 min
Pan: loaf, greased (9x5)

3½	cups	flour	
1½	tsp	baking powder	
¼	tsp	salt	Mix together.
½	cup	sugar	

1	can	beer (12oz)	Add to above. Stir just until blended. Pour into pan. Bake. (350°, glass pan) Drizzle with melted butter. Turn out on rack; cool slightly before slicing.

Darlene Nelson, Fairfield

VARIATION

3	cups	self-rising flour	
¾	cup	sugar	Follow above directions.
1	can	beer (12oz)	
1	tsp	caraway seeds (optional)	
1	tsp	herbs, mixed (optional)	Can be added to the batter.

Trina Oswald, New Haven

Scones
(English)

"Delicious with butter and homemade preserves"

Yield: 12 pieces
Bake: 450° 7-10 min
Pan: cookie sheet

1⅔	cup	flour	
½	tsp	salt	Combine.
1	tsp	baking soda	
1½	tsp	cream of tartar	
¼	cup	butter	Cut into above until fine.
⅓	cup	raisins	Stir into above.
¼	cup	sugar (optional)	
1		egg, beaten (reserve 1 tsp)	Add egg and only enough milk to form a moist dough that can be handled. Flatten into two large rounds; score each into 6 wedges.
¼-⅓	cup	milk	
		reserved egg	Brush over dough. Bake.

Joy Tait, Monroe

Chapati or Pouri
(India)

Serve with traditional Indian meal

Serves: 4
Stovetop: 2-3 min,ea
Pan: skillet (sm)

1½	cups	**whole wheat flour**	
2	Tbsp	**oil**	Mix thoroughly in bowl.
1	tsp	**salt**	

½	cup	**water,** cold (approx)	Add just enough to form a soft dough. Divide into 16 balls; roll each into a thin circle (3½" diameter x ⅛" thick).

	oil for deep frying	Heat in skillet. When hot, add one pouri. Fry (1min) until puffed; turn over and fry (1min) longer. Repeat for all pouri.

Kirti Pancholi, No. Kingstown, RI

Soda Bread
(Irish)

A great Irish tradition

Yield: 1 loaf
Bake: 350° 50-60 min
Pan: cake (9") or pudding pan

4	cups	**flour**	
2-4	Tbsp	**sugar**	
3	tsp	**baking powder**	Sift into large bowl.
1	tsp	**baking soda**	
	pinch	**salt** (optional)	

3-4	Tbsp	**margarine**	Cut into above.

2	cups	**raisins**	
1½	Tbsp	**caraway seeds** (op-tional)	Stir into above.

Combine; add gradually to flour mixture until soft dough forms. Turn out onto floured board; knead lightly (10 times). Shape into ball; pat into pan. Brush with reserved egg. Cut a cross on top (1½" deep). Bake until nicely browned. Cool (10min) then turn out onto cake rack, right side up. Cool before cutting.

2		**eggs,** lightly beaten (reserve 1 Tbsp)
1¾	cups	**buttermilk**

Kathleen Gioffre, Port Chester, NY

Oat Bran Muffins

Apples in the batter make them even better!

Yield: 10-12
Bake: 400° 15-20 min
Pan: muffin, greased

½	cup	bran cereal
½	cup	milk

Combine in medium bowl; let set a few minutes.

1		egg
¼	cup	vegetable oil
¼	cup	molasses
¼	cup	brown sugar (packed)

Add to above and mix well.

1	cup	quick oats, uncooked
⅔	cup	flour
1	Tbsp	baking powder

Combine, then add to above. Stir only until batter is moistened – do not beat.

½	cup	apples, peeled, chopped OR dates, chopped
½	cup	walnuts, chopped

Fold into above. Fill muffin cups. Bake.

Nancy Renner, West Haven

Good N' Easy Muffins

Blueberries make these special!

Yield: 10-12
Bake: 400° 20 min
Pan: muffin, greased

1		egg
½	cup	milk
¼	cup	vegetable oil
1½	cups	flour
½	cup	sugar
2	tsp	baking powder
½	tsp	salt
1	cup	blueberries

Combine ingredients in order given; mix well by hand. Pour into well greased muffin cups.

2	Tbsp	sugar
¼	tsp	cinnamon

Combine and sprinkle mixture on top of each muffin. Bake.

VARIATION: Substitute ¾ cup whole wheat flour for ¾ cup white flour or substitute ⅓ cup raw bran for ⅓ cup white flour. More nutritious!

Joan Kacin, Trumbull

For light pancakes, use club soda instead of liquid called for in your recipe.

A bit of sugar in your pancake batter will help brown them more quickly.

Sweet Potato Biscuits

Delicate flavor, so moist

Yield: 12-15
Bake: 450° 15 min
Pan: cookie sheet

¾	cup	**sweet potatoes,** cooked, mashed
⅔	cup	**milk**
¼	cup	**butter,** melted
¼	cup	**brown sugar**

Combine; mix well.

1¼	cups	**flour,** sifted
4	Tbsp	**baking powder**
½	tsp	**salt**

Mix well; add to above making a soft dough. Turn onto lightly floured board; knead lightly. Roll to ½ inch; cut and place on ungreased baking sheet. Bake.

Sally Easter, Bridgeport

O J Biscuits

"These are delicious"

Serves: 8
Bake: 425° 15-20 min
Pan: 8 custard cups, greased

1	Tbsp	**orange juice**
2	tsp	**orange rind**
½	cup	**honey**
¼	cup	**margarine**

Simmer over low heat (3min); remove; cool slightly.

¼	cup	**coconut** OR **nuts,** chopped

Add to above; divide evenly into custard cups.

2	cups	**flour,** sifted
4	tsp	**baking powder**
¼	cup	**margarine**
¾	cup	**milk** (approx)

Combine to form a soft dough. Mix well but gently. Divide into custard cups. Bake. Invert and serve hot.

Aster Seale, Bridgeport

Preheat muffin pans to make your muffins lighter yet.

BISCUITS if placed in muffin tins will be brown and crispy on all sides. Packed side by side they will be higher and brown only on top and bottom.

Wesley Waffles

Different, delicious!

Serves: 4-6
Bake: 5-7 min each
Pan: waffle iron, preheated

½	cup	**butter** OR **margarine**	Melt; set aside to cool.
2		**eggs**	
½	cup	**orange juice**	
1½-2	cups	**milk**	Place in blender bowl; blend well.
½	cup	**sweet potato**, cooked (optional)	
		reserved butter	
1¼	cups	**flour**	
¼	cup	**wheat germ**	In large bowl of mixer, mix well. Add egg mixture. Beat well (1min). Do not stir again. Spoon onto waffle iron. Bake until crisp and brown.
½	cup	**cornmeal**	
1	cup	**oatmeal**, quick	
2	Tbsp	**baking powder**	
½	tsp	**orange rind**, grated (optional)	

SUGGESTION: Serve with sliced bananas topped with Strawberry-Rhubarb Sauce (see Index) or your favorite topping.

Louise Thoman, Trumbull

French Toast "François" Style

Try this for rave reviews!

Serves: 4-6
Bake: 375° 15 min
Pan: skillet (lg); 13x9, glass

TOAST

2		eggs	
1½	Tbsp	confectioners' sugar	
2	cups	whipping cream	Combine and beat well.
	pinch	salt	
½	tsp	vanilla	
⅓	cup	rum OR brandy	

12	slices	French bread, (1" thick, cut on slant) butter for frying	Dip each slice in above mixture; sauté in skillet until golden on both sides. Arrange slices in casserole, overlapping about half way. Preheat oven.

CUSTARD SAUCE

½	cup	milk	Heat in double boiler until it bubbles; reserve.

1		egg, beaten lightly	
1	Tbsp	sugar	Combine; add hot milk stirring constantly.
	pinch	salt	
½	tsp	vanilla	

½	cup	applesauce	Mix into custard sauce; pour over golden toast.

¼	cup	confectioners' sugar	Sprinkle over casserole. Bake until hot. Serve hot with butter or maple syrup. Can be prepared ahead (1hr) and refrigerated. Bake just before serving. Increase baking time to (20-25min).

Barbara Ryan, Redondo Beach, Ca

 VANILLA BEAN is the dried bean of an orchid, abundant in Mexico.

French Toast Lorraine

Great Sunday night supper with lots of maple syrup!

Serves: 4
Soak: 4-5 hr or overnight
Stovetop: 10-12 min
Pan: heavy skillet (lg)

8	slices	**French bread,** 1" thick

2		**eggs**	Beat together; soak bread slices, turning occasionally (all liquid should be absorbed).
½	cup	**Parmesan cheese,** grated	
1	tsp	**prepared mustard**	
⅔	cup	**milk**	

	butter	Sauté slices until puffed and golden on both sides.

4	slices	**bacon,** cooked crisp, crumbled
		confectioners' sugar

Garnish.

Nancy Gray, Trumbull

Semmelklosse

(German)

The greatest dumplings!

Serves: 6
Boil: 20 min
Pan: skillet; kettle

6		**old rolls**
½	cup	**milk,** hot

Soak until milk is absorbed. Squeeze out excess.

4	slices	**bacon,** diced
1	med	**onion,** chopped

Brown in skillet. Add soaked bread.

1	cup	**flour**
1	tsp	**salt**

Stir into above. Cook well, on high heat, until mixture loosens from pan. Remove from heat. Place in bowl.

1		**egg,** separated (beat white until stiff)
2	tsp	**parsley,** fresh, chopped

Add yolk; mix in well. Fold in whites and remaining ingredients. Form into 2" balls; drop into rapidly boiling water and cook about 20min. Serve hot.

Gertrud Bargas, Trumbull

Kartoffel Kloesse
(German)

Potato dumplings to serve with soup or meats

Serves: 4-6
Stovetop: 20-25 min total
Pan: saucepan (4qt); skillet

4		**potatoes,** boiled, mashed well
2		**eggs,** beaten lightly
2	slices	**toast,** crushed fine
1	tsp	**flour**
1	tsp	**parsley,** chopped
	pinch	**nutmeg**
		salt, pepper to taste

Mix; shape into walnut sized balls. Drop, one at a time, into rapidly boiling salted water. Lift out as they rise to the top; drain.

butter

Brown the dumplings gently in a skillet. Serve hot.

Eddy Bernard, Trumbull

Almojabanas
(Puerto Rican)

Cheese-rice crullers – a great snack OR accompaniment for stew

Serves: 6
Standing time: 1½hr
Stovetop: 5 min per batch

1	cup	**rice flour**
1	cup	**milk**

Mix well then let stand at room temperature (1hr).

2-3		**eggs**
1	Tbsp	**butter,** melted

Add eggs, one at a time, along with butter; mix well. Let stand (30min).

2-3	tsp	**baking powder**
1	cup	**Puerto Rican white cheese** OR **your favorite,** grated

Add to above; mix in well.

½-1	tsp	**salt** (to taste)
		favorite seasonings to taste
		fat for deep frying

Drop by spoonful into hot fat. Fry until golden (3-5min). Serve as accompaniment to stew instead of bread OR as a snack with jelly.

Barbara Schegg, Huntington

Teisen
(Welsh)

A delicious non-sweet snack

Serves: 6-8
Bake: see recipe
Pan: see recipe

2	cups	**flour**	} Measure into medium bowl; cut fats into flour. Rub with hands until well worked in.
½	cup	**butter**	
1½	tsp	**shortening**	
½	cup	**sugar**	} Add; mix well. Form a well.
½-1	tsp	**nutmeg**	
1½	tsp	**baking powder**	
2		**eggs,** beaten	} Add just enough to form a medium firm dough; mix well.
½	cup	**buttermilk, cream** OR **milk**	
1	cup	**raisins, currants** OR **sultanas**	Add and mix in.

Cooking methods:
1. Grease 13x9 baking pan; place batter in; spread evenly. Bake: 275° (30-40min).
2. Chill dough or prepare a slightly firmer dough; roll out (½" thick) and cut into rounds (3-4"). Cook very slowly on buttered heavy griddle or electric fry pan (10min,ea side) or until golden. The Welsh use this method over an open fire.

Gwladys Dorman, Danielson

Apea Cake
(Pennsylvania Dutch)

A great no-egg snack cake

Yield: 12-16 pieces
Bake: 375° 25-30 min
Pan: (2) cake, greased (8")

4	cups	**flour**	} In large bowl, mix with pastry blender or hands, until well blended.
5	tsp	**baking powder**	
2	cups	**light brown sugar,** tightly packed	
1	cup	**shortening**	
1	cup	**water** (approx)	Add enough water to form a dough that is just stiff, bordering on soft. Pour into greased cake pans. Bake. Serve warm with butter or jam.

Harry Fillman, Dover, De

Graham Bread

"Quick! Nice dessert loaf"

Yield: 1 loaf
Bake: 350° 50-60 min
Pan: 9x5x3, greased

1	cup	**sour milk***
1		**egg,** beaten
½	cup	**sugar**
1	Tbsp	**butter,** melted
1	tsp	**baking soda**
½	tsp	**salt**
1½	cups	**graham flour****

Stir together to form a thick batter. Turn into pan. Bake then remove from pan to cool. *1 cup milk + 1 Tbsp vinegar or lemon juice **Found in specialty shops.

Julie Connery, Bridgeport

Colonial Poppyseed Loaf

A tasty Colonial legacy

Yield: 1 loaf
Bake: 350° 1 hr 15 min
Pan: 9x5x3, greased, floured

½	cup	**poppy seeds** (2oz)
¾	cup	**milk**

In large bowl, soak (3-4hr) at room temperature.

¾	cup	**butter,** softened
3		**eggs,** room temp
1¼	cups	**sugar**
1	tsp	**vanilla**
2	tsp	**baking powder**
2	cups	**flour**

Combine with the above; beat with electric mixer (1min) at medium speed. Pour into pan. Bake until cake springs back when lightly touched. Cool (5min); loosen edges and turn out on rack.

confectioners' sugar

Sprinkle over cake before serving.

Constance Detar, Stratford

CHOCOLATE – *Cacao is the raw bean; chocolate is the manufactured product; cocoa is the pulverized bean from which some of the cocoa butter has been removed.*

Nutritious Bran Raisin Bread

Great food value in every bite

Yield: 1 loaf
Bake: 375° 45 min
Pan: 9x5x3, greased, floured

1	cup	**bran flakes**
2½	cups	**whole wheat flour**
2	tsp	**baking powder**
½	tsp	**baking soda**
¼	cup	**vegetable oil**
¾	cup	**honey** OR **maple syrup**
1		**egg**
1	cup	**milk**
1	cup	**raisins***

Mix together in order given. Stir well. Bake. Let rest (5min) before removing from pan. Cool well before slicing.

*or ½ cup each raisins and nuts.

June Bartnett, Monroe

Banana Nut Bread

"A favorite in our family for four generations!"

Yield: 1 loaf
Bake: 350° 60-70 min
Pan: 9x5x3, greased

2	cups	**flour**
½	tsp	**baking powder**
½	tsp	**baking soda**
½	tsp	**salt**

Sift together; set aside.

½	cup	**shortening**
1½	cups	**sugar**

Cream together.

2		**eggs,** beaten
1	cup	**bananas,** ripe, mashed (2or3)

Add to sugar mixture.

½	cup	**buttermilk**

Stir in alternately with flour mixture, starting and ending with dry ingredients.

Stir into batter. Pour into pan. Bake until pick inserted in center comes out clean. Cool in pan (10min); remove. Cool before slicing.

1	tsp	**vanilla**
1	cup	**nuts,** chopped fine

Cornelia Brown, Weston

Chocolate Bread
(Polish)

"A longtime favorite of our family"

Yield: 1 loaf
Bake: 350° 45 min
Pan: 9x5x3, greased

2	oz	**unsweetened chocolate**	Melt together over very low heat. Set aside.
4	Tbsp	**shortening**	

3	cups	**cake flour,** sifted	
3	tsp	**baking powder**	Sift together.
1	tsp	**salt**	

1	cup	**brown sugar**	Add to dry ingredients.

1	lg	**egg,** beaten	Stir into dry ingredients; add chocolate mixture. Mix well; pour into pan. Bake. Cool in pan (3-5min); then remove to rack.
¼	cup	**milk**	

Helen Drovy, Trumbull

New England Brown Bread

Essential with hot dogs and beans!

Yield: 3 loaves
Steam: 3 hr
Pans: 3 1 lb coffee cans, greased; kettle (lg)

1	cup	**cornmeal** OR **oatmeal**	
1	cup	**graham, whole wheat** OR **rye flour**	
1	cup	**white flour**	Sift together into large mixing bowl.
1	tsp	**baking powder**	
1	tsp	**baking soda**	

1	cup	**raisins**	Add to above; mix to coat.

¾	cup	**molasses,** dark OR (6Tbsp molasses, light + 6 Tbsp brown sugar)	Add to above; mix gently. Divide batter evenly between cans. Cover tightly with foil (well greased). Place rack in bottom of kettle then cans on rack. Add boiling water to ½ of can; steam. Maintain water level in kettle. When cooked, remove from water; place in 350° oven (5-10min) to dry slightly. Remove from cans; dry on rack.
2	cups	**buttermilk** OR **sour milk**	

Molly Thoman, Foster, RI

Banana Tea Bread

Great for dieters

Serves: 8-10
Bake: 350° 30 min
Pan: 8x4x2½, vegetable spray

1		banana
2	oz	white bread, diet slice (cubed)
2		eggs
2	pkg	sugar substitute (optional)
½	tsp	nutmeg
½	tsp	lemon rind
½	tsp	baking soda
1	tsp	baking powder
1	cup	non-fat milk powder
1	Tbsp	orange marmalade, dietetic

Using electric mixer, beat well until smooth (med speed-5min). Batter will not be completely smooth. Pour into prepared pan. Bake until toothpick comes out clean. Cool then turn out. Freezes well.

Judy Webster of Thin's Inn, Monroe

Carrot Bread

"Make this bread a day ahead!"

Yield: 1 loaf
Bake: 350° 1 hr
Pan: 9x5x3, greased and floured

⅔	cup	butter OR margarine
1	cup	sugar

Add sugar gradually; cream well.

2	lg	eggs

Beat into creamed mixture.

1½	cups	flour, sifted
2	tsp	baking powder
1	tsp	cinnamon
¼	tsp	salt

Sift together; gradually add to above.

1	cup	carrots, grated fine
1	cup	raisins, seedless
1	cup	nuts, chopped

Mix together; stir into batter. Turn into prepared pan. Bake. Cool in pan (10min). Finish cooling on rack. Serve with cream cheese or butter. Store tightly covered.

Barbara Ann Sanders, Weston

Cranberry Bread

Delicious any time of year!

Yield: 1 loaf
Bake: 350° 1 hr
Pan: 9x5x3, greased, floured

2	cups	**flour**
1	tsp	**baking powder**
1	tsp	**salt**

Sift together; set aside.

¾	cup	**sugar**
¼	cup	**butter**

Cream together.

1		**egg**

Add to creamed mixture; beat well.

⅔	cup	**milk**

Add alternately with dry ingredients.

1	cup	**cranberry sauce,** whole
1	cup	**nuts,** chopped

Break up and fold into batter. Turn into prepared pan. Bake. Let cool slightly in pan before removing to rack.

Virginia Smith, Bridgeport

Zucchini Bread

Delicious and moist!

Yield: 2 loaves
Bake: 350° 50-55 min
Pan: (2) 8x4x2½, greased

3		**eggs**
1	cup	**sugar**
⅔	cup	**brown sugar**
¾	cup	**vegetable oil**
2	cups	**zucchini** OR **yellow squash,** grated
1	tsp	**vanilla**

Blend well in large mixer bowl.

2½	cups	**flour**
1½	tsp	**baking soda**
½	tsp	**baking powder**
1	tsp	**salt**
1	tsp	**cinnamon**

Mix well then add to above. Beat just enough to moisten.

½	cup	**golden raisins** (optional)
½	cup	**nuts,** chopped (optional)

Fold into batter; pour into prepared pans. Bake just until center becomes firm being careful not to overbake. Cool in pan (5min); remove to rack. Freezes well.

Joyce Reaume, Trumbull

Danish Coffee Cake

A very special treat

Yield: 2
Bake: 350° 45-60
Pan: cookie sheet

FIRST STEP

½	cup	**butter**
1	cup	**flour**
2	Tbsp	**water**

Mix as for pie crust. Form a ball; divide in half. On greased cookie sheet, pat into strips (12x3) 3 inches apart.

SECOND STEP

½	cup	**butter**
1	cup	**water**

Bring to a boil then remove from heat.

1	tsp	**almond extract**
1	cup	**flour**

Stir in to form a ball.

3	**eggs**

Add, one at a time, beating after each addition until glossy. Divide in half and spread over pastry strips. Bake until brown and crisp. Cool thoroughly.

THIRD STEP

1¼	cups	**confectioners' sugar**
1½	tsp	**vanilla**
2	tsp	**butter**
1-2	tsp	**water**

Mix together; add just enough water for a spreading consistency. Spread on cooled cakes.

walnuts, chopped fine

Sprinkle liberally over frosting. Serve COOL. Do not reheat.

Dee Maggiori, Trumbull

My Coffee Ring

Delicious served warm with fruit preserves

Serves: 10-12
Bake: 350° 25-30 min
Pan: cookie sheet, greased

RING

3	cups	**flour**
⅓	cup	**sugar**
5	tsp	**baking powder**

Mix in large bowl.

¼	cup	**shortening**

Cut into flour mixture.

1		**egg**, beaten
¾	cup	**milk**

Blend together; add to above to make a soft dough but one that can be handled. Turn out onto lightly floured surface. Roll into 2 small or 1 large rectangle, ¼-½" thick.

FILLING

¼	cup	**margarine** OR **butter**, softened

Spread over dough carefully.

¾	cup	**raisins**, golden
½	cup	**sugar** OR **brown sugar**
½	tsp	**cinnamon**
½	cup	**nuts**, chopped coarse

Sprinkle over margarine. Starting with the long side, roll as for jelly roll. Seal seam with milk. Place on prepared sheet, seamside down. Form into a ring sealing ends together by pinching. Snip deep cuts, 1" apart, around outer edge of ring twisting each so it lays over a bit.

¼	cup	**sugar**

Sprinkle over dough. Bake.

VARIATION: Instead of raisins, use prunes, dates, blueberries, apples, raspberries.

Jeannette Campbell, West Warwick, RI

 DATES can be moist, semi-dry or dry.

Great Prune Coffee Cake

Prunes are great and especially in this treat

Yield: 1 cake
Bake: 350° 55 min
Pan: tube (9"), greased, floured

1½	cups	**prunes**	Pour over prunes; let stand (5min).
		water, boiling	Drain pit and dice.
1	tsp	**lemon rind,** grated	Add; set aside.
2	cups	**flour,** sifted	Sift together. Remove ½ cup flour
1	tsp	**baking powder**	mixture and toss with prunes.
1	tsp	**baking soda**	
½	tsp	**salt**	
1	cup	**butter**	In medium bowl, cream together until
1	cup	**sugar**	fluffy.
2		**eggs**	Beat in, one at a time.
1	cup	**sour cream**	Add alternately with dry ingredients,
1	tsp	**vanilla**	beginning and ending with dry ingredients.
		reserved prunes	Fold into batter.
½	cup	**brown sugar,** light packed	Mix together for filling and topping. Pour ⅓ of batter into prepared pan.
1	Tbsp	**cinnamon**	Sprinkle with nut mixture; repeat, layering twice. Bake. Cool in pan on
½	cup	**walnuts,** chopped	rack (10min). Remove from pan.

Chris Henschel, Fairfield

PRUNES came to California commercially as late as 1870. They should be cooked slowly, just until tender and liquids should never reach the boiling point.

Nut Rolls

Filled with apples and spices

Yield: 4 rolls
Bake: 400° 35-40 min
Pan: cookie sheet, greased

DOUGH

8	cups	flour
7	tsp	baking powder
½	tsp	salt

Sift together.

1	cup	shortening
1	cup	butter

Add; cut in as for pie crust.

1	cup	sugar
5		eggs
1	pt	sour cream

Add and mix well. Knead for a few minutes. Divide dough into four equal parts. Roll out as for jelly roll and fill.

NUT FILLING

2	cups	nuts, chopped
½	cup	sugar
1	tsp	vanilla
1	tsp	almond extract
2	Tbsp	cream
1	med	apple, peeled, grated

Combine; spread over dough and roll up as for jelly roll.

1		egg, beaten

Brush top of roll. Bake.

Sophie Lapinski, Stratford

Better Butter

A wonderful "stretcher"

Yield: 2 cups

1	cup	**butter,** softened
1	cup	**oil** (safflower, soy OR corn)
2	Tbsp	**dry milk powder**
2	Tbsp	**water**
¼	tsp	**liquid lecithin*** or ½ tsp powdered lecithin

Mix in processor, blender or mixer. Keep tightly covered in refrigerator for a month or longer. Use as you would butter. Better for weight watchers and more nutricious.

*Found in health food stores.

Joan Kacin, Trumbull

Apricot-Apple Spread

A great combination

Yield: 2½ cups
Stovetop: 30 min
Pan: saucepan (2qt); 3 storage jars (8oz)

1	pkg	**apricots,** dried, snipped (8oz)
1½	cups	**apple juice**
1	can	**apple juice concentrate** (6oz)

Combine in saucepan; bring to a boil stirring occasionally then reduce to simmer. Cook until fruit is tender and ¾ liquid absorbed (approx 30min). Remove from heat.

½	tsp	**almond extract**
¼	tsp	**cinnamon**

Add to above; mix well. Pour into sterile storage container immediately, while boiling hot. Cover tightly; refrigerate.

Reisa Sukiluski

Pear-Pineapple Jam

"Honey" of a treat

Yield: 2 cups
2-3 storage jars (8oz)

3	qt	**pears,** peeled, cored

Run through food chopper, coarse; measure.

		sugar

Add 1 cup to each cup of grated pears. Cook until clear, not pink.

1	can	**pineapple,** crushed (8oz)

Add; bring to a boil. Fill sterile jars immediately. Seal while hot.

Virginia Smith, Bridgeport

Pepper Jelly

A treat over cream cheese with crackers

Yield: 2 pints
Stovetop: 15 min
Pan: saucepan (3-4qt); 4 storage jars (8oz)

1½	cups	cider vinegar
5	cups	sugar

Combine; bring to a boil.

1½	cups	red and green bell peppers, chopped (frozen can be used, 8oz)
1	Tbsp	red peppers, crushed

Add to above; return to a boil.

2	pkg	fruit pectin
	drops	red food coloring

Add; bring to a boil again. Cool; stir occasionally. Pour into sterilized jars. Stores well in refrigerator.

Connie Volante, Trumbull

"Maple Syrup"

A great way to save money

Serves: 10-12
Stovetop: 12-15 min
Pan: saucepan (2qt)

1	cup	each: water, sugar, light corn syrup
1	tsp	maple flavoring

Mix; simmer slowly until it begins to thicken, stir occasionally (it will become thicker as it cools). Store in a small-necked bottle to prevent crystalizing.

Aster Seale, Bridgeport

Grandpa's Bean Sandwich

Yield: 6-8

2	cups	baked beans
3	Tbsp	mayonnaise
1	Tbsp	onion, grated
1	tsp	mustard, prepared
1	Tbsp	chili sauce OR catsup
1	Tbsp	vinegar
		dark bread, buttered

Mix all ingredients well; mash into a spread and spread to desired thickness over crusty dark bread.

Nancy Gray, Trumbull

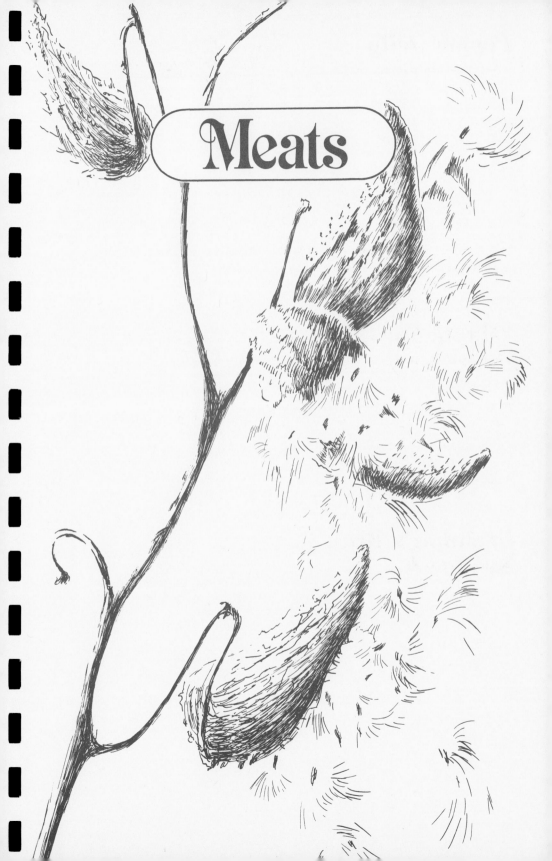

Meats

KOREAN
Seaweed: Thin Laver
Charcoal Broiled Pork
Steamed Rice
Korean Spinach Salad (cooked)
Korean Cucumber Salad
Barley Tea

BRITISH
Hearty Scotch Broth
Chicken Yorkshire
Bean Bundles
Carrots Kids Will Eat
Ginger Krakles

SWEDISH
Herring in Mustard Sauce
Swedish Cucumber Salad
Green Pepper Beef or Pork Tenderloin
Boiled Potatoes
Baked Leek
Meringue Torte

POLYNESIAN
Champagne Almond Soup
Polynesian Sliced Pork Roast
Islander Rice
Korean Salad
Bananas Bernard

POLISH
Jajka (Eggs)
Schab Pieczony (Pork)
Cielecina (Veal)
Cwikla (Relish)
Babka (Bread)
Mazurek Orzechowy (Walnut
Mazurka)

Sauerbraten

(German)

Great served with potato pancakes

Serves: 8-10
Marinate: 4 days
Stovetop: 2½-3 hr
Pan: kettle (4qt)

4	lb	**beef** (pot roast)	Place in 3-4 quart bowl; set aside.
2	cups	**wine vinegar**	
2	cups	**water**	
1	lg	**onion**, sliced	
¼	cup	**sugar**	Combine in saucepan; heat without
2	tsp	**salt**	boiling. Pour over meat; allow to cool.
10		**peppercorns**	
3		**cloves**, whole	
2		**bay leaves**	
1		**lemon**, sliced	Add; cover and refrigerate 4 days, turning meat once daily. (Can inject marinade directly into meat with baster for more even marinating.) Remove meat; drain. Strain marinade and reserve.
3	Tbsp	**butter**, melted	Brown meat on all sides (med heat). Slowly add reserved marinade. Bring to a boil; reduce heat and cover tightly. Simmer (2½-3hr). Add more marinade if necessary. Remove meat; pour liquid into bowl and set aside for gravy.
		marinated beef	
2	cups	reserved marinade	

GRAVY

¼	cup	**butter**, melted	In kettle, combine; heat until bubbly and golden brown, stirring constantly. Remove from heat.
¼	cup	**flour**	
3	cups	reserved marinade	Add gradually, stirring constantly. Return to a boil, stirring until thickened; remove from heat.
½	cup	**sour cream**	Stir in; cook slowly (2-3min) longer.

Nancy Gray, Trumbull

HERBS are rich in vitamins, aid digestion and add excitement to many every-day dishes.

BAY LEAF is a member of the laurel family from the Mediterranean region.

French Pot Roast

"Excellent"

Serves: 6-8
Stovetop: 3-3½ hr
Pans: Dutch oven (6qt); skillet (10")

4	lb	**beef roast,** top or bottom round **salt, pepper** to taste

Be sure there is a layer of fat around roast. Season well. Brown roast in Dutch oven; drain fats.

¼	cup	**brandy,** warmed

Pour over roast; ignite.

1	cup	**dry red wine**
1	cup	**beef stock**

Pour over; cover and simmer slowly (1½hr).

12	sm	**onions**
8	sm	**carrots,** halved
2	Tbsp	**butter**

In skillet, brown vegetables. Add to roast and cover; cook slowly (1hr) or until meat and vegetables are tender. Remove roast to warm platter; surround by vegetables and keep warm.

2	Tbsp	**water**
1	Tbsp	**cornstarch**

Blend; add to pan juices. Bring to a boil, cook until slightly thickened. Adjust seasonings to taste. Spoon some gravy over roast; serve remainder in sauceboat.

Emily Semonick, Trumbull

Park Avenue Beef and Vegetables

More variety with beef

Serves: 8-10
Bake: 325° 3-4hr
Pan: roaster, covered

4-5	lb	**beef roast** (2" thick)

Trim fat.

4-6	Tbsp	**lemon juice** (reserve half)
1	lg	**garlic clove,** minced **salt, pepper** to taste

Mix in bottom of roasting pan. Coat meat well by rubbing into this mixture.

2	lg	**Bermuda onions,** sliced thick
4		**green peppers,** sliced

Reserve half. Place remaining half on top of meat.

1		**eggplant,** sliced thin reserved vegetables

Arrange around meat.

		reserved lemon juice
1½	cups	**chili sauce**

Combine. Adjust salt and pepper to taste; pour over meat and vegetables. Cover tightly. Bake until tender. Freezes or reheats well.

Sonny Weintraub, Bridgeport

Swiss Steak Stew

Excellent cooked long and slow–oh so tender!

Serves: 8
Stovetop: 10-15 min
Bake: 325° 3-4 hr
Pan: Dutch oven

4-5	lb	**steak,** round or chuck (¾" thick)
1	cup	**flour**
		salt, pepper to taste

Pound; cut into serving pieces. Dredge meat well.

¼	cup	**vegetable oil**

In Dutch oven brown steak on all sides. Remove pieces as they brown; pour off fat. Return steak to Dutch oven.

½	cup	**flour**
		water

Mix into juices, then add water to cover meat.

1	can	**cream of mushroom soup** (10¾oz)
1	can	**onion soup** (10¾oz)
½	cup	**catsup**
¼	cup	**chili sauce**

Combine; pour over steak and stir in. Adjust seasonings to taste.

7		**carrots,** diced
7		**potatoes,** peeled, chunked

Add; cover. Bake until tender.

Diane Lombardi, Milford

Boolgogui
(Korean)

Oriental barbecued beef

Serves: 4-6
Marinate: 2-3 hr
Broil or barbecue: 3-5 min

1½	lb	**beef,** lean (sliced ⅛")
½	cup	**soy sauce**
1½	tsp	**garlic,** chopped
1	tsp	**pepper**
½	cup	**scallions,** chopped
2	Tbsp	**sugar**
2	Tbsp	**sesame oil**
2	Tbsp	**sesame seeds,** roasted (optional)

Combine well; add beef and marinate. Broil or barbecue just before serving.

Youngsil Rhee, Trumbull

 CASSEROLES always have a tight fitting lid and their purpose is usually to tenderize.

Beef Scaloppine Casalinga
(Italian)

A delicious change

Serves: 8
Stovetop: 30-40 min
Bake: 500° 10 min
Pans: skillet (12"); 13x9

SAUCE

¾	cup	**vegetable oil**
½	cup	**onion,** minced

Sauté until lightly browned (5min).

½	cups	**prosciutto ham,** julienned
2	cups	**mushrooms,** sliced thin
		lemon juice

Sprinkle mushrooms with lemon juice; combine with ham and add to onions. Cook slowly (10min). Pour into sieve and drain well; press to extract most oil.

2	Tbsp	**butter**

In clean skillet, heat butter; add mushroom and ham mixture.

⅓	cup	**beef gravy,** canned
1	cup	**Marsala wine**
2	Tbsp	**parsley,** minced

Add to above; blend well. Simmer (20min).

MEAT

¼	cup	**flour** (approx)
8	sliced	**beef filet rounds** (½" thick)
		oil for frying

Pound beef lightly; dredge lightly. Sauté quickly in oil over med-high heat, until golden (2min). Remove; drain. Spoon ½ mushroom sauce into baking dish; arrange meat on top and cover with remaining sauce.

8	slices	**Mozzarella cheese** (⅓" thick)

Top each meat round with a slice. Bake until hot and cheese is melted. Serve immediately.

Maria De Cesare, Trumbull

Baked Steak

Deliciously different!

Serves: 8
Marinate: 10 hr
Bake: 325° 1½ hr
Pan: 13x9

3-4	lb	**sirloin steak** (3" thick)
1	btl	**chili sauce** (12oz)
1	pkg	**mushrooms,** quartered (10oz) (optional)

Place ½ chili sauce in baking dish. Place steak over; spread remaining sauce over steak. Refrigerate to marinate. When ready, bake in chili sauce (uncovered). Surround with mushrooms. To serve, cut into thin slices.

Erna Byron, Stratford

Bracciole di Manzo

(Italian)

A delicious beef roll

Serves: 3-4
Simmer: 1½ hr
Pan: skillet (lg)

1	lb	**round steak,** sliced very thin (¼")	Cut into 6 pieces.
1	clove	**garlic,** mashed	} Mix.
1	tsp	**parmesan cheese**	
1		**garlic powder** **egg,** hard-cooked, chopped	Sprinkle over meat along with cheese mixture above. Roll; secure with toothpick.
1	tsp	**parsley,** minced	
3	slices	**bacon,** diced	
		salt, pepper to taste	
¼	cup	**olive oil**	In skillet, on low heat, sauté until limp. Add steak rolls, brown on all sides.
1		**onion,** chopped	
1	can	**Italian tomatoes** (35oz)	Combine quickly in blender; add to above.
½	tsp	**salt**	
¼	tsp	**pepper**	
1		**bay leaf**	Add; cover and simmer until tender but not dry. Remove toothpick and bay leaf. Serve with sauce.

Louise Cronan, Trumbull

Beefsteak and Kidney Pie

(British)

Serves: 4
Bake: 400° 1 hr 45 min
Pans: casserole (8-9"); baking sheet

1	lb	**stew beef,** cubed	Coat meat with seasonings; pack loosely into casserole.
1		**lamb kidney,** cubed	
2	Tbsp	**flour**	
		salt, pepper to taste	
1	med	**onion,** sliced	Add to above.
1	cup	**water** OR **stock**	Pour over all until dish is half full.

CRUST

1	cup	**flour**	Cut shortenings into flour; add water slowly to form a dough. Roll out on floured surface. Cover casserole and seal edges. Cut hole in center to vent well. Cover with foil; place on baking sheet. Place in middle of oven. Bake.
½	cup	**shortening** OR ¼cup each **butter** and **lard**	
	pinch	**salt**	
2-3	Tbsp	**water**	

Mrs. M. Crisp, Harrow, England

Green Peppercorn Beef

(Swedish)

Serve with boiled potatoes

Serves: 4
Stovetop: 10-15 min
Pan: skillet (lg)

4		**steaks**, ribeye or filet
2	Tbsp	**onion**, minced
3	Tbsp	**green peppercorns**, chopped

Mix; coat steaks, both sides

1	Tbsp	**butter**

Brown in skillet; add meat and fry (2-4min) each side (to taste). Remove to warm serving platter.

1	tsp	**salt** (to taste)

Sprinkle over meat.

1	Tbsp	**soy sauce**
1	cup	**heavy cream**

Pour into skillet; stir and bring to a boil. Remove from heat.

½	cup	**sour cream**
		lemon juice

Stir into above; adjust seasonings and add lemon juice to taste. Pour over meat and serve hot.

Kerstin Nilson, Trumbull

Cube Steak with Wine

A different way to use "cube"

Serves: 6
Bake: 350° 1 hr
Pans: skillet (lg); casserole (1½qt)

6		**cube steaks**
1		**egg**, beaten
½	cup	**bread crumbs**

Dip steaks in egg; coat with crumbs.

2	Tbsp	**vegetable oil**

Brown steaks both sides; cool slightly. Cut each into 3-4 pieces; place in casserole.

1	can	**beef broth** (10¾oz)
¾	cup	**port wine**

Pour over steaks; cover. Bake.

1	can	**mushrooms**, sliced (4oz) (optional)

Add last 10 minutes of baking. This recipe doubles easily.

Beatrix Mastrone, Trumbull

Stroganoff Rounds

Delicious served with long grain rice

Serves: 2-4
Stovetop: 15 min
Bake: 350° 20 min
Pans: skillet (10"); casserole (2-3qt)

1	lb	**beef,** sirloin tip or eye of the round	Cut in round slices ½" thick.
2	Tbsp	**butter** or **margarine**	Sauté beef until browned; cover and simmer until tender (10min).
		salt, white pepper to taste	Sprinkle over meat to season well.
1½	Tbsp	**flour**	Stir in and cook (1min).
¾	cup	**beef stock**	Add to above slowly; stir until smooth. Cook on high heat (2min); reduce heat.
½	cup	**sour cream**	Add; simmer slowly.
1½	Tbsp	**red wine**	
2	Tbsp	**onion,** chopped	Sauté until soft. Place in casserole; add meat and sauce. Bake, covered. Serve over noodles.
1	tsp	**butter** or **margarine**	

Agnes Swords, Stratford

Beef Teriyaki

Appetizer or main dish over rice

Yield: 24 pieces
Marinate: 1 hr
Stovetop: 12-20 min
Pans: skillet (12"); saucepan (1qt);
chafing dish

1	tsp	**ginger**	Blend in bowl.
⅓	cup	**soy sauce**	
¼	cup	**honey**	
1	clove	**garlic,** minced	
1	tsp	**onion,** grated	
1	lb	**beef sirloin,** strips (2x½x¼)	Add to above; marinate. Drain meat and reserve marinade.
3	Tbsp	**vegetable oil**	In skillet, brown meat in oil.
1	Tbsp	**cornstarch**	Blend in small saucepan.
½	cup	**water**	
⅛	tsp	**red food coloring** (optional)	
		reserved marinade	Add to above and bring to a boil, stirring constantly (3min). Add meat; serve in chafing dish with wooden picks.

Jan McNaughton, Fairfield

Oriental Pepper Steak

A different way to use flank steak

Serves: 6
Stovetop: 7 min
Pan: Wok or skillet (lg)

1½-2	lb	**flank steak,** partially frozen for easier cutting

Cut lengthwise into 5-6 strips (1½" wide); cut each strip into slices, across the grain (⅛").

4	tsp	**cornstarch**
4	Tbsp	**soy sauce**
2	Tbsp	**sherry,** pale dry
1	tsp	**sugar**

Combine; pour over steak and mix in well. Set aside.

1	Tbsp	**oil**
2	med	**green peppers** (1"cubes)

Stir/fry peppers in hot oil (2min). Remove and keep warm.

4	Tbsp	**oil**
4-5	slices	**ginger root** (⅛") OR ¼ tsp ground ginger

Add ginger to hot oil; stir. Add steak mixture; stir/fry quickly, just until it loses its redness. Add cooked peppers; stir. Remove ginger root. Serve at once over rice.

Louise Cronan, Trumbull

Flank Steak Teriyaki
(Japanese)

A great flavor

Serves: 4
Marinate: 8-24 hr
Broil: 20-25 min
Pan: broiler rack

1½	lb	**flank steak**

Cut into strips 1" wide.

¼	cup	**vegetable oil**
2	Tbsp	**molasses**
2	tsp	**ginger**
2	tsp	**dry mustard**
6	cloves	**garlic,** minced

Combine in glass bowl; add meat strips and coat well. Marinate, then remove meat. Roll each strip jelly roll fashion; secure with toothpick. Place on rack and broil until crisp outside.

Christine Vazzano, Huntington

GINGER comes mostly from the Orient. The lighter the color of the root the more "bite". Meats can be rubbed with raw ginger root before seasoning to "spice".

Austrian Goulash

A great tradition

Serves: 6-8
Stovetop: 2 hr
Pan: Dutch oven

4	lg	**onions,** cut in rings	Sauté in Dutch oven then remove.
⅓	cup	**butter,** melted	
2	lb	**beef,** lean (1"cubes)	Brown; return onions to pan.
1	Tbsp	**paprika**	
	dash	**cayenne**	
	dash	**garlic salt**	Add to Dutch oven.
		salt, pepper to taste	
2		**bay leaves**	
1	Tbsp	**wine vinegar**	
2-3	cups	**beef stock,** divided	Add enough to cover meat; simmer covered (2-3hr), adding liquid if necessary.
¼	cup	**flour**	Add enough stock to make a thin paste; pour into Dutch oven. Cook to thicken gravy.
		reserved beef stock	
1	cup	**sour cream**	Stir in just before serving; heat slowly to prevent curdling.
2		**dill pickles,** tart, diced, drained	Add; serve over cooked noodles.

Tony Massa, Milford

VARIATION: Instead of wine vinegar and pickles, add 1 can tomatoes (20oz) and 1½ tsp caraway seeds. (Hungarian).

Jan Simco, Bridgeport

Beef N' Biscuits

A delicious "welcome new neighbor" casserole

Serves: 4-6
Stovetop: 1 hr
Bake: 400° 20 min
Pans: skillet (12"); casserole, greased (2qt)

¼	cup	**butter** or **bacon drippings**	Sauté until golden; remove and reserve.
1	cup	**onion,** sliced	
1	lb	**steak,** round (1"cubes)	Roll steak in seasonings; brown in hot skillet.
¼	cup	**flour**	
1	tsp	**salt**	
		pepper to taste	
½	tsp	**paprika**	
1		**bay leaf** (optional)	
2½	cups	**water,** boiling	Add to steak; cover and simmer until meat is tender (50min).
2	cups	**potatoes,** raw, diced	Add to above; cover and cook (10min) longer. Pour into casserole.
1½	cups	**carrots,** sliced thick (optional)	
		reserved onions	Spread over top.
1	pkg	**biscuits,** refrigerated or scratch	Arrange over top. Bake until bubbly hot and biscuits are browned.

Constance Detar, Stratford

Gal Bi
(Korean)

Oriental barbecue sauce for short ribs, chicken, pork or spareribs

Serves: 4-5
Marinate: 3-10 hr
Broil or barbecue: 15-25 min

2½	lb	**beef short ribs** (8-10pcs)	Trim excess fat; make one deep cut into meat of each rib.
3	Tbsp	**sugar**	Sprinkle over ribs; set aside (30min).
6	Tbsp	**soy sauce**	Mix well; dip each rib into marinade. Sprinkle any that remains over the ribs; marinate a few hours or overnight, turning occasionally. When ready, broil or barbecue (10-12min) one side; turn and repeat for other side.
½	cup	**scallions,** chopped	
1½	Tbsp	**garlic,** crushed	
½	tsp	**black pepper**	
3	Tbsp	**sesame seeds,** roasted	
3	Tbsp	**sesame oil**	
3	Tbsp	**sugar**	

Jong Im Lee, Easton

Tipton's Pride Meatloaf

A zippy meatloaf

Serves: 8
Stovetop: 30-35 min
Pan: heavy skillet, covered (8")

1	lb	**ground beef**
½	tsp	**pepper**
¾	tsp	**salt**
½	tsp	**onion salt**
½	tsp	**garlic powder**
1		**egg**
¼	cup	**catsup**
2	cups	**corn flakes** (whole)

Mix together in skillet; form into circle about 1½" high. Brown on medium-high heat; turn loaf over.

¼	cup	**chili sauce**

Spread over loaf; turn heat to low. Cook, covered. When cooked, remove to warm platter.

GRAVY

½-1	tsp	**beef bouillon**

Add to pan; stir to loosen pan drippings.

¼	cup	**flour**
½	cup	**water,** cold

Combine until smooth; add to above.

1	cup	**water**
1	Tbsp	**catsup**
	dash	**salt, pepper**

Add to above; bring to a boil and stir constantly until thick and smooth. Serve hot. (Can also be baked 350° 30-35 min.)

Diane Lombardi, Milford

 MEATS – white meats should always be well cooked (poultry, pork, veal). Red meats can be cooked according to preference.

Sweet and Sour Beefloaf

A very tasty loaf

Serves: 4
Bake: 350° 1 hr
Pan: pie plate (9")

1	lb	**ground beef**	
1		**onion,** minced	
12		**snack crackers,** crushed	Combine in pie plate. Form into mound 1" smaller than plate.
¼	tsp	**pepper, salt**	
1	can	**tomato sauce** (8oz) (reserve half)	
1		**egg,** beaten	
		reserved tomato sauce	
2	Tbsp	**vinegar**	Combine; pour over meat.
¼	tsp	**dry mustard**	
2	Tbsp	**brown sugar**	
⅔	cup	**water**	Pour around edge of loaf. Bake. Serve with sauce from loaf.

Gladys Blum, Bridgeport

Meat Loaf
(Italian)

A nice change

Serves: 6
Bake: 350° 1 hr
Pan: 8x10, greased

2	Tbsp	**olive oil**	Grease casserole.
1½	lb	**ground beef**	
1	Tbsp	**parsley,** minced	
⅛	tsp	**pepper**	
2		**eggs**	
½	cup	**Parmesan cheese,** grated	Combine; pat ½ into casserole.
1	cup	**Italian bread crumbs**	
1½	tsp	**salt** (to taste)	
1	med	**onion,** chopped	
½	cup	**water**	
1	lb	**ricotta cheese**	Spread over meat.
1	cup	**Provolone cheese,** shredded	Sprinkle over all; cover with remaining meat then press down edges.
2	Tbsp	**olive oil** (optional)	Drizzle over meat. Bake then let stand (10min) before serving.

Barbara Daley, Trumbull

"Stuffed" Beef Roll

Something different in meatloaf

Serves: 4
Bake: 375° 55 min
Pan: 13x9

1½	lb	ground beef, lean	
1	tsp	salt	
½	tsp	pepper	Mix well; press into 14x10 rectangle
1	tsp	onion flakes	on waxed paper.
1		egg	
½	cup	bread crumbs	
½	cup	water	

1½	cup	Mozzarella cheese, grated OR combination of mozzarella and cheddar	Sprinkle on meat, leaving ½" border. Roll like jelly roll; place, seam side down, in pan.
1	jar	spaghetti sauce (8oz) OR your favorite	Pour half over meat roll. Bake (45min).
¼	lb	mushrooms, sliced	Add to remaining sauce; spread some over roll. Bake (10min) longer. Heat remaining sauce and serve with roll.

Lillian Thiede, Stratford

"Stephens Special"

Simple, different and delicious

Serves: 6
Broil: 16 min
Pan: broiler and rack

2	lb	ground beef	
4		eggs, lightly beaten	
2	tsp	salt	Mix well; form into 6 patties.
4	tsp	Worcestershire sauce	
4	tsp	onion, minced	

6	strips	bacon	Circle each patty as for filet mignon.
1-2	cans	green beans, drained (8oz) salt, pepper to taste	Spread over bottom of broiler pan; place rack over top. Place patties on rack. Broil (8min).
6		peach halves, canned OR fresh	Mix together to spice peaches. Turn hamburger patties over; add peach halves to rack. Broil (8min). Serve immediately.
6	Tbsp	brown sugar	
¼	tsp	cloves, ground	
4	tsp	vinegar	

Jan McNaughton, Fairfield

Danish Stuffed Cabbage

"This is one of the best we have ever had"

Serves: 6
Bake: 325° 2½ hr
Pan: Dutch oven

| 1 | lg | **cabbage,** green |

Cut out and discard center core. Remove large outside leaves; reserve. Working from bottom, use sharp paring knife to hollow out cabbage, leaving shell about ½" thick. Place shell and reserved leaves in large bowl. Cover with boiling water; let stand (10min); drain.

1½	lb	**ground beef**
1	sm	**onion,** chopped
¼	cup	**green pepper,** chopped
2		**eggs,** beaten lightly
½	cup	**rice,** cooked
1	tsp	**salt**
⅛	tsp	**pepper**
1	Tbsp	**butter**

Combine all but butter; fill cabbage shell with mixture placing any extra mixture on top. Dot with butter. Press softened outside leaves around stuffed shell. Tie with cord; place in Dutch oven.

⅛	tsp	**marjoram**
1	can	**stewed tomatoes**
1	Tbsp	**vinegar**
1	Tbsp	**sugar**

Combine; pour over cabbage. Bake. To serve, cut into wedges or spoon out.

Gemma Zingo, Bridgeport

Mock Shepard's Pie

A great use for ground beef

Serves: 6
Stovetop: 10-15 min
Bake: 350° 30 min
Pans: skillet (10"); casserole (1½qt)

| 1 | med | **onion,** chopped |
| 1 | Tbsp | **meat fat** OR **butter** |

Sauté until golden.

| 1 | lb | **ground beef** |
| | | **salt, pepper** to taste |

Add to above; brown.

| 1 | can | **green beens,** drained (8oz) |
| 1 | can | **tomato soup** (10oz) |

Add to above; pour into casserole.

5	med	**potatoes,** cooked, mashed
1½	cups	**milk**
1		**egg,** beaten
		salt, pepper to taste

Mix well; spoon, in mounds, over meat. Bake.

Virginia Smith, Bridgeport

Meatball Skillet Stew

A tasty meal in a dish

Serves: 4
Stovetop: 1 hr
Pan: skillet (lg)

1	lb	**ground beef**
¼	cup	**bread crumbs,** fine
¼	cup	**onion,** chopped
1		**egg**
1½	tsp	**salt**
¼	tsp	**pepper**
1	Tbsp	**Worcestershire sauce**
2	cans	**tomato sauce** (divided) (8oz,ea)

Combine, using ½ cup tomato sauce. Shape into 16 balls.

2	Tbsp	**oil**

Brown in hot oil.

1	lg	**onion,** quartered
4		**carrots,** 1" slices
2		**potatoes,** quartered
1	pkg	**green beans,** frozen
1	cup	**water**
1	tsp	**salt**

Add to skillet. Pour remaining tomato sauce over. Cover and simmer stirring occasionally (1hr).

1	Tbsp	**flour**

Remove ½ cup stew sauce; combine with flour then gradually pour into stew. Stir over low heat until thickened.

Jeannette Regnery, Stratford

Hamburger Stroganoff

Dill makes this one unusual

Serves: 8
Stovetop: 10-15 min
Bake: 300° 1 hr
Pans: casserole, covered; skillet (med)

1	lb	**noodles**	Cook; drain; place in casserole.
2	lb	**ground beef**	Brown and add to above.
1	lg	**onion,** sliced	Sauté until golden; add to above.
1	Tbsp	**butter** OR **margarine**	
1	can	**cream of celery**	
1	can	**cream of mushroom soup** (10oz,ea)	
1	can	**mushrooms,** chopped (3oz)	
½	pt	**sour cream**	Add to above; stir to blend. Bake covered.
½	cup	**red wine**	
1	Tbsp	**dill seed**	
½	cup	**parsley,** chopped	
		Worcestershire sauce to taste	
		salt, pepper to taste	

Jan McNaughton, Fairfield

Delicious Beef Casserole

Very rich – a little goes a long way

Serves: 5-6
Stovetop: 35 min
Bake: 350° 30 min
Pans: skillet (10"); 9x13, greased

1	lb	**ground beef**	Brown in skillet; set aside.
2	Tbsp	**margarine**	
1	clove	**garlic,** minced	
¼	tsp	**salt**	
1	tsp	**seasoned salt**	Add; bring to a boil and simmer (20min).
¼	tsp	**pepper**	
1	Tbsp	**soy sauce**	
1	can	**tomato sauce** (15½oz)	
8	oz	**noodles,** medium	Cook until just tender; drain and place in casserole.
		water	
		salt	
3	oz	**cream cheese,** softened	Spread, in layers, over noodles.
1	cup	**sour cream**	
		reserved meat mixture	
⅔	cup	**cheddar cheese,** shredded	Sprinkle over top. Bake until bubbly. Can be prepared ahead and refrigerated but does not freeze well.

Carolyn Bobkowski, Fairfield

Pelota e Frijoles Mejicano

A really tasty "chili" with chips baked in

Serves: 6-8
Stovetop: 10-15 min
Bake: 375° 35 min
Pans: skillet (10"); casserole (3qt)

2	Tbsp	**margarine**
1	cup	**onion,** chopped
2	cloves	**garlic,** crushed

Sauté until golden (3min).

1	lb	**ground beef**
1	Tbsp	**chili powder**
1	tsp	**salt**
¼	tsp	**oregano**
⅛	tsp	**pepper**

Add to above; cook, stirring often, until meat is browned (7min).

1	can	**tomato sauce** (8oz)
2	cans	**kidney beans,** un-drained (20oz,ea)
2	cups	**corn chips,** crushed coarse

Add to above; spoon into casserole.

½	cup	**corn chips,** broken
⅓-1	cup	**cheddar cheese,** grated

Sprinkle over top of casserole. Bake until bubbly.

Margaret Harris, Bridgeport

Lombardi's Chili

Different and delicious

Serves: 8
Simmer: 1 hr
Pans: Dutch oven (8qt); skillet (med)

⅓	lb	**thin spaghetti**

Break into thirds. Cook in boiling water (5min). Leave enough water to cover.

2	qt	**tomato juice**

Add to above.

1	lb	**ground beef**

Brown in skillet; break into bite-size pieces and add to spaghetti.

⅛-¼	lb	**pepperoni,** bize size
2	cans	**kidney beans,** drained (20oz,ea)

Add to above.

3	Tbsp	**chili powder**
5	Tbsp	**sugar**
1	tsp	**mixed Italian spices**
1	tsp	**garlic powder**
1	tsp	**onion salt**
2½	tsp	**salt** (to taste)
⅛	tsp	**pepper**

Add to above; simmer covered (1hr). Adjust seasonings to taste then allow to stand several hours. Reheat to serve. Will keep 1 week in refrigerator.

Diane Lombardi, Milford

Corn Tamale Pie with Cornbread Topping

Something different and delicious

Serves: 4-6
Bake: 400° 30-40 min
Pan: 13x9, greased

3	Tbsp	oil or melted fat	
1	lb	ground beef	
¾	cup	onions	
⅛	tsp	pepper	Sauté in skillet breaking up meat. Let cook 8-10 minutes longer.
2	tsp	salt	
2-3	tsp	chili powder	
½	cup	green pepper, chopped (optional)	
1	can	corn, whole kernel (12oz)	Add; bring to a boil. Pour into baking dish.
1	can	tomatoes (28oz)	

CORN MUFFIN TOPPING

1	pkg	cornbread mix, dry	Cover meat mixture. Topping will disappear then rise during baking. Bake until golden and bubbly.

Virginia Smith, Bridgeport

A Dieter's "Lasagne"

The title says it all – great

Serves: 2
Bake: 350° 35 min
Pans: 2 saucepans (lg,sm); 13x9

4	cups	tomato juice	Boil down to 2 cups.
½	lg	cabbage	Separate leaves; boil until tender.
1	lb	ground beef OR veal (lean)	Sauté.
2	Tbsp	onion flakes	
1	tsp	oregano	
1	tsp	parsley	
		garlic powder to taste	Add to ground beef.
1	can	mushrooms	
		salt, pepper to taste	
6	oz	cottage cheese	Beat in blender bowl until smooth.
1		egg	
3	oz	Mozzarella cheese, strips	Alternate layers of ground beef, Mozzarella, cabbage leaves, and cheese mixture. Bake.

Judy Webster of Thin's Inn, Monroe

Marinade for Steak

A great sauce for the less tender cuts

Yield: 1¼ cups
Marinate: 3-4 hr

2	Tbsp	vegetable oil
1	Tbsp	Worcestershire sauce
1	tsp	salt
½	tsp	garlic powder
⅓	cup	wine vinegar
2	Tbsp	soy sauce
1	tsp	prepared mustard
¼	tsp	pepper
¼	cup	catsup

Combine in blender (30sec). Pour over 1½-2" steak; marinate at room temperature, turning every half hour. Broil or barbecue to taste. Spoon extra marinade over hot steak slices.

Louise Cronan, Trumbull

St Patty's Day Special
(Irish)

A great tradition

Serves: 6-8
Simmer: 5 hr
Pan: kettle (lg)

5	lb	corned beef brisket
		water, cold

Cover corned beef with cold water in large kettle.

½	sm	onion
4		cloves
6		peppercorns
1		bay leaf
½	tsp	rosemary
2	cloves	garlic
4	strips	green pepper (½")
1	stalk	celery
1		carrot, pared, split in half
2	Tbsp	parsley, broken

Add to corned beef (may be tied in cheesecloth). Bring to a boil; cover. Simmer (4hr).

1	lg	cabbage, cut in 6ths
6		potatoes, peeled
6		carrots, pared

Add to corned beef. Cook (45-60min) longer or until vegetables are cooked and meat is fork tender. (Overcooking will make meat dry and hard to cut.) To serve, slice meat thinly against grain.

VARIATION: Can cook vegetables separately; place corned beef in oven after it is fork tender and glaze with ½ cup honey, ¼ cup brown sugar and 1 Tbsp prepared mustard. Bake: 350° (30min).

Louise Cronan, Trumbull

Corned Beef Hash Patties with Hot Sauce

Tangy delicious, a zippy meal

Serves: 4
Stovetop: 10-15 min
Pans: skillet (10"); saucepan (sm)

1	can	**corned beef hash** (16oz)
2		**eggs,** beaten
¼	cup	**bread crumbs**
1		**onion,** grated
1	Tbsp	**horseradish**
	dash	**pepper**

Mix thoroughly; shape into patties and brown.

SAUCE

1	cup	**chili sauce**
1	Tbsp	**onion,** grated
1	Tbsp	**Worcestershire sauce**
	dash	**Tabasco sauce**
2	Tbsp	**sour cream**

Combine in saucepan; heat. To serve, pour over patties.

Jeanne Elsasser, Fairfield

Carrot Tzimmes
(Jewish)

Serves: 6
Stovetop: 2½-3 hr
Bake: 350° 30 min
Pans: Dutch oven; casserole (3qt)

2½-3	lb	**beef brisket**

In Dutch oven, brown on all sides.

5	lg	**carrots,** scraped, sliced thin or diced
5	med	**potatoes,** pared, quartered
3	med	**sweet potatoes,** pared, cut in 1" thick rounds
1	sm	**onion,** whole, with 1-2 cuts at root end
1	tsp	**salt**
½	cup	**honey**
		water to cover plus 1"

Add; bring to boil. Lower heat; simmer (2½-3hr) or until meat is fork tender. Add water as frequently as required in the beginning. Do not stir; shake pot occasionally to prevent sticking. Remove onion before it becomes too mushy. When liquid has been reduced by half, turn into oven-proof casserole.

2	Tbsp	**Matzoflour,** flour or cake meal
2	Tbsp	**chicken fat** OR **shortening**

Make thickening by browning flour in shortening and adding some liquid from tzimmes. Pour over casserole. Shake to distribute. Bake until brown on top. Freezes well.

Sonny Weintraub, Bridgeport

Party Chicken and Wild Rice

Great for buffets, showers, etc.

Serves: 12-15
Simmer: 1 hr
Bake: 350° 1 hr
Pans: kettle (6qt); casserole (4qt)

2		chickens (4-5lb)	Bring to a boil in tightly covered kettle; reduce heat and simmer (1hr). Remove from heat; strain broth and chill. Skim off fat; remove meat from bones and cut into bite size pieces. Set aside.
1	cup	water	
1	cup	dry sherry OR vermouth	
1	lg	onion, quartered	
½	cup	celery, sliced	
1	tsp	curry powder	
1½	tsp	salt	
12	oz	mushrooms, fresh, sliced	Sauté; set aside.
¼	cup	butter OR margarine	
2	pkg	Long Grain and Wild Rice Mix (not instant) (6oz,ea) reserved broth	Cook according to package directions, using reserved chicken broth and water; drain and combine with above ingredients.
1	cup	sour cream	Mix well; add and pour into casserole. Cover. Bake or refrigerate until ready to use.
1	can	cream of mushroom soup (10¾oz)	

Odette Renner, Trumbull

"Stuffed" Chicken

Simple and excellent

Serves: 6-8
Bake: 350° 75 min
Pan: 13x9

4		whole chicken breasts, split	Arrange in baking pan.
1	btl	Creamy Italian Dressing (8oz)	Spread over meat.
1	pkg	dry stuffing mix (8oz) (regular or seasoned)	Spread over meat.
8	slices	bacon, cut in half	Place 2 pieces (1 strip) on top of each chicken breast. Bake.

Mary Telford, Trumbull

 CURRY is a condiment compounded from 16 different spice ingredients. In India it is prepared daily.

Barbecue Roasted Chicken

Great do-ahead meal!

Serves: 4
Bake: 375° 75 min
Pans: 13x9; saucepan (1½qt)

2	Tbsp	**butter,** melted
¼	cup	**water**
3	Tbsp	**catsup**
2	Tbsp	**vinegar**
2	Tbsp	**brown sugar**
1	Tbsp	**Worcestershire sauce**
1	tsp	**prepared mustard**
1	tsp	**paprika**
1	tsp	**salt**

Combine in saucepan; mix well and heat.

2		**whole chicken breasts,** split or chicken parts
4		**foil pieces (9x9)**

Dip 1 piece chicken in sauce and place in foil. Cover with 1 tsp sauce and wrap securely. Repeat with all pieces of chicken. Place foil packets in shallow pan. Bake (45min). When baked, remove and open packets carefully, turn pieces over and add 1 tsp sauce over chicken. Bake (30min) more with packets open. Remove and baste with remaining sauce, if any.

Mrs. H. J. Venanzi, New Canaan

Chicken Tortilla
(Mexican)

Delicious Mexican style dish

Serves: 4
Chill: 24 hr
Bake: see recipe
Pan: 14x11, buttered

4		**whole chicken breasts**
1		**bay leaf**
1	sm	**onion,** sliced
		salt, pepper to taste

Bake in foil 400° (1hr). When cool, bone, skin and cut into bite size pieces. Reserve broth; set aside.

1	can	**cream of mushroom soup (10¾oz)**
1	can	**cream of chicken soup**
1	cup	**milk**
½	cup	**onion,** chopped
½-1	can	**green chili salsa (7oz)**
		reserved chicken broth

Mix then set aside.

1½	lb	**cheddar cheese,** grated

Set aside.

12		**corn tortillas,** cut into 1" strips.

Place ½ on bottom of baking dish. Cover with half the chicken, ⅓ of the sauce then top with cheese. Repeat these layers. Refrigerate 24 hours. Bake: 300° (1½hr).

Jean Wirtz, Yorba Linda, Ca

Chicken Dijon

Zippy, tasty, variety

Serves: 4
Stovetop: 30 min
Pan: skillet (10")

4		whole chicken breasts, boned, skinned, halved	Sauté until browned and tender (approx 20min). Remove chicken from pan; keep warm.
3	Tbsp	butter	
2	Tbsp	flour	Stir into butter.
1	cup	chicken broth	Add; cook, stirring until thickened.
½	cup	light cream	
2-3	Tbsp	Dijon mustard (to taste)	Add then cover. Heat (10min). Adjust seasonings. Pour over chicken.

Agnes Swords, Stratford

Supremely Good Chicken

A hit with all those who insist "I don't like chicken"

Serves: 10-12
Marinate: overnight
Bake: 350° 55 min
Pan: 13x9

6		whole chicken breasts, boned, skinned, halved	Wipe dry.
2	cups	sour cream	
¼	cup	lemon juice	
4	tsp	Worcestershire sauce	Combine; coat chicken. Let stand in coating mixture overnight in refrigerator.
1	tsp	celery salt	
2	tsp	paprika	
4	cloves	garlic, minced	
		salt to taste	
1¾	cups	bread crumbs, dry	Following day, dip coated chicken in bread crumbs; arrange in pan in single layer.
½	cup	butter	Combine; melt then spoon half of mixture over chicken. Bake uncovered (45min). Spoon remaining butter mixture over chicken; bake another 10 minutes or until chicken is golden brown.
½	cup	shortening	

Kathy Miller, Easton

 CHICKEN is a very highly digestible meat.

Oriental Lemon Chicken

(Chinese)

A really delicious dish

Serves: 4
Marinate: 30 min
Fry: 20 min
Pans: wok; saucepan (sm)

2	Tbsp	**Chinese dark soy sauce**	
¼	tsp	**sesame oil**	Combine.
1	Tbsp	**gin**	
4		**whole chicken breasts,** boned, skinned, halved	Marinate in sauce (30min); drain.
3		**egg whites,** beaten until frothy	Dip chicken in egg whites, then coat with cornstarch.
1	cup	**cornstarch**	
		peanut oil	Deep fry chicken in oil until light brown. Drain; cut into 2" strips. Keep warm in oven (200°).

SAUCE

½	cup	**sugar**	
⅓	cup	**Oriental rice vinegar**	Bring to a boil in small saucepan.
1½	cups	**chicken stock**	
1		**lemon,** juice of	
1½	Tbsp	**cornstarch**	Combine; add to above and cook, stirring, until thickened.
2	Tbsp	**pineapple juice**	
3	sm	**carrots,** julienned	Add to sauce, heat.
3		**scallions,** julienned	
2-3	drops	**lemon extract**	Add to suit your taste. To serve, place chicken on plate then pour sauce over.

Agnes Swords, Stratford

Heat a lemon before squeezing and you will obtain more juice.
Place lemons in covered jar filled with water to store.

Stuffed Chicken Breasts

All this and low-cal too

Serves: 8
Bake: see recipe
Pan: 9x9, vegetable spray

4		**whole chicken breasts,** boned, skinned, halved	Pound into cutlets.

| 1 | cup | **Gruyere cheese,** shredded |
| ½ | cup | **onion,** chopped |

Combine in small bowl. Divide evenly placing some in center of each cutlet. Roll tightly; fasten with toothpick.

| ½ | cup | **seasoned bread crumbs** **water** |

Dip each cutlet in water then in bread crumbs to coat well. Place rolls in single layer in baking dish. Bake: 400° (40 min).

| 1 | can | **tomato sauce** (8oz) (optional) |

Pour over top if desired. Bake (15min) longer.

Judy Webster of Thin's Inn, Monroe

Chicken Marsala
(Italian)

Multiplies well – great for a party

Serves: 4
Stovetop: 10 min
Bake: 350° 20-30 min
Pans: skillet (10"); casserole, covered

| 2 | | **whole chicken breasts,** boned, skinned, halved |

Slice each into 2 pieces.

2	Tbsp	**flour**
½	tsp	**onion powder**
		salt, pepper to taste
	pinch	**thyme, savory OR 1** **bay leaf**

Coat each piece to season well. Reserve any flour not used.

| 2 | Tbsp | **butter** |

Sauté cutlets until browned; remove to casserole.

| 1 | clove | **garlic,** mashed |

Sauté gently (1-2min).

½	cup	**Marsala wine**
½	cup	**chicken stock**
		reserved flour seasoning mixture

Combine; add to skillet to loosen all pan drippings. Stir until smooth sauce is obtained. Pour over chicken. Bake covered until bubbly and chicken is tender.

Sally Easter, Bridgeport

MARSALA WINE is somewhat like sherry or Madeira, golden yellow.

Empress Chicken
(Chinese)

Part of a wonderful menu

Serves: 4-6
Marinate: 10-15 min
Stir/Fry: 5 min
Pan: wok or skillet

3	Tbsp	soy sauce	
2	tsp	sesame oil	
1	tsp	cornstarch	Combine for marinade.
1	tsp	sugar	
1	tsp	cooking wine	
	dash	salt, pepper	
12	oz	chicken breasts OR thighs, boneless, cubed	Marinate (10-15min).
3	Tbsp	vegetable oil	Sauté mushrooms in oil until soft. Remove to plate; set aside.
12	oz	mushrooms, halved	
	dash	salt	
1	Tbsp	oil	Add oil to pan; sauté scallions and chicken until cooked. Add a little water if chicken sticks to pan.
2		scallions, minced	
		reserved mushrooms	Return to pan; cook (1min). Serve.

Mable Yu, Trumbull

Chicken Chamizal
(Mexican)

Best prepared ahead and reheated

Serves: 8
Stovetop: 45 min
Pan: skillet (10")

½	lb	bacon, 1" pieces	Fry until crisp, crumble and set aside on paper towel.
1¼-1½	lb	chicken breasts, boned (1" cubes)	Dredge in flour, brown in small amount of oil.
		whole wheat flour	
2	Tbsp	vegetable oil	
6	oz	frozen orange juice concentrate	
1	cup	water	
1	can	pineapple chunks and juice (16oz)	
½	cup	currants	Add to chicken in fry pan, along with bacon bits, simmer (30min). Serve with brown rice seasoned with sautéed onions. Freezes well.
1	tsp	salt	
¼	tsp	pepper	
	dash	cayenne pepper	
⅛	tsp	cinnamon	
⅛	tsp	cloves	
¼	cup	blanched almonds, slivered or sliced (2¾oz), (optional)	

Marjorie Crump, Trumbull

Heavenly Chicken Pie With Caraway Biscuits

A very nutritious change

Serves: 4
Stovetop: 10-15 min
Bake: 350° 30 min
Pans: skillet (10"); casserole, greased (2-3qt)

2	lg	**chicken breasts,** skinned, boned, cubed
1	med	**onion,** chopped
¼	cup	**butter,** melted

Cook chicken and onion, stirring until chicken changes color (5min).

⅔	cup	**powdered milk,** dry
3	Tbsp	**cornstarch**
½	cup	**water**
½	tsp	**basil**
1	tsp	**salt**

Mix well; add to chicken. Cook over medium heat, stirring until sauce thickens (5min).

1	cup	**yogurt,** plain
1	cup	**cheddar cheese,** shredded
4	lg	**mushrooms,** sliced

Add; stir to blend well, then pour into casserole. Cover with Caraway Biscuits. Bake. Can also be served over rice.

CARAWAY BISCUITS FOR CRUST OR ...

1	cup	**flour,** unbleached
¾	cup	**flour,** whole wheat
1	Tbsp	**baking powder**
1	tsp	**salt**
½	tsp	**caraway seeds**

Mix together in bowl.

¼	cup	**oil**
½	cup	**milk**

Combine; stir into dry ingredients.

¼	cup	**flour**

Sprinkle on 12" pieces of wax paper; turn dough into paper and turn over a few times to flour. Pat out to ¾" thick; cut into biscuits. Bake separately or over casserole.

June Bartnett, Monroe

CORNSTARCH is best dissolved in cold water.

Hot Chicken "Salad"

The whole family loved it

Serves: 4-6
Stovetop: 10-15 min
Pan: wok or skillet (14")

Amount	Unit	Ingredient	Instructions
1-2	cups	**rice**	Cook; keep hot.
2		**whole chicken breasts** OR **legs** (8), boned skinned (1" cubes)	Shake to coat well; set aside.
¼	cups	**cornstarch**	
1	lg	**tomato** (8 wedges)	Prepare and set aside.
4	oz	**mushrooms**, fresh, sliced	
1	bnch	**scallions**, sliced (¼")	
1	cup	**celery**, chopped	
1	can	**water chestnuts**, drained, sliced thin (4oz)	
¼	cup	**corn oil**	Heat in wok; add chicken, browning quickly.
	dash	**garlic powder** prepared vegetables	Add; stir. Cover; reduce heat to simmer, cook (5min). Turn off heat.
1	tsp	**flavor enhancer** (optional)	
¼	cup	**soy sauce**	
2	cups	**iceberg lettuce**, chopped fine	Add; mix quickly then serve immediately, over hot rice.

Louise Cronan, Trumbull

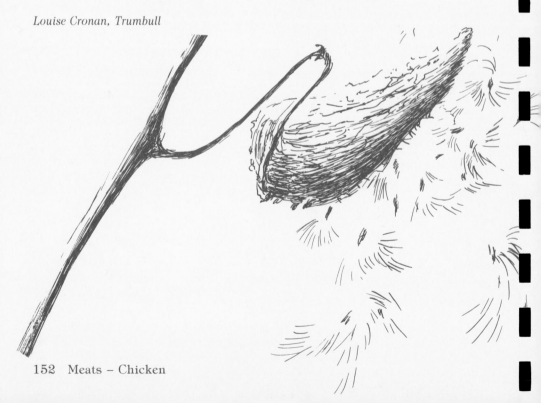

Chicken-Ham Rolls
(Italian)

A simple but elegant delight

Serves: 8-10
Stovetop: 15 min
Bake: 350° 15-25 min
Pan: skillet (lg); 11x7

6		whole chicken breasts, boned, skinned, halved	Pound into cutlets.
12	pcs	Gruyere cheese (1½x2)	Wrap cheese with ham. Place one on each cutlet. Roll each, enclosing ham completely.
12	slices	Prosciutto ham, very thin	
		salt to taste	Sprinkle over each roll.
		flour	Coat each well.
2		eggs, beaten	Dip each roll.
		Italian flavored bread crumbs	Roll each to cover well. May be refrigerated at this point for later cooking.
4-6	Tbsp	butter	Melt in skillet, add chicken rolls. Cook over moderate heat until browned on all sides (15min), adding butter as needed. Place in single layer in baking dish. Bake uncovered.
2-4	Tbsp	butter	Add to skillet; melt but do not brown.
3	Tbsp	cognac	Add to butter; set aflame and tilt to burn off all alcohol.
½	cup	heavy cream	Add and boil until shiny bubbles form. Pour over chicken just before serving.

Louise Cronan, Trumbull

MARINADE is a liquid containing spices, condiments, vegetables, herbs and a liquid of acid base in which meats are left for a period of time to enhance flavor. The acid in the marinade adds new flavor and softens the fibers of the meat.

Oriental Chicken and Peppers
(Chinese)

This makes any day a "Special Day"

Serves: 6
Marinate: 6 hr
Stovetop: 20-30 min
Pan: wok or skillet

6	med	**chicken cutlets,** cut bite size	Mix together well; refrigerate to marinate, stirring occasionally.
1	med	**onion,** chopped	
4	Tbsp	**soy sauce**	
6	Tbsp	**apple juice**	
2	cups	**rice**	30 minutes before serving, cook rice; drain and set aside.
4	cups	**water**	
½	cup	**vegetable oil**	Heat to 350°.
6	lg	**green peppers,** cut in strips	Add to oil; cook until crisp-tender then push aside.
1	tsp	**salt**	
1	tsp	**pepper**	
½	tsp	**garlic powder**	
1	cup	**mushrooms,** sliced OR	Mushrooms can be sautéed and added if you choose.
1	can	**buttom mushrooms** (optional)	
		marinated chicken	Add. Cook uncovered; turn until browned. Combine chicken and peppers. Serve immediately over rice.

Grace Parisi, Fairfield

Coq Au Vin
(French)

A great French meal

Serves: 6
Bake: 275° 2½ hr
Pans: Dutch oven; casserole (lg)

5	lb	**chicken pieces**	Dredge chicken pieces.
½	cup	**flour**	
½	cup	**butter,** melted **salt, pepper** to taste	Brown chicken well; place pieces in casserole then pour juices over.
½	cup	**ham,** chopped	Add to casserole.
10	sm	**white onions,** whole	
1	clove	**garlic,** crushed	
¼	tsp	**thyme**	
1	sprig	**parsley**	
1-2		**bay leaves**	
8		**mushrooms,** whole **salt, pepper** to taste	
2	oz	**cognac,** warm	Pour over chicken; set aflame.
1	cup	**red wine**	Add when flame dies down; cover. Bake until tender.

Dee Maggiori, Trumbull

Chicken Kiev

An elegant "do-ahead" entrée

Serves: 12
Freeze: 20 min
Bake: see recipe
Pan: jelly roll

1	cup	**butter**	Beat until soft.
2	tsp	**lemon juice**	
1	tsp	**lemon rind,** grated	
2	Tbsp	**parsley,** chopped	Add; combine well and form into 12
1	Tbsp	**chives**	balls. Freeze (20min).
1	clove	**garlic,** crushed	
1	tsp	**salt**	
⅛	tsp	**pepper**	
6	lg	**whole chicken breasts,** boned, skinned, halved	Pound into cutlets (12pcs). Place 1 butter ball on each piece. Fold ends over; roll then secure with toothpicks.
¼	cup	**flour**	Coat each breast with flour.
3		**eggs,** beaten	Dip each piece.
		bread crumbs	Roll each; place in single layer in pan. Bake: 425° (5min) then 400° (20min). Can also be fried in butter over medium heat until browned.

Pat Cervone, Fairfield

Marinated Arti-Chicken Bake

A different slant

Serves: 6
Bake: 350° 45 min
Pan: 13x9

2	lb	**chicken cutlets**	Cut into 2" strips.
		milk	Dip each piece.
		seasoned bread crumbs	Coat each piece.
		cooking oil	Fry chicken; set aside.
2	jars	**marinated artichokes** (6oz,ea)	Empty one jar artichokes and liquid into baking pan. Cover with ½ mushrooms. Place chicken on top; cover with remaining mushrooms and artichokes.
1	lb	**mushrooms,** sliced	
¼	cup	**tarragon vinegar**	Pour over; cover. Bake.

Christine Vazzano, Huntington

Chicken Breast Normandy

Juicy, tender, great flavor

Serves: 6
Stand: 2 hr
Bake: 350° 45 min
Pans: skillet (lg); 11x9

4-6		**whole chicken breasts,** boned, skinned, halved	Pound into cutlets.
½	tsp	each: **salt, pepper, thyme**	Sprinkle over the inside of each cutlet; set aside.
¼	cup	**margarine**	
½	cup	**chicken livers,** chopped	In skillet sauté slowly (5min) until liver is cooked; remove from heat.
2	Tbsp	**onion,** minced **salt** to taste	
1	can	**mushrooms,** drained (3-4oz)	Stir in; divide evenly then place in center of each cutlet. Fold sides over stuffing and fasten well.
1	cup	**Swiss cheese,** grated	
1		**egg,** beaten	Dip each piece in egg.
		bread crumbs, dry, plain or flavored	Roll each then chill uncovered, at least 2 hours, allowing coating to dry.
¼	cup	**butter**	When ready to serve, heat in skillet; add chicken and brown well. Remove to baking dish. Bake uncovered. To serve, pour a little sauce over rolls; serve the rest separately.

SUPREME SAUCE

¼	cup	**butter** OR **margarine**	Melt in saucepan.
¼	cup	**flour**	Blend in.
2	cups	**chicken stock**	Add; cook stirring constantly until sauce thickens and comes to a boil. Boil gently (3-5min) stirring.
1	Tbsp	**lemon juice**	Stir in; heat but do not boil.
½	cup	**light cream**	

Alice Targowski, Fairfield

 Natural cheese is made directly from milk curds or whey.

Arroz Con Pollo
(Puerto Rican)

Chicken or spareribs. Authentic

Serves: 8
Chill: several hours
Stovetop: 1½ hr
Pan: Dutch oven

2½	lb	**chicken pieces,** halved OR **spareribs**	Wash; pat dry

4½	tsp	**salt** (to taste)
1	tsp	**oregano**
2		**peppercorns**
2	cloves	**garlic**
2	tsp	**olive oil**
1	tsp	**vinegar**

Crush and mix well in blender. Rub into chicken pieces well. Chill several hours or overnight.

1	Tbsp	**vegetable shortening**
1	oz	**salt pork,** diced
2	oz	**ham,** diced

Brown in Dutch oven. Pour off fats; reduce heat to medium. Add chicken; brown (5-8min). Reduce heat to low.

1	sm	**onion,** chopped
1	med	**green pepper,** chopped
3		**sweet chili peppers,** seeded, chopped
1	med	**tomato,** chopped
6		**cilantro leaves** (can substitute bay leaves)

Add to Dutch oven; cook (8-10min) stirring occasionally.

1	can	**green pigeon peas** OR any kind of beans
		water

Drain juice into measuring cup; add enough water to make 2½ cups. Add to kettle; mix well.

3	cups	**rice**
½	tsp	**salt**
10-12		**olives**
¾	cup	**tomato sauce**
1	pkt	**Creole seasoning** (Sazon Goya)
1	Tbsp	**capers**

Add; cook, uncovered (moderate heat) (20min) or until rice is dry. Turn rice from top to bottom carefully. Cover; cook (low heat) (40-60min) turning rice again during first 20-25 min.

Augusto and Freda Laureano, Bridgeport

GARLIC was used by the early Egyptians for both nutrition and embalming. Rinse all utensils or hands used to handle garlic in COLD water before washing. For a SLIGHT HINT in a salad, rub a crust of bread over garlic clove, toss with salad then remove.

Chicken Fricassee
(Cuban)

Another great authentic meal

Serves: 6
Stovetop: 1½ hr
Pan: kettle (4qt)

2	sm	**chickens** quartered	
1	cup	**olive oil**, or to taste	
4	cloves	**garlic**, chopped	Fry until chicken is browned (25min).
2	lg	**onions**, chopped	
1	lg	**green pepper**, chopped	

1	can	**tomato sauce** (12oz)	
½	cup	**olives**, sliced	
¼	cup	**raisins**	Add to above; cook over low heat
2	tsp	**salt**	(1hr).
½	tsp	**black pepper**	
2	cups	**water**	

Julio and Gloria Alvarez, Bridgeport

Chicken Cacciatore
(Italian)

Delectable!

Serves: 4
Bake: 350° 1 hr
Pan: Dutch oven

2½-3	lb	**chicken**, cut up	Brown chicken (15min); remove and
¼	cup	**oil**	set aside.
2	med	**onions**, ¼" slices	Add and sauté until tender, not
2	cloves	**garlic**, minced	brown.
1	can	**tomatoes** (16oz)	
1-2		**bay leaves**	
1	can	**tomato sauce** (8oz)	
1	tsp	**salt**	
¼	tsp	**pepper**	Combine. Return chicken to pan; pour
½	tsp	**celery seed**	sauce over. Simmer (45min).
1	tsp	**oregano** OR **basil**	
1	tsp	**parsley**	
¼	tsp	**sage**	
½	tsp	**rosemary**	
¼	cup	**cooking sauterne**	Stir in and cook uncovered (20min), turning chicken occasionally. Cook until fork tender and sauce looks like chili sauce. Discard bay leaves and skim off excess fat.

Phyllis Aiello, Stratford

Chicken n' Choke

"Great! Nice flavor"

Serves: 6
Stovetop: 20-25 min
Bake: 375° 40 min
Pans: skillet (lg); 12x9

3	lb	**chicken pieces**	
1½	tsp	**salt**	Season chicken well.
½	tsp	**paprika**	
¼	tsp	**pepper**	
4	Tbsp	**butter**	Brown chicken in skillet (15-20min). Place in baking pan.
4	oz	**mushrooms,** quartered	Sauté (5min).
2	Tbsp	**butter**	
2	Tbsp	**flour**	Sprinkle over mushrooms.
⅔	cup	**chicken consommé**	Stir in; cook (5min).
3	Tbsp	**sherry**	
1	can	**artichokes** (6oz)	Arrange between chicken pieces. Pour sauce over; cover. Bake.

Julie Connery, Bridgeport

"Yorkshire" Chicken

A delicious puffy sauce

Serves: 6
Bake: 400° 1 hr
Pan: 13x9

3	lb	**chicken pieces**	
⅓	cup	**flour**	
½	tsp	**flavor enhancer** (optional)	Shake to coat meat well; place in baking dish in a single layer.
¼	tsp	**pepper**	
1	tsp	**paprika**	
½	cup	**butter,** melted	Pour over chicken, evenly. Bake (30min); remove and pour off all but ¼ cup drippings.

YORKSHIRE SAUCE

3		**eggs**	
1	cup	**milk**	Blend well in a bowl.
½	cup	**sour cream**	
½	tsp	**salt**	Add and beat well; pour over chicken evenly. Bake (30min) until puffed and brown.
1	tsp	**baking powder**	
¼	tsp	**tarragon**	

Terry Simpson, Fairfield

Chicken Paprikas with Dumplings I
(Hungarian)

Very tasty

Serves: 6
Stovetop: 1 hr
Pans: Dutch oven; kettle (4qt)

1		onion, chopped	} Sauté until golden.
4	Tbsp	shortening	
1	Tbsp	paprika	Add, stirring until blended.
3-4	lb	chicken pieces	Add to above, cover and simmer until tender (30-40min). Remove chicken and keep warm.
1	Tbsp	salt	
¾	tsp	pepper	
1½	cups	water	
2		bay leaves	
1	pt	sour cream	Add; beat until smooth. Bring to a boil then turn heat down.
4	Tbsp	flour	
1	cup	cream	Add; heat through but DO NOT BOIL. Serve over dumplings (see Index).

Ann Kovacs, Fairfield

Chicken Paprikas and Dumplings II
(Hungarian)

Try the complete menu

Serves: 4
Stovetop: 1 hr
Pans: kettle (4qt); saucepan (3qt)

1	lg	onion, chopped	} Sauté in kettle.
4	Tbsp	shortening	
2	tsp	paprika	Add; simmer until chicken is tender (1hr). Serve with dumplings (see Index).
2-3	lb	chicken pieces	
1		tomato, chopped	
2	tsp	salt	
1	cup	water	
		sour cream	Use as garnish.

Ann Howie, Stratford

Dumplings

3		eggs, beaten	Beat with spoon to form a soft dough; drop by teaspoon into boiling salted water. Cook until dumplings rise to top. Drain; rinse in cold water. Add to your main-dish pot.
3	cups	flour	
1	Tbsp	salt	
¼	tsp	baking powder	
½	cup	water, cold	

Elizabeth Marusa, Fairfield

Chicken Legs Alla Franny Fry

This is a "as much as you want, until it looks right and tastes good" recipe

Serves: your choice
Bake: 300° 1½ hr
Pans: saucepan; baking dish

Bermuda onions, sliced **carrots,** sliced diagonally **celery,** sliced diagonally	Steam (6-7min).
chicken legs **ice water** **salt**	Soak legs (5-10min); pat dry. Place legs in baking dish.
olive oil, butter OR **margarine** **salt** **pepper,** freshly ground **marjoram,** crushed	Coat chicken; cover with foil. Bake (15min); remove from oven and place steamed vegetables under chicken. Bake uncovered (10-15min) longer.
Vermouth, French or Italian 1 Tbsp **olive oil** 1 Tbsp **butter** OR **margarine** melted **marjoram,** crushed	Combine in small saucepan; brush on chicken legs. Bake (1hr) uncovered, basting often and turning legs over half way.
mushrooms, sliced, sautéed	Add just before serving. If more browning is needed, turn oven to 350° near end of cooking.

Frances Fry, Fairfield

Chicken Pie with Almond "Crust"

A great use for cooked chicken or turkey

Serves: 6-8
Bake: 350° 20-30 min
Pans: saucepan (2qt); skillet (sm);
13x9

½	cup	margarine	Melt in saucepan.
⅛	cup	flour	
2½	cups	chicken broth	
½	cup	white wine	Add and simmer.
1	tsp	lemon rind	
½	cup	onion, chopped	
½	cup	celery, chopped	Sauté until soft; add to above and combine with sauce.
⅔	cup	mushrooms, sliced	
2	Tbsp	butter	
4-5	cups	chicken, cooked, sliced	Add to sauce and place in baking dish.
		salt, pepper to taste	
½	cup	margarine, melted	Combine.
½	cup	almonds, slivered	
4	slices	bread, crusts removed	Cut each in half; dip in almond mixture and place on top of casserole, buttered side up. Spoon any extra over top of casserole. Bake. Serve piping hot.

Harriette Lindstrom, Fairfield

Hot Chicken Salad

An excellent low calorie luncheon dish!

Serves: 6-8
Bake: 400° 20 min
Pan: 9x9, non-stick spray

6	oz	low-fat cottage cheese	Combine in blender.
1	cup	skim milk	
2	cups	chicken, cooked, diced	
2	cups	celery, chopped	Mix together with above; place in prepared baking dish.
½	cup	water chestnuts, sliced	
2	Tbsp	lemon juice	
2	cups	cornflakes, crushed (4oz)	
½	cup	sharp cheddar cheese, grated	Sprinkle over top. Bake.
		salt, pepper to taste	

Joan Kacin, Trumbull

Roast Turkey with Oriental Flair

Serve with fried rice and oriental vegetables

Serves: 16
Stovetop: 45 min
Bake: see recipe
Pan: roaster (lg)

6	slices	**ginger root,** fresh	
4		**scallion stalks,** chopped	Combine in large roasting pan. Place on stovetop; bring to a boil.
3	cups	**soy sauce**	
1	cup	**sherry**	
10	cups	**water**	
2	Tbsp	**sugar**	
1	tsp	**salt** (to taste)	
½	tsp	**pepper**	

10 lb   **turkey** (preferably boneless frozen breast) — Place thawed turkey into sauce and bring to a boil again. Lower heat; simmer covered (45min). Turn turkey twice for even coating. Cover; place in oven. Bake: 350° (1hr), basting frequently. Uncover. Bake: 450° (10-15min), until browned. Remove and let cool. Thicken gravy.

Daria Dollard, Derby

Turkey–Rice Curry

"Easy and excellent!"

Serves: 8-10
Bake: 350° 2 hr
Pans: casserole (2-3qt); saucepan (sm)

6	cups	**turkey,** cooked, cubed
2	cans	**cream of mushroom soup** (10½oz,ea)
2	cans	**milk**
¾	cup	**long grain rice,** raw
2	cups	**celery,** chopped
2½	tsp	**curry powder**
¼	cup	**parsley**

Combine; place in casserole. Bake covered (1½hr). Stir once or twice. Cook until rice is done and casserole is hot and bubbly.

2	Tbsp	**margarine**
¼	cup	**bread crumbs,** dry

Combine; sprinkle over casserole. Bake (15min) until top is golden.

Marjorie Dickey, Fairfield

 Add a little water to the cavity of your unstuffed poultry (especially turkey) for a nice moist bird.

Turkey Tetrazzini

Chicken can also be used

Serves: 6
Bake: 400° 20 min
Pans: saucepan; double boiler; skillet;
    casserole, greased (4qt)

½	lb	**spaghetti**	Cook according to package directions; drain.
4	oz	**mushrooms,** fresh, sliced	Sauté then add to cooked spaghetti; set aside.
1	Tbsp	**butter**	
4	Tbsp	**butter**	Melt butter in top of double boiler; blend in flour; add broth and cook until smooth and thick, stirring constantly.
⅓	cup	**flour**	
2	cups	**turkey broth** OR **chicken consommé**	
1	cup	**light cream**	Add to sauce and divide in half.
½	tsp	**salt**	
¼	tsp	**pepper**	
2	Tbsp	**sherry**	
2	cups	**turkey,** diced	Add to half of the sauce.
		reserved spaghetti reserved mushrooms	Add to other half of sauce. Place spaghetti-mushroom mixture in casserole. Make a hole in the middle; pour turkey mixture into the hole.
½	cup	**Parmesan cheese**	Sprinkle over top. Bake, uncovered.

Julie Connery, Bridgeport

Duck with Bing Cherry Sauce

(Jewish)

Friday Sabbath main course

Serves: 6-8
Bake: 375° 2½-3 hr
Pans: roasting pan; rack; saucepan
    (sm)

| 2 | | **ducks** (4 lb, ea) | Stuff each duck with one onion to catch fat. Roast on rack, pricking constantly to let out fat. |
| 2 | med | **onions,** peeled, quartered | |

SAUCE

1	can	**bing cherries,** pitted (16oz)	Drain, reserving juice; set cherries aside.
¾	cup	**red port wine** reserved juice	In saucepan, bring to a boil.
1½	Tbsp	**cornstarch** OR **flour**	Mix; add to above and cook stirring until thickened.
3	Tbsp	**water,** cold	
		reserved cherries	Return to sauce; bring to a boil. Serve over duck or on the side.

Gail Cohen, Trumbull

Baked Pork Tenderloin

Excellent!

Serves: 6-8
Bake: 350° (1½-2½hr)
Pan: roaster

4-5 lb	**pork tenderloin** flour oil	Roll meat in flour; brown in oil.
½ cup	each: **maple syrup, catsup, water, Worcestershire sauce**	Mix sauce; place tenderloin on large piece of foil; folding edges up. Pour sauce over meat; seal foil well. Bake (30 min per lb). Cool slightly before carving.
dash	each: **salt, pepper, garlic powder**	

Diane Lombardi, Milford

Schab Pieczony

(Polish)

Roast pork loin

Bake: 325° 30-35 min/lb
Pan: Dutch oven

1	**pork loin,** boneless	
2 cloves	**garlic,** mashed	Combine; rub meat well.
1 Tbsp	**salt**	
	paprika, marjoram, caraway	Dust roast to taste. Place in Dutch oven.
	onion, sliced	Surround roast; cover and let stand room temperature (2hr).
1 cup	**water**	Add to above; cover. Bake. Serve chilled, sliced thin.

Pat McCathron, Trumbull

Crush all dried herbs before using to release flavors. ⅓ to ½ tsp dried for 1 Tbsp of fresh herbs.

"Pork Roast" Bavarian

Different and great!

Serves: 6
Bake: 325° 45 min/lb
Pan: roasting pan

6	lb	**loin of pork**

Slit each chop through to bone forming pocket.

1	lb	**sauerkraut,** drained, chopped
1	med	**apple,** diced
½	cup	**raisins**
1	sm	**onion,** diced
½	tsp	**salt**
⅛	tsp	**pepper**
¼	tsp	**caraway seeds**

Mix well; stuff each pocket and tie roast firmly with string. Bake according to weight of your roast.

Pat O'Hearne, Fairfield

Fruit Stuffed Pork with Wine Sauce

A Scandinavian specialty

Yield: 6
Stovetop: 20 min
Bake: 350° 1½ hr
Pan: Dutch oven

1	lg	**tart apple,** peeled, cored, cubed (1")
1	tsp	**lemon juice**

Sprinkle apple with lemon juice to prevent discoloration; set aside.

4½-5	lb	**pork loin,** boneless
12		**prunes,** pitted, cooked
		salt, pepper to taste
		reserved apples

Cut deep pocket in pork (cut lengthwise down loin to within ½" of the ends and within 1" of other side). Season pocket lightly; stuff with prunes and apples. Sew up opening. Tie at 1" intervals to keep shape.

3	Tbsp	**butter**
3	Tbsp	**vegetable oil**

In Dutch oven, brown pork on all sides; skim off fat.

¾	cup	**dry white wine**
¾	cup	**heavy cream**

Pour in. Whisking briskly, bring to a simmer on stovetop; cover. Bake until meat gives no resistance when pierced (approx 1½hr). Remove meat, skim off fat; bring liquid to a boil and reduce to approx 1 cup.

1	Tbsp	**red currant jelly**

Reduce heat; add jelly. Simmer briefly, stirring constantly until sauce is smooth. Remove pork; cut away string and serve 1" thick slices. Serve sauce separately.

Hillandale Gourmet Club, Trumbull

Schweinebraten
(German)

A great meat course

Serves: 6
Simmer: 2½ hr
Pan: Dutch oven

3½	lb	**pork loin,** boneless
1	tsp	**salt**
¼	tsp	**pepper**
1	tsp	**paprika**

Season meat.

2	Tbsp	**shortening**

Lightly brown meat on all sides; remove and reserve.

1	med	**onion,** sliced
4	cloves	**garlic,** crushed
2	stalks	**celery** (2" pieces)
3		**carrots** (2" slices)

Add to shortening; cook over med-high heat (5min).

2	cups	**chicken broth**
		reserved meat

Add; cover. Simmer (2½hr) or until meat is tender, turning roast occasionally. Remove meat; strain sauce, reserving large pieces of celery and carrot.

2	Tbsp	**cornstarch**
½	cup	**cream**

Blend; stir into sauce and bring to a boil. Slice meat ¼" thick. Arrange on platter; top with some gravy. Save remaining sauce for dumplings.

		parsley
		reserved vegetables

Garnish. Serve with dumplings. (see Index).

Gertrud Bargas, Trumbull

Charcoal Broiled Pork
(Korean)

Marinated slices of shoulder

Serves: 4
Marinate: 15 min
Broil: few minutes

1½	lb	**boneless pork shoulder** (Boston butt)

Trim fat; remove bone. Slice ⅛" thick then cut into 3-4" squares.

1-3	Tbsp	**soy sauce**
	dash	**pepper**
3	Tbsp	**sugar**
1		**green onion,** minced
2	tsp	**ginger,** grated
2	Tbsp	**sesame seeds**
1	Tbsp	**dark sesame oil**
1	clove	**garlic,** minced

Combine; marinate meat (15min). Broil over slow charcoal fire and serve with rice that has been cooked without salt.

Gloria Lee, Trumbull

Southeastern Pork Bake

Each chop a meal!

Serves: 6
Bake: 350° 1½ hr
Pans: skillet (med); 12x8, greased

| ½ | lb | mushrooms, sliced | } Sauté mushrooms; set aside. |
| 1 | Tbsp | margarine | |

| 6 | | pork loin chops (¾") | Place pork chops in single layer in baking dish. |

1	Tbsp	soy sauce	}
1	tsp	dry mustard	Brush on both sides of chops.
¼	tsp	hot pepper sauce (optional)	

		reserved mushrooms	}
5		green onions with tops, chopped	Top chops.
6	med	potatoes, peeled, sliced thin	

| 2 | Tbsp | margarine | Melt. |

| 1-2 | cloves | garlic, crushed | } Add to above; brush over potatoes. |
| 2 | Tbsp | soy sauce | |

| | | paprika | Sprinkle lightly; cover with foil. Bake (1hr). Remove foil and bake uncovered (30min) longer or until chops and potatoes are tender. |

| | | parsley | Garnish. |

Marie Beaudin, St. Petersburg, Fl

Sauterne Baked Pork Chops

"These are delicious"

Serves: 4-6
Fry: 5 min
Bake: 350° 60 min
Pans: skillet (lg); 13x9

| 8 | | pork chops | } Brown in skillet; remove to baking dish. |
| 1-2 | tsp | shortening | |

1	cup	Sauterne	}
½	cup	soy sauce	
⅓	cup	salad oil	
¼	tsp	ginger	Blend together; pour over chops. Bake, uncovered, turning once.
1		bay leaf, crumbled	
½	clove	garlic (optional)	
2	tsp	maple syrup	
¼	tsp	oregano	

Claudia McKenna, Trumbull

Pork Tenderloin
(Sweden)

A rich and delicious family original

Serves: 6-8
Bake: 475° (15min)
Pans: skillet; casserole, greased (3qt)

2	lb	**pork tenderloin** (½" slices)	Brown on all sides.
4-6		**tomatoes,** sliced	Cover bottom of casserole; layer meat
	dash	each: **salt, pepper**	on top. Sprinkle seasonings over.
3	Tbsp	**margarine,** melted	
½	med	**onion,** chopped	
4	oz	**mushrooms,** sliced, fresh or canned	Sauté ingredients a few minutes.
3	slices	**baked ham,** chopped	
3	Tbsp	**flour**	Combine; add to above then stir to
1½	cups	**light cream**	make sauce. Cook (5min); pour over
		adjust **seasonings**	meat. (Can be frozen at this point.)
		cheddar cheese, sliced	Cover casserole well. Bake.

Kerstin Nilson, Trumbull

Polynesian Ribs

"This tastes wonderful"

Serves: 4
Bake: 425° 20 min
Crockpot: 6-10 hr
Pans: baking dish; crockpot

2	lb	**pork spareribs** (3" pieces)	Bake (10min) to render fats; drain.
⅓	cup	**soy sauce**	Mix until smooth; brush over ribs.
1	Tbsp	**ginger**	Bake (10min) more.
¼	cup	**cornstarch**	
½	cup	**cider vinegar**	Combine in crockpot; stir well. Add
1	cup	**sugar**	browned ribs; cover. Cook on low set-
¼	cup	**water**	ting (6-10hr).
1	Tbsp	**salt** (to taste)	
½	tsp	**dry mustard**	

Jan McNaughton, Fairfield

Country Style Spare Ribs

"Terrific sauce over rice"

Serves: 6
Bake: See recipe
Pans: 13x9; saucepan (2qt)

4	lb	**spareribs**, country style	Brown ribs, both sides. Place in
½	tsp	each: **salt, pepper**	roaster.
2	Tbsp	**vegetable oil**	
1	cup	**catsup**	Combine in saucepan. Bring to a boil;
¼	cup	**Worcestershire sauce**	cook several minutes until well
	drops	**hot sauce**	blended. Pour over ribs; cover with
¼	cup	**vinegar**	foil. Bake: 325° (2-2½hr) until tender,
2	Tbsp	**brown sugar**	basting frequently. Remove cover;
1	tsp	**celery seeds**	raise heat to 350°. Bake until
1	tsp	**chili powder**	browned. Serve with rice.
¼	tsp	**pepper**	
1	cup	**water**	
1	Tbsp	**sherry** (optional)	

Diane Lombardi, Milford

 VINEGAR is made in many flavors. The acidity softens muscle fibers thus helping to digest these fibers. Add a bit to beets, cabbage, spinach, lettuce, celery and raw vegetables.

Yangfu Sweet-Sour Pork
(Chinese)

Serves: 4
Stovetop: 20-25 min
Pans: wok; skillet

"Takes time but well worth it"

1	lb	**pork steak** OR **fresh pork butt,** lean (¾" cubes)	Season pork.
1	tsp	**salt**	
1		**egg**	Mix into a batter.
¼	cup	**cornstarch**	
¼	cup	**flour**	
¼	cup	**water**	
		peanut oil for deep frying	Heat to 375°. Coat pork with batter; fry a few pieces at a time so as not to lower temp. of oil. Fry (3-4min) until crisp and golden; drain well. Keep warm. Reserve 1 Tbsp oil for sauce; discard remainder.

SAUCE

1	Tbsp	**peanut oil**	Heat.
1	clove	**garlic,** mashed	Add; stir/fry (1min).
1		**green pepper,** diced	
1		**carrot,** julienned	
½	cup	**chicken broth**	Combine; add to wok and bring to a boil.
4	Tbsp	**wine vinegar**	
3	Tbsp	**sugar**	
2	Tbsp	**catsup**	
1	tsp	**soy sauce**	
12	chunks	**pineapple**	
1	Tbsp	**cornstarch**	Dissolve then add, stirring in well but carefully.
2	Tbsp	**water,** cold	
		reserved pork	Add to wok; heat (1min) just until hot. Serve over boiled rice.

Louise Cronan, Trumbull

 PEANUTS come to us from South America. The pods grow underground.

Pork Curry with Rice

Great way to use cooked pork

Serves: 15-18
Stovetop: 35-45 min
Pan: kettle (6qt)

5	cups	**rice,** uncooked	Cook; set aside. (Crockpot good for this amount.)
10	cups	**water**	
4	cups	**cooked pork,** diced	
3	cups	**water**	
2	cups	**white raisins**	
1½	cups	**orange juice,** frozen, undiluted	Combine in kettle; simmer slowly (30min).
¾	cup	**honey**	
¾	cup	**soy sauce**	
2	Tbsp	**curry powder**	Add to above.
6	Tbsp	**cornstarch**	
¼	cup	**water**	Combine then add to kettle, stirring carefully until juices thicken.
		juice from kettle	
6	oz	**almonds,** slivered, toasted	Add just before serving to retain crispness. Serve piping hot, over boiled rice.
4	cups	**apples,** unpeeled, diced	

Hazel Peterson, Wilton

Ku Lu Jou

(Chinese)

An excellent sweet and sour pork

Serves: 4-6
Marinate: 1 hr
Pan: wok

1	lb	**pork cutlet,** cut in cubes	
2	Tbsp	**soy sauce**	
½	tsp	***five spice powder**	Marinate pork.
1		**egg**	*Found in gourmet shops or oriental markets.
	dash	**salt**	
		cornstarch	Roll each cube until coated.
		oil for deep frying	Fry until golden (4-5min). Set aside; keep warm.
5	Tbsp	each: **sugar, catsup, white vinegar**	Mix well; set aside.
½	tsp	**cornstarch**	
1	Tbsp	**oil**	
1		**tomato,** cubed	Stir/fry quickly (1min). Add above sauce; stir and cook until it boils. Add reserved pork; mix well. Serve immediately, while hot.
1		**green pepper,** cubed	
1		**scallion,** chopped	
1	can	**pineapple chunks** (13½oz)	

Mabel Yu, Trumbull

4 cans
tomato sauce

1 can concent
12 oz paste

vinegar
garlic
garlic salt
sugar
chili

Fill with water
Boil 1 1/2 hr.

Stand on end
& put sauce over

Stuffed Cabbage
(Hungarian)

A very special meal, delicious

Serves: 10-14
Stovetop: 2 hr
Pan: kettle (8qt)

2	lb	**pork** (shoulder butt)	Dice into large bowl.
2	Tbsp	**vegetable shortening**	
1	sm	**onion,** chopped	Saute until wilted; add mixture to
½	tsp	**black pepper**	pork.
½	tsp	**paprika**	
1	cup	**rice**	Soak well; rinse. Add rice to meat
		water	mixture.
1	tsp	**salt**	Add to above and mix well.
1	clove	**garlic,** minced	
4	lb	**cabbage,** cored	Soak in boiling water. Pry leaves apart. (Do not cook, just soften the leaves.) Cut out the main vein in each leaf without cutting through the leaf.
		water, boiling	

TO FORM ROLLS: Place 1 leaf on left hand, stem toward wrist; place approx. 1 Tbsp meat mixture near stem end of leaf. With right hand, roll toward finger tips. Tuck ends in tightly. Set rolls aside. Cut up left over cabbage and line bottom of kettle.

1	can	**sauerkraut** (16oz)	Spread ½ over chopped cabbage. Arrange cabbage rolls in layers. Cover with remaining sauerkraut.
2		**bay leaves**	
2	cups	**tomatoes**	Pour over cabbage. Bring to a boil; turn to low and simmer (2hr).
2	cups	**tomato juice**	
		water to cover	

Ann Kovacs, Fairfield

 SAUERKRAUT should be rinsed well to remove much of the salt brine. Add ham or pork for flavor. Chopped tart apples also enhance the flavor.

 RICE – brown, only the outer shell has been removed. This rice can be soaked (1hr) before cooking. Cook (40-50min). Unpolished white, bran coating has been removed but it is almost white. Polished white, further refined to remove all bran layers. Converted, soaked for several hours in hot water, steamed then dried again. Wild rice, is not true rice. It is the grains of grasses in North America. In Connecticut it is known as "Blackbird's Oats." It's name comes from the Menominee Indians which literally means wild rice.

Piñon

(Puerto Rican)

Ripe plantain or banana pie

Serves: 6-8
Stovetop: 25-30 min
Pans: skillet (lg); saucepan (1½qt)

3	RIPE	**Plantains,** brushed, peeled OR 6 **ripe bananas**	Slice lengthwise (¼")
		lard OR **oil** for deep frying	Fry slices until golden. Drain on absorbent paper; set aside.

*SOFRITO (sauce)

2	Tbsp	**vegetable oil** OR **lard**	
1	Tbsp	**onion,** diced	
2	cloves	**garlic,** mashed	Sauté vegetables and seasonings in hot oil until glazed; add tomato sauce and capers. Simmer slowly (10-15min).
2		**green peppers,** minced	
2		**coriander leaves** OR **Spanish parsley** (perejil)	
¼	tsp	**marjoram** (oregano)	**Sofrito is the basis of many Spanish main dishes.*
½	cup	**tomato sauce**	
1	Tbsp	**capers,** chopped	

¾	cup	**beef** OR **pork,** chopped	Add to Sofrito and cook until beans are tender; set aside.
1	cup	**water**	
1½	cups	**green beans** (1-2")	

		reserved plantain	Spread half of plantain slices over bottom of buttered skillet.
1	Tbsp	**butter**	
		reserved Sofrito	Spread over top; cover with remaining half of plantain slices.
2		**eggs,** beaten	Pour over top; simmer slowly (5-10min). Cover with plate; invert

piñon on plate then slide back into skillet and cook (5-10min) longer. Serve hot. May be baked 350°(20-25min).

Barbara Schegg, Huntington

 Use a square ended pancake turner as a mixing spoon when making foods that stick easily. The bottom scrapes a large area and slots mix juices well.

Tourtière
(Canadian)

For a traditional New Year's Day buffet

Yield: 2 pies
Simmer: 1½ hr
Bake: See recipe
Pans: saucepan (4-6qt); 2 pie plates
  (9")

Pastry for 2 2-crust pies

2	lb	**pork,** ground fine
1	lb	**beef,** ground fine
½	cup	**onion,** minced
1	tsp	**salt**
¼	tsp	**pepper**
1	tsp	**cinnamon**
½	tsp	**cloves**
¼	tsp	**nutmeg**
1	cup	**water**

Combine in saucepan; cook over medium heat, stirring often, until meats lose their pink color. Cover; cook on low heat (1hr), stirring often.

1½	cups	**potatoes,** mashed

Add; stir in well. Cook (10-15min) uncovered. Adjust seasonings; cool.

Whip with large spoon as it cools, to fluff. Line pie plates with crust; divide filling equally. Cover with crust; seal well. Cut slits; paint crust with milk. Bake: 425° (15-20min), then reduce to 350° (20-30min) until crust is golden and filling bubbly. Serve: piping hot with cranberry sauce and salad.

Jeanette Campbell, West Warwick, RI

Ca Chien Thit
(Vietnamese)

A delightful stuffed tomato

Serves: 4-6
Pan: wok

6		**tomatoes,** skinned

Cut each in half; remove seeds and set aside.

1½	lb	**pork,** ground, very fine

Chop with a knife to be sure it is very fine.

½	tsp	**sugar**
2	Tbsp	**onion,** minced
½	tsp	each: **salt, pepper**
1	Tbsp	**soy sauce**

Mix well with pork; stuff tomatoes.

	oil
	garlic, crushed

Heat in wok. Add tomatoes; cook (15min).

	rice, cooked
	soy sauce (optional)

Serve over rice.

Laura Lund, Milford

Panhandle Sauce for Barbecue or Marinade

A great tangy sauce

Yield: 3 cups
Stovetop: 15-20 min
Pan: saucepan (3qt)

1	cup	**vegetable oil**
½	cup	**butter,** melted
½	cup	**brown sugar,** light
½	tsp	**pepper**
1	tsp	**dry mustard**
½	cup	**Worcestershire sauce**
1	btl	**catsup** (14oz)
2	Tbsp	**chili sauce**
1	med	**onion,** minced
¼	cup	**lemon juice**
3	drops	**Tabasco sauce**
2	cloves	**garlic** (optional)

Over low heat, combine all ingredients, stirring constantly. Simmer, stirring frequently. Stores well for 1-2 weeks in refrigerator or freezes indefinitely. Use as a marinade or a basting sauce for poultry or ribs.

Jane Stenthal, Port Chester, NY

Chris's Barbecue Sauce

Yield: 1½-2 cups

½	cup	**cider vinegar**
½	cup	**vegetable oil**
1	med	**onion,** chopped fine
1½	tsp	**salt**
1½	tsp	**Worcestershire sauce**
⅛	tsp	**pepper**
1¼	tsp	**paprika**
¾	can	**tomato paste** (6oz)

Combine; use on pork ribs or chicken.

Chris Henschel, Fairfield

Polynesian "Roast"

Made with slices

Serves: Your choice
Bake: 350° 1 hr

	pineapple, sliced	Plan 2 slices of each per person, alternate slices; tie or skewer. Bake.
	Canadian bacon, sliced	
	OR **ham**	

GLAZE

1	cup	**brown sugar**	
1		**orange,** grated, including rind	Baste "roast" several times.
¼	tsp	**ground cloves**	

Darlene Nelson, Fairfield

Ham and Spinach Rollups

Great for that special buffet

Serves: 12
Bake: 350° 30 min
Pans: 12x8; saucepan (sm)

2	pkg	**spinach,** chopped, frozen, cooked, drained (10oz,ea)	Combine well.
2	cups	**cornbread stuffing**	
2	cups	**sour cream**	
24	slices	**ham** (⅛-¼")	Spread with above mixture; roll and place, seam side down, in pan.

SAUCE

4	cups	**milk**	Dissolve well in saucepan; heat.
4	Tbsp	**cornstarch**	
4	Tbsp	**margarine**	Add; cook until thickened, stirring. Pour over rolls. Bake, covered (15min) then uncover and bake (15min) longer. Can be frozen when cooled.
1	cup	**sharp cheese,** grated	
		pepper to taste	

Joan Mahoney, Fairfield

Ham and Mushroom Casserole

A great use for that left-over ham

Serves: 4-6
Bake: 375° 30-35 min
Pan: casserole, greased (1½qt);
    skillet (8")

1½-2	cups	**egg noodles** (med)	Cook; drain and set aside.
2	cups	**white sauce** (med) (see Roux)	Melt cheese in white sauce.
1	cup	**cheddar cheese**, diced	
1	Tbsp	**onion**, grated	
2	stalks	**celery**, sliced (¼")	Sauté vegetables in butter.
1	can	**mushrooms**, sliced (3oz)	
1	Tbsp	**butter**, melted	
1½	cups	**ham**, cooked, diced	Combine with noodles, vegetables and cheese sauce; turn into prepared casserole.
		salt, pepper to taste	(Will need very little salt.)
1	cup	**bread crumbs**, fine, buttered	Cover. Bake until crumbs brown.

Charlotte Brittain, Fairfield

"Nassi Goreng"
(Indonesian)

A great "stretch" dish

Serves: 6-8
Stovetop: 10-15 min
Bake: 350° 15 min
Pans: skillet (10"); casserole, greased
    (2qt)

¼	cup	**butter** OR **margarine**	In skillet, lightly brown onions with curry.
2	med	**onions**, chopped coarse	
1	Tbsp	**curry powder**	
3	Tbsp	**peanut butter**, chunky	Add; stir in.
2	cups	**ham**, cooked, diced	Add; mix thoroughly. Brown over low heat (5-10min).
6	cups	**rice**, cooked	
2	cloves	**garlic**, crushed	Add; stir to mix then transfer to well greased casserole. Bake covered (15min). If prepared in advance, bake until well heated (30-40min). Keep covered to prevent drying. Serve with cold raw vegetables or curried glazed fruit.
1	tsp	**salt**	
	dash	**nutmeg**	
	dash	**pepper**	

M'Lee Sampson, Stratford

Ham Sauce

A great "make ahead" sauce

Serves: 6
Stovetop: 20-30 min
Pan: double boiler

1½	cup	**sugar**	
4	tsp	**dry mustard**	Combine in top of double boiler.
1	tsp	**salt**	
2		**eggs,** lightly beaten	Gradually add to dry ingredients.
½	cup	**milk**	Cook over boiling water (20-30min).
½	cup	**vinegar**	
2	Tbsp	**butter**	Stir into sauce. Serve with baked ham. Easily made ahead and reheated.

Linda Newbauer, Weston

Cran-Shire Barbecue Sauce

Cranberry flavored barbecue sauce

Yield: 2½ cups
Stovetop: 10 min
Pan: saucepan (2qt)

1	can	**cranberry sauce,** jellied	
¾	cup	**chili sauce**	Combine in saucepan; cook until cranberry sauce is melted. Use to baste ham, pork or chicken.
2	Tbsp	**Worcestershire sauce**	
1	Tbsp	**lemon juice**	
¼	tsp	**pepper**	

Aster Seale, Bridgeport

Sausage and Peppers

A great meal or super sandwich

Serves: 12-15
Bake: 375° see recipe
Pans: roaster; Dutch oven

8	lb	**Italian sweet sausage**	Bake uncovered (45min).
3-5		**onions** (to taste) **butter** OR **margarine**	In Dutch oven, sauté.
5-6	lb	**red and green peppers,** cut in strips	Add to onions; cook (5-10min). Add to sausage.
2	cans	**tomato sauce** (15oz,ea)	Simmer together a few minutes in pan
1	lb	**mushrooms**	used to cook onions. Add to sausage

and peppers; mix lightly. Bake (45-60min) more, uncovered. Lift sausage from bottom of pan to top and baste with juice in pan, while cooking. Cut sausage into serving pieces and use as entree or on grinder rolls.

Nancy Standley, Trumbull

Sausage Stuffed Squash

"Economical, delicious, unusual!"

Serves: 6
Bake: 350° see recipe
Pans: 12x8, greased; skillet (med)

3		**butternut squash,** halved (or any winter squash)	Place, cut side down, in prepared pan. Bake (40min) or until squash is just tender.
1	lb	**Italian sweet sausage,** casings removed	While squash bakes, fry sausage until brown and crumbly.
1	lg	**onion,** chopped	Add to sausage, sauté until onion is soft.
1	clove	**garlic,** chopped	
6	slices	**bread** (½" cubes)	Stir into sausage; add water if mixture is too dry. Remove from heat. Turn squash, cut side up; scoop out seeds.
½	cup	**parsley,** chopped	
2		**eggs**	

Carefully mash squash in its skin. Spoon sausage mixture over squash. When ready to serve, return to oven. Bake (15min) or until top is golden and piping hot.

Donna Mastin, Fairfield

Sausage Popover

"A quick and easy luncheon casserole"

Serves: 4
Bake: see recipe
Pans: skillet (med); casserole (2qt)

1	lb	**sausage,** sliced (12 pieces)	Sauté sausage; reserve drippings. Pour ⅛" into casserole; add cooked sausage.
2		**eggs**	Beat together (5min); pour into casserole. Bake: 450° (20min), then 350° (15-20min) longer.
1	cup	**milk**	
1	cup	**flour,** sifted	
½	tsp	**salt**	

Christine Vazzano, Huntington

Sausage in Brew

A great summer picnic sandwich

Serves: 8
Stovetop: 3-4 hr
Pan: skillet (med); kettle (4qt)

16		**hot sausage links**	Brown in skillet. Place in kettle.
4-5	cans	**beer** (12 oz)	Pour over sausage, to cover.
2	cloves	**garlic,** crushed	Add to above. Cook on low to medium heat until mixture boils down.
4	lg	**onions,** chopped	
	pinch	**thyme**	
1	tsp	**oregano**	
1	Tbsp	**red pepper,** crushed	
		grinder rolls	Serve on rolls.

Gail Lauder, Fairfield

Kielbasa Beans for a Crowd

Great for that big summer picnic

Serves: 12
Soak: 1 hr
Stovetop: 1½ hr (approx)
Pan: Dutch oven (8qt)

1	lb	**dry pea beans**
1	cup	**dry baby lima beans**
1	cup	**dry red kidney beans**
12	cups	**water**

About 3½ hours before serving, rinse beans in cold water; drain. Add measured water; bring to a boil and cook (3min). Remove from heat; cover and let stand (1hr). Drain; rinse beans. Remove and set aside.

2	Tbsp	**vegetable oil**

Heat in same Dutch oven over medium-high heat.

2	med	**green peppers** (1" strips)
2	med	**onions,** diced
3	cloves	**garlic,** minced

Sauté in oil until tender, stirring occasionally. Return beans to Dutch oven.

3	Tbsp	**brown sugar**
4	tsp	**salt**
½	tsp	**pepper**
¼	tsp	**cloves**
6	cups	**water**

Stir into beans; bring to a boil over high heat. Reduce heat to low; cover. Simmer (1hr), stirring occasionally.

1	can	**tomatoes,** undrained (28oz)
1	can	**tomato paste** (12oz)
1-1½	lb	**kielbasa** (1½" pieces)

Add, stirring to mix well and break up tomatoes. Cover; simmer (½hr) longer or until beans are tender. Skim off excess fat.

Shirley Martikainen, Stratford

Veal Roast

(Portuguese)

Tasty hot or cold

Serves: 8
Bake: 350° 1½ hr
Pan: roaster

3-4	lb	**veal roast,** boneless, rolled
1	tsp	**salt**
		pepper to taste
1	Tbsp	**oil**
1	clove	**garlic,** minced

Preheat oven to 375°. Rub seasonings into roast; place in pan.

⅓	cup	**oil**
½	cup	**white wine**

Pour over meat.

2	Tbsp	**butter**

Dot roast; place in oven. Reduce heat to 350°. Bake until tender. Baste meat occasionally and add water if necessary. Remove meat to warm platter; make gravy with pan drippings.

Mrs. Francisco Goncalves, Bridgeport

Cielecina
(Polish)

Roast Veal

Bake: 325° 45 min per lb
Pan: Dutch oven

1		**veal shoulder roast,** boneless
2-3	cloves	**garlic,** mashed
1	Tbsp	**salt**

Combine into paste; rub over roast well.

		pepper, fresh ground
		paprika
		oil for browning

Dust roast well. Brown on all sides in Dutch oven.

1	cup	**water**

Add to roast. Bake basting occasionally replacing water as it evaporates. Serve chilled, sliced thin.

Pat McCathron, Trumbull

Veal Scaloppine with Lemon
(Italian)

An original that's a family favorite

Serves: 4-6
Stovetop: 5-8 min
Pan: skillet (lg)

2	lb	**veal cutlets,*** pounded thin
½	cup	**flour**
		salt, pepper to taste

Mix; rub seasonings into veal.
* Can use shoulder chops pounded thin, for a more economical meal.

2-4	Tbsp	**butter**
2-4	Tbsp	**olive oil**

Place 2 Tbsp each in skillet, high heat. As butter begins to brown, add veal (do not crowd slices). Brown (1min) each side, adding butter and oil as needed. Remove to warm platter.

1	Tbsp	**butter**
¼	cup	**vermouth,** dry
1	tsp	**lemon rind,** grated

Add to pan drippings; boil rapidly, scraping up particles. Spoon sauce over meat.

		lemon slices
		parsley
		mushrooms, sautéed (optional)

Garnish each cutlet.

Louise Cronan, Trumbull

VARIATION: Leave out the vermouth. To drippings in pan, add 2 Tbsp of minced garlic and 1 Tbsp minced parsley. Sauté; add 2 Tbsp butter and 1 Tbsp lemon juice. Pour over veal; serve.

Agnes Swords, Stratford

Veal "Almost" Marsala

And low in calories too

Serves: 4
Stovetop: 10-15 min
Pan: skillet (lg)

2	lb	**veal cutlets**	Pound very thin. Brown in vegetable sprayed skillet; remove to plate.
1	cup	**water**	
2	env	**vegetable bouillon**	Combine in same skillet; bring to a boil then reduce heat; add veal.
2	tsp	**sherry flavoring** **parsley**, chopped	
		lemon slices	Place over veal; simmer 5 minutes or until meat is tender. Serve hot.
3	tsp	**Parmesan cheese,** grated **parsley**, chopped	Garnish.

Judy Webster of Thin's Inn, Monroe

Veal Paprikash
(Hungarian)

An "old family favorite"

Serves: 4
Stovetop: 1 hr
Pan: Dutch oven

2	lb	**veal,** cubes (1½")	Brown meat in its own juices, over medium heat.
1	Tbsp	**shortening** (optional)	
1	Tbsp	**onion,** minced	Add; sauté until golden.
2		**beef bouillon cubes**	Dissolve; add to above.
1	cup	**water,** hot	
1	Tbsp	**paprika**	Add; cover and cook slowly on low heat (1hr) or until tender (juices should almost cover meat).
1	Tbsp	**flour,** instant	When meat is cooked, stir in and cook to thicken juices lightly.
1	cup	**sour cream**	Stir in; cook (5min) to thicken. DO NOT BOIL. Serve hot over noodles or rice. Can also be baked 350° 1 hour.

Jeanne Buynak, Bridgeport

Veal and Noodles in Sour Cream

Another great veal dish

Serves: 6-8
Stovetop: 1 hr
Bake: 350° 25 min
Pans: Dutch oven; casserole (1½qt)

2	lb	**veal**, lean, cubed
¼	cup	**flour**
1	tsp	**salt**
¼	tsp	**pepper**
	pinch	**nutmeg**

Mix; dredge veal.

¼	cup	**butter**

Brown veal on all sides.

½	cup	**onion**, minced
2	Tbsp	**celery**, minced

Add to veal; cook gently until vegetables are limp.

1	cup	**chicken broth**

Add; cover and simmer until meat is tender (1hr).

3	oz	**noodles**, cooked, drained
1	lb	**mushrooms**, sliced, sautéed
1	cup	**sour cream**

Mix with veal; adjust seasonings to taste then place in casserole.

¼	cup	**buttered crumbs**

Sprinkle over top. Bake until heated through and lightly browned on top (25min).

Bebe Stetson, Southport

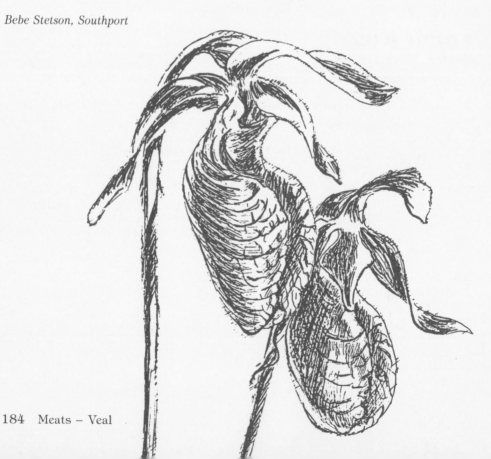

Veal Parmigiana
(Italian)

Freezes beautifully - tastes delicious

Serves: 8
Bake: 350° 25 min
Pans: skillet (lg); 13x9

2-3	cups	**spaghetti sauce** (home made or jar)	Cover bottom of baking dish with half of sauce; set aside.
8		**veal patties,** plain	(Partially frozen for easier handling.)
3		**eggs,** beaten lightly	Mix; dip veal patties individually, both sides.
¾	cup	**milk**	
1-2	cups	**seasoned bread crumbs**	Dip patties to coat.
		vegetable oil	Pour thin layer in bottom of large skillet. Over medium heat, fry patties until browned on both sides. Remove to prepared baking dish.
		reserved sauce	Cover well.
8	oz	**Mozzarella cheese,** grated	Sprinkle over top. Bake (25min) until heated through and cheese is melted. Can be prepared ahead and frozen. Bake: 250° (35min).

Shirley Collins, Milford

Lamb Roast
(Greek)

So tasty and tender

Serves: 8
Bake: see recipe
Pan: roaster

7	lb	**leg of lamb**	Make slits in meat (1" deep).
4	cloves	**garlic,** slivered	Insert into slits.
1		**lemon,** juice of	Rub entire roast well. Place in roasting pan. Bake: 450° 15min then reduce to 350°.
1	tsp	each: **salt, pepper**	
2	Tbsp	**olive oil**	
1		**onion,** sliced	Add to roast; continue roasting (3hr) until meat is tender. Baste meat occasionally; add more water if needed. Remove fat, slice and serve meat with natural juices.
2		**carrots,** diced	
4	ribs	**celery,** diced	
¼	cup	**parsley,** chopped	
2	cups	**water**	

Lemonia Bargas, Trumbull

Shashlik

A great skewered meal

Serves: 6
Marinate: 2 hr or longer
Broil: see recipe
Pan: broiler

2½	lb	**leg of lamb,** cubed **salt, pepper** to taste	Rub seasonings into lamb.

2	Tbsp	**wine vinegar**	
¼	tsp	**ginger**	Combine; marinate lamb at room tem-
¼	cup	**soy sauce**	perature, stirring occasionally.
½	cup	**olive oil**	
		red wine to taste	
		oregano to taste	

	marinated lamb	Alternate on skewers. Broil 3" from
1	**pineapple,** cut in	heat: 400° 15 min. Turn temp. to
	chunks (can use	broil. Turn meat once and brush with
	canned)	marinade. Cook to taste, watching
		carefully. Serve over Pilaf.

Sonny Weintraub, Bridgeport

Souvlakia
(Greek)

Great with Pilaf or on toasted pita

Serves: 8
Marinate: 8-10 hr
Broil: 10-15 min

3	lb	**lamb** OR **pork cubes**	Can also be a combination.

5	lg	**lemons,** juice of	
2	cups	**vegetable oil**	
2	Tbsp	**oregano**	Blend well; pour over meat and mari-
3	lg	**garlic** cloves	nate overnight.
4	med	**onions,** wedges	
		salt, pepper to taste	

		marinated meat, onions	Place on skewers alternately. Charcoal
4	lg	**green peppers,** lg cubes	broil, turning and basting frequently until tender. Serve over Rice Pilaf.
2	pts	**cherry tomatoes**	

VARIATION: Vegetables can be chopped fine, sautéed in oil, meat broiled, then both
combined and served on crispy pita bread that has been "toasted" in butter in a skillet. A delicious "sandwich" meal.

Gertrud Bargas, Trumbull

Lamb Chop Delite

Very flavorful

Serves: 4
Stovetop: 1 hr
Pan: skillet (lg)

3	Tbsp	**shortening,** melted	
4-6		**shoulder lamb chops,** lean	Season and brown chops on both sides; remove from skillet.
		salt, pepper to taste	
		paprika to taste	
	dash	**cayenne pepper** (optional)	
1		**onion,** sliced	Brown in skillet; return chops to pan.
4		**garlic cloves,** mashed	
1	can	**chicken broth** (13¾oz)	Add to above; cover and simmer (45min), until chops are tender.
½		**lemon,** juice of	
½	tsp	**oregano**	
		wine to taste (optional)	
1	Tbsp	**cornstarch**	Add to skillet; stir. Cook until thickened. Serve over rice or noodles.
		water to dissolve	

Gertrud Bargas, Trumbull

Bobotie
(South Africa)

When you're looking for the unusual

Serves: 6-8
Stovetop: 10 min
Bake: 250° 1 hr
Pans: kettle (4qt); casserole, greased (2½qt)

1	slice	**white bread** (thick)	Soak bread; mash with fork and set aside.
		milk enough to soak	
4	Tbsp	**butter,** melted	
2	med	**onions,** sliced	In large kettle, stir/fry (4min).
1		**apple,** sliced	
2	lb	**mutton,** ground (raw)	
2	oz	**curry powder** (to taste)	
1	Tbsp	**sugar**	
½	tsp	**salt**	
12		**almonds,** blanched, chopped	Add to skillet; stir well. Cook gently (3min). Place in prepared casserole.
2	oz	**currants** OR **white raisins**	
1	clove	**garlic,** crushed	
1	sm	**banana,** sliced	
2		**bay leaves**	
		reserved bread	
2		**eggs,** beaten	Mix well; pour over meat mixture. Bake until custard is set.
1	cup	**milk**	
½	tsp	**pepper**	

Nina Ravden, Bridgeport

Marinated Lamb Broil

Delicious served with Dutch Hutsput

Serves: 8
Broil: 8 min
Pan: broiler pan (lg)

3	lb	**lamb** (1" cubes)	Place in bowl that has a sealing cover.
1		**lemon,** juice of	Combine; pour over lamb and marinate at least 24 hours, shaking often. When ready to cook, pour marinade and meat into broiler pan. Broil (4min) each side.
6	Tbsp	**olive oil**	
6	Tbsp	**soy sauce**	
1		**onion,** chopped	

Claudia McKenna, Trumbull

Quick Lamb Curry

A good recipe for left over lamb

Serves: 6
Stovetop: 20 min
Pan: skillet (lg)

2	Tbsp	**bacon fat**	Sauté until golden.
2	cups	**onion,** chopped	
2	Tbsp	**flour**	Stir into onions.
½	tsp	**sugar**	
½	tsp	**salt**	
1	Tbsp	**curry powder**	
2	cups	**lamb gravy**	Add; cook, stirring until thick.
3-4	cups	**lamb,** cooked, bite-size pieces	Add lamb; heat thoroughly but do not boil. Serve over rice with condiments such as: crisp bacon, crumbled egg yolks, chopped egg whites, coconut flakes, crushed pineapple, almonds, peanuts, raisins or diced apple.

Jan McNaughton, Fairfield

FOOD PRESERVING – cooking kills the bacteria at 176°. This makes foods relatively sterile thus preserving. Freezing – stops bacterial activity though it does not kill bacteria.

Pasteles
(Puerto Rican)

A light meal with salad or part of a chicken dinner

Yield: 4-6 doz
Stovetop: 45-60 min
Pan: kettle (6qt); skillet

3		GREEN plantains*
3	lb	taniers (yautia*)
1	tsp	salt
		water

Peel; soak in salted water (5min); grate.
*OR 10-12 green bananas total.

1	Tbsp	salt
¼	cup	shortening (Annato lard preferred)
1	cup	milk (approx)

Add to above; mix thoroughly and set aside.

2	Tbsp	vegetable oil
1	lb	pork, chopped
¼	lb	ham, chopped
2	Tbsp	green pepper, chopped
¼	cup	onion, chopped
¼	cup	tomato, chopped
		salt, pepper and favorite seasonings to taste

Sauté until meat is cooked; simmer a few minutes longer.

½	cup	chick peas, cooked
½	cup	raisins
½	cup	olives, chopped
1	Tbsp	capers, chopped

Add to meat mixture; stir well and set aside.

1-1½	pkg	plantain leaves
1-2	Tbsp	shortening
		water, hot

Clean; trim then dip each leaf in hot water. Grease each leaf. Pour about 3 Tbsp of plantain mixture in center of each leaf. Spread to form rectangle. Place 2 Tbsp of meat mixture in center of rectangle. Fold leaf lengthwise and turn ends down. Tie and boil in salted water (1hr).

Barbara Schegg, Huntington

TOMATOES were used as food only around 1830. They were previously considered poisonous.

Caldo Gallego
(Puerto Rican)

A delicious Spanish stew

Serves: 6-8
Stovetop: 60 min
Pans: kettle (6qt); saucepan (1qt)

1	lb	**navy beans**
		water

} Soak overnight in large pan filled with water. In morning, leave just enough water to cover beans.

¼	lb	**ham,** cubed
1	lb	**pork** OR **beef,** cubed
¼	lb	**salt pork** OR **bacon**
2		**Spanish sausages**
		(Chorizo)
1	lb	**carrots** (1" pieces)
1	lb	**cabbage,** sliced
1	lb	**squash** OR **pumpkin**
		(optional)

} Boil (15-20min).

1½	lb	**potatoes,** cubed
½	lb	**green beans** (optional)
¼-½	lb	**Swiss chard, spinach,**
		OR **other greens,**
		chopped (optional)
	sprig	**parsley**
		salt, pepper to taste

} Add; simmer (10min) longer.

Sofrito (see index)

Prepare then pour over stew and simmer until vegetables and meat are tender. Serve hot with Almojabanas.

Barbara Schegg, Huntington

Paella
(Spanish)

Perfect for a very special occasion

Serves: 6-8
Stovetop: 35 min
Pans: kettle (4qt); skillet (lg)

3		**chicken breasts,** whole	Cut each into 6 pieces; boil in water (10-15min) until almost cooked. Remove chicken; set aside. Save broth (4cups); keep warm.
1	lb	**shrimp,** unpeeled	Add to boiling water. Boil (2min) until done. Remove seafood and set aside. Reserve broth (2cups); keep warm. Remove bay leaf.
3	lg	**lobster tails,** cut in half widthwise	
1		**bay leaf**	
		water, boiling	
3	Tbsp	**olive oil**	Heat in skillet over high heat then turn heat to medium.
1	med	**onion,** chopped fine	Add to skillet; stir/fry until onion is translucent.
2	med	**tomatoes,** peeled, chopped	
2		**chorizo** (Spanish sausage sliced ⅛")	
3	cups	**rice,** long grain	Add to skillet; stir while it absorbs color.
4	cups	reserved chicken stock	Add to skillet; mix well and bring to a boil. Reduce to slightly above a simmer.
2	cups	reserved seafood stock	
2		**chicken bouillon cubes**	
3	cloves	**garlic,** minced	Place in small cup; add some boiling stock and stir until red coloring is dispersed.
1	env	**saffron**	
¼	cup	**parsley,** fresh, chopped fine	Add to cup; stir, then add to rice mixture in skillet. Stir well; cook covered (approx 15min total).
		reserved chicken, shrimp, lobster	Place around edge of rice mixture. Cook, covered, another (5-10min) until clams open.
1	doz	**cherrystone clams,** scrubbed	
		salt, pepper to taste	

OPTIONAL GARNISHES

1		**lemon,** juice of	Use one or all; cover and let warm through.
1	can	**artichoke hearts,** drained	
1	can	**white asparagus,** drained	
1	jar	**red roasted peppers,** sliced	

Judi Barrero, Trumbull

Paella
(Cuban)

Another great version of a great dish

Serves: 10-14
Stovetop: 1½-2 hr
Pan: 2 kettles (6qt,8qt)

1¼	cups	**olive oil**
2	lg	**onions,** chopped
4	cloves	**garlic,** chopped
2	lg	**green peppers,** chopped

Sauté in large kettle (5min).

3-4	lb	**chicken,** small pieces
½	lb	**fresh pork,** 2" cubes
½	lb	**ham,** 2" cubes

Add and fry until browned (15-20min).

2		**lobsters,** shelled
2		**crabs,** shelled
1	lb	**shrimp,** shelled
2		**bay leaves**
		water to cover

In smaller kettle, place shellfish. Cover with water; boil (2-3min) until done. Remove shellfish to large kettle in which meats are cooking. Measure 4 cups broth and add also. Remove bay leaves.

4	cups	**rice**
4	cups	**dry wine**
½	lb	**fish filets**
1	can	**clams** OR **mussels**
1	can	**tomato sauce**
2½	tsp	**salt**
¾	tsp	**pepper**

Add; cover and simmer (1hr). Serve hot and delicious. Garnish with green beans, fresh or canned; pimientos, cut in strips if you would like.

Julio and Gloria Alvarez, Bridgeport

 CLAMS, hard shelled are called quohaugs in some areas; soft shelled are soft shelled clams. These grow in the waters off Rhode Island and northward.

Meat Pirohi

(Polish)

Another interesting national dish

Yield: 5-6 doz
Stovetop: 10-15 min
Pan: kettle (4-6qt)

1	lb	**ground beef**
1	lb	**ground pork**
1	sm	**onion,** chopped
		salt, pepper to taste

In large bowl, mix well. Form into small meatballs (¾-1tsp); set aside.

DOUGH

3	cups	**flour**
1		**egg**
1	tsp	**salt**

In bowl, mix.

¾-1	cup	**water**

Add only enough water to form a soft dough that can be handled; divide into 2 parts. Roll one out into a rectangle (⅛" thick). Place a line of meatballs ½" inside edge, 2 inches apart. Fold dough over. Use shot glass to cut out; crimp edges. Repeat until all dough and meatballs have been used. Fill kettle with water; add salt, bring to a boil. Drop pirohi, one at a time, into boiling water. Do not crowd. Cook about 10-15 minutes until dough is soft. Serve hot with butter.

Henry Szwolkon, Bridgeport

A Dieter's "Paella"

Very tasty

Serves: 4-6
Bake: 350° 45 min
Pans: skillet (sm); kettle (4qt);
casserole (3qt)

2	lb	**chicken breasts,** split

Broil or boil; remove skin. Drain off fats and set aside.

SAUCE:

6	slices	**salami,** diced

Brown to render fats. Remove; drain and set aside.

1	lg	**onion,** chopped
2	tsp	**salt**
	dash	**sugar substitute**
¼	tsp	**pepper**
⅛	tsp	**saffron,** crushed
1	can	**tomatoes** (28oz)
1½	cups	**water**
1		**chicken bouillon cube**

Mix; bring to a boil then add salami.

8	oz	**shrimp,** cleaned, boiled
4	oz	**pimientos,** diced
		reserved chicken

Arrange in casserole; top with sauce.

		Swiss cheese (optional)

Spread over casserole. Bake.

Jan McNaughton, Fairfield

Chicken Fricassee Pauline with Kasha

(Russian)

A really special meal

Serves: 6-8
Stovetop: 1 hr
Pans: Dutch oven; skillet (med)

1	cup	**onion,** chopped	Place on bottom of Dutch oven.
3½	lb	**chicken,** cut up with **giblets** (save liver for another meal)	Lay on top.
1	tsp	**paprika**	Sprinkle over above. Cover and simmer (15min). Stir; re-cover. While cooking, prepare the following.
2	tsp	**salt**	
½	tsp	**white pepper**	
½	tsp	**garlic powder**	
1	env	**chicken bouillon powder**	
1-1¼	lb	**ground beef,** lean	In mixing bowl, combine very well. Form meatballs (1½"). (Cold tap water on hands makes this chore easier.) Place balls on wax paper.
¼	cup	**onion,** minced	
1		**egg**	
¼	cup	**bread crumbs**	
½	tsp	**salt**	
¼	tsp	**pepper**	
¼	tsp	**garlic powder**	
1	env	**chicken bouillon powder**	
¼	cup	**water**	
		vegetable oil to cover bottom of skillet	In skillet, heat oil over which a few grains of salt have been sprinkled to prevent spattering. Sauté meatballs, shaking to prevent sticking. Brown all over; turn off heat and add to kettle. Stir in carefully; cover.
	dash	**salt**	
1	cup	**water, broth** OR **vegetable water**	Add to skillet; bring to a boil. Scrape up all residue in skillet. Pour into casserole; cover and simmer (20min) longer. May be refrigerated or divided and frozen for future use.

KASHA (groats or steamed buckwheat)

2	Tbsp	**vegetable oil**	Sauté until lightly browned.
¼	cup	**onion,** chopped fine	
1	cup	**kasha,** dried, coarse grain	Add; toss until lightly toasted.
1	tsp	**salt**	Stir in; cover tightly. Steam (20min) until liquid is absorbed and kernels
2	cups	**water**	

are separate. Serve fricassee accompanied by two bowls - one for Kasha and the other for green beans. The sauce from the fricassee is placed over the Kasha on one's plate.

Wini Suss, Harrison, NY

194   Meats – Medley

Jambalaya
(chicken/sausage/shrimp)

The best of New Orleans

Serves: 16-20
Stovetop: 2 hr
Pan: heavy kettle (8-10qt)

¼	cup	oil (vegetable, bacon, meat fats, etc.)	
1½	lb	sausage links (½" pieces) (smoked pork, Kielbasa, pepperoni, your choice except Italian with anise)	In kettle, fry (15min); remove meat and set aside.

1		chicken fryer, skinned & boned (2-3" pieces)	
½	tsp	each: salt, cayenne pepper	Season meat then fry until browned (15min); remove meat and set aside.

1	lb	shrimp, shelled (optional)	Sauté quickly; remove and set aside.

1	Tbsp	brown sugar	Add to oil in kettle; sauté to caramelize (3-5min).

4	cups	onions, chopped, coarse	
2	cups	celery, chopped, coarse	Sauté in kettle (1-2min); stir occasionally.
2	cups	bell peppers, chopped, coarse	

1	Tbsp	garlic, minced	
		reserved chicken	Add; reduce heat and simmer (5min).

5	cups	water OR stock, HEATED	Add slowly; bring to a boil. (Red Jambalaya: eliminate brown sugar, substitute 1½ cups tomato juice or V-8 for some of the water).

		reserved sausage	
3	tsp	salt	Stir in; bring to a boil then reduce heat. Cover tightly; simmer (30-40min). DO NOT PEEK. (Can be baked at 350° for 30-40min).
1	tsp	cayenne pepper	
4	cups	rice, white, long grain	

1	cup	green onions, chopped	
1	cup	parsley, fresh, chopped	Add; turn rice top to bottom, carefully. Adjust liquids if necessary. Cover; cook (15min) or until rice is cooked and liquids are absorbed.
		reserved shrimp (optional)	

TO FREEZE: Prepare up to rice; freeze. Thaw, bring to boil, add rice and continue as directed. Jambalaya was created to use anything available in the kitchen—be venturesome . . . enjoy the superb.

New Orleans School of Cooking, French Quarter, New Orleans

Sausage-Beef Dinner

Doubles well! Great for a crowd

Serves: 6-8
Bake: 375° 75-90 min
Pans: skillet (lg); casserole (3qt)

1½	lb	**Italian sausage links** (hot or sweet)	Brown in skillet; place in casserole. Drain off most fat.
1½	lb	**stew beef** (1" cubes)	Brown in skillet; turn into casserole.
1-2	lg	**onions,** sliced thick	
2	cloves	**garlic,** minced	Sauté slightly; turn out into casserole.
2	med	**green peppers,** cut in 8ths	
4	med	**potatoes,** peeled, quartered	Add to above. (Can eliminate and serve dish with rice or noodles instead.)
1	tsp	**basil**	
½	tsp	**salt**	Sprinkle; mix lightly.
¼	tsp	**pepper**	
1-2	tsp	**flour**	Mix well to remove lumps; add and
1	can	**beef stock** (10½oz)	cover. Bake until tender.

Lillian Thiede, Stratford

Veal and Peppers

Delicious with broccoli and garlic butter

Serves: 6
Stovetop: 1½ hr
Pan: Dutch oven

1	strip	**bacon**	Sauté until rendered; drain off most fat.
2	Tbsp	**olive oil** (optional)	
2	cloves	**garlic,** pressed	Add; stir.
1	lb	**Italian sweet sausage,** casings removed	Add; continue to sauté stirring to prevent sticking.
1½-2	lbs	**veal** (2" cubes)	
1-2		**green peppers** (1" strips)	Add; stir to blend then cover and simmer on low. Stir occasionally until veal is tender. Serve over broad noodles or rice.
¼	tsp	**oregano**	
1	can	**tomato sauce** (8oz)	
		salt, pepper to taste	

Louise Cronan, Trumbull

Stuffed Cabbage

"Serves an army"

Serves: 10-12
Stovetop: 2-3 hr
Pan: kettle (6qt)

1	lg	**cabbage**, green	Cook in boiling water (10min); drain. Peel and core leaves. Set aside.

1	lb	**ground beef, veal** OR **pork** OR a combination
1	lb	**sweet Italian sausage**, casings removed
1	tsp	**salt**
¼	tsp	**pepper**
1		**egg**, lightly beaten
2	med	**onions**, sautéed
1	clove	**garlic**, crushed
¼	cup	**rice**, cooked

Mix together well; place 1-2 Tbsp on each leaf. Fold sides in; roll, enclosing all stuffing. Set aside.

1	can	**sauerkraut** (27oz)
1	med	**onion**, chopped
		left-over cabbage, chopped
		reserved stuffed rolls
1	can	**stewed tomatoes** (16oz)
1	can	**tomato sauce** (8oz)

Layer in kettle:
½ of sauerkraut
½ of chopped onion
left over leaves
1 layer stuffed rolls
½ stewed tomatoes
½ tomato sauce
Repeat.

¼	cup	**brown sugar**
1	tsp	**lemon juice**
		dill, fresh, chopped

Sprinkle over top. Cover; bring to a boil then reduce to simmer. Cook until core of leaves are soft.

	sour cream
	dill, fresh, chopped

Garnish rolls as served.

Louise Cronan, Trumbull

Ham-Pork Loaves

A really flavorful loaf

Serves: 8-10
Bake: 350° 1 hr
Pan: 13x9

1	lb	**ham**, ground
1	lb	**pork**, ground
½	cup	**onion**, minced
½	cup	**tomato soup**, undiluted
⅓	cup	**milk**
1	lg	**egg**
½	cup	**bread crumbs**

Mix well; shape into small loaves (¼lb,ea).

¾	cup	**lt brown sugar**
¼	cup	**cider vinegar**
½	tsp	**dry mustard**
½	tsp	**Worcestershire sauce**

Baste loaves. Bake. Serve hot.

Kay Speck, Trumbull

Rognon Wisers
(French)

Try the whole menu

Serves: 2
Stovetop: 10 min
Pan: skillet (10")

2		veal kidneys, sliced (¼")	
1	Tbsp	butter	Fry at medium-high heat (4-5min).
		salt, pepper to taste	

2		green onions, minced	Add; mix well. Cook (1min); remove to serving plate and set aside. Keep warm.
1	Tbsp	parsley, minced	
3	cloves	garlic, minced	

1	Tbsp	butter	
4	oz	mushrooms, quartered	Sauté (3min).
1	stalk	celery, diced	
		salt, pepper to taste	

1	oz	whiskey	Pour whiskey over vegetables; ignite to flambé.

4	Tbsp	tomato sauce (preferably home made)	When flames settle, add sauce.
		reserved kidneys	Add; mix well and adjust seasonings.
		rice, cooked	Serve with rice.

Franceen Fuger-Dila, Fairfield

Stuffed Peppers
(Hungarian)

"A great favorite of our family"

Serves: 5-6
Stovetop: 1 hr
Pans: skillet (sm); kettle (6qt); saucepan (2qt)

10	sm	green peppers	Cut off tops; remove seeds and set aside.

1	med	onion, minced	Brown onion; pour into mixing bowl.
3	Tbsp	shortening	

½	lb	each: ground pork and ground beef	Add to bowl; mix well. Stuff peppers about half full; place in deep kettle.
½	cup	white rice, raw	
1	tsp	salt	
½	tsp	pepper	
1		egg	

1	pt	sour cream	Combine in small saucepan; heat through, stirring until smooth. Pour over peppers; simmer covered until rice is cooked.
1	pt	tomato juice	

Hint: To add to the flavor of any stuffed pepper, top filling with ⅓ strip of raw bacon. Bake uncovered until brown and crisp.

Joy Tuba, Fairfield

Fish & Shellfish

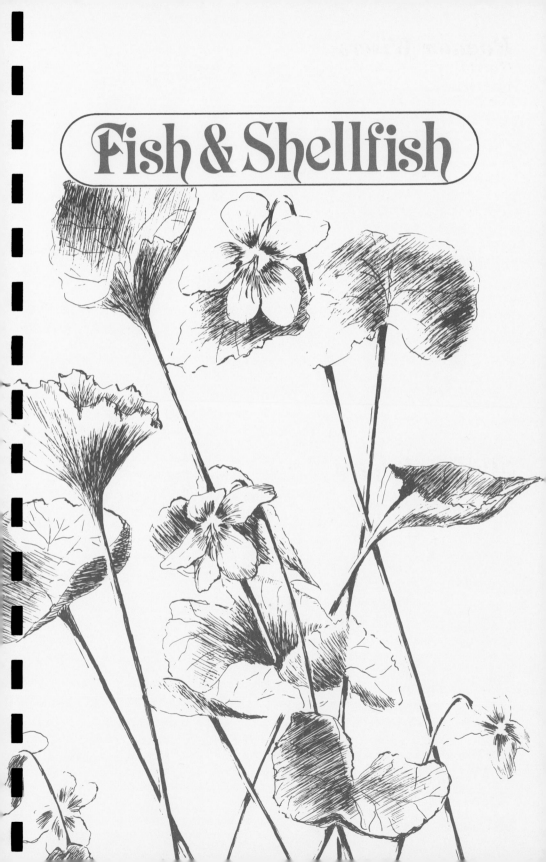

MEXICAN BUFFET (24)
Margaritas
Arizona Black Bean Dip
California Sunshine Dip
Tamale Bake
Pelota E Frijoles Mejicano (Chili)
Chicken Tortilla
Green Chili Soufflé
Romaine with Cherry Tomatoes
Oil & Vinegar Dressing
Flan
Fruit with Sour Cream Twists

POLYNESIAN
Curried Chicken Paté Mold
Pork Ribs Polynesian
Hawaiian Rice Medley
Oriental Sprout Salad
Fresh Fruit
Almond Cookies
Coffee Hawaiian

PORTUGUESE
Caldo Verde (Green Soup)
Portuguese Salad
Portuguese Fried Fish
Veal Roast
Portuguese Rice
Fresh Fruit or Flan

GERMAN
Spring Vegetable Soup
Sauerbraten
Spaetzle
Rodkaal (Red Cabbage)
Fruhlings Salat (Optional)
Apfelkuchen or Pflaumenkuchen

IRISH
Spinach Balls with Mustard Sauce
St Patty's Day Special
Irish Soda Bread
Irish Coffee

Bass – Beurre Blanc ou Rouge

An original from a renowned chef

Serves: 6
Poach: 4-5 min
Pan: skillet or poacher

BASS

	Filets of a 4 lb bass	Poach filets of bass in a Court Bouillon (see below). Let it boil (4-5min). Leave fish in until ready to serve.

BEURRE BLANC

1	cup	white wine	Reduce over medium heat until you obtain a paste.
½	cup	white wine vinegar	
4		shallots	
½	cup	heavy cream	Add and let it reduce once more. Remove from heat.
½	lb	BUTTER	Immediately beat in until it becomes thick as a hollandaise.
		season to taste	Transfer to a warm bowl and serve.

BEURRE ROUGE

Substitute red wine and red vinegar for the white wine and white vinegar. Both the appearance and the taste are very different.

COURT BOUILLON

1	qt	water	
1	cup	white wine	
2	med	carrots	
2-3	stalks	celery	
1	sm	onion	
2-3	cloves	garlic	Put all ingredients in a large pot. Bring to a boil and let cook for at least 10 minutes.
1	branch	thyme, fresh	
1	branch	tarragon, fresh	
1		bay leaf	
2-3	sprigs	parsley	
		sea salt, coarse	
5		black peppercorns	
3		coriander seeds	

Jean-Robert Pouget, Chef, Le Chambord, Westport

Recette de
• ROBERT POUGET •
Original Recipe

Autumn Ridge
Baked Fish Filets

So simple to be so tasty

Serves: 4
Bake: 350° 20-25 min
Pans: 13x9, buttered; saucepan (sm)

2		tomatoes, sliced thin	Arrange in bottom of baking dish.
⅔	cup	bread crumbs garlic salt pepper to taste parsley to taste	Combine; sprinkle over tomatoes.
2	lb	fish filets, haddock OR sole	Lay over bread crumbs.
½	cup	white wine	Heat in saucepan until butter melts; pour over fish.
¼	cup	butter	
1	Tbsp	lemon juice	
		paprika	Sprinkle over fish. Bake until fish flakes easily.
½	cup	Parmesan cheese	

Maribeth Gentile, Fairfield

Stuffed Filets

Spinach and cheese make these special

Serves: 6
Bake: see recipe
Pan: 9x7

12		flounder filets garlic salt to taste basil to taste	Lay filets flat. Sprinkle with seasonings.
12	slices	Swiss cheese	Place one slice on each filet.
1	lb	spinach, fresh, chopped fine	Place ½ cup on each filet; roll and secure with toothpick. Place in baking dish.
1	can	cream of shrimp soup (10½oz)	Spread over fish; cover with foil and seal well. Bake: 350° (20min), then 250° (15min). Serve piping hot.

Kate Benson, Fairfield

Poached Salmon and Herb Sauce

Rich creamy and special

Serves: 12
Poach: 15 min
Pan: skillet, covered (10")

1	lb	salmon steaks
		water to cover

In skillet, boil water; put in fish. Poach, on low heat (15-20min) until cooked.

SAUCE

½	cup	mayonnaise
½	cup	sour cream
1	Tbsp	parsley
1	Tbsp	chives
½	Tbsp	dill weed
3-4	drops	lemon juice
1-2	drops	Tabasco sauce
		horseradish to taste (optional)

In small bowl, mix then refrigerate. Serve hot or cold over fish.

Agnes Swords, Stratford

Fish Filets Creole Style

A meal in a pan served over rice

Serves: 4-5
Stovetop: 30 min
Pan: skillet (12")

¼	cup	butter, melted
½	cup	onion, chopped
½	cup	green pepper, chopped
1	clove	garlic, minced

In skillet, sauté vegetables until tender, but not brown.

1	can	tomatoes (16oz)
1	Tbsp	parsley flakes
1	Tbsp	instant chicken bouillon granules
¼	tsp	hot pepper sauce

Add; simmer covered (10min).

1	Tbsp	cornstarch
1	Tbsp	water, cold

Blend together; stir into tomato mixture. Cook, stirring, until thick and bubbly.

1	lb	fish filets (1"pcs)

Add fish to above stirring to coat. Return to boiling; reduce heat. Simmer, covered, (5-7min) or until fish flakes easily. Serve over rice.

Shirley Martikainen, Stratford

Crispy Fried Fish

With great flavor too

Serves: 4
Stovetop: 10-15 min
Pan: skillet (lg)

1	lb	**pan dressed fish** OR **filets**	Thaw if frozen; rinse, pat dry.
¼	cup	**flour**	Combine in shallow dish; set aside.
	dash	**garlic salt**	
1		**egg**, beaten	Combine in another shallow dish; set aside.
¼	cup	**milk**	
½	cup	**saltine crackers,** crushed fine (14)	Mix together in third shallow dish. Coat fish with flour mix, dip in egg mix then coat with crumb mix.
2	Tbsp	**Parmesan cheese,** grated	
2	Tbsp	**parsley,** chopped fine OR (2 tsp flakes)	
½	cup	**vegetable oil**	Heat in large skillet. Fry fish over medium heat (4-5min) each side or until brown and flakes easily with fork. Drain well.
		lemon wedges **parsley**	Garnish to serve.

Shirley Martikainen, Stratford

Fried Fish

(Portuguese)

More good nutrition

Serves: 6-8
Marinate: 30 min
Stovetop: 6 min each
Pan: skillet (lg)

8		**sole filets**	Marinate fish in juice and seasonings (30min).
1		**lemon,** juice of	
½	tsp	each: **salt, garlic powder**	
		pepper to taste	
1	cup	**flour**	Coat each filet.
2		**eggs,** beaten	Coat each filet well. Then dredge in flour again.
1	cup	**vegetable oil** (approx)	Heat in skillet. Fry sole filets (3min) each side.
1		**lemon,** 8 wedges	Serve with lemon wedges.

Mrs. Francisco Goncalves, Bridgeport

Skewered Swordfish

Oh, so good served over rice!

Serves: 4
Marinate: 1 hr
Broil: 10-12 min
Pans: skewers; broiler pan, foil lined

1	lb	swordfish (remnants can be used)	Cut into 2" cubes.

2	Tbsp	olive oil
2	cloves	garlic, minced
⅛	cup	red wine vinegar
4	Tbsp	butter, melted
½	tsp	salt
	dash	pepper
	pinch	tarragon
	piece	bay leaf
1	Tbsp	lemon juice
	dash	Tabasco sauce
½	tsp	dillweed, fresh, minced
1		scallion, sliced (¼")

Combine in small bowl (sauce will be thick). Coat swordfish well; set aside to marinate.

cherry tomatoes, whole
mushrooms, fresh, whole (remove stems)
onions, quartered, separated
green pepper, fresh, (bite size)

Alternate fish and vegetables on skewer (thread swordfish crossgrain). Broil 3" from heat; turn often until cooked to taste. Serve over rice, brown or white. SUGGESTION: can double amount of marinade and marinate vegetables to hasten cooking.

Louise Cronan, Trumbull

Sunshine Tuna Loaf

A light delectable tuna meal

Serves: 4-6
Bake: 350° 45 min
Pan: loaf, greased (8x4)

2	cans	tuna, drained, flaked (6½oz,ea)
1	can	cream of celery soup (10½oz)
3		egg yolks, lightly beaten (reserve whites)
1	cup	bread crumbs, fine
¼	cup	onions, chopped
2	Tbsp	parsley
3	Tbsp	lemon juice

Combine.

reserved egg whites

Beat until stiff; fold into above. Turn into prepared pan. Bake.

Hannah Bakunin, Bridgeport

Speecy-Spicy Tuna

Nice over broccoli, rice, or asparagus

Serves: 4
Cook: 5 min
Pan: skillet (10")

1	can	**cream of celery soup** (10¾oz)
3	Tbsp	**mayonnaise**
¼	cup	**dry or med sherry**
¼	cup	**Parmesan cheese**
2	Tbsp	**parsley,** chopped
1	tsp	**lemon peel,** grated
½	tsp	**Worcestershire sauce**

Mix together in skillet; heat to simmering.

1	can	**tuna,** drained (6½oz)
2		**eggs,** hard cooked, sliced

Stir into sauce; serve hot and bubbly.

Claudia McKenna, Trumbull

Tuna Casserole with Crunch

A tasty, easy to prepare meal

Serves: 4-6
Bake: 300° 40 min
Pan: casserole (2½qt)

1	can	**tuna** (6½oz)
1	can	**cream of mushroom soup** (10¾)
1	can	**mushrooms,** sliced (3oz)
1	can	**water chestnuts,** sliced (8oz) reserve liquid
4	oz	**cashews** OR **almonds,** sliced (optional)
1	cup	**celery,** diced
½-1	cup	**onions,** chopped
1	can	**chow mein noodles,** divided (3oz)

Combine all ingredients using ¼ cup liquid from water chestnuts and half the chow mein noodles. Pour into casserole. Top with remaining noodles. Bake.

VARIATION: White meat chicken for tuna. Can also be prepared stovetop in skillet.

Evelyn Fluegge, Trumbull

Salmon Ring with Olive Sauce

A delicious buffet mold

Serves: 6-8
Bake: 350° 30-35 min
Pans: ring mold, greased (8");
saucepan (sm)

SALMON RING

1	can	**salmon** (15½oz)
1	cup	**bread crumbs**
½	cup	**celery,** minced
¼	cup	**green pepper,** minced
2	Tbsp	**onion,** minced
1	Tbsp	**lemon juice**

Mix together.

1	cup	**evaporated milk**
1		**egg,** beaten

Combine and add to fish mixture; turn into greased mold. Bake. Serve with olive sauce.

SAUCE

¼	cup	**mayonnaise**
1	Tbsp	**flour**
¼	tsp	**salt**

In saucepan, mix together until smooth.

⅔	cup	**evaporated milk**
		water (to make 1¼cups)

Add slowly to mayonnaise mixture; cook over medium heat, stirring constantly, until thickened.

¼	cup	**stuffed green olives,** sliced

Stir into sauce. Serve piping hot.

Kay Speck, Trumbull

Salmon Bake

One more tasty fish meal

Serves: 4
Bake: 425° 45 min
Pans: saucepan (2qt); casserole (1qt)

2	Tbsp	**butter**
2	Tbsp	**flour**

Blend in saucepan over low heat.

1	can	**cream of shrimp soup,** frozen, thawed (10oz)
1	cup	**milk**

Combine and add to above. Cook stirring continuously until thick and bubbly; remove from heat.

½	cup	**process American cheese,** sharp, shredded

Add to above; stir until melted.

1	can	**red salmon,** drained, broken into pcs (16oz)
1	pkg	**peas,** frozen (10oz)

Stir in gently; turn into baking dish. Bake until hot and bubbly (30min).

1	cup	**biscuit mix** (see Index)

Prepare as for drop biscuits. Spoon 10 biscuits around edge of hot casserole. Bake (15min) longer, until golden.

Lee Rafferty, Fairfield

Pirok with Cream Sauce
(Eskimo)

A delicious salmon pie

Serves: 6
Bake: 350° 30 min
Pans: 8x8; skillet (sm); saucepan
    (1½qt)

PIE

		pastry for 2-crust pie	Divide dough in half; set half aside. Roll into square (10" by ⅛" thick). Line pan; set aside.
2	cups	**cream sauce,** med (see Index)	Prepare; set aside.
2	cups	**rice,** raw	Combine; spread half over bottom of crust lined pan.
½	cup	prepared cream sauce	
2	med	**onions,** sliced thin	Sauté until golden; spread over rice mixture.
2	Tbsp	**butter**	
1	can	**salmon,** flaked (16oz) OR **1 lb fresh** (½" cubes)	Layer over rice mix. Top with remaining half of rice mixture. Cover with reserved pastry and seal. Slit crust. Bake. For fresh salmon, Bake: 350° (1hr). Cut into squares and serve with sauce.
1-2		**eggs,** hard cooked, sliced OR chopped	
½	cup	**green peas,** frozen, raw (optional)	

SAUCE

1½	cups	reserved cream sauce	Melt cheese in sauce; remove from heat. Add seasonings.
½	cup	**cheddar cheese,** grated	
	sprinkle	**rosemary** OR **dill** OR your **favorite seasonings** (optional)	
½	cup	**mayonnaise**	Fold into hot sauce.

Porter Cleveland, Bridgeport

Haddock Bake

Simple but tasty

Serves: 2
Bake: 350° 20-30 min
Pans: 8x8, buttered; skillet (sm)

1	lb	**haddock filet**	Cut into serving pieces; place in prepared baking pan. Season well.
		salt, pepper to taste	
3	Tbsp	**butter** OR **margarine**	Sauté, over low heat, until soft.
2	Tbsp	**onion,** minced	
1	Tbsp	**lemon juice**	Add to skillet; mix. Spoon over fish. Bake uncovered until fish flakes easily.
2	dash	**Tabasco sauce**	
		lemon wedges	Garnish just before serving.
		parsley	

Louise Cronan, Trumbull

Imperial Crab

Fit for a Count's dinner!

Serves: 4
Bake: 450° 10-15 min
Pans: 2 saucepans (2qt); shells or
    casserole, buttered (1qt)

1	Tbsp	**butter** OR **margarine**
1	Tbsp	**flour**
½	cup	**milk**

Blend melted butter and flour in saucepan. Slowly add milk stirring constantly to form a smooth sauce. Cook, stirring, over medium heat until it comes to a boil and thickens.

1	tsp	**minced onion**, instant
1½	tsp	**Worcestershire sauce**
2	slices	**white bread**, crusts removed, cubed

Add to sauce; toss lightly and cool.

½	cup	**mayonnaise**
1	tsp	**lemon juice**
½	tsp	**salt**
	dash	**pepper**

Fold into above.

2	Tbsp	**butter**

In another saucepan, melt until lightly browned.

1	lb	**crab meat**, fins removed

Add; toss lightly. Combine with sauce. Divide into shells or pour into casserole.

		paprika

Garnish. Bake until heated and lightly browned.

Mrs. Gerald Dwyer, Boca Raton, Fl

Giovanni Crab

Great buffet dish!

Serves: 8-10
Bake: 350° 40-45 min
Pans: skillet (10"); casserole,
    greased (3qt)

2	cups	**onions**, chopped
8	oz	**mushrooms**, fresh, sliced
2	cloves	**garlic**, minced
½	cup	**butter** OR **margarine**

Sauté until tender.

½	lb	**thin spaghetti** OR **vermicelli**, cooked
2-3	cups	**crab meat** pieces
½	cup	**stuffed green olives**, sliced
½	lb	**sharp cheddar cheese**, shredded
½	cup	**sour cream**
1	can	**tomatoes** (28oz), cut up
1½	tsp	**salt**
½	tsp	**basil**

Combine all ingredients; add to above. Pour into prepared casserole. Bake until hot and bubbly. Can be prepared ahead and refrigerated. If so, allow 60 min for baking.

Sonny Weintraub, Bridgeport

King Crab Bake

A great "special occasion" meal

Serves: 6
Bake: 350° 40 min
Pan: casserole (2qt)

2	pkgs	**king crab meat,** frozen (7½oz,ea)	Thaw, separate. Place in bowl.
1	pkg	**prepared bread stuffing,** dry (8oz) (reserve ½cup)	
1½	cups	**mayonnaise**	Add to above; mix well.
½	cup	**mushrooms,** fresh, sliced	
2	cups	**light cream**	
2	Tbsp	**parsley,** minced	
4		**eggs,** hard cooked, sliced	Add; fold in gently. Spoon into casserole.
1	Tbsp	**parsley,** minced reserved dressing	Garnish. Bake uncovered.

Marjorie Dickey, Fairfield

Louauna's Crab Casserole

Elegantly delicious!

Serves: 6
Stovetop: 5-10 min
Bake: 400° 30 min
Pans: saucepan (1qt); casserole, buttered (1-2qt)

3	Tbsp	**butter**	Melt butter, blend in flour, add cream slowly. Cook, stirring, until thickened.
2	Tbsp	**flour**	
1½	cups	**light cream**	
2		**egg yolks,** beaten	Add small amount of cream sauce; stir well. Stir into remaining hot cream sauce.
1-1½	lbs	**crab meat**	Fold into sauce.
½	med	**green pepper,** chopped fine	Add; simmer (3min) or until cooked through. Pour into prepared baking dish.
2	tsp	**Worcestershire sauce**	
1	tsp	**prepared mustard**	
¼	tsp	each: **salt, pepper**	
1-2	Tbsp	**butter**	Garnish.
¼	cup	**bread crumbs**	

Louise Bollman, Bridgeport

Crabmeat Crepes

A very special luncheon or party entrée using any kind of shellfish

Yield: 24 crepes
Bake: 400° 20 min
Pans: 2 skillets (6")(12"); 2 (9x13)
   buttered

CREPES

1	cup	milk
1	cup	water, cold
4		eggs
1	tsp	salt
2	cups	flour, sifted
4	Tbsp	butter, melted

Combine all ingredients; blend well. Use ¼ cup batter per crepe. Cook (6" skillet) until lightly golden each side. Separate each crepe with toweling; keep warm. (Can be prepared ahead and frozen.)

FILLING

8	Tbsp	butter

Melt in large skillet.

½	cup	green onions, minced
2	lbs	king crabmeat, flaked
		salt, pepper to taste

Stir in onion, then crab; toss lightly. Cook a few minutes.

½	cup	vermouth (white)

Add and boil rapidly until liquid is almost evaporated. Scrape into bowl; set aside.

SAUCE

⅔	cup	vermouth, white

Add vermouth to same skillet and boil rapidly until reduced to 2 Tbsp; remove from heat.

¼	cup	cornstarch
¼	cup	milk

Mix together; stir into boiled down vermouth. Return to low heat.

4	cups	heavy cream
		salt, pepper to taste

Add slowly to above; cook several minutes until slightly thickened. DO NOT BOIL.

2½	cups	Swiss cheese, grated
		(reserve 1 cup)

Stir into above; cook until melted and well blended. Adjust seasonings.

TO FILL CREPES

Blend half of sauce with crabmeat. Check seasoning again. Put a large spoonful on each crepe and roll. Place seam side down in baking dish.

		reserved sauce
1	cup	reserved cheese
		butter

Spoon over crepes. Sprinkle cheese over all. Dot with butter; refrigerate until 30 min before cooking. Bake until hot and bubbly. Freezes well before or after putting together.

Carole Manjoney, Trumbull

Crab Cakes

Maryland favorites

Serves: 6
Chill: 30 min
Stovetop: 6-10 min
Pan: Dutch oven OR deep skillet

1	tsp	*Old Bay Seasoning
¼	tsp	salt
1	tsp	parsley
1		egg, beaten
1	Tbsp	mayonnaise
	dash	hot sauce

Mix well.
*Available in many markets and fish markets. Other seafood seasonings can be substituted.

1	lb	**crab meat

Add; mix well with fork. Form into cakes.
** 2 cups minced oysters, clams, shrimp OR lobster can be substituted.

½	cup	bread crumbs
		lemon wedges

Roll cakes to coat lightly. Chill in freezer (30min). Fry in enough oil to cover ½ of cakes until browned (3min, ea side). Serve immediately, while piping hot with lemon wedges.

Betty Butler, Bridgeport

Celestial Scallops

A delicious stir/fry meal

Serves: 4
Stir/fry: 15-20 min
Pan: wok or skillet (lg)

1	Tbsp	oil

Heat in wok.

1	can	bamboo shoots (8oz)
1	med	onion, sliced
1	cup	carrots, sliced
1	can	mushrooms, drained (3oz)

Add to above; stir/fry on high heat (2-3min). Remove; keep warm.

1	pkg	broccoli spears, frozen (10oz) OR fresh

Thaw and slice lengthwise. Drain well. Stir/fry (2min); push to the side.

1	lb	scallops

Add to center of wok; cook on high (3min).

reserved vegetables

Return to wok.

2	Tbsp	water
2	tsp	cornstarch
1	tsp	sugar
½	cup	sherry
1	tsp	instant beef bouillon granules
		salt, pepper to taste

Stir to dissolve. Add to wok; cook and stir until bubbly (3-4min). Season to taste.

Jane Fulton, Trumbull

Crêpes Coquilles

Elegantly delicious!

Serves: 6
Stovetop: approx 20 min
Bake: 350° 20-25 min
Pans: skillet (6"); 2 saucepans
(2qt)(1qt); baking dish
(7x11)

CREPES

2		eggs
3		egg yolks
½	cup	milk

Beat together well.

½	cup	flour

Sift into above; beat until smooth.

½	cup	milk
½	cup	heavy cream
½	tsp	salt
2	Tbsp	butter, melted

Beat in until smooth. Let stand (1 hr). To cook, heat skillet with a small amount of butter; spoon in 1½-2 Tbsp batter. Roll to cover skillet. Crepes should be thin and lightly browned. Stack between layers of paper toweling. (May be frozen)

SCALLOPS

1¼	lb	bay scallops, quartered

Wash, drain well; place in saucepan.

1	cup	white wine, dry
1	Tbsp	lemon juice
½	tsp	salt
⅛	tsp	pepper, white
	pinch	thyme
	small	bay leaf
1	Tbsp	onion, minced, sautéed (1min)

Add to above; simmer (10min).

4	oz	mushrooms, chopped coarse

Add and simmer (2min).

5	Tbsp	butter
4	Tbsp	flour

In small saucepan, mix and melt over low heat without browning. Strain liquid from simmering scallops; add while stirring.

1	cup	heavy cream
1	tsp	parsley, chopped

Add; cook, stirring until smooth and thick. Pour ¾ of this sauce over scallops. Mix thoroughly.

	reserved crepes

Spoon 2-3 Tbsp scallop/cream mixture onto center of each crepe. Roll and place in shallow baking dish. Pour remaining cream sauce over top.

	parsley, chopped

Garnish. Bake until hot and bubbly.

Teresa Frillici, Fairfield

Coquilles St. Jacques Parisienne

(French)

Well worth the effort

Serves: 6
Bake: 350° 10-15 min
Broil: 30 sec
Pans: saucepan (1qt)(3qt); skillet (med); shells or 4" baking dishes, buttered

1½	cups	chicken stock	
1½	cups	white wine	
3		scallions, sliced	In small saucepan, boil over high heat. Reduce heat, simmer uncovered (20min). Strain through a sieve into a skillet or electric fry pan.
3		celery tops with leaves (2" pcs)	
1		bay leaf	
10		peppercorns	

¾	lb	mushrooms, fresh, sliced	Add to skillet; cover and simmer (5min). Remove with slotted spoon to a medium bowl and set aside. Boil remaining bouillon down to 1 cup; set aside.
2	lbs	bay scallops, whole	

SAUCE PARISIENNE

4	Tbsp	BUTTER	In 3qt saucepan, melt over medium heat until foam subsides; remove from heat.
5	Tbsp	flour	Stir in; return to low heat and cook stirring constantly (2min). DO NOT BROWN. Remove from heat.
1	cup	reserved bouillon	Pour in slowly, whisking constantly. Return to high heat, cook, whisking, until it thickens and is ready to boil. Reduce heat; simmer (1min).
¾	cup	milk	
2		egg yolks	In small bowl, mix well then stir in 2 Tbsp of the hot sauce. Add 2 more Tbsp hot sauce; whisk well. Whisk all the cream mixture into the hot sauce in pan. Bring to a boil over moderate heat, stirring constantly (30sec). Remove from heat.
¼	cup	cream	
	drops	lemon juice	Add. (If too thick, add a bit more cream, up to ¼ cup.)
1	tsp	salt	
	dash	white pepper	
		reserved scallops mushroom mixture	Drain liquid. Pour in about ⅔ Sauce Parisienne; folding gently. Spoon mixture into shells or baking dishes. Cover with remaining sauce.
¼	cup	Swiss cheese, grated	Sprinkle over top. If using shells, place on cookie sheet for baking. Place

vessels in top third of oven (10-15min) or until sauce begins to bubble. Then slide under a hot broiler (30sec) to brown gently. Serve at once.

Carole Manjoney, Trumbull

Maryland Seafood – Rice Bake

Could substitute crab, white fish chunks. Delectable!

Serves: 6-8
Stovetop: 20-30 min
Bake: 325° 20-30 min
Pans: saucepan (3qt); skillet (12");
    casserole, greased (3qt)

RICE

1	pkg	**long grain and wild rice**	In large saucepan, cook rice in broth and enough water to total the amount of liquid called for on package; drain.
1	can	**beef broth** (10¼oz)	
		water	
½	cup	each: **celery, onion, green pepper,** chopped	Sauté in skillet (2-3min). Add cooked rice; set aside.
6	Tbsp	**butter**	

SEAFOOD AND SAUCE

6	Tbsp	**butter**	Make a roux in skillet; cook gently (2-3min).
¼	cup	**flour**	
1	cup	**lobster** OR **crab,** cooked	
2	cups	**shrimp,** cooked	
1	can	**mushrooms,** sliced (4oz)	Add to skillet; cook until heated through.
¼	tsp	**paprika**	
1	tsp	**salt**	
3	Tbsp	**dry sherry**	
2	cups	**light cream** (1pt)	Add to skillet; simmer until thickened. (DO NOT BOIL.) Spread over bottom of casserole.
½	cup	**American cheese,** grated	Sprinkle half over seafood.
		reserved rice mixture	Layer over top. Bake until hot and bubbly.
		reserved cheese **Parmesan cheese,** grated, to taste	Garnish.

Betty Butler, Bridgeport

Seaman's Catch Baked

Shrimp and filets in a rich sauce and cheeses

Serves: 6-8
Stovetop: 15-20 min
Bake: 350° 50 min
Pans: skillet (10"); 13x9, greased

9		lasagna noodles, cooked, drained	Arrange 3 noodles over bottom of baking dish; set aside.
1	lg	onion, chopped	Sauté in skillet until soft.
2	Tbsp	vegetable oil	
1	pkg	spinach, frozen (10oz)	Thaw; chop well; press to remove all moisture. Add to onion.
3	oz	cream cheese, softened	
1	cup	cottage cheese, creamed	Add to skillet; mix well. Spread ⅓ mixture over noodles in dish.
1		egg, beaten	
1	tsp	Italian herb seasoning	
		salt, pepper to taste	
1	can	condensed cream of celery soup (10¾oz)	
⅓	cup	milk	Combine; spread ⅓ fish mixture over cheese layer. Repeat these three layers twice.
8	oz	shrimp, frozen, cooked	
1	lb	fish filets, cubed (fresh or frozen)	
3	Tbsp	parmesan cheese, grated	Combine; sprinkle over casserole. Bake (45min).
2	Tbsp	seasoned bread crumbs, fine	
⅓	cup	sharp cheddar cheese, grated	Sprinkle over top; dot with butter. Bake (5min). Let stand (20min) before serving.
		butter OR margarine	

Marjorie Dickey, Fairfield

North Shore Lobster Bake

So simple but so tasty

Serves: 4
Bake: 350° 30 min
Pan: casserole (1½qt)

48	**Ritz crackers**	Blend or crush coarse.
	salt, pepper to taste	
¼ tsp	**onion salt** (optional)	
1 tsp	**parsley,** chopped (optional)	Add to above and mix well.
1 cup	**butter,** melted	
1 lb	**lobster pieces,** bite size	Fold in. Can prepare to here early in the day; refrigerate.
½-⅔ cup	**milk**	Pour over casserole just before baking. Bake uncovered until hot and lightly browned on top. Serve piping hot.

Ruth Gilchrist, Wenham, Ma

Saucy Seafood Stuffing

Tasty and versatile

Serves: 6
Stovetop: 5 min
Bake: 400° 15-20 min
Pans: skillet (med); casserole, buttered

½ cup	**margarine**	Sauté until golden.
4 Tbsp	**onion,** chopped	
4 Tbsp	**parsley,** chopped	
¼ cup	**white wine**	Add liquids to skillet; simmer (3-5min).
1 can	**clams,** minced (10oz) (reserve clams)	
1 cup	**prepared stuffing mix,** dry	
1 cup	**shrimp,** raw, chopped (optional)	Add to above; mix well and place in casserole. Bake. Excellent as appetizer in shells; on crackers as side dish OR stuffing for chicken. Freezes well.
	reserved clams	
	salt, pepper to taste	
1 tsp	**Worcestershire sauce**	

Jane Stenthal, Port Chester, NY

A Southerner's Shrimp Stew

A great gulf state delicacy

Serves: 6
Stovetop: 30-40 min
Pans: 2 saucepans (3qt); kettle (4qt); ring mold (9"), oiled

4	cups	**water**	Cook in kettle; drain and set aside. Keep warm.
2	cups	**rice,** raw (6 cups cooked)	
		season to taste	
2	cups	**shrimp,** shelled	Boil (1min) in saucepan; set aside.
		water to cover	
2	Tbsp	**shortening**	Sauté in deep saucepan.
2		**onions,** sliced	
1	cup	**celery,** diced	
1	Tbsp	**flour**	Sprinkle over vegetables; stir to blend well.
1	tsp	**salt**	
1-1½	tsp	**chili powder**	
1	cup	**water,** warm	Stir in gradually; simmer covered, stirring occasionally until thickened (10-15min).
2	cups	**tomatoes,** canned (16oz)	Add; simmer (10min).
2	cups	**peas,** fresh or frozen	
1	Tbsp	**cider vinegar**	
⅓	cup	**cooking sherry**	Stir in; simmer (2-3min). Keep stew warm. Pack hot rice in ring mold; unmold on platter. Fill center with stew. Can also spoon stew over rice in soup plates.
		reserved shrimp	

Porter Cleveland, Bridgeport

Peking Shrimp

(Chinese)

Wok meals are so much fun – try them all

Serves: 4
Stovetop: 10-15 min
Pan: wok or skillet (lg)

2	Tbsp	**oil**	Heat in wok.
¼	cup	**dark corn syrup**	Add to oil; cook until mixture has thickened.
¼	cup	**water**	
2	Tbsp	**soy sauce**	
2	Tbsp	**sherry**	
1	Tbsp	**cornstarch**	
1	clove	**garlic**	
¼	tsp	**ginger**	
1	lb	**shrimp,** shelled	Add to above; stir until cooked (5min). Serve with rice.
1	sm	**tomato** (1" pcs)	
½	cup	**green pepper,** chopped coarse	

Annabel Christy, Weston

Seafood in Shells

Great for that special luncheon

Serves: 4
Freeze or chill
Bake: 250° 15-25 min
Pans: Dutch oven; 5" casseroles or
     shells

1	pkg	**crab**, frozen (7½oz)	Can use any combination of fresh,
1	lb	**shrimp**, fresh, cooked, diced	canned or frozen shellfish. Combine and set aside.
⅓	cup	**butter**	Melt in Dutch oven then remove from heat.
⅓	cup	**flour**	
¾	tsp	**salt**	Combine; stir into above until
⅓	tsp	**paprika**	smooth.
⅛	tsp	**white pepper**	
⅓	cup	**light cream**	Gradually add stirring until smooth. Bring to a boil, stirring constantly.
½	cup	**white wine**, dry	Simmer (2min); stir in reserved seafood.
			Combine; toss until coated. Fill casseroles or shells with seafood mixture; top with bread crumbs. Can be prepared ahead and chilled or frozen.
¼	cup	**butter**, melted	Chilled: Bake (15min). Frozen: Bake
1	cup	**bread crumbs**	(25min) or until bubbly and golden. Serve over rice.

Barbara Clark, Westport

Shrimp Creole Earl

Delicious served with rice and a green salad

Serves: 4
Stovetop: 45-60 min
Pan: skillet (10")

4	Tbsp	**margarine** OR **olive oil**	Brown butter and flour to form a roux
4	Tbsp	**flour**	(see Index).
½	cup	each: **green onions, celery, green pepper**, diced	Add to roux; cook a few minutes until glazed.
2	cloves	**garlic**	
1		**bay leaf**, crushed	Add; sauté a few minutes longer.
1	tsp	**thyme**	
		salt, pepper to taste	
1	can	**tomatoes** (16oz)	Add to above, slowly. Cook until tomatoes are brown and all moisture is evaporated.
1	qt	**shrimp stock** (from boiled heads and tails OR 1 btl clam juice)	Add and simmer until consistency of thick cream.
1	lb	**shrimp**, shelled	Add to sauce; simmer (3-5min). Serve
8	oz	**mushrooms**, sliced	hot over rice along with a green salad.

Abby Catledge, New Orleans, La

Fairfield Shrimp Supreme

Great for a special buffet

Serves: 12
Stovetop: 20-30 min
Bake: 325° 40-50 min
Pans: saucepans; skillet (med); 13x11

¾ cup	**wild rice** (1 box)	Cook separately according to package directions. Drain; set aside to dry a bit.
½ cup	**white rice** (NOT instant)	

½ cup	**BUTTER**	Sauté (2-3min).
1 cup	**onion**, chopped	
½ cup	each: **celery, green pepper**, chopped	
10 oz	**mushrooms**, fresh, thick slices	
	salt, pepper to taste	

1 can	**cream of mushroom soup**, undiluted (10¾oz)	In large bowl, combine with all of above. Spread in casserole.
2½ lbs	**shrimp**, cooked	
1 pkg	**crabmeat**, frozen	

1¼ cups	**sharp cheddar cheese**, grated	Sprinkle cheese over top. Pour sauce over but DO NOT STIR. Bake until hot and bubbly.
1½ cups	**cream sauce**, medium (see Index)	

Pat O'Hearne, Fairfield

Baked Shrimp – California Style

Crisp and delicious

Serves: 6-8
Bake: 375° 15 min
Pan: 9x13, lightly oiled

2 cups	**cheese crackers**, crushed fine	Mix well.
1 tsp	**dill**, dried	
1 tsp	**paprika**	
2 lb	**shrimp**, large, raw, shelled	Roll in crumb mixture.
⅔ cup	**evaporated milk**	Roll in milk, then in crumbs again. Place in baking dish.
½ cup	**butter**, melted	Drizzle over shrimp. Bake until golden but be careful not to overbake.
	lemon wedges	Garnish.

Mrs. William Wirtz, Ojai, Ca

Kan Shao Hsia Jen
(Chinese)

Shrimp with hot sauce

Serves: 4-6
Marinate: 1 hour
Stovetop: 7-10 min
Pan: wok or skillet

1	lb	**shrimp,** shelled
1		**egg white**
1	tsp	**cooking wine**
1	tsp	**salt**
1½	tsp	**cornstarch**

Marinate shrimp in other ingredients (1hr).

4	cups	**oil** for frying

Deep fry shrimp until pink (90% done). Remove shrimp; discard all but 2 Tbsp oil. Keep shrimp warm.

2	Tbsp	**scallions,** chopped
1	Tbsp	**ginger root,** chopped

Reheat oil; add and stir/fry quickly.

2	Tbsp	**catsup**
1	Tbsp	**hot pepper paste**
3	Tbsp	**chicken broth**
½	tsp	**salt**
½	tsp	**sugar**
1	tsp	**sesame oil**

Combine and add to above; bring to a boil then boil only a few seconds. Stir in shrimp.

1½	tsp	**cornstarch**
		water

Add just enough water to form a paste; stir into wok. Heat through well. Serve immediately.

Mabel Yu, Trumbull

Grammy's Herb Shrimp

Very good!

Serves: 6
Stovetop: 8 min
Pans: skillet (lg); chafing dish

½	cup	**butter**

Melt in skillet.

4	Tbsp	**lemon juice**
2	tsp	**parsley,** chopped
2	tsp	**chives,** chopped
1	tsp	**tarragon**
1	tsp	**dry mustard**
1½	tsp	**season-all**
¼	tsp	**cayenne**
¼	tsp	**garlic powder**

Add to skillet; mix well.

2	lb	**raw shrimp,** cleaned, deveined OR **scallops**

Sauté in herb butter, over medium heat, until pink. Turn as needed. Serve over rice.

Jan McNaughton, Fairfield

Shrimp–Clams Fra Diavalo
(Italian)

Another great Italian delicacy

Serves: 4
Stovetop: 1 hr
Pan: skillet (12")

2	Tbsp	**olive oil**
2	med	**onions,** chopped
4	cloves	**garlic,** minced
1	Tbsp	**parsley,** minced

Sauté (2-3min).

		red pepper, crushed (to taste)
2	cans	***tomatoes in puree,** crushed

Add; simmer uncovered (30min). *For a lighter, less sweet consistency, use imported Italian Plum Tomatoes (not water pack); crush through strainer.

1	lb	**shrimp,** shelled
1½	doz	**clams,** small, scrubbed

Add to sauce; cover and cook until clams open (approx 15min). Serve over spaghetti.

Agnes Swords, Stratford

Shrimp Curry

Simple and delicious

Serves: 4
Stovetop: 5 min
Pan: skillet

⅓	cup	**butter** OR **oleo**
½	cup	**onions,** chopped
¼-½	cup	**green peppers,** chopped
2	cloves	**garlic,** minced

Sauté carefully until tender and golden (2-3min).

2	cups	**sour cream**
2	tsp	**lemon juice**
2	tsp	**curry powder**
¾	tsp	**salt**
½	tsp	**ginger**
	dash	**chili powder**
3	cups	**shrimp,** fresh OR canned, cooked, split

Add to above; cook only until heated through. Serve over rice.

Nancy Johnson, Shelton

Vegetables

Cherry Tomatoes – Sauté gently in skillet in which you have melted butter, shaking skillet to roll tomatoes until warmed through. Season with salt and basil or oregano, to taste.

Green Peas – Lay one lettuce leaf over top while cooking, for a different taste.

Tomato halves – Sprinkle with salt and pepper and a few drops of white wine then bake or broil.

Green Peas – Sprinkle with mint while cooking for a pleasant difference.

Mushrooms – Sauté then freeze to prevent loss if you can't use them soon. Add to vegetables as they are heating.

Carrots – Slice; add a small amount of water, some honey, butter, salt and pepper. Cook until tender.

Carrots – Slice 3 or 4; dot with butter, salt and pepper. Wrap in foil. Place in oven to bake with roast for at least 1 hour. (1 lb carrots sliced into casserole, cover then bake with roast at least 1 hour).

Celery – Simmer in chicken broth then use as vegetable dotted with butter. Broth makes a delicious drink.

Summer Squash – Slice; sauté in skillet in which butter has been melted. Season with salt, pepper and onion powder.

Tomato halves – Bake. When warm, spread with mayonnaise then sprinkle with Parmesan cheese, salt and pepper. Return to oven until hot and luscious.

Mushrooms – Sauté in heavy skillet sprinkled with salt only – delicious, dry and golden.

Green beans – Wrap in foil (can add a slice or two of tomatoes); season to taste then bake with roast for one hour.

Topping – a little mayonnaise, some sour cream, season with a little curry; spread over fish or tomato halves then broiled makes a delicious puffy topping.

Those odds-and-ends of vegetables – Grease a casserole; layer prepared vegetables according to hardness. Pour a small can of tomatoes or one of the green vegetables over the top. Season to taste. Bake with roast for one hour.

Green Beans or Carrots –Add a tablespoon or two of coconut cream to the liquid in which your beans are being cooked for a different flavor.

Torta di Palmito
(Brazilian)

Something different—a heart of palm pie

Serves: 6-8
Stovetop: 15 min
Bake: 350° 45 min
Pans: saucepan (3qt); 10" round

CRUST

3	cups	**flour**	} Combine.
½	tsp	**salt**	

½	cup	**margarine**	Cut in.

1		**egg**	Add; mix well until dough forms a ball. Using ⅔ of crust (reserve ⅓ for top), line pan. Patching will be necessary.

FILLING

2		**eggs**, hard cooked	Slice; set aside.

3	med	**onions,** chopped, coarse	} Sauté until tender.
3	cloves	**garlic,** minced	
¼	cup	**oil**	

4		**tomatoes**	Cut into bite-size pieces; add; cook slowly (10min).
2	cans	**heart of palm** OR **artichoke hearts**	

2	cups	**milk**	Mix well; add. Stir until absorbed; cook (5min).
2	Tbsp	**cornstarch**	

		salt, pepper to taste	Fold in gently; spoon into crust lined pan and cover with remaining dough.
		reserved sliced eggs	
12		**olives,** ripe, halved	

1		**egg yolk,** beaten	Brush on crust. Bake. Serve hot.

Celeste Jardim, Trumbull

Broccoli al Limone
(Italian)

A compliment to most any meat dish

Serves: 6-8
Stovetop: 10 min
Pan: skillet (12")

1	bunch	**broccoli,** trimmed **salt** to taste	} Split each stalk lengthwise into 3 pieces. In skillet, over medium heat, in 1" boiling water, cook covered (10min) or until crisp-tender. Do not overcook. Arrange on platter.

3-4	Tbsp	**olive oil**	} Mix and pour over broccoli.
2-3	Tbsp	**lemon juice,** fresh	

		garlic powder to taste	Sprinkle over and serve hot.

Maria DeCesare, Trumbull

Emerald Barley Casserole

A change from potatoes—unusual and tasty

Serves: 4-6
Bake: 350° 1 hr
Pans: saucepan (1½qt); casserole
    (1½qt)

½	cup	**butter**	
1	cup	**pearl barley**	In saucepan, sauté lightly.
1	med	**onion,** chopped	
1	pkg	**dehydrated onion soup** (2oz)	
2	cups	**chicken broth**	Add; mix thoroughly and pour into casserole. Bake covered, adding liquid if needed.
1	can	**water chestnuts,** drained, sliced (5oz)	
½	cup	**almonds,** slivered	
1	can	**mushrooms** (3oz)	

Jean Beard, Pine Knoll Shores, NC

Fresh Broccoli Puff

A glamorous vegetable

Serves: 6-8
Bake: 350° 50-60 min
Pans: saucepan (3qt); casserole,
    buttered (2qt)

½	cup	**butter**	Sauté until tender.
2	Tbsp	**onion,** chopped	
½	cup	**flour**	Blend in.
4	cups	**milk**	Stir in gradually; cook, stirring continuously until sauce thickens and comes to a boil. Remove from heat.
3		**eggs**	Beat in small bowl; stir in a small amount of hot sauce; return to saucepan.
1-2	tsp	**salt**	Add; mix well.
¼	tsp	**pepper**	
1	bunch	**broccoli,** chopped fine	Stir in; turn into casserole. Bake until top is golden and tip of knife inserted in center comes out clean. Let stand (5min). Serve.

Joan Attolino, Trumbull

When cooking cabbage or cauliflower, put a piece of bread on top to absorb the unpleasant odors.

BARLEY is one of the oldest cereals cultivated. It was grown in ancient times by Greeks and Romans.

Rodkaal

(Scandinavian)

Cabbage at its best! Great with pork

Serves: 8
Stovetop: 1 hr
Pan: saucepan (4qt)

3	lb	**red cabbage leaves,** shredded
¼	cup	**butter**

In saucepan, cook (3-4min) stirring.

½	cup	**water**
2	Tbsp	**red wine vinegar**
1	Tbsp	**sugar**
		salt, pepper to taste

Add; cover. Simmer (1hr).

½	cup	**red currant jelly**

Add; mix then serve hot. Best made a day ahead and reheated.

Hillandale Gourmet Club, Trumbull

Carrots Kids Will Eat

The title says it all

Serves: 4
Stovetop: 20 min
Pan: saucepan (2½qt)

1	lb	**carrots,** thin diagonal slices
1	cup	**raisins,** golden
1	cup	**water**
1	tsp	**salt**

Combine; cover and simmer until tender. Drain well.

½	cup	**brown sugar,** packed

Sprinkle over carrots.

4	Tbsp	**butter**
2	Tbsp	**lemon juice**

Add to above; cook (10min) longer, until glazed.

Claudia McKenna, Trumbull

Red Cabbage

Serves: 4
Stovetop: 10 min
Pan: saucepan(1½qt)

1	jar	**red cabbage** (1lb)
¼-½	cup	**red wine**
1-2		**apples,** chopped

Combine in saucepan. Simmer.

Patricia Braun, Trumbull

Carrot Pudding

Another nice change

Serves: 6-8
Bake: 350° 1 hr
Pan: 12x8, buttered

2	cups	**carrots,** cooked, mashed
6	slices	**white bread,** fresh, crusts removed
¼	cup	**sugar**
¼	cup	**brown sugar**
½	cup	**vegetable shortening**
2		**eggs**
¾	cup	**milk**
2	tsp	**baking powder**
	dash	**nutmeg**

Mix together well, put into baking dish. Bake. Serve hot.

Cissy Moffat, Cold Spring Harbor, NY

Carottes Glacées

(French)

Tasty and attractive

Serves: 8
Stovetop: 30-40 min
Pan: skillet (10")

12	med	**carrots** (2" pieces)
1½	cups	**beef** OR **chicken stock**
4	Tbsp	**butter**
2	Tbsp	**sugar**
½	tsp	**salt**
	dash	**pepper,** fresh ground

Combine in skillet; cover. Bring to a boil then simmer until tender. Shake skillet occasionally to roll carrots in liquid. Juices should become a brown, syrupy glaze. If stock reduces too quickly, add more. If it does not reduce enough, remove carrots, boil to reduce. Before serving, shake to glaze carrots. Remove to heated dish.

2	Tbsp	**parsley,** chopped

Garnish.

Hillandale Gourmet Club, Trumbull

Corn Pudding

A must for Thanksgiving dinner

Serves: 8
Bake: 350° 1 hr
Pan: 13x9, greased

add cracker crumbs

¾	cup	**butter,** melted
½	cup	**sugar**
4		**eggs**
3	Tbsp	**flour**
2	cans	**corn,** cream style (16oz,ea)
2	tsp	**vanilla**
1¾	cups	**milk**

Mix. Bake until firm.

Chris Henschel, Fairfield

Concombre Maître d'Hôtel

Hot cucumbers, great with fish

Serves: 4
Cook: 20 min
Pan: saucepan (3qt)

1	cup	**water,** boiling
½	tsp	**salt**
3	lg	**cucumbers,** firm, peeled, quartered lengthwise, seeds removed, sliced 1" thick

Boil cucumbers, covered, over medium heat until tender (10min). Drain; return to pan. Toss in pan over low heat to remove moisture.

1	Tbsp	**butter**
1	Tbsp	**parsley,** chopped
1	Tbsp	**chives** OR **dill,** chopped
⅛	tsp	**pepper**

Add; toss again (1min). Adjust seasonings; serve hot.

Gemma Zingo, Bridgeport

Korean Cucumber Salad

Try the whole menu

Serves: 4
Marinate: 30 min
Chill

3		**cucumbers,** Kirby OR pickling type

These cucumbers are not as watery nor do they require peeling. Slice very thin.

1	Tbsp	**salt,** Kosher

Mix with cucumbers to coat; let stand (30min) then rinse. Place in damp cloth; gently but firmly squeeze out excess liquid.

1	tsp	**sesame seeds,** toasted

Add to above.

1	clove	**garlic,** crushed
1	tsp	**sesame oil,** dark
1	tsp	**sugar**
	dash	**salt**
	dash	**cayenne pepper**

Combine; add to cucumbers and mix well. Serve at room temperature or chilled.

Gloria Lee, Trumbull

 Line bottom of your vegetable compartment with layers of paper towels to absorb excess moisture. Helps prevent molding and keeps vegetables fresh longer.

Raita
(India)

Another interesting dish, part of a delicious menu

Serves: 4
Chill: 2-4 hr

8	oz	**yogurt,** plain

Drain on 4-5 layers paper towels (1hr) to remove liquids.

1	sm	**cucumber,** peeled, grated
¼	tsp	**salt**

Combine; squeeze well to remove liquids. Mix with above.

¼	tsp	**salt**
½	tsp	**sugar**
⅛	tsp	**pepper**
1		**hot pepper,** minced

Add and stir in well. Chill thoroughly.

Kirti Pancholi, No. Kingstown, RI

Skillet Eggplant

Simple, quick and still tasty

Serves: 6
Stovetop: 20 min
Pan: skillet (10")

2		**eggplants,** peeled, diced
2		**green peppers,** chopped coarse
2	sm	**onions,** chopped coarse
3	Tbsp	**vegetable oil**

Sauté until lightly browned.

6		**tomatoes**
3	tsp	**salt** (to taste)
1	tsp	**paprika**
	dash	**pepper**

Add to above; cook until eggplant is tender. Serve immediately.

June Logan, Stratford

Bohnen und Karotten Gemuse
(German)

Green beans and carrots with summer savory

Serves: 6-8
Stovetop: 15-20 min
Pans: 2 saucepans (3qt,4qt);
skillet (6")

1	lb	**carrots,** fresh (sliced)
1½	lb	**green beans,** fresh, whole

Cook separately to taste. Arrange on serving platter (green beans in middle, carrots around edge).

6	Tbsp	**butter**
1	Tbsp	**summer savory**
1	Tbsp	**bread crumbs**
		salt, pepper to taste

In skillet melt butter; add seasonings. Mix well; pour over vegetables. Serve immediately.

Gertrud Bargas, Trumbull

Tomato-Eggplant Delight

A tasty luncheon treat

Serves: 6
Stovetop: 10 min
Bake: 375° 35 min
Pans: saucepan (2qt); 11x7, buttered

3	Tbsp	**onion,** chopped	
1	clove	**garlic,** minced	Sauté; set aside.
3	Tbsp	**butter**	

1	lg	**eggplant,** peeled, cubed	
1½	tsp	**salt** (to taste)	In saucepan, simmer until soft; mash.
½-1	cup	**water**	

2		**eggs,** beaten	
		reserved onion mixture	
½	cup	**bread crumbs**	Add to above; mix well.
⅓	tsp	**pepper**	
½	tsp	**oregano, thyme, marjoram** OR **basil**	

2	lg	**tomatoes,** sliced	Place half over bottom of casserole. Place mound of eggplant mixture on each slice, top with remaining slices forming "sandwiches."

½-1	cup	**Cheddar cheese,** grated (2oz)	
¼	cup	**Parmesan cheese,** grated	Sprinkle on top. Bake.
	dash	**paprika**	

Joyce Greene, Weston

Dals

(chick peas) (India)

One part of a delicious meal

Serves: 4
Stovetop: 10-15 min
Pan: saucepan (2qt)

2	Tbsp	**vegetable oil**	Sauté seed in oil until browned; lower heat.
1	tsp	**cumin seed**	

3		**cloves,** whole	
2		**cinnamon sticks**	Add and sauté until golden (2min).
1	med	**onion,** chopped	

1	clove	**garlic,** minced	Add; sauté (1min). Stir well.

2	med	**tomatoes,** chopped	
1	tsp	**salt**	
1	tsp	**paprika**	Add and stir in well. Cook (2min).
2	tsp	**coriander powder**	
1	tsp	**sugar**	

1	can	**chick peas,** undrained (20oz)	Add; bring to a boil then lower heat. Simmer (10min). Serve hot.
2	cups	**water,** warm	

Kirti Pancholi, No. Kingstown, Ri

"Stuffed" Eggplant

Freeze in summer for easy winter meals

Serves: 6-8
Bake: 350° 35-40 min
Pan: 13x9

1	med	**eggplant,** sliced length- wise (⅛" slices)	Dip into egg, then crumbs or flour. Fry until crispy brown on both sides; set aside.
2-3		**eggs,** beaten	
¾	cup	**bread crumbs,** OR **flour** **vegetable oil** for frying	
1		**egg,** beaten	Mix; spread 1 heaping Tbsp on each eggplant slice. Roll and secure.
15	oz	**Ricotta cheese** **salt, pepper** to taste	
1	jar	**tomato sauce** (16oz) OR your favorite	Spread half of sauce over bottom of baking dish; place eggplant rolls in single layer; cover with remaining sauce.
½	cup	**Parmesan cheese,** grated OR	Sprinkle over top. Bake. Freezes well. Can prepare eggplant, freeze, then put together when ready to use.
4	oz	**Mozzarella cheese,** grated	

Beatrix Mastrone, Trumbull

Yu Hsiang Ch'ien Tzu

(Chinese)

Eggplant Sze-chuan style

Serves: 6
Stovetop: 10-15 min
Pan: wok or skillet

1	lb	**eggplant**	Wash; remove both ends (do not peel). Cut into finger-sized pieces.
6	Tbsp	**oil**	Heat to very hot; add eggplant and reduce heat. Stir/fry until soft. Press out excess oil while in skillet; remove eggplant and set aside.
½	Tbsp	**ginger,** chopped	Add to oil in wok; stir a few seconds.
1	tsp	**garlic,** chopped	
1	Tbsp	**hot bean paste**	
2	Tbsp	**soy sauce**	Add; bring to a boil. Return eggplant and cook (1min) or until liquids are absorbed.
1	tsp	**sugar**	
1	tsp	**salt**	
½	cup	**chicken broth**	
½	Tbsp	**brown vinegar**	Add; stir in well.
½	Tbsp	**sesame oil**	
1	Tbsp	**scallions,** chopped	Garnish.

Mabel Yu, Trumbull

Baked Leeks

(Swedish)

A nice recipe for a badly neglected vegetable

Serves: 6-8
Bake: 400° 15 min
Pans: casserole, greased (2qt);
saucepan (3qt,1qt)

2	lb	**leeks,** sliced **water,** lightly salted	Boil until soft (save 1 cup water); arrange in casserole.

SAUCE

2	pkts	**Hollandaise sauce mix** reserved vegetable water **milk**	Follow packet directions using water and milk; remove from heat.
¾	cup	**sour cream**	
2-3	tsp	**mustard**	Add to sauce; mix and pour over leeks.
1½	Tbsp	**lemon juice,** fresh	
	dash	**cayenne pepper**	
		salt, pepper to taste	
		Parmesan cheese	Garnish. Bake.

Kerstin Nilson, Trumbull

Lentils and Rice

(Lebanese)

Great source of vegetable protein

Serves: 4-5
Stovetop: 35 min
Pan: saucepan (3qt)

1	cup	**lentils,** rinsed, sorted	Cook over medium heat (20min).
8	cups	**water**	
1	cup	**rice,** uncooked	Add; cook (15min).
2	tsp	**salt** (to taste)	
½	cup	**vegetable oil**	Sauté until golden; add to above and
4	lg	**onions,** chopped coarse	mix. Serve hot or cold.

Fran Thompson, Fairfield

 LEEK is in the onion family. It is the National Emblem of Wales.

 LENTILS have nearly twice as much protein as wheat or oats plus phosphorous and B vitamins also.

Croquetas de Gandules

Pigeon pea croquettes

Serves: 4
Stovetop: 6-10 min
Pan: Dutch oven

2	cups	**pigeon peas** OR your favorite legume, cooked	Put through sieve or vegetable press.
1	Tbsp	**onion juice**	
¼	tsp	**garlic juice**	Add to above and mix well. Shape into desired form (chill if hard to handle).
1	Tbsp	**butter**	
¼	tsp	**celery salt**	
⅛	tsp	**pepper**	
1		**egg,** beaten	
1	cup	**bread crumbs**	Roll each croquette.
1		**egg,** beaten	Dip each in egg then roll in crumbs again.
		oil for deep fat frying	Fry in hot fat until golden brown; drain on absorbent paper. Serve hot with cheese or tomato sauce.

Serving Suggestion: Make croquettes cone shaped; fry then place in center of serving platter on a bed of plain boiled rice. Place a border of boiled sliced carrots around edge then a row of cooked green peas or beans. Pour 1 cup cream sauce (med) over vegetables or croquettes. Serve hot.

Barbara Schegg, Huntington

Green Bean Bake

A zesty flavor

Serves: 6
Stovetop: 15-20 min
Bake: 350° 15-20 min
Pans: 2 saucepans (2qt,4qt); 13x9, buttered

2	slices	**bacon,** chopped	Heat in saucepan, to render fats.
1	cup	**onion,** chopped	Add to above and cook until wilted.
3	med	**tomatoes,** peeled, chopped **salt, pepper** to taste	Add to above; bring to a boil then simmer (15min).
1	lb	**green beans,** fresh (2")	Cook in boiling water, in large saucepan, until crisp-tender. Spread over bottom of baking dish.
½	cup	**heavy cream**	Heat to boiling point; add to tomato sauce; pour over beans.
1	cup	**Parmesan cheese,** grated	Sprinkle over top. Bake until hot, then broil slightly to glaze cheese. (Can be prepared ahead, reheated: 350° 30min)

Marguerite Weeks, Monroe

Tasty Crunchy Green Bean Casserole

Not too rich, just right

Serves: 8
Bake: 350° 35 min
Pan: casserole (2qt)

18-20 oz	**green beans,** frozen, French style	Cook until crisp-tender (4min).
1 can	**water chestnuts,** sliced (5oz)	Layer with green beans in casserole.
1 can	**cream of celery soup** (10¾oz)	} Combine; pour over vegetables and cover. Bake (25min).
1 cup	**milk**	
⅛ tsp	**pepper**	
¼ cup	**almonds,** slivered	Sprinkle over top. Bake (10min) longer, uncovered.

Phyllis Aiello, Stratford

Green Bean "Bundles"

Sort of special

Serves: 6
Stovetop: 6-8 min
Broil: 3-4 min
Pans: saucepan; broiling pan

1 lb	**green beans,** fresh	Cook to crisp-tender; divide into 6 bundles. (Can use canned vertical pack beans.)
3 strips	**bacon,** halved	Wrap one piece around each bundle. Secure with toothpick. Place on rack; broil until bacon is crisp. Remove to warm platter.

SAUCE

2-3	Tbsp	**butter**	} Combine; simmer (1-2min). Pour over hot bundles.
3	Tbsp	**vinegar**	
½	tsp	**salt** (optional)	
1	tsp	**paprika**	
1	Tbsp	**parsley**	
1	tsp	**onion, chopped**	

Gretchen MacArthur, Fairfield

 Add a teaspoon or two of coconut milk to cooking vegetables. Adds a new and different flavor.

Mushrooms
(Polish)

Prepare ahead, refrigerate, heat and serve

Serves: 6
Bake: 375° 15 min
Pans: skillet (10"); 8x8, buttered

¾	lb	**mushrooms,** sliced	Place in fry pan.
1	Tbsp	**lemon juice,** fresh	Sprinkle over mushrooms.
1	Tbsp	**onion,** minced	
3	Tbsp	**butter**	Add; cover tightly. Simmer over me-
¼	tsp	**salt**	dium heat (5min).
⅛	tsp	**pepper**	
1	Tbsp	**flour**	Stir in; cook (3-4min) stirring occa-
2	Tbsp	**Parmesan cheese,** grated	sionally. Place in baking dish.
1	cup	**cream,** heavy*	Beat together; pour over mushrooms.
2		**egg yolks,** beaten lightly	*Skim evaporated milk can be susti- tuted to help dieters.
2	Tbsp	**bread crumbs**	Sprinkle over top.
1	Tbsp	**butter**	Dot crumbs.
	dash	**paprika**	Garnish. Bake.
1	Tbsp	**tarragon,** crushed	

Alberta Kinne, Trumbull

Mushroom-Artichoke Casserole

Very nice

Serves: 6-8
Bake: 350° 20 min
Pan: casserole (1qt)

1	pkg	**artichoke hearts,** frozen* (10oz)	Cook; drain and set aside. *Canned can be substituted.
3	cups	**mushrooms,** halved	
½	cup	**scallions** (with tops) sliced	Sauté (3-4min); remove and set aside.
4	Tbsp	**butter** OR **margarine**	
2	Tbsp	**flour**	Blend into pan drippings.
½	tsp	each: **salt, pepper**	
¼	cup	**milk**	
¼	cup	**water**	
1	pkg	**instant chicken granules**	Add; mix and cook gently. Add ar- tichokes and mushroom mix. Cook until bubbly then turn into casserole.
1	Tbsp	**lemon juice**	
	dash	**nutmeg**	
¼	cup	**bread crumbs**	Mix then sprinkle around edge.
1	Tbsp	**butter,** melted	

Maribeth Gentile, Fairfield

Onions Baked with Sherry

A very tasty recipe for a neglected vegetable

Serves: 4
Stovetop: 10 min
Bake: 350° 30-40 min
Pan: casserole (2qt)

6	med	**onions**
	pinch	**salt, pepper**
1	tsp	**water**

Cut 1" deep cross into the base. Arrange all in casserole.

2-3	Tbsp	**butter**

Dot onions.

2-3	Tbsp	**Sherry**

Pour over; cover. Bake (30min) or until crisp-tender.

TOPPING

½	cup	**commercial cornbread* stuffing**, crushed
1	Tbsp	**Romano cheese**, grated
1	Tbsp	**bacon bits**
1	Tbsp	**butter, melted**
		salt, pepper to taste

Mix; spoon over onions. Bake uncovered (15min) or until onions are soft and crumbs brown and crisp.
*Seasoned bread stuffing, corn flake crumbs or cracker crumbs can be used.

Ester Sealy, Bridgeport

veg492

Okra

(Greek)

Part of a delicious menu

Serves: 6
Marinate: 30 min
Stovetop: 25-30 min
Bake: 350° 1 hr
Pans: skillet (lg); casserole (3qt)

2	lb	**okra**, fresh or frozen, washed, stemmed
2	cups	**wine vinegar**

Place in bowl; marinate (30min). Drain well; place okra in casserole.

½	cup	**olive oil** OR **meat drippings**
¼	cup	**butter**
1½	cups	**onions**, chopped

Sauté in skillet until golden.

1	can	**tomatoes**, drained (16oz)
2	Tbsp	**parsley, chopped**
2	tsp	**salt** (to taste)
		pepper to taste

Add to skillet; cook (15min). Pour over okra and cover with foil. Bake: 30 minutes; remove foil. Bake 30 minutes longer until okra is tender.

Gertrud Bargas, Trumbull

veg493

The mild shallot sauteed in butter makes a delicious sauce for peas or asparagus.

Potatoes
(British)

Add a sprig or 2 of **mint** to your boiling **new** small unpeeled potatoes for a different flavor.

Margaret Lindsay, Trumbull

Baked Mashed Potatoes

A great "do-ahead" vegetable for a group

Serves: 8
Bake: 350° 30 min
Pan: casserole, buttered (2qt)

8	lg	**potatoes,** peeled, quartered	Boil until tender (15-20min); drain.
½-1	cup	**butter**	Add; mash well.
1	cup	**sour cream**	
8	oz	**cream cheese,** softened **garlic salt** to taste **pepper** to taste	Add to above; whip with electric mixer. Put into casserole. Bake.

VARIATION: ¼ to ½ tsp basil, thyme, parsley, marjoram, your choice, can be added. Garnish with chives.

Agnes Swords, Stratford

Janssons Temptation
(Swedish)

Rich, creamy and delicious

Serves: 4
Bake: 400° 45 min
Pan: casserole, buttered (1½qt)

4	cups	**potatoes,** raw, peeled, julienned	Soak in cold water to convert starch and prevent sticking; dry well.
1	Tbsp	**butter**	Sauté.
1	cup	**onion,** sliced	
1	can	***Swedish anchovy filets** (reserve juice) *found in gourmet shops	In casserole, layer potatoes, onion, anchovies; repeat, ending with a layer of potatoes. Sprinkle with 1 Tbsp of anchovy juice.
¼	cup	**butter** OR **margarine**	Dot.
1	cup	**cream,** light	Pour over casserole. Bake until potatoes are tender and golden brown.

Kerstin Nilson, Trumbull

Hasselbackspotatis
(Scandinavian)

Attractive and delicious

Serves: 8
Bake: 450° 45 min
Pan: casserole, buttered (3qt)

12	med	**potatoes,** oval shaped, peeled

Place on a tablespoon, cut into thin slices (do NOT cut through–Tbsp helps prevent this). Place, sliced side up, into well buttered casserole.

1	tsp	**salt**
		pepper to taste

Sprinkle.

3	Tbsp	**butter** OR **margarine**

Dot. Bake 450° (20min), basting occasionally.

4	Tbsp	**Parmesan cheese,** grated
2	Tbsp	**bread crumbs**

Garnish. Bake (25min) longer without basting.

Hillandale Gourmet Club, Trumbull

Kugali
(Lithuanian)

Worth the effort

Serves: 6-8
Bake: see recipe
Pans: saucepan (4qt); loaf, greased (8x4)

3	lg	**eggs,** beaten

Set aside.

2½	lb	**potatoes,** peeled

Dry well and keep wrapped.

2	Tbsp	**butter**
1½	Tbsp	**vegetable shortening**
½	cup	**onion,** minced

In saucepan, sauté onion gently.

	reserved potatoes

Grate quickly; drain off as much liquid as possible; add to saucepan.

		reserved eggs
2	Tbsp	**heavy cream**
1½	tsp	**salt**
1	Tbsp	**sugar**

Add and mix. Pour into prepared pan. Bake: preheated 450° (20min). (This is mandatory to prevent darkening.) Reduce to 350° (40-50min) longer. Serve in 1" thick slices.

	sour cream
	applesauce

Garnish (your choice).

Hint: Stores well in refrigerator if sealed with plastic wrap. To reheat, broil slices or heat whole loaf in oven. Doubles very well.

Nancy Craig, New Canaan

Potato Kuku

"An old family favorite"

Serves: 6
Bake: 350° 45-50 min
Pans: casserole (2qt); saucepan (2qt)

1	lb	**potatoes** (3 med) **water**, salted	Boil until tender; cool slightly then peel and mash.
¼	cup	**milk**	Add and whip.
¼	cup	**onion**, grated	
1	tsp	**salt**	
¼	tsp	**pepper**	Stir into potatoes.
2	Tbsp	**parsley**, chopped	
6		**eggs**, beaten well	Beat in a large bowl; add potato mixture and beat to combine well.
¼	cup	**butter**, melted	Pour into casserole and coat well. Top with potato mixture. Bake until tester inserted in center comes out clean. Serve immediately.

Ginny Moreno, New Canaan

Dutch Hutspot

This recipe gets 3 vegetables into "kids" of all ages, plus nutritious cheese

Serves: 4
Stovetop: 20 min
Broil: few min
Pans: saucepan (2qt); casserole, buttered (2 qt)

4		**potatoes**, peeled, sliced	
4		**carrots**, peeled, sliced	Cook in covered saucepan until
2		**onions**, peeled, sliced **salt** to taste	tender. Drain very well.
¼	cup	**evaporated milk**	
3	Tbsp	**butter**	Add to above; mash well. Transfer to
1	tsp	**salt**	buttered casserole.
½	tsp	**pepper**	
4	slices	**Cheddar cheese**, sharp	Top casserole; broil a few minutes until melted and brown. Watch carefully.

Claudia McKenna, Trumbull

 CARROTS are a good source of vitamin A. Should be scraped as thinly as possible and never peeled so as to retain their vitamins during cooking.

Two-Potato Puff

Excellent with sausage, pork, sauerkraut

Serves: 6-8
Bake: 350° 50-60 min
Pans: saucepan (med); casserole,
    greased (2½qt)

3	cups	**potatoes,** peeled, cubed	Boil until tender; drain and mash. Set aside.
3	cups	**sweet potatoes,** peeled, cubed	
3	Tbsp	**margarine**	Brown in saucepan.
½	cup	**onions,** chopped	
½	tsp	**nutmeg**	
¼	tsp	**pepper**	
¾	tsp	**salt**	
1½	cups	**milk, warm**	Mix flour with small amount of milk to prevent lumping; add remainder. Pour into saucepan; bring to a boil.
3	Tbsp	**flour**	
3		**egg yolks,** lightly beaten	Add to sauce; mix well.
2	Tbsp	**parsley,** snipped	Add; mix well.
		reserved potatoes	
3		**egg whites,** beaten stiff	Fold gently into potato mixture; turn into prepared baking dish. Bake.

Elizabeth Kappus, Trumbull

Sweet Potato Puff

A well-flavored dish

Serves: 8
Bake: 325° 25 min
Pan: casserole (3qt)

3	lb	**sweet potatoes,** boiled in jackets	Cool; peel and mash.
1	cup	**applesauce**	Add; mix well. Adjust any ingredient to taste.
4	Tbsp	**butter**	
¼	cup	**brown sugar**	
¼	cup	**milk**	
¼	cup	**maple syrup**	
2	tsp	**lemon juice**	
1	can	**crushed pineapple,** (8oz)	
12		**marshmallows**	Place over top. Bake until they soften and brown.

Sonny Weintraub, Bridgeport

The Best Sweet Potatoes

Oh the compliments you'll get

Serves: 10-12
Stovetop: 10 min
Bake: 350° 20 min
Pan: casserole, buttered (3qt)

3	cups	**sweet potatoes,** boiled, mashed
¼-½	cups	**sugar**
½	cup	**butter,** melted
2		**eggs,** beaten
1	tsp	**vanilla**
⅓	cup	**milk**

Mix well, then pour into prepared baking pan.

⅓	cup	**butter,** melted
¾	cup	**light brown sugar**
⅓-½	cup	**flour**
1	cup	**pecans,** broken

Mix; sprinkle on top. Bake. Doubles well and freezes well.

Hillandale Gourmet Club, Trumbull

Orange Glazed Sweets

Always a favorite

Serves: 6
Stovetop: 10 min
Bake: 350° 30 min
Pans: saucepan (sm); 7x11, greased

6		**sweet potatoes,** boiled or baked, peeled

Cook until barely tender; place in prepared dish.

1	cup	**orange juice**
2	tsp	**orange rind,** grated
1	Tbsp	**cornstarch**
3	Tbsp	**butter,** melted
⅓	cup	**sugar**
⅓	cup	**brown sugar**
⅛	tsp	**salt**

In saucepan, combine; bring to a boil. Pour over potatoes. Bake, basting occasionally.

Hillandale Gourmet Club, Trumbull

Baked Sweets

Can be refrigerated and baked when needed

Serves: 4
Stovetop: 15-20 min
Bake: 350° 30 min
Pans: saucepan; 12x8

6		**sweet potatoes,** long thin

Boil until tender; peel. Cut in half lengthwise; arrange in baking dish.

1	cup	**butter** OR **margarine**

Drizzle over potatoes.

salt, pepper, paprika, nutmeg OR **mace** to taste

Sprinkle over potatoes. Turn and sprinkle other side. Bake until golden.

Diane Lombardi, Milford

Spinach-Rice-Cheese-Mélange

A great quick vegetable

Serves: 6
Stovetop: 5-6 min
Bake: 350° 1 hr
Pans: skillet (sm); saucepan (2qt);
　　　casserole (2qt)

¾	cup	**onions, chopped**	In skillet, sauté until golden; pour into casserole.
½	cup	**margarine**	
2	pkg	**spinach,** chopped (10oz,ea)	Cook in saucepans; drain well. Mix into above.
1	cup	**rice**	
1	jar	**cheese food** (lg)	Add ¾ of the jar; mix in. Spread remainder over top. Bake uncovered.

Gail Lauder, Fairfield

Spinach Bake with Onion Rings

Also delicious using broccoli

Serves: 4
Bake: 400° 30 min
Pan: 11x7

1	pkg	**spinach,** frozen, chopped (10oz)	Cook and drain well; reserve liquid.
1		**egg,** beaten	Combine, then add spinach. Mix carefully. Bake until bubbly; remove from oven.
3	oz	**cream cheese,** softened	
1⅓	pkg	**G Washington season-** **ing**	
⅓	cup	**spinach liquid**	
1	Tbsp	**butter**	
1	tsp	**onion,** minced **salt, pepper, nutmeg** to taste	
1	can	**fried onion rings**	Spread over top. Bake: (3min).

Marion Child, Bridgeport

SWEET POTATOES will be more dry if their skins are yellow. They will be sweet and sugary if the skins are whitish or reddish. Never refrigerate – keep in a dry place (50-60degrees).

Squash au Gratin

Winter squash delight

Serves: 4-6
Bake: 350° 20-30 min
Pan: casserole, greased (2-3qt)

1	cup	**bread crumbs,** dry	Place in bowl.
3	Tbsp	**bacon drippings** OR **butter**	Combine and heat to melt fats. Pour over bread crumbs.
1	cup	**milk**	
2	cups	**winter squash,** cooked, mashed	Add to above; mix in well.
½	cup	**cheese,** grated	
1	Tbsp	**onion,** grated	
		salt, pepper to taste	
¼	cup	**cracker crumbs**	Sprinkle over top. Bake
½-1	cup	**cheeese,** grated	

Virginia Smith, Bridgeport

Zucchini Bake

A nice use for squash

Serves: 8
Stovetop: 5 min
Bake: 350° 25 min
Pans: saucepan (4qt); 11x7, buttered

3	lb	**zucchini** OR **yellow squash,** sliced	Boil (5min); drain.
1	sm	**onion,** chopped	
1	cup	**sour cream**	Combine; add to squash and mix. Set aside.
1	can	**cream of chicken soup** (10¾oz)	
1	cup	**carrot,** grated	
½	cup	**margarine,** melted	Combine; layer ½ in casserole. Top with zucchini mixture. Spread remaining stuffing mix on top. Bake.
1	pkg	**prepared stuffing mix** (8oz)	

Lily Westberg, Stratford

 FREEZING – blanching is essential when freezing vegetables. This process inactivates enzymes and stops the natural loss of color and flavor. It helps retain vitamins and destroys bacteria.

Italian Style
Zucchini Casserole

Good for family or guests

Serves: 10-12
Bake: 350° 20 min
Pans: skillet (med); 13x9, greased

8	med	**zucchini,** ¼" slices
1	cup	**water**
		salt to taste

Boil (5min); drain. Set aside.

8	slices	**bacon**

Sauté to render fat.

1	lg	**onion**

Add to bacon; sauté (5min); drain well. Stir bacon-onion mix into zucchini.

1	clove	**garlic,** minced
4	slices	**bread,** white
2	cups	**cheese,** shredded
1	tsp	**salt**
1	tsp	**Italian seasoning**
1	can	**tomato sauce** (15oz)
	dash	**pepper**

Add; toss until well mixed. Pour into baking dish.

⅓	cup	**Parmesan cheese,** grated

Sprinkle over top. Bake until bubbly.

Maribeth Gentile, Fairfield

Zucchini Corn Bake

A different combination

Serves: 6
Bake: 350° 40 min
Pans: saucepan (2qt); skillet (sm); casserole (1qt)

1	lb	**zucchini,** unpeeled, sliced 1" thick
1	cup	**water**
		salt to taste

Cook in boiling salted water until tender (15-20min); drain. Mash with fork; set aside.

¼	cup	**onion,** chopped
1	Tbsp	**margarine**

Sauté until tender.

2		**eggs,** beaten
1	pkg	**corn** frozen (10oz) OR 2 cups fresh
1	cup	**Swiss cheese,** cubed
¼	tsp	**salt**

Combine with zucchini and onion; put into casserole.

¼	cup	**bread crumbs,** dry
2	Tbsp	**Parmesan cheese,** grated
1	Tbsp	**margarine,** melted

Mix together; sprinkle on top of casserole. Bake; let stand (10min) before serving.

Charlotte Brittain, Fairfield

Zucchini Fritters with Cheese Sauce

Very tasty

Serves: 4-6
Deep fry: 375° 3 min
Pans: deep fryer; saucepan (2qt)

1½	cups	**flour**	
2	tsp	**baking powder**	Mix together in medium bowl.
¾	tsp	**salt**	

1		**egg**, beaten	Combine; add to dry ingredients. Mix
1	cup	**milk**	just until all ingredients are moist-
1	cup	**zucchini,** chopped fine	ened.

vegetable oil — Drop by tablespoon into deep hot fat (375°). Fry a few at a time, until golden, turning once (about 3 min). Drain on paper towel. Serve with cheese sauce. (see Index)

Rose Sayles, Trumbull

Harvest Bounty Casserole

Biscuits baked right in

Serves: 10-12
Bake: 350° 45-50 min
Pan: 13x9, greased

3	cups	**green beans,** cut, cooked, drained	Spread in baking dish.
3	med	**green peppers,** chopped	

6	med	**tomatoes,** chopped	Sprinkle over beans and peppers.
3	cups	**Cheddar cheese,** shredded (12oz)	

1	cup	**biscuit mix**	Beat with hand beater until smooth;
2	tsp	**salt**	pour over vegetables and cheese. Bake,
1	tsp	**cayenne pepper**	uncovered, until golden brown. Let
1	cup	**milk**	stand (10min) before serving.
6		**eggs**	

Marjorie Dickey, Fairfield

 BROCCOLI and cauliflower are in the cabbage family and came to us from Cyprus.

Ratatouille

Good as a side dish or served with pita bread

Serves: 12-16
Stovetop: 30 min
Pan: kettle (4-6qt)

2	Tbsp	**oil**	
1	lg	**onion,** chopped	Sauté (3-5min).
1		**green pepper,** chopped	
2	cloves	**garlic,** chopped	

2		**tomatoes,** chopped	
2		**zucchini,** chopped	
1	med	**eggplant,** chopped	Add; simmer, stirring occasionally un-
½	tsp	**basil,** crumbled	til mixture thickens and vegetables
1	cup	**tomato juice**	are soft (15-20min). Serve hot. This
3	Tbsp	**oil**	vegetable can be frozen and reheated.
1	Tbsp	**vinegar**	
2	tsp	**salt**	
½	tsp	**pepper**	

Carol Longo, Hamden

Mixed Vegetable Bake

Another great use for summer's bounty

Serves: 10
Bake: 350° 1 hr
Pan: casserole, oiled (3qt)

1	can	**tomatoes,** chopped (28oz) (reserve juice)	
1½	lb	**zucchini,** sliced ¼"	
2	lg	**carrots,** sliced ¼"	Layer in prepared casserole.
1	lb	**potatoes,** sliced ¼"	
2		**onions,** sliced ¼"	
1	pkg	**okra,** frozen (10oz)	

2	cloves	**garlic**	
½	cup	**parsley**	
1	Tbsp	**oregano**	Sprinkle over vegetables.
½	cup	**olive oil**	
		salt, pepper to taste	

reserved tomato juice	Pour over casserole; cover. Bake.
croutons	Top casserole just before serving. This casserole can be prepared a day ahead, baked just before serving.

Eleanor Weinhaus, Stratford

Vegetable Chow Mein and Fried Noodles

Great! A special treat

Serves: 4
Cook: 15-18 min
Pans: skillet, covered (lg); saucepan
(3qt); deep fryer

CHOW MEIN

4-6	cups	**fresh vegetables:** (except tomato) carrots, celery, broccoli, beans, turnips, parsnips, mushrooms, potatoes, green peppers, etc.)	Wash; drain and cut in pieces (1x¼x¼) then set aside.
2	Tbsp	**oil**	
1-2	cloves	**garlic,** minced	Stir fry (2min); add chopped vegetables and stir to coat with oil. Cover; cook over low heat (5min).
1	lg	**onion,** chopped	
1	piece	**ginger root,** chopped fine	
2	Tbsp	**soy sauce**	Add and stir in.
½	cup	**water**	Blend together; pour over vegetables. Cook, stirring until thickened. Top with fried noodles and serve immediately.
1	Tbsp	**soy sauce**	
2	Tbsp	**cornstarch**	

FRIED NOODLES

2	cups	**egg noodles,** fine	Drop noodles into water to which oil has been added. Return to boil; cook (5min). Drain; rinse with cold water and dry on paper towels.
1	Tbsp	**vegetable oil**	
1	qt	**water, boiling**	
½	cup	**vegetable oil**	Heat oil (2min) in very hot skillet. Reduce heat to medium. Fry noodles stirring constantly until they start to turn brown.
1	cup	**wheat germ**	Add; continue to cook stirring until noodles are brown.
1	tsp	**salt**	Add; stir well. Remove and drain.

June Bartnett, Monroe

 CELLULOSE is found in the outer layers of cereals and legumes. They are a good source of fiber.

Meatless Patties
with Spanish Sauce

A great meatless main dish or vegetable

Serves: 5-6
Stovetop: 10-15 min
Bake: 350° 30-40 min
Pans: skillet (lg); saucepan (2qt);
13x9

PATTIES

4		**eggs**
1	cup	**Mozzarella cheese,** shredded
1	cup	**pecans, cashews** OR **walnuts,** chopped
⅓	cup	**evaporated milk**
¾	cup	**prepared stuffing mix,** dry
1	med	**onion,** chopped
1	tsp	**salt**
¼	cup	**oatmeal**
1		**zucchini,** shredded (optional)

Combine all ingredients. Form into patties, ¼ cup each.

vegetable oil

Lightly brown patties in hot oil; arrange in baking dish. Set aside.

SAUCE

3	med	**onions,** sliced or chopped
2	Tbsp	**butter** OR **oil**

Sauté.

2	Tbsp	**flour**
4	cups	**tomato juice**
1		**bay leaf**
1	tsp	**brown sugar**

Add to onions; cook, stirring (10min). Remove bay leaf. Pour ½ of sauce over patties; cover. Bake. Serve remainder of sauce, warmed, with patties.

Edith Skoog, Trumbull

Squash and Tomato Casserole

A delicious way to use up those summer vegetables

Serves: 8
Bake: 350° 30 min
Pan: casserole, buttered (2qt)

3-4		**tomatoes,** peeled, sliced
1	lg	**onion,** sliced very thin
3	cups	**yellow squash,** ¼" slices

} Layer in casserole.

		pepper to taste
	pinch	**thyme**

} Sprinkle over squash.

½-1	cup	**cheddar cheese,** shredded OR ¼ cup **Romano** OR **Parmesan** cheese, grated

Sprinkle over casserole.

½-1	cup	**bread crumbs**
1	Tbsp	**butter,** melted

} Combine and sprinkle over top. Bake until hot and bubbly.

Marguerite Weeks, Monroe

A Simple Zucchini Casserole

Easy but tasty

Serves: 6
Stovetop: 5 min
Bake: 350° 40-45 min
Pan: casserole (2-3qt)

8-10	med	**zucchini,** cut up
½	tsp	**garlic powder**
½	tsp	**basil**
½	tsp	**pepper**

} Parboil along with seasonings; drain.

½	lb	**Monterey Jack cheese,** shredded
½	lb	**cheddar cheese,** shredded
8	oz	**sour cream**

} Add to above; pour into casserole.

½	cup	**Italian seasoned bread crumbs**
		Parmesan cheese

} Sprinkle over top.

Jean Wirtz, Yorba Linda, Ca

A Simple Hollandaise Sauce

Yield: 1 cup

1	cup	**sour cream**	
1-2	Tbsp	**lemon,** juice of OR **dry sherry**	Mix in top of double boiler. Stir OVER hot water until thickened.
2		**egg yolks**	
½	tsp	**salt**	
¼	tsp	**paprika**	

Mustard Sauce

Great with sauteed fish filets, sausage in pastry, ham, plus much else

Yield: 1½-2 cups
Cook: 15 min
Pans: double boiler

2½	Tbsp	**dry mustard**	Mix together in small bowl. Can adjust mustard to taste.
1	Tbsp	**flour**	
¼	tsp	**salt**	
¼	cup	**milk**	
¾	cup	**milk**	Heat together in double boiler until sugar is dissolved. Stir in mustard mixture, heat.
¼	cup	**sugar**	
2		**egg yolks**	Slowly stir a small amount of warm sauce into egg yolks, then pour back into pan. Cook until thick.
½	cup	**white vinegar**	Add to sauce, continue cooking until thickened.

Agnes Swords, Stratford

Cheese Sauce

Yield: 2 cups

2	Tbsp	**butter,** melted	Combine in saucepan to form roux.
2	Tbsp	**flour**	
	dash	**white pepper**	
1¼	cups	**milk**	Add; cook, stirring, over medium heat until mixture is thick and bubbly.
½	cup	**American cheese,** shredded	Add; cook, stirring, until cheese is melted.
½	cup	**process Swiss cheese,** shredded	

Rose Sayles, Trumbull

Roux

White, blond or brown, your choice

Yield: 1 cup
Stovetop: see recipe
Pan: saucepan (2qt)

For each cup of sauce you desire:

WHITE: (Bechamel or cream sauce) for vegetables, souffles, creamed dishes, etc.

2	Tbsp	each: **BUTTER*** and **flour** *unsalted is best.	Melt fat. When sizzling add flour and blend; cook over low heat (3-5min) stirring constantly. DO NOT BROWN. Cool slightly.
1	cup	**milk,** scalded	Stir in slowly; cook until thickened.
		season to taste	Serve hot.

BLOND: for poultry, fish, vegetables, etc.

2	Tbsp	each: **BUTTER*** and **flour** *unsalted is best.	Melt fat. When sizzling add flour and blend; cook over low heat until light brown (10min) stirring constantly. Cool slightly.
1	cup	**water** OR **milk,** heated	Stir in slowly; cook until thickened.

BROWN: gumbos, green vegetables, beef, pork, gravies, etc.

2	Tbsp	each: **fat** and **flour** (bacon, sausage, meat fats, oil, etc.)	Melt fat. When sizzling add flour and blend, cook until it reaches the desired color and smell. Low heat (up to 20-25min). High heat (5min). Watch carefully, stir almost continuously, to prevent scorching. Cool.
1	cup	**water** OR **broth,** HOT	Add slowly; stir and cook until thickened. Browned flour without liquid added can be stored in refrigerator for

long periods, tightly covered. Add liquids and cook when needed.
Seasonings: chives, onion powder or juice, nutmeg, celery salt, savory, dill, sherry, parsley, whatever compliments your entrée.

Mornay Sauce

Yield: 3 cups

¼	cup	**butter,** melted	Combine in saucepan over medium heat, to form a roux.
⅓	cup	**flour**	
1-1½	cups	**vegetable liquid**	Add; cook stirring until thickened.
½-1	cup	**cream**	
¼	cup	**Parmesan cheese,** grated	Stir in; cook until well blended and thickened. Pour over favorite vegetables. Bake: 350° 30 min uncovered.
2	Tbsp	**white wine**	
	pinch	**nutmeg** and **thyme**	

Cissy Moffatt, Cold Spring Harbor, NY

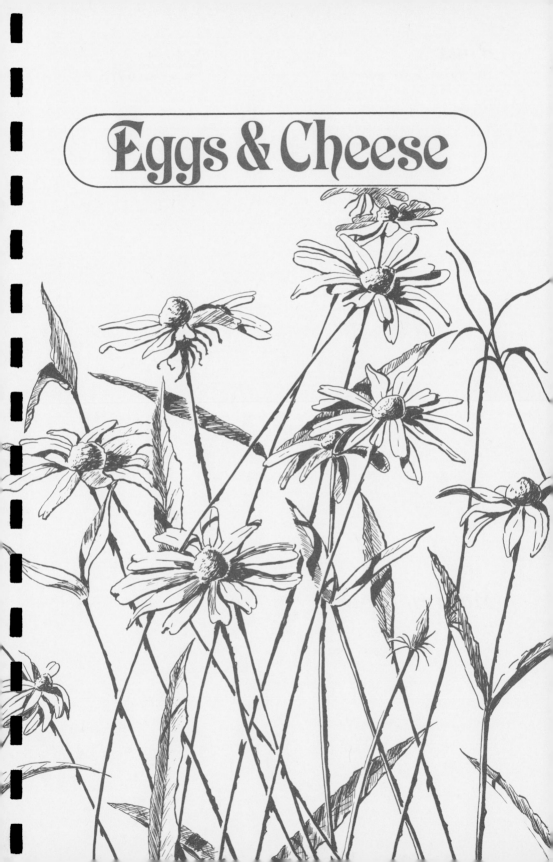

Eggs & Cheese

"LITE" FARE
Cream of Lettuce Soup
Veal "Almost" Marsala
Vegetable Chow Mein with Fried
Noodles
Leaf Salad
Banana Tea Bread

BREAKFAST
Zippy Tomato Juice Toddy
Jewel's Company Breakfast or
Oeuf aux Jambon et Fromage
Toasting Loaf
Apricot-Apple Jelly
Fresh Fruit Tray

LUNCHEON
Champagne Fruit Cup
Torta di Palmito or
Crepes Coquilles
Spinach Salad
Rolls
Better Butter
Chocolate Cheesecake

SUNDAY BRUNCH OR EVENING
Bruce's Oriental or Frozen Coconut
Daiquiri
French Toast "Francois" Style with
Maple Syrup
Fresh Fruit or Ambrosia

Baked Asparagus and Cheese "Sandwich"

And ham makes it even better

Serves: 6
Bake: 325° 40 min
Pan: 13x9, greased

6	slices	**bread,** thick, crust removed
6	slices	**Swiss cheese** (3½-4")
6	slices	**ham** (optional)

In greased baking dish, cover each slice of bread with cheese and ham.

4		**eggs,** beaten
2	cups	**milk**
1	tsp	**salt**
⅛	tsp	**pepper**
¼	tsp	**nutmeg**
1	Tbsp	**onion,** chopped fine

Combine; pour over above (can be refrigerated, to be completed later). Bake (25min). Remove from oven.

18	spears	**asparagus,** canned
½	cup	**cheddar cheese,** shredded

Top each "sandwich" with 3 spears, sprinkle with cheese. Bake (10-15min) longer until set. Let stand (5min) before serving.

Mary MacInnis, Fairfield

Pannickaku Suomalainin

Serve with fresh fruit

Serves: 4
Bake: 425° 25 min
Pan: 7x9

4		**eggs**
¼	cup	**honey**
¾	tsp	**salt**
2½	cups	**milk**

Blend in bowl with whisk or mixer.

1	cup	**flour,** unsifted

Add; beat until smooth. May be set aside at this point. Remove from refrigerator (30min) before baking.

4	Tbsp	**butter**

Melt in baking dish; heat until hot. Pour batter into pan. Bake; serve immediately.

		peaches, sliced
		honey

Top with peaches; drizzle with honey.

Christine Powers, Wallingford, Vt

Jewel's Company Breakfast

A special way to start the day

Serves: 8
Chill: overnight
Bake: 350° 45 min
Pans: skillet (lg); 13x9

1	lb	**mushrooms**, sliced	
8		**green onions**, sliced	Saute until golden then set aside.
½		**green pepper**, chopped	
1-2	Tbsp	**margarine**	
12	slices	**bread**	Lay along bottom of baking dish.
1	lb	**bacon**, diced	Fry, drain and place on top of bread.
½	lb	**boiled ham**, diced	
		reserved vegetables	Spread over meat.
1½	lb	**Swiss cheese**, grated	Sprinkle over casserole.
12		**eggs**	Beat together; pour over casserole. Refrigerate overnight. When ready to serve, bake (45min) or until knife inserted in center comes out fairly clean. Serve immediately.
2	cups	**milk**	
½	tsp	**nutmeg**	

Jewelette Thompson, Fairfield

Oeuf au Jambon et Fromage

Muenster and cottage cheese

Serves: 10-12
Bake: see recipe
Pans: skillet (sm); 13x9

½	cup	**butter**	Melt in baking dish. Remove half; set aside. Coat baking dish with remainder.
2	cups	**ham**, diced	Sauté lightly in skillet; set aside.
1	Tbsp	**butter**	
12		**eggs**, beaten	
	dash	**salt, pepper**	
5-6	drops	**Tabasco sauce**	
½	cup	**flour** (scant)	Combine well; pour into prepared baking dish. Bake: 400° (15min). Reduce heat. Bake: 350° (10-15min) longer or until puffed and golden. Best served immediately.
1	tsp	**baking powder**	
1	lb	**Muenster OR Monterey Jack cheese**, shredded	
1	pt	**cottage cheese** (sm curd)	
		reserved ham	
		reserved butter	

Hannah Burke, Farmington

Jajka
(Polish)

Various sauces for traditional hard-cooked eggs   **Yield:** 1½ cups each sauce

MAYONNAISE SAUCE

1	cup	**mayonnaise**
1	tsp	**sharp brown mustard**
2	tsp	**vinegar** OR **lemon juice**
	dash	**salt**
1	Tbsp	**confectioners' sugar**

Fork blend; chill.

SPRING SAUCE

1	cup	**mixed greens** (chives, green onions, radishes and cucumbers), minced
1	Tbsp	**dill,** minced
1	tsp	**lemon juice**
1	cup	**sour cream**
		salt, pepper to taste
	dash	**confectioner's sugar** (optional)

Fork blend; chill.

HORSERADISH SAUCE

1	cup	**sour cream**
½	cup	**horseradish,** non creamed
3		**egg yolks,** hard-cooked, sieved
1	tsp	**lemon juice**
	dash	**salt**
1-2	Tbsp	**confectioners' sugar**

Fork blend; chill. Pour any or all of these sauces over whole or halved hard-cooked eggs arranged on a bed of lettuce for a traditional Polish welcome. "Wesolego Alleluja!"

Pat McCathron, Trumbull

To poach eggs, drop into SIMMERING water. Never let it boil.

Process cheese is made of one or more natural cheeses.
Process cheese food is made with more milk or water and less cheese.
Process cheese spread has an edible stabilizer added.

Egg Scramble

A great brunch dish

Serves: 10
Bake: 350° 30 min
Pans: skillet (lg); 12x8

CHEESE SAUCE

2	Tbsp	**butter,** melted
2	Tbsp	**flour**
½	tsp	**salt**
⅛	tsp	**pepper**

Blend in frying pan, over low heat.

2	cups	**milk**

Add to above; stir and cook until bubbly.

1	cup	**American cheese,** shredded

Add to above; stir until melted. Remove from heat.

CASSEROLE

3	Tbsp	**margarine**
1	cup	**Canadian bacon,** diced
¼	cup	**green onions,** chopped

In large skillet, cook bacon. Sauté until onion is tender but not brown.

1	doz	**eggs,** beaten

Add to above; scramble until just set.

1	can	**mushroom pieces**

Fold into cheese sauce along with egg mixture. Turn into baking dish.

TOPPING

2	tsp	**butter,** melted
2¼	cups	**bread crumbs,** soft
⅛	tsp	**paprika**

Combine; sprinkle over top and chill (30min). Bake uncovered until hot and bubbly. Can be prepared, covered and refrigerated 12 hours.

Catherine Merillat, Boynton Beach, Fl

Great Spinach Quiche

Muenster cheese forms the crust!

Serves: 6
Bake: 325° 30 min
Pan: pie plate, buttered (9")

16	oz	**Muenster cheese,** cut in long slices

Line plate, starting from center, having half of each slice overhang the plate edge.

2	pkg	**spinach,** frozen, chopped (10oz,ea)

Cook; drain and squeeze out liquid.

2		**eggs,** beaten
2	Tbsp	**onion,** chopped
1	cup	**Ricotta cheese**
		salt, pepper to taste
		nutmeg to taste

Mix thoroughly; add spinach. Spoon over cheese; cover with overlapping slices of cheese. Bake. Cool (15min) before serving.

Lillian Thiede, Stratford

Chicken Quiche

Swiss cheese

Serves: 6
Bake: 375° 15 min
Pan: pie plate (9")

	1	**pastry shell,** unbaked	Line plate.
½-1	cup	**chicken,** diced	Arrange in shell.
3	Tbsp	**almonds,** slivered	
1½	cups	**Swiss cheese,** shredded	Sprinkle over chicken.
3		**eggs,** lightly beaten	
1½	cups	**milk**	
½	tsp	**salt**	Combine; pour over cheese.
¼	tsp	**mace**	
⅛	tsp	**pepper**	
2	Tbsp	**Parmesan cheese,** grated	Sprinkle over quiche. Bake until knife inserted in center comes out clean. Allow to stand (10min) before serving.

Pat Edwards, Bridgeport

"South of the Border" Quiche

Cream and Swiss cheeses

Serves: 6-8
Bake: see recipe
Pan: pie plate (10")

1		**pastry shell,** baked	Brush baked shell with butter.
2	Tbsp	**butter,** melted	
8	oz	**cream cheese,** diced	Arrange in shell; chill until butter is set.
2	cans	**green chilies,** drained, chopped (4oz,ea)	
1	cup	**Swiss OR Monterey Jack cheese,** shredded	Sprinkle over cream cheese in layers.
5		**eggs,** beaten	Combine; pour evenly over all. Bake:
1½	cups	**heavy cream**	400° (15min); reduce to 350° (30min)
½	tsp	**salt**	longer.
	dash	**pepper**	

Hannah Burke, Farmington

 MACE is from the covering around the nutmeg seed though very different in flavor.

Crabmeat Quiche

Gruyere cheese

Serves: 8
Bake: 375° 30-40 min
Pan: pie plate (9")

1		**pastry shell,** baked	Set aside.

2		**eggs**
1	cup	**light cream**
¾	tsp	**salt**
1	tsp	**onion,** grated

Beat together.

1	can	**crabmeat,** flaked (6½oz)
3	oz	**Swiss cheese,** grated
3	oz	**Gruyere cheese,** grated
1	Tbsp	**flour**

Combine with egg mixture; pour into shell. Bake.

Rita Madore, Fairfield

Quiche – Bacon or Ham

Swiss and Parmesan cheeses

Serves: 6
Bake: 375° 25 min
Pan: pie plate (9")

1		**pastry shell,** unbaked	Line pie plate.
6	slices	*****lean bacon,** diced, cooked	Sprinkle over bottom of shell.

3		**eggs**
1	cup	**heavy cream**
½	tsp	**salt**
	dash	**pepper**

Beat together in large bowl.

½	cup	******Swiss cheese,** grated
½	cup	**Parmesan cheese,** grated

Add to above; gently ladle over bacon leaving ⅛" for expansion.

2	Tbsp	**butter,** chilled, cut in small pieces

Dot over above. Bake until puffed and brown and knife inserted in center comes out clean.

VARIATIONS: * Canadian bacon or ham may be substituted.
**Cheese: ¾ cup Swiss cheese can be substituted for half Swiss and half Parmesan.

Virginia Smith, Bridgeport

Swiss Cheese Pie
with Seafood Sauce

A very special luncheon dish!

Serves: 6-8
Bake: see recipe
Pans: pie plate (9"); saucepan (1qt)

CHEESE PIE

1		**pastry shell**	Bake: 450° (7min). Remove, reduce oven to 350°.
4		**eggs,** separated (reserve yolks)	Beat egg whites, in small bowl, until stiff peaks form.
		egg yolks	
1½	cups	**light cream**	Combine; fold in beaten egg whites.
½	tsp	**salt**	
⅛	tsp	**nutmeg**	
6	oz	**Swiss cheese,** shredded (1½cups)	Fold into egg mixture; gently pour into pie shell. Bake at 350° (40-45min) until knife inserted in center comes out clean. Let stand (5min).

CRABMEAT SAUCE

1	can	***crabmeat,** drained, flaked (7½oz)	Heat gently.
2	Tbsp	**butter** OR **margarine**	*Delicious using scallops, shrimp or lobster also.
2	Tbsp	**flour**	
⅛	tsp	**salt**	Blend into crabmeat.
	dash	**onion powder** (optional)	
1	cup	**light cream**	Add; cook, stirring until thickened.
1	Tbsp	**sherry** (optional)	Spoon over slices of pie just before serving.

Joan Kacin, Trumbull

 PASTRY, adding water – the amount varies with the temperature and rate of adding water. Less water is needed for warm, fine ingredients but more will be needed if added quickly. Less water makes pastry tender.

Sausage-Cheese Strata

Just great

Serves: 6-8
Chill: 24 hr
Bake: see recipe
Pan: casserole, buttered (3qt)

1	lb	**sausage links** (1" slices)	Fry; remove and drain well. Set aside.
2	cups	**bread cubes,** white or wheat	Prepare; set aside.
1	cup	**cheddar cheese,** grated	
6		**eggs,** beaten lightly	Mix; add all above ingredients. Pour into casserole and chill overnight. Bake: 350° (45min) or 325° (1hr). Watch carefully.
2	cups	**milk**	
½	tsp	**dry mustard**	
		salt, pepper to taste	

VARIATION: Use 6-8 bread slices; remove crusts. Add ½ cup sautéed, sliced mushrooms or bits of cooked broccoli; 1 cup cooked shrimp with or instead of sausage. Add ½ tsp onion powder, ½ tsp dill. Layer bread, vegetables, meats; pour egg mixture, to which seasonings have been added, over all; chill. Bake: 325° (1hr) or until done. Serve with salad, fresh fruit compote or creamed beef or chicken, hot curried fruit. Spiced grape preserves are a good condiment for this.

Mary Alice McHugh, Trumbull

Turkey "Sandwich" Strata

Another great luncheon dish

Serves: 4
Bake: 325° 50-60 min
Pan: 9x9, buttered

8		**white bread slices** **prepared mustard**	Remove crusts; spread mustard on bread, very thinly.
½	lb	**turkey,** cooked, sliced	Prepare 4 sandwiches; place in baking dish.
¼	lb	**Swiss cheese**	
4		**eggs,** beaten	Blend well; pour over sandwiches. Bake until set and golden. Can be prepared ahead, refrigerated. Bake a bit longer.
2	cups	**milk**	
2	tsp	**seasoned salt**	
¾	tsp	**thyme,** crushed	
¼	cup	**onion,** minced	

Edith Curran

 Soufflés will remain light and fluffy longer if you add ¼ tsp cream of tartar to egg whites while beating.

Green Chili "Soufflé"

Great with hot slices of ham

Serves: 6-8
Bake: 350° 45 min
Pan: casserole (2qt)

2	cans	**green chilies**, seedless (4oz,ea)	Layer chilies, cheese in casserole; repeat.
½	lb	**cheddar cheese**, grated	
½	tsp	**oregano**	
1	tsp	**salt**	Combine; pour over above. Bake.
¾	cup	**sour cream**	
4		**eggs**, beaten	

Nancy Hogan, Denver, Co

"Gypsy" Eggs by Wanda

A great breakfast or brunch

Serves: 4
Stovetop: 20 min
Pans: saucepan (sm); skillet (sm)

2	Tbsp	**butter**	Melt in saucepan.
½	Tbsp	**flour**	Blend in.
½	tsp	**meat extract**	
½	cup	**water**, boiling	Combine well; add to saucepan. Cook
1	tsp	**tomato paste**	(5min); set aside.
	dash	**salt, pepper**	
4	oz	**mushrooms**, sliced	Meanwhile, sauté mushrooms (5min);
1	Tbsp	**butter**, melted	add to sauce.
4	slices	**toast**	Place 1 slice on each plate.
4		**eggs**, poached	Place on on each toast; pour sauce over.
1	tsp	**parsley**, chopped	
1	Tbsp	**Parmesan cheese**, grated	Sprinkle over each. Serve immediately.

Wanda Violante, Bridgeport

 Store cottage cheese upside down and it will keep much longer.

Cheese Blintzes
(Jewish)

A great appetizer, entrée or dessert

Serves: 3-4 main dish
6 side dish
Stovetop: see below
Pans: skillet (6"); Dutch oven

Make 12 crepes (see Index). Pancakes can be cooked on one side, filled then rolled and deep fried on outside.

CHEESE FILLING

1¼	lb	**Farmer cheese** (soft) OR **pot style cottage cheese**
1		**egg**, lightly beaten
	pinch	**salt**
¼	cup	**sugar**
¼	tsp	**cinnamon** (optional)

Sieve cheese well then mix all together well. Put one well-rounded teaspoon of filling in middle of each pancake. Fold in edges, roll and seal so all filling is tucked in. Be careful not to break pancake.

¼	cup	**vegetable oil** OR **butter**

Heat to very hot in large pan. Place 6 blintzes in oil, folds down. Turn heat to medium; cook until brown. Turn over; cook until brown (10min). Serve hot or cold with yogurt, sour cream or hot cherry sauce. Great as a dessert served with preserves. Freezes well. Blintzes can also be baked 425° until browned.

Marge Scheir, New Haven

BLUEBERRY FILLING

1	pt	**blueberries**, washed drained
¼	cup	**sugar**
¼	tsp	**cinnamon**
2	tsp	**cornstarch**

Sprinkle over berries. Fill pancakes on browned side; roll and brown in melted butter. Serve with yogurt or sour cream.

HOT CHERRY SAUCE

1	can	**cherries, dark**, sweet, pitted
2	Tbsp	**sugar**
1	Tbsp	**lemon juice**
1	Tbsp	**cornstarch**, dissolved in water

Drain juice from cherries into saucepan; add sugar and lemon juice. Bring to a boil; add cornstarch mixture. Boil and stir constantly until slightly thickened; add cherries. Serve hot.

Sonny Weintraub, Bridgeport

 COTTAGE CHEESE or pot cheese is made from milk. It was devised by small farmers to use up soured milk. It is a good source of calcium.

 CHEDDAR is one of the oldest of English cheeses made from milk.

Enchiladas
(Mexican)

Try it, you'll like it!

Serves: 6
Bake: 400° 20 min
Pans: skillet (9"); saucepan (2qt)

12		corn tortillas
		vegetable oil
1	cup	Monterey Jack cheese, shredded
1	cup	Cheddar cheese, shredded
1	med	onion, diced

Heat tortillas, in warm oil in skillet, just enough to soften. (Can be done without oil in microwave - 2 at a time (25-30sec). Place 1 Tbsp of each cheese and onion in center of each tortilla; roll up. Place seam side down in baking dish (can be secured with toothpick).

SAUCE

4	Tbsp	butter
4	Tbsp	flour
2	cups	chicken broth

Cook stirring until thickened. (Can substitute cream of chicken soup.)

1	cup	sour cream

Stir in but DO NOT BOIL.

2-3		Jalapeño peppers, seeded, chopped

Add and stir. Pour hot sauce over enchiladas.

1	cup	Cheddar OR Jack cheese, shredded

Sprinkle over top. Bake.

Susan Farley, Monroe

Beer Rarebit Fondue

Serve with French bread cubes

Serves: 6-8
Cook: 20 min
Pan: fondue cooker or saucepan

4	cups	sharp cheese, shredded (2lb)

Shred when cold; let stand until room temperature.

½	cup	beer

With electric mixer, beat cheese and beer until fluffy, in small bowl.

2	tsp	Worcestershire sauce
½	tsp	dry mustard
⅛	tsp	garlic powder
	dash	hot pepper sauce

Add; beat well. Melt cheese mixture in fondue cooker or stove.

1	Tbsp	cornstarch
2	Tbsp	water

Blend together; add to cheese. Cook, stirring, until thickened.

Jeanne Elsasser, Fairfield

Vegetarian's Casserole

A great meatless main dish

Serves: 8-10
Stovetop: 5 min
Bake: 350° 40 min
Pan: 13x9, buttered

4	Tbsp	**butter**	
1	cup	**onion,** chopped	
2-3	cloves	**garlic,** crushed	Sauté until onions are golden and soft.
8	oz	**mushrooms,** chopped	
1	tsp	each: **basil, thyme, marjoram**	

4		**eggs,** lightly beaten	
2	cups	**cottage** OR **Ricotta cheese**	
1	cup	**Mozzarella cheese,** grated	Combine and mix with vegetables above. Spread in prepared casserole.
2	Tbsp	**tamari**	
		salt, pepper, cayenne to taste	
2	cups	**soybeans,** cooked	
2	cups	**brown rice,** cooked	
2	med	**tomatoes,** sliced thin	Place over top of casserole.
½	cup	**Parmesan cheese,** grated	Combine then sprinkle over tomatoes.
½	cup	**bread crumbs**	Bake uncovered.

Joyce Greene, Weston

Scotch Eggs
(British)

Very good

Yield: 8
Pans: saucepan (3qt) or
deep fryer, 5-6 min

8		**eggs,** hard cooked, peeled	Coat eggs with flour.
¼	cup	**flour**	
1	lb	**sausage,** cut into 8 pieces	Pat one piece of sausage around each egg.
2		**eggs,** beaten	Combine; roll eggs to coat well.
¾	cup	**bread crumbs,** dry	
½	tsp	**sage,** ground	Roll eggs to coat well.
¼	tsp	**salt**	
		oil for deep frying	Heat 1½-2" oil in saucepan to 360°. Fry eggs (4 at a time) turning occasionally (5-6min). Drain well. Serve hot or cold.

Margaret Lindsay, Trumbull

266   Eggs and Cheese

Rice, Noodles & Pastas

BUFFET FOR 12-16
Rum Fruit Punch
Tourtière (Canadian Meat Pie)
Salmon Ring with Olive Sauce
Party Chicken and Wild Rice
Vegetable Marinade
Oat Bran Muffins
Gâteau au Chocolat
Tropical Orange Cake

"LITE" FARE
"Lifesaver" Soup
Dieter's Lasagne
Leaf Salad
"Rice" Pudding

A PREPARE-AHEAD LUNCHEON
Mmmm-Mimosa Cocktail
Sausage-Cheese Strata
Marinated Mushrooms and Green
Beans
Dilly Bread
Frosty Cranberry Pie

A DO-AHEAD FAMILY DINNER
Pepper Jelly over Cream Cheese
Layered Garden Surprise
Crispy Fried Fish
Tasty Crunchy Green Bean Casserole
Baked Mashed Potatoes
Settlers Poppy Seed Cake

Islander Green Rice

Delightful flavor

Serves: 5-6
Sauté: 5 min
Bake: 400° 25 min
Pans: saucepan (2qt); 11x7

1	cup	**rice,** raw	Cook until just tender.
3	Tbsp	**green onions,** chopped fine	Sauté in saucepan (5min).
¼	tsp	**curry powder**	
3	Tbsp	**butter**	
⅓	cup	**almonds,** toasted, slivered	Combine with rice and onions; place in baking dish.
1	tsp	**salt**	
1		**pimiento,** chopped fine	
⅓	cup	**parsley,** chopped fine	
12-14		**spinach leaves,** trimmed	Lay on top of rice mixture.
¼	cup	**water**	Pour over all. Bake.

Hillandale Gourmet Club, Trumbull

Fried Rice for Lindsay

With pork, chicken or beef

Serves: 6
Chill: rice
Stir/fry: 5 min
Pan: wok or skillet

3	cups	**rice,** cooked	Chill.
¼	cup	**soy sauce**	Combine in small bowl; set aside.
1½	tsp	**brown sugar**	
2	tsp	**cider vinegar** OR **sherry**	
⅛-¼	tsp	**red pepper,** crushed	
2	Tbsp	**vegetable oil**	Stir/fry (1min) in hot oil.
½	cup	**onions,** chopped	
1	clove	**garlic,** crushed	
2	cups	**chicken, beef** OR **pork,** cooked and cubed	Add, using fork to break up egg as it cooks.
1		**egg,** lightly beaten	
		reserved cold rice	Add; stir/fry (2-3min).
		reserved soy mixture	
1½	cups	**broccoli** (or other green vegetable), cooked (1" pcs)	Add and stir/fry (1min) or until heated through. Serve immediately.

Judy Perkins, Fairfield

Rice
(Portuguese)

Great "red" rice

Serves: 8
Stovetop: 5-8 min
Bake: 350° 35 min
Pan: skillet (lg); casserole (2qt)

| ½ | cup | olive oil |
| 1 | med | onion, chopped fine |

Sauté until tender.

| 2 | cups | rice, raw |
| 1 | can | mushroom caps (8oz) |

Add to above; stir constantly, until lightly browned.

3½-4	cups	water
1	can	tomato sauce (8oz)
1	tsp	salt

Add and stir well; pour into casserole. Bake until tender.

Mrs. Francisco Goncalves, Bridgeport

Rice Pilaf
(Greek)

A tasty tradition

Serves: 6-8
Simmer: 30-40 min
Pan: skillet (lg)

| 4 | tsp | butter |
| 1 | sm | onion, minced |

Sauté until transparent.

2	cups	rice, raw
½	tsp	salt
	dash	pepper

Add to above; stir until coated with butter.

| 4 | cups | chicken OR beef broth (divided) |

Add 2 cups broth. Simmer until liquid is absorbed; add more liquid as necessary until rice is tender.

| | | parsley, chopped |

Garnish.

Gertrud Bargas, Trumbull

Rice Pilaf
(Armenian)

Great instead of potatoes

Serves: 4
Stovetop: 25 min
Pan: saucepan (3qt)

| ½ | cup | butter |
| ½ | cup | noodles, fine, crushed |

In saucepan, melt butter. Add noodles; stir until browned (3-5min).

| 1 | cup | rice, long grain, raw |

Add to above; sauté a few minutes.

| 2 | cups | chicken broth, hot |
| | | salt to taste |

Add to above; bring to a boil. Cover; simmer (15-20min).

Dorothy Noreiks, Stratford

Hawaiian Rice Medley

Pineapple and coconut of the islands

Serves: 6
Stovetop: 20 min
Pan: saucepan (3qt)

1	can	**pineapple chunks,** unsweetened (20oz)
		water

Drain juice into measuring cup; add enough water to make 2½cups. Bring to a boil in large saucepan.

1	cup	**rice,** raw
1	Tbsp	**butter** OR **margarine**
1	tsp	**salt**

Add; stir. Reduce heat; cover and simmer (20min).

reserved pineapple

Stir in; remove from heat. Let stand covered until all liquid is absorbed (5min). When ready to serve, remove to casserole.

¼	cup	**coconut,** toasted

Sprinkle over top. Serve with any meat instead of potato.

Terri Trinkley, Fairfield

Pilau
(India)

Part of an interesting meal

Serves: 4
Soak: 1 hr
Stovetop: 15-20 min
Pan: saucepan (2qt)

1	cup	**rice,** long grain, raw
		water to cover

Soak (1hr); drain.

¼	cup	**butter,** melted
1	tsp	**cumin seeds**
3-4		**cloves,** whole
3		**cinnamon sticks**
2		**bay leaves**
2-3		**cardamon** OR **cumin** seeds

Sauté gently over low heat.

reserved rice

Add; sauté, stirring until light brown.

2	cups	**water**
¼	cup	**green peas**
¼	cup	**carrots,** chopped

Add; bring to a boil.

2	tsp	**salt** (to taste)
1	tsp	**cumin powder**
1	tsp	**coriander powder**
¼	tsp	**turmeric powder**
¼	cup	**raisins**

Add; lower heat. Cover and simmer (15-20min) until rice is cooked. Serve hot.

Kirti Pancholi, No Kingstown, RI

Baked Stuffed Rice
(Italian)

An old family favorite

Serves: 12-16
Bake: 350° 45-60 min
Pans: skillet; 13x9

2⅓	cups	**rice,** par boil, drain
		salt to taste
½	lb	**ground beef,** sautéed
¼	lb	**boiled ham** (1" pcs)
¼	lb	**Genoa salami** (1" pcs)
½	stick	**pepperoni** (1" pcs)
3		**eggs,** hard cooked, sliced
4	oz	**sharp cheddar cheese,** strips
¼-⅓	cup	**Romano cheese,** grated
3	cups	**tomato sauce**

Layers:
Cover bottom of baking dish with to-mato sauce (⅓).
Sprinkle with grated cheese.
Spread rice over cheese (½).
Cover rice with more sauce (⅓).
Sprinkle with grated cheese.
Spread hamburg, ham, salami, pepper-oni, egg slices, over all.
Cover with cheddar strips.
Cover with rice (½).
Cover all rice with sauce (⅓).
Sprinkle with grated cheese.
Cover casserole tightly.
Bake until sauce has been absorbed.

Carole Manjoney, Trumbull

The Best Pasta Yet

Serves: 2-3

2	cups	**flour**
3		**eggs**

Blend well (best in processor) until mixture leaves sides of bowl. Cover and let dough rest (15-20min) before rolling. Roll to thickness desired and cut size desired or use pasta machine. Cook just until tender (3-4min) for fresh or (7-9min) if pasta was allowed to dry.

John Santilli, Fairfield

Mom's Spaghetti Sauce
(Italian)

Great over spaghetti, veal, eggplant—anything Italian

Serves: 8-10
Stovetop: 6 hr
Pan: kettle (6qt)

2	Tbsp	**olive oil**
½	cup	**onions,** chopped
¼	cup	**green pepper,** chopped
2	cloves	**garlic,** pressed
3	links	**Italian sweet sausage**

Sauté in kettle, until vegetables are soft. (Do not use aluminum.)

1	can	**Italian tomatoes,** peeled, mashed (35oz)
1	can	**water,** cold
2	cans	**tomato paste** (6oz,ea)
2	cans	**water**
2	tsp	**salt**
2	tsp	**sugar**
1½	tsp	**rosemary**
⅛	tsp	**black pepper**
¼	tsp	**Italian seasoning**
⅛	tsp	**red pepper flakes**
1	tsp	**oregano**

Add to above; mix well. Bring to a boil on high heat, stirring. When sauce comes to a boil. turn heat to low. Cover and simmer. (Cover can be left ajar a few hours to reduce liquids faster.) Cook until reduced to about half. Freezes well.

Louise Cronan, Trumbull

Mom's Meatballs
(Italian)

Great for pasta or appetizer

Yield: 2-3 doz
Stovetop: 25-35 min
Pan: skillet (10")

½	lb	**ground beef**
½	lb	**ground pork**
¾	cup	**bread crumbs,** Italian
1	Tbsp	**Parmesan cheese,** grated
1	Tbsp	**parsley,** minced
1		**egg,** beaten
1	tsp	**salt**
¼	tsp	**pepper**

Mix well; shape into 2" balls for entrée or ¾" for appetizer.

2	Tbsp	**olive oil**
1	clove	**garlic,** minced

Brown meatballs in skillet with garlic; drain well. Add to spaghetti sauce ½ hour before serving. For appetizer, place meatballs on aluminum foil covered cookie sheet. Bake: 450°, shaking several times to rotate balls until cooked on all sides. Drain well; cover with 1-2 cups your favorite sauce.

Louise Cronan, Trumbull

"Connecticut" Spaghetti Sauce

A great use for those left over meats and gravies

Serves: 10-12
Stovetop: 4-6 hr
Bake: 35-45 min
Pans: kettle (8qt); skillet (lg)

SAUCE

2	Tbsp	**oil**	
2	Tbsp	**butter**	In kettle, sauté gently (1min).
1	lg	**onion,** chopped	
1	clove	**garlic,** crushed (optional)	
1	can	**tomato paste** (6oz)	Add to above; sauté (2-3min) stirring constantly.
2	cups	**water**	Add to above; mix.
1	tsp	**sugar**	
1-2	tsp	**salt**	Add; mix well.
½	tsp	**pepper**	
2	cans	**Italian plum tomatoes** (35oz)	Purée in blender; add to above and mix well. Simmer slowly, uncovered
2	cans	**tomatoes** (25oz)	(2hr); stir occasionally.

MEAT

1		**chicken breast,** whole, bone in, cut into 4-6 pieces
4		**pork country ribs,** cut into serving pieces
8		**sausage links** (your choice flavor)

Bake until browned: 350° (35-45min). Add to sauce after it has been cooking 2-3 hours.

½	cup	**water,** hot

Pour into pan to loosen any bits of meat and juices; add to sauce. Simmer slowly, uncovered (1hr).

MEATBALLS

½	lb	**ground beef** and/or **pork**
½	cup	**bread crumbs**
1	sm	**onion,** chopped
2		**eggs**
¼	cup	**milk**
		salt, pepper to taste

Combine well; form into balls. Sauté until browned; add to sauce. Simmer uncovered (1hr) or until sauce is thick and aromatic. Stir gently to prevent sticking. Serve over your favorite pasta.

Louise Thoman, Trumbull

Manicotti with Cheese Filling

(Italian)

The real thing!

Serves: 12
Stovetop: 15 min
Bake: 350° 45-60 min
Pans: skillet (6"); 13x9

CREPES (12)

1	cup	**flour**
1	cup	**water**
4		**eggs**
¼-½	tsp	**salt**
		vegetable oil

Beat well in mixer or blender. Lightly grease skillet; place on moderate heat. Pour scant ¼ cup batter per crepe. Tip skillet to cover bottom evenly. Cook until lightly browned. Loosen edge with spatula and lift. Turn over; cook other side (30sec). Remove to warm plate. Repeat until all batter is used. Separate each crepe with absorbent or waxed paper.

FILLING

1-2	lb	**Ricotta cheese**
1-2		**eggs**
½	cup	**Romano cheese,** grated
8	oz	**Mozzarella cheese,** shredded
		salt, pepper to taste
2	Tbsp	**parsley,** chopped

Mix thoroughly in large bowl.

tomato sauce, your favorite

Cover bottom of dish with sauce; fill each crepe with 2-3 Tbsp filling. Fold ends over; roll and place over sauce, seam side down. Repeat, filling as many crepes as you need. Cover with tomato sauce. Bake until hot and bubbly. (Unused crepes can be stacked with absorbent or waxed paper, tightly wrapped and frozen.)

Carole Manjoney, Trumbull and
Bernadette Dioguardi, Stratford

FRUITS are great to stimulate an appetite, improve digestion and give variety in your diet. Most nutriments: banana, date, fig, prune and grape.

Lasagne
(Italian)

A truly hearty meal

Serves: 10
Stovetop: 45 min
Bake: 375° 30 min
Pans: saucepan (3qt); 13x9

1	lb	**Italian sweet sausage, bulk** OR (1lb **ground beef**)	Brown slowly; spoon off excess fat. (A combination of these meats can also be used.)
1	clove	**garlic,** minced	
1	Tbsp	**parsley flakes**	
1	Tbsp	**basil**	Add to above; simmer uncovered until thick (35-40min). Stir occasionally.
1½	tsp	**salt**	
2	cups	**tomatoes** (16oz)	
2	cans	**tomato paste** (6oz,ea)	
1	pkg	**lasagne noodles** (10oz)	Cook until just tender. (See Popeye's version for another method.) Drain and rinse in cold water; set aside.
		water, boiling	
		salt	
3	cups	**Ricotta cheese** (12oz) OR 2 ctns **Cottage Cheese,** lg curd, cream style (12oz,ea)	Combine well. Spread small amount of meat/sauce mixture over bottom of baking dish. Cover with ½ of noodles then ½ the cheese mixture.
2		**eggs,** beaten	
2	tsp	**salt**	
½	tsp	**pepper**	
2	Tbsp	**parsley flakes**	
1	lb	**Mozzarella cheese,** sliced thin	Place ½ over top of cheese mixture. Spread ½ of meat/sauce mixture.
½	cup	**Parmesan cheese,** grated	Sprinkle ½ over top. Repeat these layers ending with Parmesan. Bake. Let stand (10-15min) before cutting.

Helen Tucker, Westport

Popeye's Version of Lasagne

Don't cook the noodles, it's great!

Serves: 8-10
Bake: 350° 1 hr 15 min
Pan: 13x9, greased

1½	lb	**cottage cheese,** small curd or **Ricotta cheese**	
1½	cups	**Mozzarella cheese,** shredded (reserve ½ cup)	In large bowl, mix all well.
1		**egg**	
1	pkg	**spinach,** frozen, thawed, chopped and drained	
1	tsp	**salt**	
¾	tsp	**oregano**	
⅛	tsp	**pepper**	
3	jars	**spaghetti sauce** (15½oz,ea) or your favorite	Layers: spread ½ cup sauce over bottom, cover with ⅓ of raw noodles. Spread ½ of cheese mixture. Repeat. Top with remaining noodles then the remaining sauce. Sprinkle with reserved Mozzarella.
8	oz	**lasagne noodles,** uncooked **reserved Mozzarella**	
1	cup	**water**	Pour around edges of pan. Cover tightly with foil. Bake until hot and bubbly then let stand (15min) before serving.

Skillet Lasagne

A great "quick" meal

Serves: 6
Stovetop: 20-30 min
Pan: skillet (12")

10		**lasagne noodles** (8oz)	Cook; rinse and set aside to cool.
1	lb	**ground beef**	Sauté over medium heat until meat is browned (10min).
1	sm	**onion,** minced	
1	jar	**spaghetti sauce** (15oz) (reserve ⅓)	Add your favorite sauce to meat in skillet. Cook until heated through. Remove half of meat mixture to small bowl and keep warm. Reduce heat; continue simmering meat.
15	oz	**Ricotta cheese**	Combine in medium bowl then layer over meat in skillet: spoon ½ Ricotta mixture, ½ noodles, ½ Mozzarella. Repeat then top with reserved ⅓ cup of sauce and Mozzarella on top. Cover; simmer (5min). Serve hot and delicious.
1		**egg**	
¼	tsp	each: **salt, pepper**	
14	oz	**Mozzarella cheese,** shredded	

Gemma Zingo, Bridgeport

Pasta and Cheese Bake

"A great last minute meal"

Serves: 6-8
Bake: see recipe
Pans: skillet (lg); casserole (lg)

2	lb	**ground beef**
2	Tbsp	**oil**

Sauté until browned; drain.

2	med	**onions,** chopped
1	clove	**garlic,** crushed
1	jar	**spaghetti sauce** (14oz)
1	can	**tomatoes,** stewed (16oz)
1	can	**mushrooms,** undrained (3oz)

Add to skillet; simmer (20min). Reserve half.

8	oz	**shell macaroni**

Meanwhile, cook to just tender; drain and rinse with COLD water. Pour ½ into deep casserole; cover with ½ of meat sauce.

1	pt	**sour cream**
8	slices	**Provolone cheese**
8	oz	**Mozzarella cheese,** shredded
		salt, pepper to taste

Layers: ½ of sour cream; top with 4 slices Provolone, ½ Mozzarella. Repeat all layers then cover. Bake: 350° 35-40min. Uncover: Bake 5-10 minutes longer.

Nancy Henry, Fairfield

Salsa Rossae Vongole

(Italian)

red clam sauce with linguini

Serves: 4-6
Stovetop: 15 min
Pans: skillet (med); 13x9

6	oz	**linguini** (see Pasta)	Cook until just tender; set aside.
¼	cup	each: **olive oil** and **butter**	
3	Tbsp	**parsley**, chopped	Sauté on medium heat (2min).
4	cloves	**garlic**, pressed	
3	med	**tomatoes**, fresh, peeled, seeded, chopped	
¼	tsp	**salt**	Add; simmer (10min) stirring occasionally; continue on low heat.
⅛	tsp	**pepper**	
2-3	drops	**hot pepper sauce**	
½	tsp	**oregano**	
4	doz	**hard-shell clams**, chopped OR 1-2 cans **minced clams** with juice (6½oz,ea)	Add clams and juice to above; cook only enough to heat well. Serve hot over linguini.

Hint: Freeze clams ½-1hr before opening. Shells will relax, juices will congeal — no struggle, mess or waste. Save shells, wash, dry, place in plastic bag and use for stuffed clams. Always grease shells before stuffing.

Louise Cronan, Trumbull

Fettucini with Zucchini and Mushrooms

Delicious as vegetable also

Serves: 8
Stovetop: 15-20 min
Pans: kettle (4qt); skillet (lg)

1	lb	**fettucini**	Cook until just tender; drain well.
½	lb	**mushrooms**, fresh, sliced	
3	sm	**zucchini**, unpeeled, sliced thin	Sauté (3min).
¼	cup	**butter** **salt** to taste	
		reserved noodles	
¾	cup	**Parmesan** OR **Romano** **cheese**	Add; cook (1-2min) longer until blended and hot.
½	cup	**parsley**, snipped	

Mary Telford, Trumbull

White Clam Sauce
(Italian)

Appetizer or main dish

Serves: 4
Stovetop: 15-20 min
Pans: saucepan (2qt); kettle (4qt)

2	cans	**clams,** minced (10½oz,ea)	Drain (reserve liquid); set aside.
¼	cup	**butter** OR **margarine**	
1	Tbsp	**onion,** minced	In saucepan, sauté (3min) gently.
1	clove	**garlic,** minced	
2	Tbsp	**flour** (optional)	Sprinkle over top; blend well.
		reserved clam liquid	
¼	cup	**white wine,** dry	
⅓	cup	**parsley,** chopped	Add and simmer, uncovered, (10min).
½	tsp	each: **salt, pepper, oregano**	
		reserved clams	Stir in; heat thoroughly. DO NOT BOIL.
1	lb	**linguini** (see Pasta)	Cook to taste; drain. Pour clam sauce over. Serve piping hot.

Margaret Galluzzo, Bridgeport

Pastitsio
(Greek)

A tasty change from potatoes or rice

Serves: 12
Bake: 375° 45-60 min
Pan: 11x7, buttered

1	lb	**elbow macaroni**	Cook until just tender; remove and drain. Rinse with cold water; place in baking dish.
6		**eggs**	Beat in large bowl.
1	lb	**cottage cheese**	
½	lb	**Feta cheese,** crumbled	
½	lb	**Romano** OR **Parmesan** cheese, grated	Add; mix well. Pour over macaroni. Add 1 cup milk poured evenly over mixture, if sauce does not cover maca-roni.
3	cups	**milk**	
1	cup	**heavy cream**	
1	med	**onion,** chopped (optional)	
1	tsp	each: **salt, pepper**	
½	cup	**butter**	Dot casserole. Bake until lightly browned; remove from oven. Cool (10min); cut into squares.

Lemonia Bargas, Trumbull

Ziti con Salsiccia
(Italian)

Very good and different

Serves: 4
Stovetop: 20 min
Pans: skillet (lg); 2 saucepans
(2qt,ea); kettle (4qt)

1	lb	**ziti**	Boil to desired firmness; set aside.
½	lb	**broccoli**, fresh	Boil until tender-crisp.
¼	lb	**sausage**, sweet or hot (½" slices)	Boil (10min).
⅔	cup	**olive oil** (to taste)	Sauté carefully until lightly browned. Add broccoli and sausage; sauté (3-4min). Drain off oil.
3	cloves	**garlic**, sliced thin	
6	Tbsp	**white wine**	
⅔	cup	**beef broth**	
¼	cup	**butter**	
2-4	Tbsp	**Romano cheese**, grated	Add and sauté (3-4min) longer; serve piping hot.
1-2	Tbsp	**parsley**, chopped	
	pinch	**salt**	
4		**hot cherry peppers**, chopped (optional)	
		reserved pasta	

Florence Massey, Trumbull

Fettucini Alfredo
(Italian)

Your choice entrée or appetizer

Serves: 4
Pans: kettle (6qt); bowl (lg)

1	lb	**fettucini noodles**	Cook according to package directions; drain and pour into warm bowl.
¾	cup	**butter**, melted	Pour over noodles.
2	pt	**heavy cream**	Combine; pour half over noodles and toss. Reserve remaining half.
3		**egg yolks**	
1½	cups	**Parmesan cheese**, grated	Combine; sprinkle half over noodles; toss lightly. Reserve remaining half.
		salt, pepper to taste	
		reserved cream and cheese	Pour over noodles, do not toss.
1	Tbsp	**parsley**, chopped (optional)	Garnish; serve immediately.

Christine Vazzano, Huntington

Cappelletti alla Carbonara

(Italian)

A superb, rich sauce — appetizer or main course

Serves: 4-6
Stovetop: 20-25 min
Pans: skillet (med); kettle (4qt)

¼	lb	**bacon,** lean (1" pcs)	Sauté in skillet until crisp; drain well and set aside. Pour off fat.
3	Tbsp	**olive oil**	Sauté until wilted.
2	med	**onions,** chopped fine	
		salt, pepper (fresh ground, to taste)	Add to skillet; cover and simmer over low heat (5-10min) stirring often.
5	Tbsp	**parsley,** chopped	*If you substitute fontinella cheese, add to sauce during the last minute or two only.
½	cup	**prosciutto ham,** chopped	
½	lb	**fontina cheese*,** diced reserved bacon	
1	pkg	**cappelletti** (pasta)	Cook according to package directions; drain and place in serving bowl.
4		**eggs,** beaten	Add eggs; toss well. Add sauce; toss again. Serve immediately
		Parmesan cheese, grated	Garnish.

Maria DeCesare, Trumbull

Pesto Sauce for Pasta

(Italian)

A great quick meal

Serves: 4
Stovetop: 12-15 min
Pan: kettle (4qt)

1	pkg	**thin spaghetti** OR **noodles** (8oz)	Cook as package directs; drain and keep warm.
1	cup	**parsley,** chopped	Combine thoroughly to make a sauce. Place hot, well drained spaghetti in large bowl. Pour sauce (room temp) over; toss lightly to coat thoroughly. Serve with additional Parmesan to garnish. (To store sauce for several days, cover with thin layer of oil in covered jar; refrigerate. Return to room temperature before using.) Can also be frozen.
1	Tbsp	**basil leaves,** dried	
1	tsp	**salt**	
⅛	tsp	**white pepper**	
2	cloves	**garlic,** crushed	
½	cup	**olive oil**	
2	Tbsp	**butter** OR **margarine**	
2	Tbsp	**water,** boiling	
¾	cup	**Parmesan cheese,** grated	
¼	cup	**walnuts,** chopped fine OR **pine nuts,** whole	

Rose Sayles, Trumbull

Noodle Pudding Kerekes

Super instead of potatoes

Serves: 6
Stovetop: 1½ hr
Pans: saucepan; covered skillet (lg)

5	oz	**egg noodles** (½")	Cook noodles (8min) in boiling salted water; drain, rinse, then return to saucepan.
2	qt	**water,** boiling	
2	tsp	**salt**	
4	Tbsp	**butter,** melted	Stir into noodles.
3		**eggs,** beaten	Combine; mix into noodles to coat well.
¾	tsp	**salt**	
⅛	tsp	**pepper**	
¼	tsp	**nutmeg,** to taste	
1	Tbsp	**butter**	Butter well bottom and sides of skillet. Turn noodles into skillet. Cover; cook over low heat (30min). Slip

spatula around sides and bottom to loosen pudding and prevent possible sticking. Continue to cook until pudding is brown and crisp on underside. Loosen with spatula then turn over to brown other side.

Gemma Zingo, Bridgeport

Denise's Noodle Pudding

(Italian)

Ricotta cheese

Serves: 12
Bake: 350° 1½ hr
Pan: 13x9, greased

6		**eggs,** beaten	Beat together well.
2-3	Tbsp	**vanilla**	
2	cups	**milk,** scalded, cooled	
1½	cups	**sugar**	
3	lb	**ricotta cheese**	Add; mix well.
½	lb	**fine egg noodles**	Cook; drain well, cool; fold into above. Pour into prepared baking pan. Bake until knife inserted in center comes out clean.
		water	
		NO salt	

Denise Pellegrino

Kugel
(Jewish)

Try the whole menu!

Yield: 12 pieces
Stovetop: 15 min
Bake: 375° 40 min
Pans: kettle (4qt); skillet (sm); 13x9,
       greased

½ cup	**onion,** diced	} Brown onion, cool slightly.
¼ cup	**chicken fat** OR **oil**	

3	**eggs,** beaten	} Combine in bowl; add onions. Turn into baking dish. Bake uncovered. Serve as a starch with your meal.
6 cups	**fine noodles,** cooked	

Gail Cohen, Trumbull

Spaetzle
(German)

A delicious noodle

Serves: 4-6
Boil: 5-8 min
Pan: saucepan (3qt)

BATTER

1½ cups	**flour**	} In medium bowl, stir by hand until batter is smooth. It will be thick enough to creep to the edge of the bowl when poured.
2	**eggs**	
½ tsp	**salt**	
½ cup	**water**	

2 qt	**water,** boiling	} In saucepan, heat water. Tip bowl so batter comes to the edge. Cut ½ tsp batter off with a sharp knife letting it drop into the boiling water. Repeat until half
2 tsp	**salt**	

the batter has been used. (Dip knife into boiling water frequently to prevent sticking.) Boil gently (5-8min); remove to a warm bowl. Repeat with other half; drain well.

¼ cup	**butter,** melted, lightly browned	Pour over Spaetzle and mix gently. Serve hot.

Hint: These noodles should be light and fluffy. Test the first ones. If they are not, add a small amount of water to lighten the batter. Can be used as noodles in soup.

Florence Cummings, Trumbull

Desserts

YANKEE FARE
Apple Fritters
Hearty Fish Chowder
Haddock Bake
Corn Pudding
Green Peas
Indian Pudding

A NEW ENGLAND SUPPER
Tomato Relish and a Cottage Cheese
Tray
Ham-Pork Loaves
Sliced Cucumbers and Tomatoes
Harvest Bounty Casserole
Blueberry Buckle

MORE YANKEE FARE
Tomato Juice Toddy
Lobster Stew
Basic White Bread Plus
Tomato-Cucumber Salad
Kyle's Apple Pie a la Mode

A SOUTHERN DINNER
Jazzland Crabmeat Balls
Southerner's Shrimp Stew
Rice
Collards or Mixed Greens
Bishop Whipple Pudding

Ambrosia

A summer favorite

Serves: 8
Chill: several hours

1	can	**pineapple chunks,** halved (20oz)	
2	cans	**mandarin oranges** (11oz,ea)	Drain; place in medium bowl.
1	cup	**maraschino cherries**	
1½	cups	**marshmallows**	Add.
1	cup	**coconut**	
1	cup	**sour cream**	Fold in just enough to blend. Pour into serving bowl; chill.
		mint leaves	Garnish.

Anne Mercurio, Stratford

Hot Applesauce & Fruit Compote

A yummy fruit dessert

Serves: 8-10
Bake: 350° 1 hr
Pan: baking dish (3qt)

1	jar	**applesauce,** divided (20oz)	Spread half over bottom of baking dish.
1	can	**apricot halves** (20oz)	
1	can	**pineapple,** crushed (20oz)	
1	can	**peaches,** sliced (20oz)	Drain; layer over above in order listed. Cover with reserved applesauce. Bake. Serve hot.
1	can	**pitted cherries,** dark (16oz)	
1	pkg	**raspberries,** frozen, thawed (10oz)	

Avor Breiner, Trumbull

 PINEAPPLE should look fresh, have an orange-yellow color, be fragrant, be heavy and the leaves should pull out easily.

Cold Fruit Compote

Flavors improve with time

Serves: 8-10
Chill: 2-7 days
Pans: saucepan (2qt);
refrigerator container

1	can	each:**apricot halves, peach halves, pine-apple chunks, pear slices** (8oz,ea)

Drain syrup into saucepan. Place fruit in refrigerator container.

1	cup	**sugar**
1-2	Tbsp	**lemon juice** (to taste)
½	tsp	**lemon rind,** grated

Add to syrup; bring to a boil, then simmer (20min). Remove from heat.

½	tsp	**vanilla**

Add to above; cool. Pour syrup over fruit. Refrigerate, covered, up to a week.

1	cup	**strawberries,** fresh or frozen, halved
1	cup	**blueberries,** fresh or frozen

When ready to serve, add berries to refrigerated fruits. Serve over ice cream, sherbert, or frozen yogurt.

Cornelia Brown, Weston

Pastel de Manzana
(Spanish)

A delightful taste of apples & mint

Serves: 6
Bake: 350° 45 min
Pan: 8x8, well buttered

1	cup	**sugar**
1	cup	**flour**
½	tsp	**baking powder**

Sift into mixing bowl; form a well.

1		**egg**

Drop into above. Mix only until egg is absorbed; set aside.

2	lb	**apples,** tart cooking, peeled, sliced (¼")

Place in large mixing bowl.

1	Tbsp	**mint leaves,** dried, crushed
1	Tbsp	**cinnamon**

Mix; toss with apples until coated. Arrange in baking dish.

reserved flour mix

Scatter over apples. Spread and press gently to form a smooth layer covering the apples completely. Bake until top is crusty; cover and set aside to cool. Serve at room temp.

1	cup	**cream** (optional)

Whip then garnish.

Hillandale Gourmet Club, Trumbull

Bananas Bernard

Rich and tasty

Serves: 2-4
Bake: 350° 30 min
Pan: 11x7, buttered

2		bananas, green tipped
2	Tbsp	honey
2	Tbsp	butter

Peel; roll in honey until coated. Place in baking dish. Dot with butter. Bake until tender, puffy and brown.

½-1	cup	thick coconut cream

Mix well; spoon over top of hot bananas. Bake (2-3min). Serve hot. (Can use home-made cream or commercial.)

Eddy Bernard, Trumbull

Creamy Blueberry Squares

A very versatile dessert

Yield: 36 (1x3)
Stovetop: 5 min
Chill: overnight
Pans: saucepan (med); 13x9, foil lined

¼	cup	cornstarch
½	cup	sugar
½	cup	water
3	cups	blueberries, rinsed, drained

Combine in saucepan; cook, stirring until sauce bubbles and thickens. Set aside to cool.

1	pkg	graham crumbs (13½oz)
¾	cup	butter OR margarine, melted

Combine and set aside.

16	oz	cream cheese, softened
1½	cups	sugar
2	tsp	vanilla

Combine well.

18	oz	frozen whipped topping, thawed

Fold into cheese mixture; set aside.

Layers: (1) press ½ graham crumb mixture into bottom of pan.
(2) Spread ½ of cheese mixture.
(3) Gently spoon all of blueberry mixture.
(4) Spread ½ of cheese mixture.
(5) Top with remaining ½ of crumb mixture. Chill overnight. Use foil to raise dessert from pan; place on platter and cut into squares.

VARIATION: canned pie filling (any flavor) can be substituted for blueberries.

Mary Hudak, Easton

Fruit Dessert Pizza

Different and yummy

Serves: 10-12
Bake: see recipe
Chill: few hours
Pan: pizza or flan ring (12")

		favorite pastry (cookie, flan, butter-crust, etc.)	Roll to 14" circle. Place in pan; flute edges and prick well. Bake: 350° (15-20 min) to set only.
16	oz	**cream cheese**	Blend well.
¾	cup	**sugar**	
3		**eggs**	Add; beat well.
½	cup	**nuts**, chopped	Add; pour into partially baked shell. Bake: 350° (10min); cool.
1	tsp	**vanilla**	
2	cans	**cherry** OR **strawberry pie filling** (21oz,ea)	Spoon over cheese layer; chill.
1	pt	**whipping cream** (optional)	Whip; decorate then chill. To serve, cut in wedges.

Helene Liolin, Fairfield

Cherry Nightingale

Rich, light, delicious

Serves: 9
Chill: 24 hr
Pan: 8x8

1	cup	**maraschino cherries,** halved	Drain well; set aside.
¾	cup	**pineapple**	
¾	box	**vanilla wafers,** crushed	Spread ½ in pan (reserve half).
1	cup	**butter**, softened	Beat well with electric mixer.
1	cup	**confectioners' sugar**	
2		**eggs**	Add, one at a time, beating well after each addition. Spoon over crumbs; spread to edges with knife. Chill (2hr).
1	cup	**heavy cream** reserved fruit	Whip cream; fold in fruit and nuts. Spoon carefully over egg mixture.
½	cup	**walnuts**, chopped	
		reserved crumbs	Sprinkle over top. Chill (24hr).

Erica Byron, Stratford

Cherry Cream Crunch

A new twist in cherry desserts

Serves: 9-12
Bake: see recipe
Chill: thoroughly
Pan: 12x8

CRUST

1	cup	**flour**
½	cup	**brown sugar**, firmly packed
½	cup	**butter**, softened
½	tsp	**salt**
½	tsp	**cinnamon**
1	tsp	**vanilla**

In large mixer bowl, mix until well blended.

1	cup	**coconut**, flaked or shredded
½	cup	**oatmeal**, quick
½	cup	**nuts**, chopped

Stir into above; press 2½ cups over bottom of ungreased baking dish. (Reserve remainder for topping.) Bake: 375° (12min).

LEMON FILLING

1	can	**sweetened condensed milk** (14oz)
2		**eggs**
4	tsp	**lemon peel**, grated
¼	cup	**lemon juice**
¼	tsp	**salt**

Mix in small bowl until slightly thickened. Spread over baked crust.

1	can	**cherry pie filling** (21oz)

Spread over above.

reserved crumbs

Sprinkle over top. Bake: 375°(15-18min) until lightly browned. Chill thoroughly before serving. Spoon into sherbet glasses for a pretty as well as tasty dessert.

Hillandale Gourmet Club, Trumbull

Date Roll

"A holiday tradition at our house"

Serves: 6
Chill: several hours

12		**graham crackers,** crushed (reserve 2Tbsp)
1	pkg	**dates,** cut up (8oz)
14	lg	**marshmallows,** cut up OR 1 cup small marshmallows
1	cup	**nuts,** chopped, coarse
½	cup	**light cream** (or milk)

Mix; shape into roll and sprinkle with reserved crumbs. Wrap in waxed paper; refrigerate. To serve, top with whipped cream or vanilla ice cream.

Jane Fulton, Trumbull

Southern Baked Alaska

Grapefruit served hot and so delicious

Serves: 6
Bake: 500° 1 min
Pan: 13x9

3		**grapefruits**

Chill. Section and remove membranes; return sections to shells. Set aside.

MERINGUE

3		**egg whites**
⅛	tsp	**salt**

In medium bowl, beat until frothy.

6	Tbsp	**sugar**
½	tsp	**vanilla**

Add to above gradually; beat until peaks form. Set aside.

1	pt	**vanilla ice cream**

Place 1 scoop over grapefruit sections in each shell; cover with meringue. Bake.

Suggestion: fruit and meringue can be prepared ahead and refrigerated until ready to assemble. Can section 1 extra grapefruit; dividing equally for larger portions.

Christine Vazzano, Huntington

 MERINGUE – for a HIGH, fluffy, dry meringue add 1 Tbsp sugar to each egg white. For a SWEETER, more flavorful, less fluffy meringue add 2-3 Tbsp sugar to each egg white. Bake at a low oven temperature or it will be tough and will shrink. 1 tsp of cold water added for each white will help it to whip better and make more meringue. Grated orange peel can be added for a nice delicate flavor. A pinch of baking soda will help it to stand high. ¼ tsp cream of tartar will help keep it nice and firm.

Peach Cobbler

One of the delights of the summer

Serves: 6
Bake: 400° 25-30 min
Pans: saucepan (2qt); casserole (2qt)

¼	cup	**sugar**	} In saucepan, mix together.
1	Tbsp	**cornstarch**	
½	tsp	**cinnamon**	

| 4 | cups | **peaches**, fresh, sliced | } Add to above; mix. Cook, stirring until mixture thickens and boils. Cook (1min) longer, stirring continuously. Pour into casserole and keep warm. |
| 1 | tsp | **lemon juice** | |

TOPPING

| 1 | cup | **flour** | } Cut shortening into flour until mixture resembles fine crumbs. |
| 3 | Tbsp | **shortening** | |

1	Tbsp	**sugar**	} Add to above.
1½	tsp	**baking powder**	
½	tsp	**salt**	

| ½ | cup | **milk** | Add; stir only until flour is moistened. Drop 6 rounded Tbsp onto hot peach mixture. Bake until topping is golden. |

CINNAMON WHIPPED CREAM

3	Tbsp	**sugar**	} Chill bowl and beaters. Whip cream; add sugar and cinnamon. Spoon over warm cobbler.
½	tsp	**cinnamon**	
1	cup	**whipping cream**	

Laura Biasucci, Derby

Liebesbirnen

(German)

Love pears

Serves: 8
Stovetop: 10-15 min
Pan: saucepan (2qt)

4	med	**pears**, fresh, peeled, halved, cored	} Combine; simmer until cooked but not soft. Cool in the wine. When cooled, drain pears (reserve juice). Chill pears.
1	cup	**white wine**	
¼	cup	**sugar**	

| 8 | | **shortcake rounds** | Moisten with reserved juice. |
| | | **currant jelly** | Spread over shortcakes. Place 1 pear half on each cake, cut side up. |

| ½ | pt | **cream**, whip | } Mix; place dollop in cavity of each pear. Serve. |
| ½-1 | tsp | **sugar** | |

Gertrud Bargas, Trumbull

Apple Walnut Cobbler

Great use for those tangy fall apples

Serves: 8
Bake: 325° 55 min
Pan: 8" round, greased

4	cups	**apples,** peeled, sliced (¼")	Place in baking dish.
½	cup	**sugar**	
½	tsp	**cinnamon**	Sprinkle over apples; set aside.
½	cup	**nuts,** chopped	
1	cup	**flour**	
1	cup	**sugar**	Sift together in medium bowl; set
1	tsp	**baking powder**	aside.
¼	tsp	**salt**	
1		**egg,** well beaten	Combine; add all at once to above and
½	cup	**evaporated milk**	mix just until smooth; pour over
⅓	cup	**butter,** melted	apples.
¼	cup	**nuts,** chopped	Sprinkle over top. Bake. Serve with cinnamon whipped cream (see Index), ice cream, fresh fruit or a dollop of your favorite preserves.

Lillian Thiede, Stratford

Baked Pineapple

A great non-sweet treat

Serves: 6
Bake: 350° 40 min
Pan: 8x8, buttered

2½	cups	**pineapple,** crushed	
½	lb	**cheddar cheese,** grated	
¾	cup	**sugar**	Mix; pour into prepared dish.
2	Tbsp	**flour**	
½	tsp	**salt** (optional)	
2-3	Tbsp	**breadcrumbs,** buttered	Sprinkle over top. Bake.

Teresa Callan, Trumbull

Pineapple Dessert

As refreshing as the tropics!

Serves: 10-12
Bake: 325° 30 min
Pan: 13x9

42		**Waverly Wafers** (each wafer counts as 3), crushed fine	Combine; spread in pan. Pat down lightly.
½	cup	**butter**, softened	
4		**egg whites** (reserve yolks)	Beat whites; add sugar gradually. Beat until stiff peaks form. Spread over crust. Bake, then cool.
1	cup	**sugar**	

FILLING

1	can	**pineapple**, crushed (16oz)	Combine and cook over medium heat until thickened; cool and spread over crust.
1	Tbsp	**sugar***	
		reserved egg yolks	*Unsweetened pineapple, use 2 Tbsp.
1	Tbsp	**cornstarch**	
	pinch	**salt**	
		whipped topping (8oz) OR **whipped cream** (1pt)	Garnish.

Marion Bender, Trumbull

Ice Box Cake

Easy and tasty too

Serves: 12
Chill: 8-9 hr
Pan: 8x8 or 9x9

1	cup	**butter**, unsalted	Cream until fluffy.
1	cup	**confectioners' sugar**	
2		**eggs**	Add, one at a time.
1		**lemon, juice of**	Add, while beating constantly, until light.
1		**orange, juice of**	
2	doz	**lady fingers**, split	Line pan with ⅓ of lady fingers. Spread ½ mixture over them. Repeat ending with remaining lady fingers. Chill. Serve with whipped cream and strawberries or any fresh fruit.

Jessie MacLennan, Merrillville, In

Grandma's Chocolate Ice Box Cake

Great for Passover too

Serves: 10-12
Chill: overnight
Pan: spring form

2-3 pkg	**lady fingers,** plain	Line pan, sides and bottom; set aside.
4 squares	**bitter chocolate**	Melt, stirring constantly until very thick.
1 cup	**milk**	
1 cup	**sugar**	Add to above and continue to stir until thick again. Remove from heat. Allow to cool.
4	**eggs,** separated (reserve whites)	Add yolks one at a time. Mix in well.
	reserved egg whites	Beat until stiff then fold into chocolate mixture.
1 tsp	**vanilla**	Mix into above. Pour half over lady fingers in pan.
	remaining lady fingers	Arrange over filling then add remaining filling. Chill overnight.
1 cup	**cream,** whipped	Top just before serving.

PASSOVER: Prepare sponge cake by cutting off top, hollow out cake leaving shell. Fill with ½ of chocolate mixture; replace cake parts gently. Replace top; pour 2nd half of chocolate filling over top. Chill.

Chris Henschel, Fairfield

Summer Dessert for a Crowd

Easily prepared ahead of time

Serves: 24-36
Bake: 350° 20 min
Chill: overnight
Pan: 13x9, greased

1	can	**pineapple,** crushed (20oz)	Drain thoroughly; eliminate grapes. Set aside.
1	can	**fruit cocktail** (30oz)	
3		**egg whites**	Combine in large bowl; beat until foamy.
½	tsp	**baking powder**	
1	cup	**sugar** (scant)	Gradually beat into egg whites. Continue beating until stiff glossy peaks form.
40		**Ritz crackers,** crushed fine	Fold into meringue; mix well. Spread into prepared pan. Bake. Cool on rack to room temperature.
1	cup	**walnuts** OR **pecans,** ground	
8	oz	**cream cheese,** softened	Beat cheese until light.
9	oz	**frozen whipped topping,** thawed	Fold into cream cheese along with reserved fruit. Spread over cooled crust.
		coconut, (optional) (3½oz)	If desired, sprinkle over above. Cover; refrigerate overnight. Cut in squares to serve.

VARIATION: Squares of dessert may be placed in paper muffin cups, overwrapped with freezer wrapping and frozen till needed. Thaw in refrigerator 3 hours before serving.

Shirley Martikainen, Stratford

Spiced Prunes

With a cookie – delicious and healthful

Yield: 1 qt
Simmer: 10-15 min
Pan: saucepan (3qt)

1	lb	**prunes,** pitted	Combine in saucepan.
3-4		**lemon slices**	
1½	cups	**water**	
1	stick	**cinnamon**	Tie in cheesecloth; add to above. Cover and simmer until cooked. Remove from heat and discard spices.
1	tsp	**allspice,** whole	
½	tsp	**cloves,** whole	
2	Tbsp	**lemon juice**	Add to above; serve hot or cold.
½	cup	**brown sugar** (optional)	

Chris Henschel, Fairfield

Pineapple-Cheese Baklava

A very special dessert

Serves: 10-12
Bake: 350° 50 min
Pan: pyrex 13x9, well buttered;
saucepan (1qt)

1	can	**crushed pineapple,** in syrup (20oz)	Drain (reserve ½ cup syrup). Set pineapple aside.
8	oz	**cream cheese,** softened	
1	cup	**ricotta cheese**	
½	cup	**sugar**	Blend then stir in pineapple; set aside.
2		**egg yolks**	
1	tsp	**lemon peel,** grated	
1	tsp	**vanilla**	
½	lb	**phyllo pastry leaves**	Wrap in waxed paper; place between damp towels to prevent drying.
½	cup	**butter,** melted, clarified	Place 1 leaf of phyllo on bottom of baking dish; brush with butter. Repeat with 3 more leaves. Spread the pineapple-cheese mixture over evenly. Top with 4 more phyllo leaves, buttering each. Mark pastry into diamond shapes with point of sharp knife by carefully cutting through to filling. Bake until golden brown. Cool slightly placing pan on wire rack.
		reserved pineapple syrup	Cook until thickened; spoon, while hot, over baked baklava. Cool, then cut into diamonds. Can be served warm or cool.
½	cup	**sugar**	
1	tsp	**lemon juice**	

Doris Hadad, Trumbull

Baklava

(Greek)

A very rich traditional dessert

Yield: 36 pieces
Bake: 325° 1 hr
Pan: 11x7, buttered

1	pkg	**phyllo,** frozen (1lb)	Defrost; wrap well in damp towel to prevent drying.

SYRUP

1	cup	**water**
3	cups	**sugar**
1	Tbsp	**lemon juice,** fresh
½		**orange,** sliced
1	stick	**cinnamon**
6	whole	**cloves**

Combine in saucepan; bring to a boil. Simmer (10min); strain and set aside.

LAYERS

1	lb	**sweet butter,** melted
		phyllo leaves

Place 1st sheet on bottom of buttered pan. Brush top lightly with butter. Repeat, using 10 sheets.

½	lb	**almonds,** chopped
½	lb	**walnuts,** chopped
½	tsp	**cinnamon**
1	tsp	**cloves,** ground

Mix; sprinkle ⅓ evenly over top phyllo layer. Add 5 more sheets buttering each. Add ⅓ of nut mixture. Add 5 more sheets, buttering each. Add remaining ⅓ of nut mixture. Add remaining phyllo leaves, buttering each. Cut diagonally across, making diamond shaped pieces, with a sharp knife. Bake until golden. Remove from oven and cool in pan.

reserved syrup

Pour over top then let cool. Serve from pan at room temperature.

Lemonia Bargas, Trumbull

Mazurek Orzechowy

(Polish)

Walnut-meringue waffle Easter tradition

Serves: 4-6
Bake: 325° 20 min
Pan: double boiler

Your favorite waffles for 4 or 6 people.

5		**egg whites,** beaten stiff
2	cups	**confectioners' sugar**

Combine in bowl of double boiler. Cook over boiling water, beating continuously until mixture thickens.

2	Tbsp	**honey**
1½	cups	**walnuts,** ground (5oz)
¼	tsp	**vanilla**

Add to above and stir until smooth. Spread over oplatek or waffle up to one inch in thickness. Bake.

Pat McCathron, Trumbull

Bunuelos de Viento

(Puerto Rican)

Fried "balloons" with syrup

Yield: 4-5 doz
Stovetop: see recipe
Pans: 2 saucepans (2qt); Dutch oven

| 3½ | cups | **flour** | } | Make a paste in saucepan. |
| 3 | cups | **water** | | |

| 2 | Tbsp | **butter** | Add to above; work in well. Cook (5-8min) stirring constantly. Remove from fire; cool. |

| 12 | | **eggs** | Add one at a time stirring in well after each addition. Stir well until it forms a soft paste. |

| | | **shortening** for frying | Drop by spoonful into hot fat. Turn only once. Remove when golden brown. |

SYRUP

| 2 | cups | **sugar** | } | In saucepan, over medium heat, stir until sugar is dissolved then simmer until "syrup" consistency (10min). Do not stir or it will crystalize. Pour over "bunuelos" when ready to serve. |
| 1 | cup | **water** | | |

Barbara Schegg, Huntington

Crêpes Suzettes

Butter-rich orange filling melts out ready for flaming

Serves: 4-6
Stovetop: ½ min ea side
Pans: skillet (6"); chafing dish

Prepare 8-12 of your favorite crêpes or (see Index).

FILLING

| ½ | cup | **butter** OR **margarine,** softened | } | Cream until fluffy. |
| 1 | cup | **confectioners' sugar** | | |

| 3 | Tbsp | **orange flavored liqueur** (Cointreau, Curacao, Triple Sec) | } | Blend in (mixture will be thick). Spread 1 Tbsp on each crêpe; fold into quarters. Arrange in chafing dish in a circle; refrigerate. |
| 2 | tsp | **orange rind,** grated | | |

| ¼ | cup | **brandy,** warmed | When ready to serve, heat over low heat until filling starts to melt and flow out. Drizzle brandy over top and ignite. Serve. |

Odette Renner, Trumbull

Cream Cake
(Norwegian)

A celebration cake

Serves: 10
Chill: 1-2 days

2		**8 or 9" yellow layer cakes** OR **9" sponge cake**	Split into 4 layers.
1	can	**pineapple, crushed, drained well** (16oz)	Fruit: remove ¼ cup for garnish. Juice: pour into small bowl.
4	Tbsp	**sherry** reserved juice	Add to pineapple juice and mix. Pour over each cake layer to moisten well; set aside.

PINEAPPLE FILLING

1	cup	**heavy cream**	Beat well.
2	Tbsp	**sugar** drained pineapple	Add to cream and mix well; set aside.

WALNUT FILLING

1	cup	**heavy cream**	Beat well.
2	Tbsp	**sugar**	Add to cream and mix well. To assemble, alternate these 2 layers of filling starting with pineapple, covering each cake layer well. Refrigerate at least overnight but best 2 days.
½	cup	**walnuts,** chopped	

FROSTING

2	cups	**heavy cream**	Beat until thick.
4	Tbsp	**sugar**	Add; mix well. Frost cake, top and sides, shortly before serving.
		reserved pineapple **fruit, nuts** (optional)	Garnish. Strawberries can be substituted for pineapple.

Ginny Bergethon, Trumbull

MILK – to whip evaporated milk, milk, bowl and beaters must be thoroughly chilled. It also helps to set bowl in a bowl of cracked ice. Evaporated milk scalded in double boiler (5-10min) then chilled quickly is easier to whip. 2 Tbsp lemon juice added helps the flavor, makes the cream more permanent.

Easy but Special Mocha

"Anything this fattening should be harder to make"

Serves: 12-15
Bake: 350° 20 min
Chill: several hours
Pan: 13x9

1	cup	**flour**	} Cut in.
½	cup	**margarine**	

| 1½ | cups | **peanuts,** chopped fine (reserve ½ cup) | Stir into above; press over bottom of pan. Bake. |

| 16 | oz | **cream cheese,** softened | In small bowl, beat on low speed until light and fluffy. |

| 2 | cups | **confectioners' sugar,** sifted | } Beat in sugar and 4 oz whipped topping. Spread over crust; chill. |
| 8 | oz | **whipped topping,** thawed (reserve ½) | |

1	pkg	**instant chocolate pudding** (4oz)	} Beat well in large mixer bowl (2-3min). Spoon over cream cheese layer. Chill until firm (several hr).
1	pkg	**instant coffee pudding** (4oz) OR (2 pkg chocolate)	
3	cups	**milk**	

| | | reserved peanuts reserved topping | } Garnish. |

Esther Sayles, Bridgeport

Rainbow Torte

Best when prepared a day ahead

Serves: 10
Chill: overnight
Pan: spring form (9")

1	pkg	**black cherry gelatin** OR **orange** (3oz)	} Add 1½ cups water to each package. Make separately. Chill overnight.
1	pkg	**lemon gelatin** (3oz)	
1	pkg	**lime gelatin** (3oz) **water,** hot	

| 1 | pkg | **gelatin, unflavored** | } Soften gelatin in water. |
| ½ | cup | **water,** cold | |

| 1 | cup | **pineapple juice,** hot | Add gelatin; mix to dissolve then let cool well. |

2	cups	**cream,** medium	} Whip together; fold in gelatin mixture. Unmold the 3 flavors of gelatin; cube. Carefully blend into cream.
1	tsp	**vanilla**	
½	cup	**sugar**	
24		**graham crackers,** crushed	Line pan with crumbs (reserve some for topping). Pour torte into pan; chill thoroughly.

Gloria DeCarli, Trumbull

302   Desserts – Confections

Cherry Torte Glacé

Elegant, luscious, special

Serves: 10-12
Bake: 375° 30-35 min
Pan: round (10") OR tube (10"),
    greased

TORTE

2	cans	**cherries,** sour, pitted (1lb,ea)	Drain; chop; set aside. Reserve syrup.
6	Tbsp	**butter**	In mixing bowl, cream well adding sugar gradually.
1½	cups	**sugar**	
2		**eggs,** beaten	Add to above.
1½	cups		
+ 2	Tbsp	**flour**	Sift together; add to creamed mixture alternately with chopped cherries.
½	tsp	**baking powder**	
¾	tsp	**baking soda**	
⅛	tsp	**salt**	
1	cup	**walnuts,** chopped	Fold into above; turn into greased pan. Bake. Cool on rack (5min) then remove from pan. Cool completely; spread with topping.

TOPPING

1½	tsp	**unflavored gelatin**	Soften gelatin in measuring cup. Set cup in pan of hot water, stirring until gelatin is dissolved; cool slightly.
2	Tbsp	**water,** cold	
1	cup	**heavy cream**	Beat until stiff; gradually beat gelatin into cream. Spread over cooled cake as smoothly as possible; refrigerate while making glaze.

GLAZE

1	cup	**reserved syrup**	
½	cup	**sugar**	Combine in saucepan; cook, stirring, until transparent. Cool, stirring frequently until almost cold. Spread on cake, covering most of whipped cream.
2	Tbsp		
+½	tsp	**cornstarch**	
½	tsp	**red food coloring** (optional)	

Diane Gorman, Trumbull

Meringue Torte
(Swedish)

Serves: 8
Bake: 300° 35 min
Pans: 2 (9") springform, greased, floured

Make cake ahead then fill and assemble just before serving

¼	cup	**margarine**	} Cream together.
½	cup	**sugar**	
4		**eggs,** separated (reserve whites)	Add yolks, one at a time, to above stirring after each addtion.
½	cup	**flour**	} Mix together.
1½	tsp	**baking powder**	
¼	cup	**milk**	Add alternately with flour; divide and spread into two prepared pans (batter need not reach to edge).
1	cup	**walnuts,** chopped	Sprinkle over batter in pans.

MERINGUE

		reserved egg whites	Beat until foamy with mixer at high speed.
¾	cup	**sugar**	Gradually add to egg whites, beating constantly, until meringue is formed. Spread meringue over chopped nuts. Bake. Cool.

TOPPING

			Beat together until stiff. Invert one layer on plate, meringue side down. Spread cream. Place other cake on top with meringue facing up. Vanilla, almond or anise flavoring can be added for variation. Chill if not served immediately.
1	cup	**heavy cream,** whip	}
1-2	Tbsp	**confectioners' sugar**	

Kerstin Nilson, Trumbull

ANOTHER TOPPING

1	pt	**heavy cream,** whip	} Prepare cakes as directed above. Spread one with cream then cover with a layer of pineapple. Cover with second layer of cake. Chill.
½	can	**pineapple,** crushed, drained (8oz)	

Nancy Henry, Fairfield

Hazelnut Torte

Rich and delicious

Serves: 10-12
Bake: 300° 35 min
Pan: 2 cake pans (8"), removeable
bottoms, buttered, floured

MERINGUE LAYERS

5		**eggs**, separated (reserve yolks)	Beat whites until stiff.
¾	cup	**sugar**	Fold into above; spread in prepared
1½	cups	**hazelnuts** OR **filberts**, ground	pans. Bake. Remove from pans while warm; let cool. (Layers will be thin.)
3	Tbsp	**cocoa**	

BUTTERCREAM FROSTING

		reserved egg yolks	Heat in saucepan, stirring constantly
⅔	cup	**sugar**	until thickened. DO NOT BOIL. Re-
½	cup	**light cream**	move from heat; stir until lukewarm.
⅔	cup	**butter**, unsalted	Melt together; add to above. Refriger-
3½	oz	**unsweetened chocolate**	ate until spreading consistency. Spread between layers, on top and sides.
		almonds, blanched, flaked, toasted	Garnish. Torte will be 2" thick when completed.

Teresa Frillici, Fairfield

Ruggelah
(Jewish)

A nice ending to a traditional meal

Serves: 8-10
Chill: 1 hr
Pan: cookie sheet, lightly greased

PASTRY

2	cups	**flour**	
2	tsp	**baking powder**	
¾	cup	**sugar**	
2	Tbsp	**vegetable shortening** (heaping)	
2		**eggs,** beaten	Mix; divide into 3 pieces. Chill (1hr); roll each into a long rectangle.
1	tsp	**vanilla**	
	pinch	**salt**	
½		**orange,** juice of and rind	
½		**lemon, juice of and rind**	

FILLING

	jelly (your favorite)	Spread over each rectangle.
	raisins, chopped **nuts,** chopped **coconut, cinnamon** to taste	Sprinkle over jelly; roll each as for jelly roll, starting with long side. Place on cookie sheet, seam side down. Make indentations where slices will be made after baking. Bake. Slice while warm.

Gail Cohen, Trumbull

Chocolate Cheesecake

Chocolate lovers beware

Serves: 20-25
Bake: 350° 50 min
Chill: overnight
Pan: spring form (12")

2	pkg	**chocolate wafer cookies** (8½oz,ea)	Crush well.
½	tsp	**cinnamon**	Add to above. Press firmly into bottom and sides of pan; chill.
½	cup	**butter,** melted	
1	cup	**sugar**	Beat until light and fluffy.
4		**eggs**	
1½	lb	**cream cheese,** softened	Add to above gradually; beat well after each addition.
16	oz	**semi-sweet chocolate,** melted	Add to above.
1	tsp	**vanilla**	Add, beating continuously.
2	Tbsp	**cocoa**	
3	cups	**sour cream**	
¼	cup	**butter,** unsalted, melted	Add; mix well. Pour into shell. Bake; cool then refrigerate. Remove from refrigerator 1 hour before serving.

Cheesecake with Sour Cream Topping

A very nice small sized treat

Serves: 6-8
Bake: see recipe
Pan: 8" layer cake

CRUST

1	cup	Zwieback crumbs (12pcs)
¼	cup	sugar
½	tsp	cinnamon
4	Tbsp	butter, melted

Combine all ingredients. Processor works well for this. Press firmly over bottom and sides of pan; chill.

FILLING

½	cup	sugar
1	inch	lemon wedge, seeded, diced

Process until lemon is very fine.

2		eggs
½	cup	lt cream OR half and half
½	tsp	vanilla
⅛	tsp	salt
1½	cups	cottage cheese OR cream cheese (12oz)
2	Tbsp	flour

Add to above and process (30sec) or beat until very smooth. Pour into crust. Bake: 325° 45-50 min, only until set. Do not overbake.

TOPPING

1	cup	sour cream
1-2	Tbsp	sugar
¼	tsp	vanilla (optional)

Combine; spread gently and evenly over hot cheesecake. Return to oven (5min). Cool then chill. Remove from refrigerator one half hour before serving. Can be served topped with fresh or frozen strawberries lightly sweetened.

Carol Caputa, Huntington

Place oranges or grapefruit in hot oven before peeling – no white fiber will remain on fruit.

Store fresh limes in covered jar in refrigerator.

Steffie's Best Cheesecake

Large and delicious

Serves: 15
Bake: see recipe
Pan: 10" spring form

CRUST

		Zwieback crust (see Index)	Grease sides of pan only. Press crust into bottom of pan.

FILLING

1½	lb	cream cheese	Beat until fluffy.
1	lb	cottage cheese	
1½	cups	sugar	
1	pt	sour cream	Add to above; mix well. Bake: 350° (1hr), then 375° (5min). Turn off heat and leave cake in oven 1 hour longer with door open.
	pinch	salt	
1	Tbsp	vanilla	
4		eggs	
3	Tbsp	flour, sifted	

Jean Brauer, Monroe

Creamy Cheesecake

"Easy to prepare and excellent"

Serves: 10-12
Bake: see recipe
Pan: 9" spring form

1		Graham Cracker Crust (see Index)	Pat over bottom and sides of pan.
2½	lb	cream cheese, softened	Beat in large bowl, until fluffy.
1½	cups	sugar	
2	Tbsp	flour	Add to above; beat until smooth.
⅛	tsp	salt	
5		eggs, whole	Add one at a time.
2		egg yolks	
½	cup	heavy cream	Add to above; beat well. Pour into pan. Bake: 475° (10min) then 225° (1hr). Turn off oven; open door and let cake sit (15 min) before removing. Cool thoroughly then refrigerate until ready to use.
1	tsp	vanilla	

Jeanne Elsasser, Fairfield

Strawberry-Rhubarb Cheesecake

Elegant and worth the effort

Serves: 12
Bake: 375° 45-50 min
Pans: 9" spring form; 2 saucepans
(1qt, 2qt)

1½	cups	**zwieback,** crushed fine	
⅓	cup	**sugar**	Combine; press into pan and chill.
¾	tsp	**cinnamon**	
6	Tbsp	**butter,** melted	

3   **eggs**   Beat until foamy.

16	oz	**cream cheese,** softened	
1	cup	**sugar**	
2	tsp	**vanilla**	Add to above; beat until smooth.
½	tsp	**nutmeg**	
¼	tsp	**salt**	

3 cups   **sour cream**   Add to above; pour into chilled crust. Bake, until filling is just set. Cool.

½	cup	**sugar**	In 2 quart saucepan, heat and stir un-
½	cup	**water**	til sugar dissolves.

2 cups   **rhubarb,** fresh, (1" pcs)   Add to above; bring to a boil then reduce heat. Simmer (1min). Remove from heat. Lift out rhubarb with slotted spoon. (Reserve ½ cup liquid.)

GLAZE

¾	cup	**strawberries,** hulled	In blender, blend until smooth.
½	cup	reserved liquid	

2	tsp	**cornstarch**	In 1 quart saucepan, blend. Add strawberry mixture. Cook, stirring un-
	dash	**salt**	til thick and bubbly. Cook (1min)
1	Tbsp	**water**	longer. Remove from heat. Cool to room temperature.

1	pt	**strawberries** (halved) reserved rhubarb	Arrange strawberries; cover with rhubarb. Spoon glaze over top. Cover and chill.

Rose Sayles, Trumbull

Peaches and Cream Cheesecake

Great any time of year

Serves: 4-6
Bake: 350° 30 min
Pan: 9" spring form, greased

CRUST

¾	cup	**flour**
1	tsp	**baking powder**
½	tsp	**salt**
1	pkg	**vanilla pudding mix** (not instant) (3½oz)
1		**egg**
½	cup	**milk**

Combine; beat (2min). Pour into pan.

FILLING

1	can	**peaches,** sliced, drained (15-20oz)

Reserve juice. Place peaches over batter.

8	oz	**cream cheese**
½	cup	**sugar**
3	Tbsp	**reserved juice**

Combine; beat (2min). Spoon mixture to within one inch of edge.

1	Tbsp	**sugar**
½	tsp	**cinnamon**

Combine; sprinkle over filling. Bake. Filling will appear soft.

Charlotte Mack, Trumbull

N.Y. Style Cheese Cake

Great! No crust

Serves: 12
Bake: 325° 1 hr; set 2 hr
Pan: 9" spring form, greased

2	lb	**cream cheese,** softened
1½	cups	**sugar**
3	Tbsp	**flour**
3	Tbsp	**cornstarch**
4		**eggs**

Mix together; beat (10min).

1	tsp	**vanilla**
1½	tsp	**lemon juice**
¼	lb	**butter,** melted
1	pt	**sour cream**

Add to above; beat (5min). Pour into pan. Bake. After baking, turn off oven; leave cake in oven for 2 hours. DO NOT OPEN DOOR.

Janet Kent, Southport

Soufflé Grand Marnier

A very special dessert

Serves: 4
Bake: 400° 12-15 min
Pan: soufflé dish

To prepare dish: butter lightly all over. Then heavily coat inside edge of bowl with sweet butter (almost ⅛"). This is an important detail. While the soufflé is baking, the butter melts along the side of the bowl making the soufflé rise higher and more evenly.

3	tsp	**sweet butter**	Cream, blend to a paste-like consistency. (This is called a beurre manié.)
4	Tbsp	**flour**	
1	cup	**milk**	Heat together. As it starts to boil, add beurre manié, stirring constantly, letting it boil (1min). Remove from heat.
½	cup	**sugar**	
few	drops	**vanilla**	
4		**egg yolks** (reserve whites)	Add and blend (30sec). Pour into a bowl.
5		**egg whites**	Beat until stiff but not dry; fold gently into above.
			Add; pour batter into prepared "bols à soufflé". Bake. Serve topped with Crème Anglaise (see Index) OR melted ice cream OR melted ice cream mixed with whipped cream to which a few more drops of Grand Marnier have been added.
few	drops	**vanilla**	
½	oz	**Grand Marnier**	

Jean-Robert Pouget, Chef, Le Chambord, Westport

Recette de
• **ROBERT POUGET** •
Original Recipe

Blintz Soufflé

Best served warm

Serves: 16
Bake: 375° 45 min
Pan: 13x9

2	pkg	**blueberry blintzes,** frozen	Arrange in single layer in pan.
½	cup	**margarine,** melted	Pour over blintzes.
1	pt	**sour cream**	Blend. Pour over blintzes.
¾	cup	**sugar**	
4		**eggs**	
		cinnamon	Sprinkle over pan. Bake.
		whipped cream OR **vanilla ice cream** (optional)	Garnish.

Jane Fulton, Trumbull

Cold Chocolate Almond Soufflé

Elegance personified

Serves: 10-12
Chill: 3-4 hr
Pans: soufflé (2qt); saucepan

Make waxed paper collar for soufflé dish. Brush inside of collar with vegetable oil. Sprinkle with sugar.

2	Tbsp	**gelatin, unflavored**
½	cup	**light rum**

In heat-proof dish, sprinkle gelatin into rum. Set in pan of boiling water to dissolve.

8	oz	**dark sweet chocolate** (Maillard)
2	cups	**light cream**

In saucepan, melt chocolate in cream. Beat with whisk until smooth.

1	cup	**confectioners' sugar**
½	tsp	**salt**

Beat into chocolate along with dissolved gelatin. Chill until almost set (1hr).

4	cups	**heavy cream**

Beat until very stiff. Beat in chocolate mixture, a little at a time. Beat after each addition until smooth.

½	cup	**almonds,** slivered

Fold into above; pour into prepared dish and chill. Remove collar before serving.

1	cup	**heavy cream,** whipped
¾	cup	**chocolate,** shaved

Decorate.

Hannah Burke, Farmington

Brandy Alexander Soufflé

A very special dessert

Serves: 8-10
Chill: until firm
Pans: saucepan (1qt); soufflé (1½qt)

¾	cup	**sugar**	Combine sugar and gelatin in saucepan. Gradually add water; stir over low heat until dissolved and remove from heat.
2	env	**gelatin, unflavored**	
1¾	cups	**water**	

4		**egg yolks,** beaten (reserve whites)	Blend into above; return to heat. Cook (2-3min).

8	oz	**cream cheese,** softened	Gradually add gelatin mixture to cheese. Blend well.

3	Tbsp	**brandy**	Stir into above; chill until slightly thickened.
3	Tbsp	Crème de Cacao	

4		**egg whites**	Beat egg whites until soft peaks form. Gradually add sugar. Fold egg whites and whipped cream into cream cheese mixture. Wrap 3" foil collar around top of soufflé dish; pour in mixture. Chill until firm. Remove collar; serve garnished with nutmeg or chocolate shavings.
¼	cup	**sugar**	
1	cup	**heavy cream,** whipped	

Rita Madore, Fairfield

Fresh Strawberry or Raspberry Soufflé

You really should try it

Serves: 6-10
Chill: 3-4 hr
Pans: soufflé dish (2qt); saucepan (1qt)

2	pt	**strawberries** OR **raspberries,** fresh	Wash; hull; purée. Pour into large bowl.

2	env	**gelatin, unflavored**	Combine in saucepan. Cook over medium heat, stirring constantly, until dissolved and liquid just begins to boil. Remove from heat; cool slightly.
½	cup	**water**	
⅔	cup	**sugar**	

1	Tbsp	**lemon juice**	Add to above then add this mixture to strawberries. Chill until consistency of unbeaten egg white.

4		**egg whites**	Beat whites until foamy; add sugar gradually then beat until stiff peaks form. Fold into above.
½	cup	**sugar**	

1	cup	**cream, heavy**	Whip; fold into above. Attach 3" waxed paper collar around soufflé dish; pour mixture in. Chill. Remove collar just before serving.

Jeanne Buynak, Bridgeport

Charlotte Russe

A very special chocolate dessert

Serves: 8-10
Chill: at least 8 hr
Pan: spring form (8x3)

1	Tbsp	**gelatin,** unflavored	Soften gelatin.
2	Tbsp	**water,** cold	

3	oz	**unsweetened chocolate**	Melt, over low heat, stirring constantly; remove from heat. Add softened gelatin; stir to dissolve thoroughly and set aside.
½	cup	**water**	

4		**eggs,** separated (reserve whites)	Beat yolks until thick and lemon-colored.

½	cup	**sugar**	Add gradually to above; beat well.

1	tsp	**vanilla**	Gradually stir in; cool. Stir again until smooth; set aside.
	dash	**salt**	
		reserved chocolate mixture	

		reserved egg whites	In separate bowl, beat until soft peaks form.
½	tsp	**cream of tartar**	

¼	cup	**sugar**	Add gradually; beat until stiff peaks form.

		reserved chocolate mixture	Fold into beaten egg whites.

1	cup	**heavy cream,** whipped	Fold into chocolate mixture.
½	cup	**walnuts,** chopped (optional)	

3	doz	**lady fingers,** single (reserve 10)	Line bottom of pan, cutting to fit. Stand on ends to line edges. Pour in ½ chocolate mixture; spread remaining lady fingers, then top with remaining chocolate mixture. Chill.

whipped cream **maraschino cherries** **grated nuts**	Optional garnishes.

Dee Maggiori, Trumbull

Trifle
(British)

A wonderful traditional dessert

Serves: 8-10
Pans: saucepan (3qt);
serving bowl (2qt)

½	cup	**sugar**	
3	Tbsp	**cornstarch**	Mix in saucepan.
¼	tsp	**salt**	
3	cups	**milk**	Gradually stir into above. Heat to boiling, stirring constantly; boil (1min). Remove from heat.
½	cup	**dry sherry**	
3		**egg yolks**	Add one at a time, beating after each addition.
3	Tbsp	**butter**	Stir in; cover and refrigerate at least 3 hours.
1	Tbsp	**vanilla**	
2	pkg	**lady fingers**, split (3oz,ea)	Spread lady fingers with jam. Cover bottom of bowl with ¼ of the lady fingers (cut sides up). Line sides of bowl with lady fingers, upright, cut sides in.
½	cup	**strawberry** OR **raspberry preserves**	
1	pkg	**strawberries** OR **raspberries,** thawed reserved pudding	Layer half of strawberries then half of pudding over lady fingers. Repeat layers of lady fingers, berries, pudding. Cover and refrigerate.
1	cup	**whipping cream,** chilled	Beat until stiff; add sugar then spread over dessert.
2	Tbsp	**sugar**	
2	Tbsp	**almonds,** toasted, slivered	Garnish.

Margaret Lindsay, Trumbull

Whipped Cream Roll

Creamy and luscious

Serves: 8
Bake: 350° 18 min
Pan: jelly roll, buttered

4		egg whites (reserve yolks)	In large bowl, beat until stiff.
½	cup	sugar	Add gradually; beat well. Set aside.
		reserved egg yolks	
½	cup	sugar	
2	Tbsp	water	In separate bowl, mix.
1	tsp	vanilla	
¼	tsp	salt	
⅓	cup	flour	Sift into egg yolk mixture; mix well. Fold into egg whites. Spread in prepared pan. Bake. Turn onto clean dish towel that has been sprinkled with confectioners' sugar; roll. Cool on rack (30min).
⅓	cup	cocoa	
1	tsp	baking powder	
1	pt	heavy cream	Beat until stiff.
1-2	tsp	vanilla	Add; mix well. Unroll cake and spread with cream; roll up again. Chill at least 8 hours.
2-3	Tbsp	sugar	

Agnes Swords, Stratford

Almond Carob Mousse

Good for digestion!

Serves: 4
Pans: 4 dessert cups

3		egg yolks (reserve whites)	
½	cup	carob powder	
⅓	cup	milk	Blend at medium speed (30sec).
½	tsp	almond extract	
2	tsp	honey	
		reserved whites	In bowl, beat until stiff. Gently fold carob mixture into egg whites. Spoon into cups or bowls.
4		almonds	Top each dessert with an almond. Chill, or serve immediately.
		cream, whipped	
		honey	Optional topping.
		vanilla	

June Bartnett, Monroe

Avocado Mousse

(Puerto Rican)

An avocado delight

Serves: 4
Freeze: 4-6 hr
Pan: mold

4	Tbsp	**sugar** OR **honey**	Combine in saucepan; stir until sugar is dissolved. Boil (3min); chill.
¼	cup	**water**	
½	pt	**heavy cream***	Beat until stiff; add above syrup slowly. *OR coffee cream with ½ tsp plain gelatin added.
1	med	**avocado*** (reserve ¼ cup, thin slices)	Mash remainer of fruit (½cup). *OR papaya.
3	Tbsp	**sugar** OR **honey**	Add to mashed avocado. Beat until very light. Fold in reserved slices; pour into mold and freeze.
1		**egg white**	
1	tsp	**lemon juice**	

Barbara Schegg, Huntington

Dark Chocolate Mousse

Chocolate lovers beware

Serves: 6-8
Chill: 12-24 hr
Pan: double boiler

4	oz	**unsweetened chocolate**	Combine in top of double boiler. Cook over boiling water, stirring constantly until chocolate is melted and mixture is smooth. Remove from heat; leave over hot water.
¾	cup	**sugar,** superfine	
¼	cup	**coffee**	
5		**eggs,** separated (reserve whites)	Beat yolks, one at a time, into above. Remove top of double boiler from water; cool.
1½	tsp	**vanilla**	Add to cooled mixture.
2-3	Tbsp	**brandy** OR **coffee liqueur**	
		reserved egg whites	Beat until stiff but not dry. Fold gently into chocolate mixture. Spoon into 6-8 individual dishes. Cover; refrigerate 12-24 hr.
1	cup	**heavy cream,** whipped	Garnish.
¼	cup	**pistachio nuts** OR **almonds,** chopped	

Miki Fetzer, Trumbull

Crème Anglaise

Serves: 4-6

1	cup	**milk**
2	Tbsp	**sugar**

} Boil (1min).

2		**egg yolks,** lightly beaten

Gradually pour milk mixture over yolks in a thin stream while continuing to whisk. Stir continuously and continue to cook over low heat until mixture coats back of spoon. DO NOT BOIL. Strain through double cheesecloth or very fine chinois.

VARIATION: Vanilla, Grand Marnier or any other ingredient can be added to this cream to modify the basic taste.

Jean-Robert Pouget, Chef, Le Chambord, Westport

Zabaglione Parfait
(Italian)

Can be made up to two weeks ahead

Serves: 6
Pan: double boiler
parfait glasses (6oz)

6		**egg yolks**
¼	cup	**sugar**

} In double boiler, over hot, not boiling water, beat until thick (5min).

½	cup	**Marsala wine**

Add to above; continue beating until mixture is fluffy and mounds slightly when dropped from a spoon. Cover and refrigerate until slightly cooled (30min).

1	cup	**whipping cream**

In small bowl, with mixer at medium speed, beat cream until soft peaks form. (Reserve ¼ cup for garnish.) Fold cream into cooled egg yolk mixture. Spoon into glasses. Garnish. Cover and freeze until firm (3hr). To serve: let stand at room temperature (10min) to soften slightly.

Maria DeCesare, Trumbull

 STRAWBERRIES were so named because they were brought to market strung on straws to prevent damage. They were cultivated as early as the 15th century.

Quick Flan

An easy way to make an elegant dessert

Serves: 10-12
Chill: 4-6 hr
Pans: 2 saucepans (2qt);
casserole (2qt)

6	cups	**milk**	In saucepan, bring to simmer.
2	pkg	**vanilla pudding** (4½oz,ea)	Add to milk. Cook according to package directions; remove from heat.
2	cups	**sugar**	Place in 2nd saucepan; melt down to light caramel. Pour into casserole,

coating entire surface. Pour in pudding; chill. To serve, turn out onto deep serving dish. Cut and serve.

Mrs. Francisco Goncalves, Bridgeport

Caramel Custard Mold with Fruit

An elegant custard dessert from the Pennsylvania Dutch

Serves: 10
Bake: 325° 55-60 min
Pan: heavy skillet; bundt (lg)

1	cup	**sugar**	Sprinkle evenly over bottom of heavy skillet. Cook over LOW heat, stirring

occasionally with wooden spoon until sugar melts to a golden syrup. Be careful not to burn. *Immediately* pour syrup into bundt pan; tilt pan while syrup is still liquid, to coat bottom and sides (syrup will harden). Let cool.

10		**eggs**	Beat together, in large bowl, using wire whisk.
1	cup	**sugar**	
½	tsp	**salt**	
2	tsp	**vanilla**	
7	cups	**milk**	Add gradually, beating until smooth but not frothy. Place bundt pan in

shallow baking pan; pour in egg mixture. Place baking pan on center rack in oven; pour hot water into pan 1" deep around mold. Bake until knife inserted 1" from edge comes out clean. Do not overbake. Remove mold to rack to cool, then refrigerate (can be made a day ahead). To serve: loosen edge of custard with spatula; place serving plate upside down on top; invert and shake gently to unmold. Caramel will run down sides.

1	cup	**pineapple chunks,** drained	Toss together lightly; fill center of custard with fruit. Spoon caramel sauce over each serving.
½	lb	**seedless grapes,** halved	
1		**banana,** sliced, sprinkled with lemon juice	

Hillandale Gourmet Club, Trumbull

Bread Pudding with Whiskey Sauce

Or any flavor you choose

Serves: 16-20
Bake: cold start to 375° 75 min
Pan: 9x9 casserole, buttered

1	cup	**raisins** **whiskey** }	Soak raisins in whiskey or your choice of liquid (see variations), 2 hr or overnight.
1	loaf	**French bread**, stale* (10oz) or 6-8 cups any type dry bread, crumbled	Combine well in large bowl. *To "stale" your bread: place in 200° oven (2hr) or set out for 2 days.
4	cups	**milk**	
2	cups	**sugar** (to taste)	
4	Tbsp	**butter**, melted	
2	Tbsp	**vanilla**	
3		**eggs**, lightly beaten	
		reserved raisins, drained (reserve liquid for sauce)	Add to above (mixture should be moist not soupy). Adjust milk or bread as needed. Pour into baking dish. Place in COLD oven. Bake until pudding is brown but center still jiggles slightly. Serve hot with sauce.
1	cup	**coconut**, shredded	
2	cups	**pecans**, chopped coarse	

VARIATIONS: **Bread:** Use stale cinnamon rolls, danish, etc.
Milk: Replace ½ cup with ½ cup coconut cream, chocolate milk, etc.
Sugar: Can use honey.
Eggs: Add as many as you choose, the more eggs the more custardy.
Vanilla: Can use almond or rum extract to match flavor you choose for sauce.
Fruit: Can use 1 cup chopped apples, rolled in cinnamon-sugar, bananas, pineapple, blueberries, strawberries, etc. instead of raisins or in addition to.
Nuts: Can use walnuts, almonds, etc.
Seasonings: Can use cinnamon or nutmeg for additional flavor.
Pineapple-upside-down Pudding: Place pineapple rings over bottom of buttered casserole, place maraschino cherries in center of each ring. Pour pudding batter over then bake according to pudding directions.
Apple Upside-down Pudding: Roll enough apple slices in cinnamon-sugar to cover bottom of dish in a design. Fill spaces with chopped walnuts and or coconut. Pour pudding batter over. Bake.

WHISKEY SAUCE

½	cup	**butter** }	Combine, adding enough sugar to absorb butter. Cream well.
1	cup	**confectioners' sugar**	
1		**egg yolk**	Blend in; cream well. This is the basic sauce for any variation you choose.
½	cup	**bourbon** (to taste)	Pour in slowly, stirring well. (Can use any combination of juices and liquors

being careful to maintain ½-1 cup liquid). Simmer 1 minute longer to evaporate alcohol. Sauce will thicken as it cools. Serve hot over warm pudding. **MICROWAVE:** Pour sauce over bread pudding, place in microwave 45 sec. to 1 min. Sauce blends and bubbles into pudding.

VARIATIONS: Rum, brandy, plain or fruit flavored; dark creme-de-cacao; Amaretto; chocolate-mint liqueur; Grand Marnier; lemon juice and water.

SUGGESTED COMBINATIONS: Rum over pineapple upside down; chocolate-mint over chocolate pudding; Amaretto over almond flavored pudding; cinnamon-bourbon over apple upside down.

New Orleans School of Cooking, Old Quarter, New Orleans, La

An Uncommon Bread Pudding

The brown sugar makes a delicious sauce

Serves: 4
Stovetop: 1 hr
Pan: double boiler

3	slices	**bread,** white or soft wheat	Remove crusts; butter and cube bread. Set aside.
1	Tbsp	**butter** OR **margarine**	
1	cup	**brown sugar**	Place in top of double boiler; top with bread cubes.
2		**eggs**	Beat together; pour over bread. DO NOT STIR. Cover and cook over boiling water (1hr). Turn over onto deep serving dish. See Bread Pudding with Whiskey Sauce for variations.
2	cups	**milk**	
½	tsp	**vanilla**	

Gloria Schleicher, Weston

Riz à l'Amande

(Scandinavian)

Very rich and delicious

Serves: 8
Stovetop: 1 hr
Pan: saucepan (2½qt)

1	can	**evaporated milk** (13oz)	Combine in saucepan. Bring to a boil; lower heat to simmer. Cook over low heat (40min) stirring frequently; remove from heat.
3½	cups	**rice,** cooked	
¾	cup	**sugar**	Stir in; cover with waxed paper to prevent crusting as it cools. Refrigerate. Remove ½ hour before completing.
1	Tbsp	**almond extract**	
1	pt	**heavy cream,** whipped	Fold into rice mixture; refrigerate until ready to serve.
1	pt	**strawberries,** fresh, chopped OR frozen, thawed (10oz)	Garnish.

Hillandale Gourmet Club, Trumbull

Custard Pudding

One basic recipe, four variations!

Serves: 6
Bake: 325° 45 min
Pan: casserole (1qt) OR 6 custard
cups, greased

3		**eggs,** lightly beaten
3	cups	**milk**
½	cup	**sugar**
1	tsp	**vanilla**
¼-½	tsp	**cinnamon** OR **nutmeg**

Mix together; let stand until bubbles on surface disappear. (If making a variation, add grapenuts, rice or bread at this time.) Put casserole or cups in larger baking pan. Pour hot water in outer pan to within ½" of top. Bake until tester comes out clean but custard is still shakeable in center. Remove from oven; cool on rack. Refrigerate.

VARIATIONS: **grapenut:** add ⅓ cup grapenuts
rice: add 1 cup cooked white rice, ½ cup raisins
bread: add 1 cup bread pieces (crusts removed) soaked in a little milk, ½ cup raisins

Dorilda Heon, West Warwick, RI

Baked Fudge Pudding

Ecstasy!

Serves: 8
Bake: 350° 45-50 min
Pan: 8x8, greased

1	cup	**flour,** sifted
2	tsp	**baking powder**
¾	tsp	**salt**
½	cup	**sugar**
2	Tbsp	**cocoa**

Sift into bowl.

¾	cup	**nuts,** chopped
½	cup	**milk**
1	tsp	**vanilla**
2	Tbsp	**butter,** melted

Stir into above. Spread in prepared pan.

¼	cup	**cocoa**
¾	cup	**brown surgar,** firmly packed

Mix then spread over batter.

1¾	cups	**water,** boiling
1	tsp	**vanilla**

Combine; pour gently over all. Bake. Serve warm or cold topped with ice cream.

Pat Braun, Trumbull

Baked Indian Pudding

A favorite at Thanksgiving time

Serves: 8
Bake: 275° 2 hr
Pan: double boiler; 2 qt casserole, buttered

3	cups	milk	Heat in double boiler.
1	cup	milk	Mix together; stir into hot milk. Cook until slightly thickened; remove from heat.
¾	cup	yellow cornmeal	

¼	cup	molasses	
1	tsp	cinnamon	
½	tsp	nutmeg	Mix together; stir into above.
1	cup	brown sugar, firmly packed	
½	tsp	salt	

½	cup	margarine, softened	Beat into above; pour into casserole. Bake. Serve hot, topped with sour cream or vanilla ice cream.
2		eggs, beaten	

Florence Bolcer, Trumbull

1		apple, peeled, sliced	Add before cooking, for another flavor. Yummy!

Judy Perkins, Fairfield

Date Pudding

Serves: 8
Bake: 350° 45 min
Pan: 11x7, buttered

SYRUP

2	cups	brown sugar, packed	Boil together (10min).
2½	cups	water	

1	Tbsp	butter	Add to above; pour into baking dish.
1	tsp	vanilla	

BATTER

1	cup	dates, chopped	
1	cup	nuts, chopped	
½	cup	sugar	
2	tsp	baking powder	Mix together.
½	cup	milk	
2	Tbsp	butter, softened	

2-4	Tbsp	flour	Add enough flour to make a stiff batter. Drop batter by heaping Tbsp into syrup in baking dish. Bake.

Diane Lombardi, Milford

A Bishop Whipple Pudding

A delicious date dessert

Serves: 6-8
Bake: 350° 20-30 min
Pans: 9" layer cake, greased;
saucepan (2qt)

2		**eggs**

Beat until thick and lemon colored.

¼-½	cups	**sugar**

Stir in.

⅔	cup	**flour**
1	tsp	**baking powder**

Sift together; add to above. Beat until well blended.

1	cup	**dates,** chopped
1	cup	**nuts,** chopped coarse

Fold in; spoon into prepared pan. Bake. Serve warm with sauce.

BROWN SUGAR SAUCE

⅓	cup	**butter** OR **margarine**
½	cup	**cream,** heavy
2	cups	**light brown sugar,** packed
¼	tsp	**salt**
⅓	cup	**corn syrup,** light

Mix in saucepan; bring to a boil and cook rapidly (3min). (220° on candy thermometer.)

Porter Cleveland, Bridgeport

"Rice Pudding"

A great low-cal dessert

Serves: 6
Bake: 350° 30 min
Pan: pie plate (9")

1	lb	**cottage cheese** OR **farmer's cheese,** mashed

1	env	**unflavored gelatin**
1	cup	**pineapple tidbits** in own juice, drained (reserve fruit)

Soften gelatin in juice.

1		**egg**
2-4	pkts	**artificial sweetener** (optional)
1	tsp	**vanilla**
1	tsp	**lemon juice**

Combine; add all of the above ingredients. Pour into pie plate.

	dash	**nutmeg** OR **cinnamon**

Sprinkle over top. Bake; cool then refrigerate.

Judy Webster of Thin's Inn, Monroe

Coffee Tortoni

A light ending to a nice meal

Serves: 8
Freeze: 4-5 hr
Pan: 2 oz cups

1		egg white
1	Tbsp	instant coffee
⅛	tsp	salt

Combine; beat until stiff.

2	Tbsp	sugar

Add to above gradually.

1	cup	cream, heavy

Beat until stiff.

¼	cup	sugar
1	tsp	vanilla
⅛	tsp	almond extract
¼	cup	almonds, chopped

Add to cream then fold into egg whites. Fill cups then freeze.

Jeanne Davidson, Southport

Easy Spumoni

A really attractive dessert

Serves: 8-10
Freeze: see recipe
Pan: mold (2qt) Chill
mold in freezer. Do NOT oil.

1	pt	French vanilla ice cream
2	Tbsp	rum
6	red	maraschino cherries, chopped

Soften ice cream until it can be stirred. Stir in rum, cherries; refreeze until workable. Spread in layer over bottom and sides of mold. Refreeze until firm.

1	pt	French vanilla ice cream, softened
½	tsp	pistachio extract
¼	cup	pistachio nuts, chopped fine
2-4	drops	green food coloring

Mix together; freeze until workable. Spread to cover first layer completely; freeze until firm.

½	cup	heavy cream
¼	cup	chocolate instant drink powder

Whip until peaks form. Spread over previous layer but do not go up the sides. Freeze until firm.

½	cup	heavy cream
	dash	salt

Whip until peaks form.

¼	cup	strawberry jam
2-4	drops	red food coloring

Fold into above. Spread over previous layer. Freeze, covered with foil. To unmold, dip in warm water for an instant or wrap in linen towel wrung in hot water. Turn out onto chilled platter. Cut frozen.

VARIATION: Almond extract, blanched almonds substituted for pistachios.

Alice Barreca, Weston

Frozen Pumpkin Joy

A delicious end of meal treat

Serves: 18
Freeze: 5 hr
Pan: 13x9

½ gal	**vanilla ice cream**	Soften in a large chilled bowl.

1 can	**pumpkin** (1 lb)	
1 cup	**sugar**	
1 tsp	**salt** (optional)	
1 tsp	**ginger**	Combine well; fold into above.
1 tsp	**cinnamon**	
½ tsp	**nutmeg**	
1 cup	**pecans,** chopped	

36	**gingersnaps**	Line pan with ½ of the gingersnaps. Spread half ice cream mixture over. Cover with remaining gingersnaps. Cover with remaining ice cream. Freeze until firm. Cut into squares.

	whipped cream **pecan halves**	Garnish. Thaw 30-40 minutes before serving.

VARIATION: Crush gingersnaps, add 3 Tbsp melted butter, press over bottom of pan. Save ½ cup for topping. Cover with pumpkin mixture; freeze.

Terri Trinkley, Fairfield

Cherry Bisque

A delightful, simple dessert

Serves: 8-12
Freeze: 1-2 hr
Pan: muffin

2	**egg whites**	Beat whites until foamy. Add sugar gradually. Beat until stiff.
2 Tbsp	**sugar**	

⅓ cup	**grapenuts**	
¼ cup	**almonds,** toasted, chopped	
¼ cup	**maraschino cherries,** quartered	
1 Tbsp	**cherry syrup**	Fold into above.
½ tsp	**vanilla**	
1 cup	**heavy cream,** whipped	
¼ cup	**confectioners' sugar,** sifted	

	grape nuts	Sprinkle in bottom of cup cake liners place in muffin cups. Pour in mixture. Sprinkle grapenuts on top then freeze.

Joyce Green, Weston

Strawberry Jam Delight

A very nice molded dessert

Serves: 4-6
Freeze: 1 hr
Pan: saucepan (med)

| ¼ | cup | **water** | Combine; set aside to dissolve. |
| 2 | Tbsp | **gelatin, unflavored** | |

| 1 | can | **pineapple,** crushed (8¼oz) drained (reserve juice) **water** | Add enough water to juice to make 2 cups. Pour into saucepan. |

| 1 | cup | **strawberry jam** | Add; bring to a boil, stirring constantly. Add gelatin; lower heat and stir until dissolved (5min). Remove from heat. |

| | | reserved pineapple | Add; cool. Place in freezer (1hr). Remove and break into pieces. Beat (1min). |
| 1 | tsp | **lemon juice** | |

| ½ | pt | **whipping cream** | Beat until thick. Stir ½ cup into strawberry mixture. Chill until ready to serve. |

| ½ | tsp | **honey** | Drizzle over remaining whipped cream and stir in vigorously. Garnish. |

June Bartnett, Monroe

Frosty Lime Mold

Can be used as dessert or salad

Serves: 12
Chill: several hours
Pans: mold (5cup); saucepan (sm)

1	cup	**water,** boiling	Stir gelatin into water until it dissolves.
2	pkg	**lime gelatin** (3oz,ea)	

1	can	**pineapple,** crushed (8oz) drained (reserve juice) **water**	Add water to make 1½ cups liquid. Add to gelatin mixture. Pour into medium-size bowl.

1	ctn	**sour cream** (8oz)	Add to above; beat with electric mixer until smooth. Stir in pineapple. Pour into mold; chill until set.

	whipped cream, yogurt, nuts, chopped (optional)	Great garnishes.

VARIATIONS: Strawberry gelatin with 1 package frozen strawberries (10oz)
Peach gelatin with 1 small can diced peaches
Orange gelatin and 1 small can mandarin oranges halved
Apricot gelatin with 1 small can apricots
Apple gelatin with 1 apple diced

Anne Mercurio, Stratford

Ribboned Fruit Mold

Salad or dessert – good for buffet

Serves: 14-16
Chill: 4-5 hr
Pan: 13x9

1	pkg	**strawberry gelatin** (3oz)	Dissolve all gelatins together in boiling water.
1	pkg	**mixed fruit gelatin** (3oz)	
1	pkg	**lemon gelatin** (3oz)	
2½	cups	**water,** boiling	

1	pkg	**strawberries,** frozen, sliced, thawed (10oz)	Add to above.
1	can	**pineapple,** crushed (20oz)	

1½	cups	**water,** cold	Add to above; mix then pour ½ of mixture into dish. Chill to set. (Keep remaining half at room temp.)
3		**bananas,** mashed	

1	pt	**sour cream**	Carefully spread over set gelatin mixture. Spoon remaining mixture over top. Chill until set.

Joan DelGrande, Bridgeport

Honey Cake
(Jewish)

Traditionally served on happy occasions

Serves: 12
Bake: 350° 55-60 min
Pan: tube (9"), ungreased

3½	cups	**flour,** sifted
2½	tsp	**baking powder**
1	tsp	**baking soda**
1	tsp	**cinnamon**
½	tsp	**cloves**
¼	tsp	**ginger**
1	cup	**sugar**

Mix and sift into large bowl; make a well.

3		**egg yolks** (reserve whites)
¼	cup	**vegetable oil**
1⅓	cups	**honey**
1⅓	cups	**coffee,** black, warm

Add to above; beat well.

¼	tsp	**cream of tartar**
		reserved egg whites

Beat until stiff peaks form. Gently fold batter into egg whites.

1	cup	**almonds,** slivered (optional)

Fold in if desired; pour batter into pan. Bake until cake springs back when gently touched. Remove from oven; invert cake pan on wire rack. Cool cake in pan until completely cooled then remove. Serve with fresh fruit over which coconut has been sprinkled.

Hannah Bakunin, Bridgeport

Walnut Cake

"This cake keeps them coming back for more"

Serves: 8-10
Bake: 325° 40-45 min
Pan: 2 cake (8"), lightly greased

16	oz	**walnuts,** ground fine (until dry crumbs)
1	cup	**sugar**
8		**eggs**

Combine in large bowl; beat (10min) with electric mixer and pour into prepared pans. Bake until sides come away from pan. Cool on racks (10min); remove from pans.

FROSTING

½	cup	**butter,** unsalted
1-2	Tbsp	**coffee,** strong
2	Tbsp	**sugar**
⅛	tsp	**vanilla**

Cream well; spread between layers only.

Sidnee Finik, New Canaan

Pepparkaka

(Swedish)

A yummy spice cake, even better with lemon frosting

Serves: 8
Bake: 350° 35 min
Pan: Bundt (8cup), greased

¾	cup	**sugar**	
¾	cup	**brown sugar**	Cream well.
¼	cup	**butter** OR **margarine**	
2		**eggs**	Add; beat well.
1½	cups	**flour,** sifted	
¼	tsp	**salt**	
1	tsp	**baking soda**	
1	tsp	**ginger**	Sift together.
1	tsp	**cinnamon**	
1	tsp	**allspice**	
½-1	tsp	**cloves**	
1	cup	**sour cream**	Mix together; add alternately with dry ingredients to creamed mixture. Pour into prepared pan. Bake until toothpick comes out clean.
½	tsp	**vanilla**	

Yelva Person, Fairfield

Pumpkin Cake

A delicious light Fall treat

Serves: 10-12
Bake: 350° 30-35 min
Pan: 2 cake (8") lined with wax paper

½	cup	**shortening**	
1	cup	**brown sugar,** packed	Cream together well, in large bowl.
½	cup	**sugar**	
2		**eggs**	Add; beat well.
¾	cup	**pumpkin,** canned	
2¼	cups	**cake flour,** sifted	
3	tsp	**baking powder**	
¼	tsp	**baking soda**	Combine well.
1½	tsp	**cinnamon**	
½	tsp	**ginger**	
½	tsp	**allspice**	
¾	cup	**buttermilk** OR **sour milk**	Add alternately with flour mixture; beat well after each addition. Pour batter into prepared pans. Bake until

center springs back when pressed lightly. Frost with butter cream or cream cheese frosting with (1Tbsp) marshmallow cream added to prevent crusting.

Esther Sayles, Bridgeport

Toffee Coffee Cake

A "sweet" treat

Serves: 12-16
Bake: 325° 45-50 min
Pan: bundt (9or10"), greased, floured

¼	cup	**sugar**
1	tsp	**cinnamon**

Mix together; set aside.

1	cup	**sugar**
½	cup	**butter,** softened
1	cup	**sour cream**
2		**eggs**
1	tsp	**vanilla**

Combine in large bowl.

2	cups	**flour**
1½	tsp	**baking powder**
1	tsp	**baking soda**
¼	tsp	**salt**

Mix; add to above. With electric mixer, blend then beat (3min) at medium speed, scraping bowl occasionally. Spoon half of batter into prepared pan; spread to edges then sprinkle with 2 Tbsp cinnamon mixture. Spoon remaining batter over; top with remaining cinnamon mixture.

3		**chocolate-toffee bars** (1-1/16oz,ea) coarsely crushed
¼	cup	**walnuts,** chopped

Sprinkle over batter.

¼	cup	**butter,** melted

Drizzle over top. Bake until top springs back when lightly pressed in center. Cool upright in pan (15min). Remove from pan; sprinkle with confectioners' sugar. (Can also use a 13x9 baking dish.)

Lillian Mierzejewski, Stratford

Donna's Marble Chiffon Cake

Makes a great birthday cake

Serves: 12-16
Bake: see recipe
Pan: tube (10"), ungreased

7		eggs, separated (reserve yolks)
½	tsp	cream of tartar

Beat egg whites and cream of tartar together until very stiff peaks form.

2¼	cups	cake flour, sifted
1½	cups	sugar
3	tsp	baking powder
1	tsp	salt

Sift together into bowl; make well in center.

½	cup	vegetable oil
		reserved egg yolks
¾	cup	water, cold
1	tsp	vanilla

Add to dry ingredients in order listed; beat until satiny smooth. Slowly pour this batter, in a thin stream, over entire surface of the egg whites; fold in gently. Remove ⅓ of batter and set aside.

2	oz	no-melt unsweetened baking chocolate
2	Tbsp	sugar
¼	cup	water, boiling

Blend together then gently fold into reserved ⅓ of batter. Spoon ½ of light batter into ungreased tube pan; top with ½ of chocolate batter. Repeat these layers until all batter is used.

Gently swirl layers. Bake: 325° (55min) then 350° (10min). Cake is done if it springs back when pressed lightly. Invert pan to cool cake. Frost with favorite chocolate frosting (see Index).

Joan Kacin, Trumbull

VARIATION: Instead of no-melt chocolate, use ¼ cup cocoa; ¼ cup sugar; ¼ cup water, boiling.

Dorothy Noreiks, Stratford

SIFTING FLOUR – Stir your canister of flour with a french whisk until light and fluffy. Spoon into your measuring cup then level. No sifting needed.

Oatmeal Cake

A delicious spice cake with broiled frosting

Serves: 12
Bake: 350° 50-55 min
Pan: 9x9, greased, floured

1	cup	**oatmeal,** uncooked	Pour water over oats; let stand (20min).
1¼	cups	**water,** boiling	
½	cup	**margarine**	
1	cup	**sugar**	Cream together.
1	cup	**brown sugar,** firmly packed	
2		**eggs**	Add to creamed mixture; mix well then stir in oats.
1	tsp	**vanilla**	
1½	cups	**flour**	
1	tsp	**baking soda**	
½	tsp	**salt**	Add to above; mix well then pour into prepared pans. Bake.
¾	tsp	**cinnamon**	
¼	tsp	**nutmeg**	

FROSTING

¼	cup	**margarine,** melted	
½	cup	**brown sugar,** firmly packed	
3	Tbsp	**light cream**	Combine and spread over cake. Broil until bubbly.
½	cup	**walnuts,** chopped	
¾	cup	**coconut**	

Diane Gorman, Trumbull

Cream Cheese Icing

¼	cup	**butter,** softened	Cream together until smooth.
3	oz	**cream cheese,** softened	
2	cups	**confectioners' sugar,** sifted	Add; beat until smooth.
½	tsp	**vanilla**	

Sally Trinkley, Bridgeport

8	oz	**cream cheese,** softened	
¼	cup	**confectioners' sugar**	Beat well with mixer.
5	oz	**cool whip**	

Marge Schneider, Stratford

Settlers Poppy Seed Cake

Outstanding served plain or with chocolate or fruit sauce

Serves: 12-16
Soak: 3 hr
Bake: 350° 1 hr
Pan: bundt (12cup) OR 2 (6cup)

⅔ cup	**poppy seeds**	Soak 2-3 hours at room temp.
¾ cup	**milk**	
⅔ cup	**butter**	Cream butter; add sugar gradually.
1½ cups	**sugar**	
2 cups	**cake flour,** sifted	Sift all a second time.
3 tsp	**baking powder**	
½ tsp	**salt**	
¼ cup	**milk**	Add to creamed butter alternately with flour mixture, in about 3 additions, beating well after each addition.
1 tsp	**vanilla**	
4	**egg whites**	Beat until stiff but not dry; fold into batter. Pour into prepared pan. Bake until cake springs back when lightly pressed.

Esther Sayles, Bridgeport

Mocha Cake with Icing

A delicious treat, rich & yummy

Serves: 15-20
Bake: 300° 30-35 min
Pans: saucepan (sm); 13x9 greased, floured

¾ cup	**butter** OR **margarine**	Cream well.
2 cups	**sugar**	
2	**eggs**	Add to above and beat in well.
½ cup	**sour cream**	
2 cups	**flour**	Combine; set aside.
½ cup	**cocoa**	
1 tsp	**baking soda**	
½ tsp	**salt**	
1 tsp	**instant coffee**	Combine; add to creamed mixture alternately with dry ingredients. Blend well; pour into prepared pan. Bake until cake springs back when pressed lightly. Frost with Cooked Chocolate Icing (see Index).
1 cup	**coffee,** strong, hot	

Kathy Thoman, Austin, Tx

Gâteau au Chocolat

A very rich treat

Serves: 10-12
Bake: 350° 25 min
Pans: 2 round (8"), greased, floured

1	cup	**unsalted butter,** softened	Place in large mixing bowl.
10	oz	**semi-sweet chocolate squares** OR **morsels**	Combine; melt in top of double boiler. Add to above.
6	Tbsp	**milk**	
6		**eggs,** separated (reserve whites)	Add yolks; mix well.
1	cup	**sugar,** scant	Add; mix thoroughly and beat (2min) longer.
1	cup	**cake flour**	
		reserved egg whites, stiffly beaten	Fold small amount of beaten egg white into batter to lighten it then fold batter back into whites; Pour into prepared pans. Bake. Cool in pans (10min); remove to racks and cool completely. Frost tops of layers.

FROSTING

6	oz	**sweet chocolate**	Heat in top of double boiler stirring until smooth and chocolate is melted; turn off heat.
¼	cup	**water**	
¼	cup	**sugar**	
4		**egg yolks**	Add one at a time, beating well after each addition; cool to lukewarm.
6	Tbsp	**butter,** softened	Add a little at a time, beating after each addition; cool to a good spreading consistency.

Jo Gardner, Fairfield

To melt baking chocolate, place it on a piece of aluminum foil in its own wrapper, place in oven that is preheating or top of a double boiler. It will be ready when needed.

Chocolate "Sauce" Cake

Something different

Serves: 9
Bake: 350° 40-45 min
Pan: 9x9, greased

1	Tbsp	**butter**	} Cream together.
¾	cup	**sugar**	

1	cup	**flour,** sifted	}
1½	Tbsp	**cocoa**	Add to creamed mixture.
1	tsp	**baking powder**	
	pinch	**salt**	

½	cup	**milk**	Add; mix to form batter then spread in prepared pan.

½	cup	**walnuts,** chopped	Sprinkle over batter.

½	cup	**brown sugar**	}
½	cup	**sugar**	Combine; sprinkle over nuts.
½	cup	**cocoa**	

1¼	cups	**water,** boiling	Pour over all just before placing pan in oven. Bake (cake will rise to top,

sauce will settle). Invert on plate; serve upside down either warm or cold. Can be topped with whipped cream or ice cream.

Marie Coope, Trumbull

Spiced Apple Cake

Great for meetings and "just friends"

Serves: 14
Bake: 350° 50-60 min
Pan: 9x12 or tube (10")

4	lg	**apples,** peeled, chopped	Put into large bowl.

2	cups	**sugar**	Pour over apples.

3	cups	**flour**	}
2	tsp	**baking soda**	
1	tsp	**salt**	Combine; add to above.
1	tsp	**nutmeg**	
2	tsp	**cinnamon**	

1	cup	**vegetable oil**	} Add; mix well. Pour into prepared
3		**eggs,** beaten lightly	pan. Bake until toothpick comes out
1	cup	**raisins**	clean.

Joan Kacin, Trumbull

Apfelkuchen
(German)

A delicious apple cake with variations

Serves: 12
Bake: 400° 30-35 min
Pan: 13x9, greased

1¼	cups	**flour,** sifted
¼	cup	**sugar**
1½	tsp	**baking powder**
½	tsp	**salt**

Sift together in medium bowl.

¼	cup	**butter**

Cut in with pastry blender until mixture resembles coarse crumbs.

1		**egg,** beaten
¼	cup	**milk**
1	tsp	**vanilla**

Add; stir with fork (about 1min).
Spread evenly in bottom of pan.

5	cups	**tart apples,** pared, sliced thin

Arrange in parallel rows over batter, thin ends down and overlapping.

TOPPING

¼	cup	**sugar**
1	tsp	**cinnamon**
¼	cup	**butter,** melted

Mix well; sprinkle over apple slices. Bake until apples are tender. Remove to wire rack.

⅓	cup	**apricot preserves**
1	Tbsp	**water,** hot

Mix; brush over apples. Serve warm.

		whipped cream

Use as a topping.

VARIATIONS: Add chopped nuts. Double sugar, butter and preserves for a richer topping. Can use brown sugar. Spread blueberries over top.

Rotraut Ragusin, New Canaan

Julieapple Cake

A delicious, moist apple cake, best warm

Serves: 10-12
Bake: 425° 20-30 min
Pan: 9x9, greased

4-6		apples, peeled, sliced in wedges	Cover; set aside.
2	cups	flour	
2	tsp	baking powder	Combine in medium bowl.
3	Tbsp	sugar	
6	Tbsp	vegetable shortening	Cut into flour mixture.
1		egg (optional)	Add to above; mix with spoon just until moistened. Spread in pan.
⅔	cup	milk	
		reserved apple slices	Arrange in rows, thin side down, covering ⅔ of apple with dough.
1	cup	brown sugar, packed	Sprinkle over top of batter.
1-2	tsp	cinnamon	Sprinkle over top of sugar.
½	cup	margarine, melted (cooled slightly)	Drizzle over cake. Bake until golden and bubbly. Cake is best eaten while hot. Serve garnished with ice cream or whipped cream or plain.

VARIATIONS: Can add or substitute nuts, coconut, fresh blueberries, sliced fresh peaches.

Louise Thoman, Trumbull

Apricot Crumble Cake

Cake, jam and topping – so good

Serves: 12-15
Bake: 350° 35-40 min
Broil: 1-2 min
Pan: 13x9, greased, floured

8	oz	cream cheese, softened	
½	cup	butter OR margarine	Blend thoroughly.
1¼	cups	sugar	
2		eggs	
¼	cup	milk	Add to creamed mixture.
1	tsp	vanilla	
2	cups	flour	
1	tsp	baking powder	Sift together; add to above; mix well.
½	tsp	baking soda	Pour half of batter into prepared pan.
¼	tsp	salt	
1	jar	apricot preserves (12oz)	Spread over batter in pan; top with remaining batter. Bake.
2	cups	coconut, shredded	
⅔	cup	brown sugar	Combine; spread on baked cake. Broil (1-2min) until golden brown (watch closely).
1	tsp	cinnamon	
⅓	cup	margarine, melted	

Terri Trinkley, Fairfield

Sourdough Applesauce Cake

Delicious and moist

Serves: 12-16
Bake: 350° 45-50 min
Pan: 13x9, greased

1	cup	**Sourdough Starter II**	
1	cup	**applesauce,** thick (canned)	Blend in mixing bowl; set aside.
¼	cup	**powdered skim milk**	
1	cup	**flour**	

½	cup	**sugar**	
½	cup	**brown sugar**	Cream well in separate bowl.
½	cup	**butter**	

1		**egg**	Add to creamed mixture; blend well.

2	tsp	**baking soda**	Combine then add to above stirring just until blended. Pour into prepared pan. Bake until toothpick inserted in center comes out clean. Cool in pan. Can frost with a thin layer of butter icing (see Index).
½	tsp	**nutmeg**	
½	tsp	**allspice**	
½	tsp	**cloves**	
½	tsp	**salt**	
1	tsp	**cinnamon**	
		reserved sourdough mixture	

VARIATIONS: Raisins and nuts can be added. Cake can be made in layers 2 (8") (reduce baking time) OR a tube pan (10").

Mary MacInnis, Fairfield

Banana Cake

Always a favorite

Serves: 12-15
Bake: 350° 35 min
Pan: 2 layers (9") greased, floured

½	cup	**butter** OR **margarine**	Cream together.
1½	cups	**sugar**	

2		**eggs**	Add; beat well.

1	cup	**bananas,** mashed	Add; beat.

1	cup	**flour**	
1	cup	**cake flour**	
1	tsp	**baking powder**	Sift together.
1	tsp	**baking soda**	
½	tsp	**salt**	

¾	cup	**buttermilk**	Add alternately with dry ingredients, starting and ending with the dry ingredients; pour into prepared pan. Bake. Frost with your favorite frosting or serve plain.
1	tsp	**vanilla**	

Julie Jacob, Stratford

German Apple Cake

Delicious served warm

Serves: 8-10
Bake: 350° 40-45 min
Pan: 8x8, greased

1	cup	**sugar**	
½	cup	**vegetable oil**	Combine in medium bowl.
2		**eggs,** beaten	
1	cup	**flour**	
1	tsp	**cinnamon**	
1	tsp	**baking powder**	Add; stir until well blended.
1	tsp	**baking soda**	
½	tsp	**salt**	
3	cups	**apples,** sliced thin	Stir in; turn batter into prepared pan. Bake.
		whipped cream OR **ice cream**	Serve warm with either topping. Can also be served cold.

Odette Renner, Trumbull

Blueberry Maple Syrup Loaf

So nice for that cup of coffee with friends

Serves: 10-12
Bake: 350° 40-50 min
Pan: loaf (9x5), greased

⅓	cup	**butter,** softened	Cream together until light and fluffy.
½	cup	**sugar**	
3		**eggs,** well beaten	Add one at a time; beat in well.
¾	cup	**maple** syrup	Stir in.
2¼	cups	**flour**	Sift together.
3	tsp	**baking powder**	
½	cup	**milk**	Add dry ingredients alternately with milk, beginning and ending with the dry.
2	cups	**blueberries,** fresh, or dry pack frozen	Dust lightly with flour; fold into batter; pour into prepared pan. Bake until top is browned. Cool.
		confectioners' sugar	Dust cake.

Rita Madore, Fairfield

Blueberry Cake or Cherry or Apple, etc.

Uses pie filling that's right on the shelf

Serves: 24
Bake: 350° 1 hr
Pan: 13x9, greased, floured

2¾	cups	**flour**	} Cut in shortening until mixture is like coarse meal.
1¾	cups	**sugar**	
1	tsp	**baking powder**	
1	tsp	**baking soda**	
1	cup	**shortening**	

½	cup	**milk**	} Add; blend until sticky. (Do not use electric mixer.) Spread ¾ of batter evenly over bottom and sides of prepared pan.
1		**egg**	
½	tsp	**vanilla**	

1	can	**pie filling** (21oz) apple, blueberry, etc.	Spread over batter. Drop remaining batter by spoonfuls over pie filling.
		sugar-cinnamon mixture (optional)	If desired, sprinkle with mixture. Bake.

This cake goes a long way, freezes well, is very attractive cut in squares and placed on cupcake papers then arranged on a plate.

Beth Schless, Trumbull

Blueberry Buckle

Fresh "blues" make it special

Serves: 8
Bake: 375° 35 min
Pan: 9x9, greased

¼	cup	**butter**	} Cream together lightly.
¾	cup	**sugar**	
1		**egg**	Add; beat well.

2	cups	**flour**, sifted	} Sift together.
2	tsp	**baking powder**	
½	tsp	**salt**	

½	cup	**milk**	Add alternately with dry ingredients, beating until smooth.
2	cups	**fresh blueberries,** washed	Dust with flour then fold in. Pour batter into prepared pan.

¼	cup	**butter**	} Blend together; sprinkle over batter. Bake until toothpick comes out clean.
½	tsp	**cinnamon**	
⅓	cup	**sugar**	
⅓	cup	**flour**	

Patricia Daley, Weston

Butternut Squash Cake

A moist, flavorful confection

Serves: 12-16
Bake: 350° 50 min
Pan: tube (10") greased, floured

2		eggs, beaten	
1	cup	sugar	Mix together, by hand.
½	cup	vegetable oil	
1½	cups	butternut squash, cooked, mashed, cooled	Add to above; mix well.
2	cups	flour	
2	tsp	baking powder	
2	tsp	baking soda	Combine; add to squash mixture.
¾	tsp	salt	
1½	tsp	cinnamon	
1	cup	bran cereal	Stir into batter; turn into tube pan. Bake until it springs back when lightly pressed in center. Cool in pan (10-15min) before removing.
1	cup	raisins OR dates	
¾	cup	nuts	

Marion Wallin, Devon

Company Carrot Cake

Better the next day

Serves: 10-12
Bake: 350° 45-60 min
Pans: 2 rounds (9") greased

2	cups	flour	
2	cups	sugar	
2	tsp	baking soda	Mix together.
2	tsp	cinnamon	
1	tsp	salt	
1	cup	vegetable oil	Add to above.
⅓	cup	milk	
4		eggs	Add, one at a time, beating well after each addition.
3	cups	carrots, grated fine (1lb)	Add; mix well then pour into prepared pans. Bake. Cool before frosting with Cream Cheese Icing (see Index).

Susan Lewis, Easton

Summer Lemon Layers

A lovely light confection

Serves: 8-12
Bake: 350° 45 min
Pans: 3 layers (8"), buttered, dusted

6		**eggs,** separated (reserve whites)
¾	cup	**sugar**
2	Tbsp	**lemon juice**
		rind of 1 lemon, grated
	pinch	**salt**

Beat yolks with other ingredients until light and fluffy (5min).

1	cup	**cake flour**

Sift; blend into above mixture.

reserved egg whites — Beat until stiff but not dry. Fold gently into mixture. Place equal amounts of batter into prepared cake pans. Bake. When finished, invert on wire racks. When cool, loosen edges and remove from pans.

TOPPING

1		**egg**
⅔	cup	**sugar**
		rind of 1 lemon, grated

Beat together until foamy.

		juice of 1 lemon plus enough **water** to make ⅔ cup
¼	cup	**flour**

Add; cook in top of double boiler, stirring constantly, until smooth and thick. Cool.

1¼	cups	**heavy cream,** whipped

Fold in gently. Spread over 2 layers. Stack; cover top and sides with cream.

½	cup	**almonds,** toasted, chopped

Pat firmly around sides of cake.

Marie Caldana, Fairfield

 Dust a little flour or cornstarch over your cake before frosting it to prevent frosting from running off.

Tropical Orange Cake

Fruity glaze makes it moist and delicious

Serves: 12-14
Bake: 350° 50-60 min
Pans: saucepan (sm); 9" spring form,
    greased, floured

2		**oranges**, peeled (reserve fruit)	Slice peel; place in blender.
1	cup	**buttermilk**	Add; blend well; set aside.
1	cup	**margarine**	Cream well in large mixer bowl.
1	cup	**sugar**	
2		**eggs**	Add; beat well.
2½	cups	**flour**, sifted	Mix; add alternately to creamed mixture with reserved orange peel mixture and beat well. Pour into prepared pan. Bake. Do not remove from pan.
2	tsp	**baking powder**	
1	tsp	**baking soda**	

TOPPING

		reserved fruit, cut into pieces	Combine in saucepan; boil (5-7min). Prick cake; spoon topping over hot cake while still in pan; continue to prick cake until topping is absorbed. Cool slightly; remove from pan.
4	Tbsp	**rum**	
2-3	Tbsp	**coconut cream**	
1	cup	**sugar**	
½	cup	**nuts**, chopped	Garnish.
½	cup	**coconut**	

Louise Thoman, Trumbull

Sunshine State Fruitcake

A great date loaf

Serves: 10-12
Bake: 300° 2 hr (Cold oven start)
Pan: loaf (9x5), greased, floured

4		**eggs**	Combine; beat well with electric mixer.
1	cup	**sugar**	
½	cup	**vegetable oil**	
1	tsp	**salt**	Add; mix well by hand. Pour into prepared pan; place in cold oven. Bake.
1	cup	**flour**, sifted	
1	lb	**dates**, pitted	
4	cups	**pecan** OR **walnut** halves	

Bernie Pratt, Trumbull

Yum Yum Cake

Freezes well without the frosting

Serves: 20
Bake: 350° 45-50 min
Pan: 13x9, greased, floured

2	cups	**sugar**
2½	cups	**coffee**, brewed
½	cup	**margarine**
1	pkg	**raisins**, dark, seedless (15oz)
2	tsp	**cinnamon**
⅛	tsp	**cloves**
¼	tsp	**nutmeg**

Mix together in saucepan; boil (5min). Remove from heat; let cool (1hr); pour into large bowl.

3	cups	**flour**, sifted
2	tsp	**baking soda**
1	cup	**walnuts**, chopped

Add to cooled mixture; mix well then turn into prepared pan. Bake until toothpick inserted in center comes out clean. Frost with cream cheese or butter cream frosting (see Index).

Marie Beaudin, St Petersburg, Fl

Sherry Fruitcake

Full of fruits, nuts and delicious

Yield: 3 loaves
Bake: 300° 1 hr
Pans: 3 loaf (8x4), greased, floured

2	cups	**butter**, softened
1¾	cups	**sugar** (half brown, half white)
2	tsp	**vanilla**

Cream together in large bowl.

7		**eggs**

Add one at a time, beating well after each addition.

4	cups	**flour**, sifted
2	tsp	**baking powder**
2	tsp	**nutmeg**

Combine.

1	cup	**sherry**, sweet
½	cup	**pineapple juice**, unsweetened

Add flour mixture and liquids alternately to creamed mixture; beat until smooth after each addition.

1½	cups	**flour**, sifted
1	cup	**red glace cherries**, halved
1	cup	**candied pineapple**, sliced
3	cups	**coconut**, shredded
3½	cups	**golden raisins**
2	cups	**walnuts**, chopped coarse
2	cups	**pecans**, chopped coarse

Mix all together to coat fruit; add to batter. Mix well; turn into prepared pans. Bake until cake tester inserted in center comes out clean. Cool partially, in pans. Loosen edges; turn out on wire rack to cool completely. Sprinkle cakes with additional sherry. Wrap in sherry soaked cheesecloth; overwrap with foil then refrigerate about 1 week. If cake dries, sprinkle with more sherry.

Joy Tuba, Fairfield

Queen Elizabeth Cake
(British)

A great date treat

Yield: 36 pieces
Bake: 350° 35 min
Pan: 13x9, greased

CAKE

1	cup	**water**, boiling	Pour water over dates and soda; let stand; cool.
1	cup	**dates**, chopped	
1	tsp	**baking soda**	
1	cup	**sugar**	Cream together.
¼	cup	**butter**	
1		**egg**, beaten	Add to above.
1	tsp	**vanilla**	
1½	cups	**flour**, sifted	sift together; add to above and mix well.
1	tsp	**baking powder**	
½	tsp	**salt**	
		reserved date mixture	Add to above; stir in and pour into pan. Bake then cool.
½	cup	**nuts**	

ICING

5	Tbsp	**brown sugar**	Boil (3min); spread on cake.
2	Tbsp	**butter**	
5	Tbsp	**cream**	
		coconut OR **nuts**	Sprinkle on cake.

Gwladys Dorman, Danielson

Date Nut Bran Loaf

A rich delicious loaf cake

Yield: 2 loaves
Bake: 350° 50-60 min
Pan: 2 loaf (8x4), greased

1	cup	**dates**, chopped	In large bowl, pour water over dates and shortening; let cool.
2	Tbsp	**vegetable shortening**	
1½	cups	**water**, boiling	
1		**egg**, lightly beaten	Add to above; mix but do not beat.
2	cups	**flour**, sifted	Mix together; add to date mixture. Stir in just enough to moisten.
2	tsp	**baking soda**	
½	tsp	**cinnamon**	
2	cups	**light brown sugar**	Add then mix in.
1½	cups	**bran cereal**	Stir in gently; pour into prepared pans. Bake. Serve with cream cheese.
⅔	cup	**nuts**, chopped	

Aster Seele, Bridgeport

Pineapple Cream Cake

Fresh fruit would also be a nice topping

Serves: 10-12
Chill: overnight
Pan: spring form (10")

2	pkg	**lady fingers** (3oz,ea)	Line sides and bottom of pan.
11	oz	**cream cheese**, softened	
½	cup	**sugar**	Beat together; set aside.
1	tsp	**vanilla**	
1	pt	**whipping cream**	Beat together until stiff. Fold into cream cheese mixture; pour into lined pan.
¼	cup	**sugar**	
1	can	**pineapple**, crushed (16oz)	Top with pineapple; chill overnight.

Diane Gorman, Trumbull

Pineapple Upside Down Cake

A nice "old" favorite

Serves: 8
Bake: 350° 45 min
Pan: 9" cake

2	tsp	**butter**	Melt in heavy pan (iron skillet is great for this.)
1	cup	**brown sugar**	
1	can	**pineapple**, sliced, drained (16oz)	Arrange pineapple over syrup in pan. Place a cherry in center of each slice.
10		**Maraschino cherries**	
3		**eggs**, separated (reserve whites)	Beat yolks until light and creamy.
1	cup	**sugar**	Gradually beat in.
½	cup	**pineapple syrup**	
1	cup	**flour**	Sift together; mix into above batter.
1	tsp	**baking powder**	
		reserved egg whites	Beat until stiff then fold into batter. Pour into pan. Bake. Invert onto serving plate while still hot.

Virginia Smith, Bridgeport

Prune Spice Cake

Troop 65 BSA's greatest fundraiser

Serves: 10-12
Bake: 350° 1 hr
Pans: saucepan (3qt); tube (9"), greased

CAKE

2	cups	**cake flour**, sifted	
1	tsp	**baking soda**	
¼	tsp	**salt**	Sift together; set aside.
1	Tbsp	**cinnamon**	
1	Tbsp	**nutmeg**	
1	Tbsp	**allspice**	
1	cup	**corn oil**	Beat together in large bowl of electric mixer.
1½	cups	**sugar**	
3		**eggs**	Add one at a time beating well after each addition.
1	tsp	**vanilla**	Add.
1	cup	**buttermilk**	Blend in alternately with dry ingredients (do not beat).
1½	cups	**prunes**, pitted, cooked, chopped	Stir into batter; pour into prepared pan. Bake until done.
1	cup	**walnuts**, chopped	

TOPPING Prepare (15min) before cake is done.

1	cup	**sugar**	Mix all ingredients in saucepan. Bring to a boil over medium heat; boil (10min) stirring occasionally. Remove from oven. While hot, gently and slowly pour glaze over cake. Baste until all glaze is absorbed. Cool completely before removing from pan. Use spatulas to remove, do NOT invert.
½	cup	**buttermilk**	
2-4	Tbsp	**butter**	
¼	cup	**light corn syrup**	
½	tsp	**baking soda**	
½	tsp	**vanilla**	

Al and Eunice Rusinak, Trumbull

Pflaumenkuchen

(German)

Best served the same day but you'll never have any left to worry about

Serves: 12-14
Bake: 425° 45 min
Pan: 13x9, greased

1½	cups	**flour,** sifted	
½	cup	**sugar**	Sift together.
2	tsp	**baking powder**	
½	tsp	**salt**	
1		**egg,** beaten	Combine; stir into dry ingredients.
⅔	cup	**milk**	Mix only enough to dampen flour;
3	Tbsp	**butter,** melted	pour into prepared pan.
4	lb	**purple plums,** fresh	Halve; remove pits. Place in even rows (cut side down) close together, pushing into dough so half of plum sticks out.
2	Tbsp	**butter**	
2	Tbsp	**sugar**	Combine; sprinkle over plums. Bake
¼	cup	**flour**	until done.
½	tsp	**cinnamon**	
		whipped cream	Garnish each serving.

Rotraut Ragusin, New Canaan

Self-Icing Cocoa-Date Cake

A nice addition to your recipe file

Serves: 16
Bake: 350° 30 min
Pan: 14x10, greased

CAKE

1¼	cups	**water,** boiling	Pour water over dates; add soda and
1½	cups	**dates,** chopped	stir. Cool.
1	tsp	**baking soda**	
¾	cup	**vegetable shortening**	
1	cup	**sugar**	Mix together.
2	Tbsp	**cocoa**	
2		**eggs**	
1½	cups	**flour**	Add to above mixture alternately with date mixture. Combine well; beat
¼	tsp	**salt**	(1min); pour into prepared pan.

TOPPING

1	cup	**chocolate morsels**	Combine; sprinkle on top of batter.
½	cup	**nuts,** chopped	Bake.
½	cup	**brown sugar**	

Joyce Reaume, Trumbull

Dark Fruit Cake

Always nice at holiday time

Yield: 1 cake
Bake: 250° 3-4 hr
Pan: 10x3, waxpaper lined

¾	cup	**lard,** melted
4	cups	**sugar**
6		**eggs**

Beat well in large mixing bowl.

3½	cups	**coffee,** black
¼	cup	**whiskey**

Combine.

6	cups	**flour**
2½	tsp	**soda**
½	tsp	**salt**
4	tsp	**cinnamon**
3	tsp	**cloves**

Combine; add to sugar mixture, alternately with above liquids.

¾	cup	**walnuts,** chopped
1	jar	**cherries** (6oz)
1	can	**pineapple,** crushed (8oz)
2	lb	**dried fruit,** mixed
3	lb	**raisins,** mixed
½	cup	**flour**

Coat fruit with a little flour; fold into above then pour into pan. Bake.

Helen Amante, Bridgeport

Round About Marble Cake

A lovely confection

Serves: 16
Bake: 350° 70-80 min
Pan: tube (10"), greased, floured

3	cups	**flour**
2	cups	**sugar**
2	tsp	**baking powder**
½	tsp	**salt**
1	cup	**milk**
1	cup	**butter,** softened
1½	tsp	**vanilla**
3		**eggs**

Combine in large bowl; beat (3min) on medium speed. Pour 4 cups batter into prepared tube pan.

¾	cup	**chocolate syrup**
¼	tsp	**baking soda**

Add to remaining batter; blend then pour over yellow batter in tube pan; swirl. Bake until toothpick comes out clean, then cool (30min). Remove from pan.

GLAZE

¾	cup	**confectioners' sugar**
¼	cup	**chocolate syrup**
1	tsp	**vanilla**
1-2	tsp	**water**

Blend then spoon over cooled cake.

Sophie Lapinski, Stratford

Yankee Plum Pudding

This is a very rich cake. A small piece goes a long way

Yield: 25-30 pieces
Mold: 10 cup, greased
Steam: 4½ hr
Pan: kettle with rack (8qt)

2	cups	**carrots,** cooked, mashed

1	cup	**butter**	
½	cup	**honey**	} Add to carrots then set aside.
1½	Tbsp	**rum**	

2	cups	**flour**	
1	tsp	**cinnamon**	
½	tsp	**cloves**	
½	tsp	**nutmeg**	
¾	lb	**raisins**	
¾	lb	**dates,** chopped	
4	oz	**candied pineapple,** chopped	
4	oz	**candied cherries,** halved	
⅔	cup	**walnuts,** chopped coarse (reserve enough fruit and nuts to decorate mold)	

Combine all but reserved fruit in large bowl. Coat well then add mashed carrots; mix well. Decorate bottom of mold. Spoon mixture in carefully and cover tightly. Place mold on rack in kettle. Add boiling water to within 2" of top of mold. Cover kettle tightly and steam until tester comes out clean. Remove mold from water and allow to cool (30min). Remove pudding from mold when it is completely cooled. Wrap cake in cheesecloth that has been soaked in rum. Wrap again with foil. Place in tightly closed container; store in a cool place (4-6 weeks).

½	cup	**rum** (optional but good)

At 2-week intervals, pour ¼ cup rum over cake for livelier flavor.

To reheat: Place pudding, covered as is, into oven-proof container; cover. Place in 325° oven 30min OR leave wrapped as is and place on rack in kettle; pour in just enough water to reach bottom of pudding (not touch). Cover and simmer (15-20min). Serve with hot lemon sauce. Freezes beautifully for as much as a year.

Plum Pudding Lemon Sauce

Great over gingerbread, too

Yield: 1 cup
Stovetop: 6 min
Pan: saucepan (2qt)

½	cup	**sugar**	} Mix well in saucepan.
1	Tbsp	**cornstarch**	

1½	cups	**water,** boiling

Add slowly, stirring constantly until thickened. Cook 5 minutes longer.

1½	tsp	**lemon juice**	} Add; mix well. Serve hot.
1	tsp	**butter**	

Louise Thoman, Trumbull

Genuine English Christmas Pudding

A wonderful import

Serves: 8
Steam: 4 hr
Pan: crockery bowls or molds (2½qt)
buttered

1	lb	beef suet, chopped
4		eggs, beaten
1	lb	bread crumbs
1	lb	brown sugar
1	lb	raisins
1	lb	currants
½	lb	citron peel, chopped
2		apples, minced
12		almonds, chopped fine
2	cups	flour
½	tsp	baking powder
½	tsp	salt
1	tsp	cinnamon
1	tsp	mace
½	tsp	cloves, ground
1		lemon, juice and rind

Combine well in large bowl.

1	cup	milk
1	cup	whiskey, rum OR brandy

Add only enough liquids to moisten thoroughly. Mix well; pour into prepared molds and cover with buttered paper. Steam in large kettle, in hot water to cover at least ⅔ of mold. Serve with a hard sauce or lemon sauce. Reheat pudding in boiling water (30min).

Alice Simpson, Trumbull

Bien Me Sabe

(Puerto Rican)

"Tastes me good" coconut creme over your favorite cake

Yield: 1 pt
Stovetop: see recipe
Pans: saucepan (2qt); double boiler

3	cups	sugar
⅔	cup	water

In saucepan, over medium heat, stir until sugar melts. Cook without stirring (10-12min).

1⅓	cups	coconut, shredded
3		egg yolks, lightly beaten

Combine in double boiler; pour the above syrup over mixture slowly, while stirring constantly. Cook stirring constantly until well blended and thickened. Pour hot or cold over slices of your favorite cake.

Barbara Schegg, Huntington

Strawberry-Rhubarb Sauce

Great on so many things

Serves: 4-6
Simmer: 5-7 min
Pan: saucepan (2½qt)

1	pkg	**strawberries,** frozen
1	pkg	**rhubarb,** frozen

Thaw; remove ½ cup juice and reserve. Heat fruit in saucepan just enough to warm through.

¼-½	cup	**sugar**
2	Tbsp	**cornstarch**
		reserved juice

Combine then add to fruit; stir constantly. Bring to a boil then turn down heat; cook until juice is thickened and clear (5min). Serve hot over waffles, pancakes or biscuits. Can also be served cold over ice cream, cake or cheesecake.

VARIATION: Can also use 1 pt fresh strawberries and 1 pt fresh rhubarb; add ¼ cup water to juices when mixing with cornstarch.

A Dreamer's Chocolate Sauce

So simple and so good

Yield: 2 cups
Simmer: 30 min
Pan: double boiler

½	cup	**butter**
2¼	cups	**confectioners' sugar**
⅔	cup	**evaporated milk**
3	oz	**unsweetened chocolate,** chopped

Place all ingredients in top of double boiler over simmering water; cover. Cook (30min) (do not stir). Remove from heat; beat with wire whisk until smooth.

To microwave: Assemble in same manner, using pyrex bowl. Cover with plastic wrap. Cook on high (5-6min) then beat until smooth.

Jewelette Thompson, Fairfield

Rum Glaze

½	cup	**sugar**	
½	cup	**orange juice**	In saucepan, cook until dissolved; remove from heat.
½	cup	**rum**	Add to above; mix well. Drizzle slowly over favorite plain cake.

Eileen Buckley, Weston

Orange Glaze

1	cup	**confectioners' sugar,** sifted	
2	Tbsp	**butter** OR **margarine,** melted	Combine; pour and spoon over favorite plain cake.
		grated orange peel	*Add enough to obtain desired consistency.
		orange juice, warm*	

Dorothy Avery, Trumbull

Cooked Cocoa Icing

½	cup	**margarine**	
6	Tbsp	**milk**	Combine in saucepan. Bring to a boil. DO NOT COOK.
4	Tbsp	**cocoa**	
1	lb	**confectioners' sugar,** sifted	Mix well.
1	cup	**pecans,** chopped	Add; mix well. Spread over cake while both are hot.

Jan Anderson, Trumbull

Brandied Sour Cream Topping

1	cup	**sour cream**	
2	Tbsp	**confectioners' sugar**	Mix thoroughly, then chill well. Serve very cold over plain cake, apple pie, fresh or frozen fruit.
2	tsp	**brandy**	
1	tsp	**vanilla**	
⅛	tsp	**nutmeg**	

Sally Easter, Bridgeport

Cocoa Whipped Cream

Yield: 2 cups

1	cup	**heavy cream,** whipped
½	tsp	**vanilla**
2	Tbsp	**cocoa**
2	Tbsp	**sugar**
	dash	**salt**

Mix well then chill. Fill and frost tops of layers.

Doris Bonuomo, Fairfield

Cooked Chocolate Icing

Yield: enough for 13x9 cake
Pan: saucepan (med)

½	cup	**butter**
2	cups	**sugar**
½	cup	**cocoa**
½	cup	**milk**

Combine in saucepan and boil (3min). Cool slightly.

1	tsp	**vanilla**

Add to above then let cool before frosting cake.

LaRay Roiz, Rio Hondo, Tx

La Sauce Chocolat

"So easy you can't believe it"

Yield: 2½ cups
Simmer: 5 min
Pan: saucepan (1½qt)

1	can	**chocolate syrup** (16oz)
1	can	**sweetened condensed milk** (14oz)
½	cup	**butter**

Combine in saucepan; cook over low heat, stirring until butter is melted.

½	tsp	**vanilla**

Add; serve or store.

Virginia Wier, Fairfield

Confectioners' Icing

Regular and chocolate   Yield: Enough for 1 layer

1	cup	**confectioners' sugar**
1	oz	**chocolate**, melted (for chocolate flavor)
2	Tbsp	**milk**, scalded

Combine.

2	Tbsp	**butter**, melted

Add just enough for spreading consistency.

Hint: Add just enough liquid for spreading consistency then add 2-3 tsp marshmallow creme. This prevents crust from forming on any confectioners' sugar frosting.

Barbara Clark, Westport

Super Fluffy Frosting

Yield: enough for 9" cake

1	pkg	**instant pudding** (any flavor) (3⅛oz)
1¼	cups	**milk**

Prepare pudding as directed on box, using milk; set aside.

½	cup	**margarine**
½	cup	**vegetable shortening**
1	cup	**sugar**

In medium bowl, beat well. Add pudding; mix and beat at least 5 minutes on high speed. This is very important.

Jan Simko, Bridgeport

"Cream" Frosting

Tastes just like real cream

Yield: enough for 9" cake
Stovetop: 5 min
Pan: saucepan (2qt)

1	cup	**milk**
1	tsp	**vanilla**
3	Tbsp	**flour**
½	tsp	**salt**

Mix together in saucepan. Cook, over medium heat, stirring constantly, until thickened; cool.

1	cup	**margarine**, softened
1	cup	**sugar**

Beat together; add cooled flour mixture. Beat, using electric mixer on high speed until smooth and light (5-10min).

Gail Lauder, Fairfield

A Variety of Great Icings

Coconut-pecan, chocolate or vanilla

Yield: for 3 rounds (8") or a 13x9

3 ROUNDS	13 x 9	
1 cup	1½ cups	**evaporated milk**
1 cup	1½ cups	**sugar**
3	3	**egg yolks**
½ cup	½ cup	**butter**
	1 tsp	**vanilla**
	3 sq	**semi-sweet chocolate** (optional for chocolate flavor)
1 cup	1 cup	**nuts,** chopped
1⅓ cups	1½ cups	**coconut**

Combine in saucepan; cook over medium heat (12-15min). Stir to prevent scorching. When thickened, add nuts or coconut as desired. Beat lightly with large spoon until thick enough to spread over cooled cake. Great over chocolate or any other cake.

Porter Cleveland, Bridgeport

Flaky Pie Crust

Even better after freezing

Yield: 2 crusts (9")

1 CRUST	2 CRUSTS		
1¼ cups	2 cups	**flour**	Combine in large bowl.
⅓ tsp	½ tsp	**salt**	

½-⅔ cup	1 cup	**vegetable shortening**	Cut in (there is enough shortening when dough almost holds together without liquid).
3 Tbsp	¼ cup	**water,** cold, OR **orange juice**	Add gradually only enough to hold dough together, then mix only enough to moisten. HANDLE GENTLY. Roll out on floured surface.

 Ice water changes the texture of crust. Refrigerate (24hr) after shell has been formed for an even flakier crust that shrinks less. Make fruit pies, freeze, then bake frozen for an even better pie crust.

Esther Sayles, Bridgeport

A Never-Fail Short Crust
(British)

Yield: 2 crusts (9")

1	cup	**vegetable shortening**	} Cream well.
½	cup	**water,** boiling	

1	tsp	**salt**	} Add all at once; stir well. Form into ball; wrap. Chill at least 1 hr. Keeps up to 3 weeks.
3	cups	**flour,** sifted	

Mrs. M. Crisp, Harrow, England

Butter Crust

Yield: 1 crust (9")

1½	cups	**flour**	} Combine in small bowl or processor.
1	tsp	**sugar**	

6	Tbsp	**butter,** cold	Cut into above.
3-4	Tbsp	**ice water**	Add gradually, only enough to hold dough together. Stir only enough to

moisten. Chill (1-2hr). Use with Mississippi Mud Pie or your favorite filling.

Dorothy Ann Webb, Stratford

Pâte Brisée Shell
Great for dessert flan

Yield: 1 crust (9")

2	cups	**flour**	} Cut into flour until mixture is the size of a small pea. (Processor great for this.)
½	tsp	**salt**	
½	cup	**butter,** chilled	
¼	cup	**vegetable shortening**	

3-4	Tbsp	**ice water**	Add, gradually, just enough to hold ingredients together. Form a ball; chill

1 hr or more. When ready to use, knead gently 5-6 times. Roll out gently on lightly floured board; fill with favorite filling and bake according to recipe directions. To bake empty crust, prick well; chill again. When ready, line with buttered waxed paper; fill with beans.

Fully baked: 350° (30min), remove weight and paper; reduce heat 325° (20-25min) longer.

Partly baked: 375° (20-25min) or until pastry has set.

"Cornflake" Crust

Yield: 1 crust (8-9")
Bake: 375° 15 min

1-1½	cups	*flaked or puffed breakfast cereal, crushed well	
¼	cup	**sugar	
¼-½	tsp	cinnamon	

*Approx 4-6 cups whole cereal.
**Eliminate sugar if you use sugared cereal. Combine well.

⅓-½	cup	butter OR margarine, melted

Add; mix well. Press firmly into pie plate; chill. Bake as directed in recipe or bake empty: 375° (15min).

Toasted Almond Crust

Yield: 1 crust (9")
Bake: 400° 10-12 min

1¼	cups	flour
½	cup	butter, softened
¼	cup	almonds, toasted, chopped fine
3	Tbsp	sugar
¼	tsp	salt

Mix well, with hands, until pliable. Press against bottom and sides of plate; flute edges and prick bottom. Bake until golden, then cool completely.

Charlotte Brittain, Fairfield

Graham Cracker Crust

So many variations possible

Yield: 1 crust (9")
Bake: 300° 15 min

1½	cups	graham crumbs, fine*
¼	cup	sugar**
1	tsp	cinnamon (optional)

*OR chocolate or vanilla wafers, zwieback, gingersnaps.
**OR confectioners' sugar.
Mix well.

4-6	Tbsp	butter OR margarine, melted

Drizzle over crumbs; combine. Reserve ¼ cup for topping. Pat over bottom and sides of pan; chill then fill with favorite filling. Without filling: Bake 300° (15min). Cool before filling.

A Cream Cheese Pastry

Great for tarts and turnovers

Yield: 1 crust (9")

1	cup	**flour**, sifted
¼	tsp	**salt**

} Mix.

½	cup	**butter** OR **margarine**
4½	oz	**cream cheese**, softened OR **dry cottage cheese**

} Cut into above well; wrap with waxed paper; refrigerate (12-14hr). Freeze (8-10hr). Roll out between layers of waxed paper to ⅛" thick; fill with favorite filling. Bake as directed in recipe.

Sour Cream Pastry

Great for little meat pies and turnovers

Yield: 1 crust (9")

2	cups	**flour**
½	tsp	**salt** (optional)
¾	cup	**butter**, chilled

} Cut in until mixture is like coarse corn meal.

½	cup	**sour cream**

Add; mix gently with a fork. Knead gently, 3-4 times, on lightly floured board. Wrap in waxed paper; chill at least 2 hr. Can be refrigerated 2 days or frozen 3-4 weeks. Defrost in refrigerator. Bake as directed in recipe.

Chocolate Cookie Crust

Yield: 1 crust (9")

1	pkg	**plain chocolate wafers** (8½oz)

Crush or blend until fine.

½	cup	**margarine**, softened

Add to crumbs in blender; combine.

½	cup	**nuts**, ground fine (optional)
½	tsp	**cinnamon** (optional)

} Add to above; press into pie plate and fill with Hershey Bar pie, cream filling or your favorite.

Nancy Renner, West Haven

Rice Crust

Great for quiches

Yield: 1 crust (9")
Bake: 425° 25 min

1½	cups	**rice,** brown or white, cooked
1		**egg**
1½	oz	**Swiss** OR **sharp cheese** **salt** to taste

Combine; press over pie plate in an even layer. Bake.

Pat Alessio, Trumbull

Kyle's Apple Pie

Always welcome

Serves: 6-8
Bake: see recipe
Pan: pie plate (9")

		flaky Pie Crust (2crust)
1-2	tsp	**oatmeal,** quick
6-10	lg	**apples,** tart, juicy
¼	cup	**brown sugar**
1¼-1½	cups	**sugar**
⅔-1	tsp	**cinnamon**
1	Tbsp	**frozen orange juice** concentrate, undiluted

Line pie plate; set aside.

(Amount depends on how juicy apples are.) Sprinkle over bottom of crust.

Peel; slice; generously fill shell.

Sprinkle over apples; cover with top crust and seal. Cut slits. (Freezes well at this point.) When ready to bake, brush crust with milk or diluted orange juice or a combination of both. Bake: 425° (25min) then 375° (30min) then 325° (30min) longer. Long slow cooking makes the difference – juices thicken like candy.

Hint: To freeze, use aluminum disposable pans. To bake, place frozen, in a heavy skillet. This catches juices and helps brown bottom crust.

Louise Thoman, Trumbull

Harvest Apple Pie

Fall's great bounty

Serves: 6-8
Bake: see recipe
Pan: pie plate (9")

		pastry for 1-crust pie (see Index)	Line plate; set aside.
6-8		**apples,** peeled, sliced	Combine in large bowl to coat fruit well.
2	tsp	**lemon juice**	
½	cup	**sugar**	Combine; pour over apples; toss then arrange apples in shell. Sprinkle remaining sugar over top. Bake: 450° (10min). Reduce to 350° (25min).
½	cup	**brown sugar**	
¼	cup	**flour**	
½	tsp	**cinnamon**	
¼	cup	**heavy cream**	Pour over hot apples, slowly. Bake: 350° (10min). Serve hot.

Fran Sanders, Wenham, Ma

Celestial Dream Pie

"Absolutely delicious"

Serves: 6-8
Bake: 275° (1hr)
Chill: 24 hr
Pans: pie plate (10");
        double boiler

MERINGUE CRUST

4		**egg whites**	Beat in small bowl until stiff.
1	cup	**sugar**	Combine; add to above slowly while continuing to beat until stiff peaks form. Pour into pie plate; form nest. Bake; cool.
¼	tsp	**cream of tartar**	

FILLING

4		**egg yolks**	Cook over hot water, stirring, until mixture is very thick (8-10min); set aside to cool.
½	cup	**sugar**	
⅛	tsp	**salt**	
4	Tbsp	**lemon juice**	
1	Tbsp	**lemon rind,** grated	
1	pt	**heavy cream,** whipped (reserve half) (light cream, add 2 tsp unflavored gelatin)	Fold into egg yolk mixture; spread in meringue shell. Cover with reserved cream.
3¼	oz	**coconut,** grated	Sprinkle on pie; chill. (Grated nuts, chocolate sprinkles can be used as garnish.)

Virginia Smith, Bridgeport

Date Chiffon Pie

A quick, easy dessert

Serves: 6-8
Bake: 325° 25-30 min
Pan: pie plate (8") well greased

12		dates, chopped fine
12		saltines, crushed fine
½	cup	nuts, chopped fine
1	cup	sugar
½	tsp	baking powder

} Mix together well.

3		egg whites

Beat until stiff but not dry.

1	tsp	almond extract

Add to above; mix in then fold into date mixture. Pour into pie plate. Bake; cool thoroughly.

½	pt	cream, whipped

Garnish. (Chiffon pies can be frozen if there is at least ½ cup whipping cream in batter.)

Charlotte Hendry, Stratford

Easy Cranberry Meringue

Serve warm or cold

Serves: 6-8
Bake: 350° 45-50 min
Pan: pie plate (8") buttered

2	cups	cranberries, fresh OR frozen
¼	cup	nuts, chopped
⅓	cup	sugar

} Mix; spread in plate; set aside.

1		egg
½	cup	sugar

} Beat well; add sugar 1 Tbsp at a time, beating until dissolved.

½	cup	flour
4	Tbsp	butter, melted

} Add to above separately; beat well. Pour over berries. Bake until golden. (Double: use 13x9.)

		ice cream OR whipped cream

Serve with garnish of your choice.

Catherine Merillat, Boynton Beach, Fl

Harvest of Sunshine Pie

Lemon slices right in the filling

Serves: 8
Bake: 400° 30-35 min
Pan: pie plate (9")

		pastry for 2-crust pie (see Index)	Line pie plate; set aside.
1	lg	**lemon,** peeled, cut into paper thin slices	Place over bottom of crust.

FILLING

1¼	cups	**sugar**	
2	Tbsp	**flour**	Mix.
⅛	tsp	**salt** (optional)	
¼	cup	**butter,** soft	Cut into above.
3		**eggs,** beaten well (reserve 1 tsp white)	Add; blend well. Pour over lemon slices. Cover with top crust. Seal edges; cut slits.
1	tsp	**lemon rind,** grated	
½	cup	**water**	
		reserved egg white	Brush over crust.
1	tsp	**sugar**	Mix; sprinkle over crust. Bake.
¼	tsp	**cinnamon**	

Esther Sayles, Bridgeport

To avoid soggy pie crusts, brush with beaten eggwhite then sprinkle lightly with flour.

Lemon Sponge Pie

Light and yummy

Serves: 6-8
Bake: see recipe
Pan: pie plate (9")

	pastry for 1-crust pie (see Index)	Line plate; set aside.
2	**eggs**, separated (reserve whites)	Beat yolks until lemony.
¼ cup	**butter**, softened	
1 cup	**sugar**	
pinch	**salt**	Add to above; mix well.
2 Tbsp	**flour**	
1 med	**lemon, juice of**	
1 tsp	**lemon rind**, grated	
1 cup	**milk**	Add to above; beat until well blended.
	reserved egg whites	Beat until stiff; fold into above. Pour into shell. Bake: 400° (10min), 350° (15-20min).

Mary Telford, Trumbull

Peaches 'n Cream

"A nice homey dessert"

Serves: 6-8
Bake: see recipe
Pan: pie plate (9")

	pastry for 1-crust pie (see Index)	Line plate; set aside.
¾ cup	**sugar**	Combine; spread half over bottom of shell.
3 Tbsp	**flour**	
5	**peaches**, fresh, peeled, halved	Cover bottom with peach halves, cut side down. Slice remainder; arrange to fill spaces. Sprinkle remainder of sugar mixture over peaches.
¾ cup	**medium cream**	Pour over peaches.
¼ tsp	**cinnamon**	Sprinkle over top. Cover edge of pie crust with strips of foil to prevent

excessive browning; remove last 15 min of baking. Bake 450° (10min), reduce to 350° (30-35min). Serve warm.

Nancy Henry, Fairfield

 Always use only enough liquid in pie dough to just hold together. Too much liquid will make doughs tough.

Pineapple Pie Like Mom's

A delicious "old fashioned" pie

Serves: 6-8
Bake: 425° 25-30 min
Pans: pie plate (9"); saucepan (med)

		pastry for 2-crust pie (see Index)	Line plate; set aside.
1	can	**pineapple,** crushed, undrained (20oz)	Place in saucepan.
3	Tbsp	**cornstarch**	Combine; add to above; mix. Cook, over medium heat until clear and thickened; remove from heat.
¾	cup	**sugar**	
1		**lemon, juice of**	Add to above; cool. Pour into shell; top with crust and slit crust to vent. Bake until golden.
1	tsp	**lemon rind**	
3	Tbsp	**butter** OR **margarine**	

Gloria Schleicher, Weston

Peaceful Valley Pumpkin Chiffon Pie

An original and delicious

Serves: 8-10
Pans: deep pie plate (10"); saucepan (med)

		pastry for 1-crust pie (see Index)	Line plate; prick. Bake: 500° (10-12min). Cool.
2	env	**gelatin,** unflavored	
⅓	cup	**lt brown sugar,** firmly packed	Combine in medium saucepan.
½	tsp	**salt**	
2	tsp	**pumpkin pie spice**	
3		**eggs,** separated (reserve whites)	Beat egg yolks lightly; add to above.
1½	Tbsp	**molasses**	Add to above; combine well. Bring to a boil, while stirring. Remove from heat; pour into large bowl. Cover; chill (1½-2hr).
½	cup	**milk**	
1	can	**pumpkin** (1lb)	
		reserved egg whites	Beat egg whites until stiff; add sugar gradually, while beating. Fold into pumpkin mixture.
½	cup	**sugar**	
1	cup	**heavy cream,** whipped	Fold gently into above; pour into cold shell.
		walnut halves	Garnish; chill several hours.
		whipped cream	

Elisabeth Kappus, Trumbull

Raisin-Nut Custard Pie

"Very rich"

Serves: 6-8
Bake: 350° 30-35 min
Pan: pie plate (9")

		pastry for 1-crust pie (see Index)	Line plate; set aside.
6	Tbsp	**butter** OR **margarine,** melted	Combine.
1⅛	cups	**sugar**	
3		**eggs**	Add to above, mix well.
¾	cup	**raisins**	
¾	cup	**coconut,** shredded	Stir into above; pour into shell. Bake.
¾	cup	**pecans,** chopped	
1½	tsp	**vanilla**	
		ice cream OR **whipped cream**	Garnish, your choice.

Charlotte Brittain, Fairfield

Pecan Pie

"It was great"

Serves: 8
Bake: 350° 40-50 min
Pan: pie plate (9")

		pastry for 1-crust pie (see Index)	Line plate; set aside.
½	cup	**butter,** very soft	Cream well.
1	cup	**sugar**	
1	cup	**corn syrup,** dark	
½	tsp	**salt**	Add; beat well.
1½	tsp	**vanilla**	
3		**eggs**	Add; beat gently just until blended.
2	cups	**pecans,** chopped coarse	Fold in; pour into shell (place on cookie sheet to protect oven from

drippings). Bake until top is brown and filling is just set when pie is shaken.

Joan Kacin, Trumbull

 To avoid shrinkage of pie crust, place in pie plate without stretching.

Midnight Madness

A rich, creamy, delicious chocolate cheesecake pie

Serves: 8
Chill: overnight
Bake: 350° 30-35 min
Pans: saucepan (1qt);
 pie plate (8")

1		**chocolate cookie crust** (see Index)	Line pie plate; set aside.
8	oz	**cream cheese,** softened	In blender or processor, on high speed, beat until smooth.
½	cup	**mayonnaise**	
½	cup	**sugar**	Add to above; pour into bowl.
2		**eggs**	
6	oz	**semi-sweet chocolate bits,** melted	Combine; add to above mixture and mix well. Pour into reserved shell. Place on cookie sheet. Bake until set; chill.
1	tsp	**vanilla**	

Nancy Gray, Trumbull

Chocolate Angel Pie

Heavenly

Serves: 8
Bake: 300° 50-55 min
Chill: several hr
Pans: saucepan (1qt);
 glass pie plate (9"), greased

MERINGUE SHELL

2		**egg whites**	In small bowl, beat until frothy.
⅛	tsp	**salt**	
⅛	tsp	**cream of tartar**	
½	cup	**sugar**	Gradually add to above, beating until stiff.
1	tsp	**vanilla**	Add; blend.
½	cup	**walnuts** OR **pecans,** chopped fine	Fold into meringue; spoon into prepared plate forming a nest. Bake. Cool thoroughly.

FILLING

4	oz	**German sweet chocolate**	Combine in saucepan; melt, then cool completely.
3	Tbsp	**water**	
1	cup	**heavy cream,** whipped	Combine; fold into chocolate mixture. Spoon into meringue shell. Chill several hours or overnight.
1	tsp	**vanilla**	

Suggestion: Garnish with pecans, walnuts or pistachios, grated; maraschino cherries, chopped fine; coconut; color meringue green.

Zel Finkenstadt, Trumbull

Mississippi Mud Pie

Winner of "Way up North in Mississippi Picnic in Central Park" contest judged by Craig Claiborne

Serves: 8
Bake: 350° 35-40 min
Pans: pie plate (9");
    saucepan (1qt)

1		Buttercrust (see Index)	Line plate; set aside.
½	cup	butter	Combine in saucepan; heat slowly, stirring until melted, then set aside.
3	oz	unsweetened chocolate	
3		eggs	In small bowl, beat until light and frothy.
3	Tbsp	corn syrup, light	Stir into beaten eggs. Add reserved chocolate mixture, stirring continuously. Pour into pie shell. Bake until top is slightly crunchy and filling is set. Do not overcook. Filling should remain soft inside. Best served warm with a scoop of vanilla ice cream on top, but can be served room temp or cold.
1½	cup	sugar	
1	tsp	vanilla	

Dorothy Ann Webb, Stratford

Frozen Raspberry Cream Pie

"Great summer dessert for company"

Serves: 6-8
Freeze: 6-8 hr
Pan: pie plate (9")

		Toasted almond crust (see Index)	Line pie plate as directed. Bake.
2		egg whites	Combine in large mixer bowl. Beat (5min) at medium speed. Increase to high speed; beat until stiff peaks form (10min).
1	pkg	raspberries, frozen, thawed (10oz)	
¾	cup	sugar	
1	Tbsp	lemon juice	
½	tsp	almond extract	
1	cup	heavy cream, whipped	Gently fold into raspberry mixture. Spoon into crust; freeze until firm. Remove (10-15min) before cutting.

Charlotte Brittain, Fairfield

Frosty Cranberry Pie

Pretty at holiday time or a warm summer eve

Serves: 6-8
Freeze: 1 hr or more
Pan: pie plate (9")

1		**pastry shell** OR **crumb crust,** baked, cooled (see Index)	
1	cup	**cranberry orange relish**	Combine.
¼	cup	**crushed pineapple,** drained	
1	qt	**vanilla ice cream,** softened slightly	Blend with above; spoon into shell. Freeze until firm.
½	cup	**cream**	Whip, then garnish pie.
1	tsp	**confectioners' sugar** (optional)	
1-2	Tbsp	**almonds,** slivered, toasted	Sprinkle over top.

Charlotte Mack, Trumbull

Frozen Mocha Pie

Simple but elegant pie for ice cream lovers

Serves: 6-8
Bake: see recipe
Freeze: 24 hr
Pan: pie plate (8-9")

1		**Graham cracker crust** (cinnamon optional) (see Index)	Line pie plate. Bake 375° (5-8min). Cool.
1	pkg	**instant chocolate pudding** (3oz)	In lg bowl, beat well.
1	cup	**milk**	
1	pt	**coffee ice cream,** softened slightly	Gradually add, beating after each addition. Pour into shell; freeze.
			Remove from freezer 15 min. before serving.
		chocolate curls, whipped cream, nuts	Garnish, your choice.

VARIATIONS: Could be made with chocolate cookie or butter crust. Easily doubled and made in 9x13 or 12" spring form pan; decorated for a special occasion.

Theresa Callan, Trumbull

Peanut Butter Pie

So simple, so delectable

Serves: 8
Freeze: 24 hr
Pan: pie plate (9")

1		graham cracker crust (see Index)	Line pie plate; set aside.
4	oz	cream cheese, softened	
⅓	cup	peanut butter, smooth OR chunky	Beat with electric mixer until fluffy.
1	cup	confectioners' sugar	Add, beat until smooth.
½	cup	milk	Add gradually; beat again.
8	oz	whipped topping	Fold in; pour immediately into prepared crust. Freeze; remove when ready to serve.

Nancy Pierce, Salem, NH

Almond Cookies
(Chinese)

A great tradition

Yield: 40 cookies
Bake: see recipe
Pan: cookie sheet, greased

40		almonds, whole	Roast in 325° oven (12-15min); set aside.
2½	cups	flour, sifted	
1	tsp	baking powder	
¼	tsp	salt	Mix together in bowl.
1¼	cups	sugar	
2	cups	almonds, blanched, ground fine	
¾	cup	butter	Add to dry ingredients; work in using hands.
1	Tbsp	sesame seed oil	
2		eggs, beaten	Add to above; mix 1 minute longer. Break off tablespoon size pieces of dough; shape into balls and place on cookie sheet, at least 1 inch apart.
1	tsp	almond extract	
		sesame seed oil	Brush lightly on cookies.
		reserved almonds	Place one on each cookie; press in lightly. Bake: 375° (5min); reduce temp to 325° (8-12min) longer. Cool on rack.

June Prescott-Cohen, Bridgeport

Mandelbrot

(German)

A tea time favorite

Yield: 3 doz
Bake: see recipe
Pan: 2 cookie sheets, greased

½	cup	**vegetable shortening**	Cream well.
1	cup	**sugar**	Add gradually, creaming well.
3		**eggs**	Add, one at a time, beating well after each addition.

3	cups	**flour,** sifted	
3	tsp	**baking powder**	Combine; stir into above.
½	tsp	**salt**	

1	cup	**almonds,** blanched, chopped fine OR **walnuts,** chopped fine	Add to above; stir in well. Divide dough into 2 pieces. Shape each into a roll (8x3). Bake: 350° (30-35min), until golden and tester comes out clean. With serrated knife, slice each

roll crosswise into ½" slices. Place, cut side up, on cookie sheets. Return to oven; toast until golden; turn to brown other side. Cool on rack.

VARIATION: Add 2 Tbsp grated lemon peel, 1 tsp vanilla, ¾ tsp almond extract OR 1 tsp anise flavoring (Italian).

Hannah Bakunin, Bridgeport

Kosut Kifli

(Hungarian)

Delicate half-moon shaped tea cookies

Yield: 3 doz
Bake: 350° 20 min
Pan: 15x10x1, greased

1	cup	**sugar**	Cream well. (Salt free butter helps prevent sticking.)
½	cup	**butter** OR **margarine**	
6		**egg yolks** (reserve whites)	Beat yolks; add to above and mix.

1	cup	**flour**	
¼	tsp	**salt**	Add; mix well.
1	tsp	**baking powder**	

1	Tbsp	**lemon rind**	Mix into above.
1	Tbsp	**lemon juice**	

		reserved egg whites	Beat until stiff; fold into above mixture. Pour into prepared pan.
½	cup	**walnuts,** chopped	Sprinkle over batter. Bake. When cake is cool, cut with round cutter (2½-3").

The first circle will be round. Then move along cutting half circles which form crescents. Remove each piece as you cut. Outside circle of a donut cutter is good for this.

	confectioners' sugar	Sprinkle over each and serve.

Rose Ruskay, Trumbull

Kourabies

(Greek)

Delicious butter cookies!

Yield: 4-5 doz
Bake: 300° 30 min
Pan: cookie sheet

2	cups	**unsalted butter**	} Cream well.
½	cup	**margarine**	
1		**egg**	} Add to above; beat well.
½	cup	**confectioners' sugar**	
¼	cup	**orange juice**	
6	cups	**flour**	Add to batter; mix with hands until dough no longer sticks. Shape dough into long rolls 1" in diameter. Cut on the bias, in 2" pieces, creating a diamond shape. Bake then cool.

confectioners' sugar — Sprinkle heavily over cookies.

Hope Banquer, Fairfield

Hungarian Cookies

Delectable

Yield: 4-5 doz
Bake: 350° 15-20 min
Chill: 10 to 48 hr
Pan: cookie sheets, ungreased

4	cups	**flour**	} Blend well.
2	cups	**butter**	
3		**egg yolks**	Add to above; mix well. Form into 3 balls; chill thoroughly. When ready, roll one ball out to ¼" thickness. (Keep others refrigerated.) Cut into squares (2½").
1	cup	**sour cream** (8oz)	
1	tsp	**vanilla**	

prepared filling* (NOT jams or jellies) — Place scant teaspoon of filling on each square (use sparingly). Bring 2 opposing corners to the center and pinch. Place on cookie sheets. Bake until golden. Cool.

confectioners' sugar — Sprinkle over each before serving.

*Varied FILLINGS can be purchased in bulk in food specialty stores. In supermarkets, cans of fruit, nut or poppy seed fillings can be found; also jars of Lekvar (prune or apricot).

Vivian Kral, Trumbull

Ice Box Hungarian Pastry

Well worth the effort

Yield: 6-8 doz
Bake: 400° 7-10 min
Pan: cookie sheet, ungreased

1½	cups	**butter,** melted	
4½	cups	**flour**	
½	tsp	**salt**	Mix together.
1	Tbsp	**baking powder**	
1	Tbsp	**sugar**	
4		**egg yolks,** beaten	Stir in.
2	cakes	**yeast**	Dissolve yeast in liquids; add to above and mix well. Let rest overnight in cool place. Divide in half, roll out on sugared surface. Cut with cookie cutter or into 1" squares.
½	cup	**milk**	
½	tsp	**vanilla**	
		jam, walnuts OR **poppyseeds**	Place filling (½tsp) on each pastry. Bring four corners to center; pinch. Place on cookie sheets. Bake.
		confectioners' sugar	Sprinkle on pastry.

Sophie Lapinski, Stratford

Scotch Shortbread

Truly Scotch! They melt in your mouth

Yield: 4-5 doz
Chill: 1-2 hr
Bake: 275° 55-60 min
Pan: cookie sheet

1	cup	**butter**	Cream well.
½	cup	**sugar**	Add to above; beat until well blended.
2	cups	**flour**	Add gradually to above, using more flour if needed to obtain a medium stiff dough. Form into a large ball and chill. Roll out on floured surface to ¼" thick; cut into strips ¾x1½". Place on baking sheet ½" apart. With fork, make 3 rows of perforations in each cookie. Bake until lightly browned.
	pinch	**salt**	

Alternate: Pat dough into jelly roll pan (15x10) spread evenly, to edges, using rolling pin. Bake as above. Immediately cut into desired shape then pierce as above.

Mary Telford, Trumbull

Mandelflarn
(Scandinavian)

"Light, delicate, delicious"

Yield: 2 doz
Bake: 300° 16 min
Pans: saucepan (2qt); cookie sheet,
    greased, floured (see below)

¾	cup	**BUTTER**

In saucepan, melt over low heat.

1½	cups	**almonds,** ground
1	cup	**confectioners' sugar**
½	cup	**flour**
¼	cup	**milk**

Add; stir until butter is melted. DO NOT BOIL. (Use shortening or vegetable oil to grease cookie sheet. Salt in butter will cause cookies to stick.) Drop by teaspoonful at least 4" apart to allow for spreading. Bake until light brown. After baking, leave on cookie sheet (2min). Remove carefully; place on brown paper until cool.

Hillandale Gourmet Club, Trumbull

Sour Cream Twists

A great treat

Yield: 4-5 doz
Chill: overnight
Bake: 400° 15-20 min
Pan: cookie sheets, greased

3½	cups	**flour**
1	tsp	**salt**

Mix in a large bowl.

1	cup	**butter** OR **margarine,** softened

Cut in; set aside.

1	cup	**sour cream**
1	cake	**yeast,** crumbled

Place in small bowl; combine and mix until yeast dissolves.

1		**egg**
2		**egg yolks**
1	tsp	**vanilla**

Add to above; blend well. Add to flour mixture; stir until blended. Cover and chill.

1½	cups	**sugar**

Sprinkle (approx 2 Tbsp over area about 18x10). Roll out ⅓ of dough on this sugared area to ¼" thick. Sprinkle sugar as needed to prevent sticking. (Use a total of approx ½ cup for each third of dough.) Cut into strips (1x4). To form cookie, fold as shown at left. Place on cookie sheets. Bake. Repeat using all remaining dough.

Fold Line

Fold Line

Odette Renner, Trumbull

Swedish Cream Wafers

So delicate

Yield: 5 doz
Chill: 1-3 hr
Bake: 375° 7-9 min
Pan: cookie sheet, ungreased

COOKIE

1	cup	BUTTER, softened
⅓	cup	heavy cream
2	cups	flour

Mix thoroughly; chill at least 1 hr. Roll out to ⅛" thickness; cut into rounds (2").

	waxed paper
	sugar

Transfer rounds to paper, heavily sprinkled with sugar. Turn over to coat both sides; place on cookie sheet and prick each in 4 places. Bake until puffy but NOT brown.

CREAM FILLING

¼	cup	BUTTER, softened
¾	cup	confectioners' sugar, sifted
1		egg yolk
1	tsp	vanilla

Mix well; spoon ½ to 1 tsp filling onto half of the cookies. Form a sandwich with remaining half of cookies.

Esther Sayles, Bridgeport

Italian Cookies

Melt in your mouth

Yield: 5-6 doz
Bake: 375° 12-15 min
Pan: cookie sheet, ungreased

6		eggs

Beat until light and fluffy.

5	cups	flour
1½	cups	sugar
3	tsp	baking powder
¾	cup	vegetable oil with some shortening (can use butter)
1	tsp	nutmeg
1	tsp	vanilla
½	tsp	cinnamon
		juice of 1 lemon OR orange

Add to above; mix well. Knead by hand until smooth; roll into 1" balls. Place on baking sheets. Bake until lightly browned but be careful not to overbake. Frost with Butter Cream Frosting (see Index).

Virginia Smith, Bridgeport

Poppy Seed Cookies

A great New England favorite

Yield: 4-6 doz
Chill: 1-2 hr
Bake: 425° 6-8 min
Pan: cookie sheet, greased

¼	cup	**butter,** softened	Cream until smooth.
¼	cup	**vegetable shortening**	
1	cup	**sugar**	Add to above gradually, continue beating.
1		**egg**	Add; beat until fluffy.
3	cups	**flour,** sifted	Sift together well.
¾	tsp	**baking soda**	
½	tsp	**salt**	
½	cup	**buttermilk**	Add alternately with flour, beating well after each addition.
2	Tbsp	**lemon juice**	Add; mix in thoroughly. Chill then roll out on floured surface. Cut in desired shape; place on cookie sheets. Bake until lightly browned; cool on rack.
2	Tbsp	**lemon rind,** grated	
½	cup	**poppy seeds**	

Aster Seale, Bridgeport

Buttercrunch Cookies

A crunchy bar cookie

Yield: 3-4 doz
Bake: 375° 20 min
Pan: 15x10x1, greased lightly

1	cup	**butter,** melted	Mix well.
1	cup	**brown sugar,** dark (packed)	
1		**egg yolk** (reserve white)	Add and mix well.
2	cups	**flour,** sifted	Add; mix well to form firm dough. Pat dough evenly in prepared pan.
1	tsp	**vanilla**	
	pinch	**salt**	
		reserved egg white	Beat lightly; brush over dough.
1	cup	**walnuts,** chopped fine	Sprinkle generously covering all of dough. Bake then cool (3-5min). Cut into squares.

Sonny Weintraub, Bridgeport

Yummy Cookies

Full of fiber and good taste

Yield: 4 doz
Bake: 350° 10 min
Pan: cookie sheets, greased

2		eggs
⅔	cup	vegetable oil
⅔	cup	honey
1	tsp	vanilla
1½	cups	whole wheat flour
½	cup	sunflower meal*
1	tsp	baking soda
1	tsp	salt (optional)

Mix Well.
* Put seeds in blender to make "meal" or use extra ½ cup flour.

1	cup	granola**
½	cup	walnuts OR almonds,** chopped
1	cup	raisins OR dates**
¼	cup	coconut**

Add to above; mix then drop by teaspoon onto prepared cookie sheets. Bake. Let cool 3-4 minutes before removing. Place on brown paper bag to cool.
**Use any combination to yield 2¾ cups total.

June Bartnett, Monroe

Mathew's Favorite Giants

Delicious fun!

Yield: 20-24
Freeze: 3-4 hr
Bake: 375° 22-25 min
Pans: saucepan (2qt); cookie sheets, foil lined

1	cup	BUTTER

In saucepan, melt over low heat.

¾	cup	brown sugar, light, packed
¾	cup	sugar

Stir into above until mixture looks like caramel sauce.

1	tsp	vanilla

Stir in; cool sauce slightly.

2¼	cups	flour
1	tsp	baking soda
1	tsp	salt

Mix in medium bowl; set aside.

2		eggs

Add to cooled butter mixture; stir well. Add all to flour mixture; stir.

2	cups	semi-sweet chocolate morsels (12oz)
2-3	cups	walnuts, chopped

Stir into above; place dough in freezer until stiff (can be kept for weeks). To bake, spoon off ⅓ to ½ cup dough; form into a ball then place on lined cookie sheet. Do not flatten. Bake until golden. Cookies will be 1" thick.

Barbara Ryan, Redondo Beach, Ca

Commissary
Chocolate Chips

Everyone loves chip cookies

Yield: 4-5 doz
Bake: 350° 12-15 min
Pans: cookie sheets

1	cup	brown sugar
1	cup	white sugar
1	cup	butter

Cream together well.

2	tsp	vanilla
2	Tbsp	milk
2		eggs, beaten

Add to above; mix well.

2	cups	flour (can be 1 cup whole wheat)
1	tsp	baking powder
1	tsp	baking soda
1	tsp	salt (optional)

Add to above and blend well.

2½	cups	oatmeal
12	oz	chocolate morsels
1½	cups	nuts, chopped

Stir in. Drop by teaspoonful, or larger if you choose, onto cookie sheets. Bake.

Edith Filliettaz, Southport

Double Chocolate
Bourbon Balls

Great flavor

Yield: 4-5 doz
Stovetop: 3-5 min
Pan: double boiler

2¼	cups	chocolate wafers, crushed (8½oz)
1	cup	nuts, chopped fine
½	cup	confectioners' sugar

Combine in large bowl.

1	cup	semi-sweet chocolate morsels (6oz)

Melt in top of double boiler over hot (not boiling) water; remove from heat.

3	Tbsp	corn syrup
½	cup	bourbon

Stir into above; add to wafer mixture and stir until blended. Let stand 30 minutes then shape into 1" balls.

granulated sugar

Roll balls in sugar. Store in air tight container at least 12 hours to season.

Catherine Merillat, Boynton Beach, Fl

Chocolate Cookies

Decorate for any occasion

Yield: 30-36
Bake: 300° 12 min
Pan: cookie sheet

½	cup	**butter,** softened	} Cream together.
1	cup	**brown sugar,** packed	
1		**egg**	Add to above; cream well.
½	cup	**milk**	Add to above mixture.
1⅔	cups	**flour**	} Sift and add to above.
½	tsp	**salt**	
1	tsp	**baking soda** (scant)	
1	tsp	**vanilla**	} Mix into above; drop by teaspoonful onto cookie sheet. Bake. Frost when cooled. Use Confectioners' Icing (see Index).
2	oz	**unsweetened chocolate,** melted	

Barbara Clark, Westport

Mother's Chocolate Cookies

A great hand-me-down recipe

Yield: 3 doz
Bake: 325° 12-18 min
Pan: cookie sheet, greased

½	cup	**vegetable shortening**	} In medium bowl, cream well.
1	cup	**sugar**	
2		**eggs,** beaten	Add; beat well.
2	sq	**unsweetened chocolate,** melted	} Add; mix well.
½	tsp	**vanilla**	
1	cup	**flour**	} Combine; stir into above.
1	tsp	**baking powder**	
½	tsp	**salt**	
1	cup	**coconut**	} Stir in; drop ty teaspoon onto cookie sheets. Bake.
½	cup	**walnuts,** chopped	

Barbara Gustafson, Lyme

A slice of fresh bread placed in with cookies will keep them fresh longer and will also soften cookies that have hardened.

Fudge Cups

Rich and yummy

Yield: 2 doz
Bake: 350° 15-20 min
Pans: double boiler; cupcake (1¾")

1	cup	**flour**, sifted	Sift together.
¼	tsp	**baking powder**	
¼	tsp	**salt**	
⅓	cup	**butter** OR **margarine**	Cut into above until size of small peas.
1		**egg**, lightly beaten	Sprinkle 3-4 Tbsp egg over above, stirring with fork to form dough. Roll out on floured surface to ⅛" thickness; cut into 3" rounds. Fit one into each cupcake round.
1	cup	**semi-sweet chocolate morsels** (6oz)	Melt in top of double boiler.
⅓	cup	**sugar**	Stir into chocolate. Remove from heat.
1	Tbsp	**milk**	
1	Tbsp	**butter** OR **margarine**	
1	tsp	**vanilla**	
1		**egg**, beaten	Blend into chocolate mixture. Place scant Tbsp filling in each pastry shell.
24		**pecan halves** OR **whole almonds**, blanched	Top each with a nut. Bake.

Odette Renner, Trumbull

Snow Caps

For a special occasion

Yield: 2½ doz
Bake: 325° 20 min
Pan: cookie sheet, brown paper lined

2	lg	**egg whites**	Beat until soft peaks form.
½	tsp	**peppermint extract**	Add slowly.
	dash	**salt**	
⅛	tsp	**cream of tartar**	
¾	cup	**sugar**	Add gradually, beating until stiff.
1	cup	**chocolate chips**	Gently fold in; drop by teaspoon onto lined cookie sheet. Bake.

Kate Benson, Fairfield

Coffee Time Fingers

Great finger food

Yield: 4 doz
Chill: 2-4 hr
Bake: 350° 8-10 min
Pan: cookie sheet, greased

1	cup	**butter**	} Cream until fluffy.
¼	cup	**sugar**	

2½	cups	**flour**	} Add to above; mix thoroughly and chill. Roll out to thickness of a finger; cut in strips (2").
½	tsp	**almond extract**	

1		**egg,** beaten	Brush strips with egg.
15		**pecans,** chopped	} Combine; sprinkle over strips. Bake until golden.
2	Tbsp	**sugar**	

Esther Johnson, Bridgeport

Nutmeg Butter Fingers

A lovely addition to your cookie assortment

Yield: 6 doz
Bake: 350° 13-15 min
Pan: cookie sheet, greased

1	cup	**butter**	} Cream well; beat until fluffy.
¾	cup	**sugar**	

1		**egg**	} Add to above; mix well.
2	tsp	**vanilla**	

3	cups	**flour**	} Combine; add gradually to above; blend well. Shape into fingers (½x3); flatten. Bake. When cool frost with Confectioners' Icing to which rum and vanilla flavorings have been added.
¾	tsp	**nutmeg**	

		nutmeg	Sprinkle lightly over top.

Lillian Thiede, Stratford

 MOLASSES – When molasses is used in a recipe it must be accompanied by baking soda. If honey is substituted no baking soda is needed but baking powder must be increased 1 tsp for each ¼ tsp of soda eliminated.

Grandma Kennedy's Hermits

Dreams of childhood

Yield: 5 doz
Bake: 375° 10-12 min
Pan: cookie sheets, greased

1	cup	sugar	} Cream well.
⅔	cup	vegetable shortening	
⅔	cup	milk	} Add and beat in well.
1	cup	molasses	
1		egg	
3¾	cups	flour	} Combine; add to above and cream well.
1	tsp	salt	
1	tsp	baking powder	
1	tsp	baking soda	
1	tsp	cloves	
1½	tsp	cinnamon	
1	tsp	nutmeg	
1½	cups	raisins	Stir in; drop by teaspoon onto cookie sheets. Bake.

VARIATION: Reduce sugar to ¾ cup; chill or freeze dough thoroughly. Do not grease cookie sheets. Spoon out approx 1 cup dough; shape into 1½" thick rope (8" long). Place on cookie sheets and bake (20min). While still warm, cut into 4" pieces.

Betty Kennedy, E. Greenwich, RI

Ginger Krakles

Spicy, yummy!

Yield: 6-8 doz
Chill: 2 hr
Bake: 350° 8-10 min
Pan: cookie sheets

1½	cups	shortening	} Cream well.
2	cups	brown sugar	
½	cup	molasses	
2		eggs	
5	cups	flour	} Combine; add to above and mix well. Chill until dough can be handled. Form into 1" balls.
4	tsp	baking soda	
2	tsp	cinnamon	
1-2	tsp	ginger	
1	tsp	cloves	
		sugar	Roll each ball to coat well. Place on cookie sheet 3" apart. Bake but do not brown.

Barbara Gustafson, Lyme

Pepparkakor
(Swedish)

A spicy cookie

Yield: 5-6 doz
Chill: overnight
Bake: 350° 5 min
Pan: cookie sheet

1	cup	**butter,** softened	
1½	cups	**sugar**	Cream well.
1	Tbsp	**molasses**	
1		**egg**	

3	cups	**flour**	Sift together; add to creamed mixture above and mix well. Chill thoroughly. Roll dough to ⅛" thickness; cut into desired shapes. Bake. Variation: For a less spicy cookie, can cut seasonings to 1 tsp each cinnamon, ginger and cloves; add 1 tsp cardamom, crushed (optional).
1½	tsp	**baking soda**	
½	tsp	**baking powder**	
3	tsp	**cinnamon**	
3	tsp	**ginger**	
3	tsp	**cloves**	

Nancy Johnson, Shelton

Branfruit Cookies

And good for you, too

Yield: 6-7 doz
Bake: 350° 10-12 min
Pan: cookie sheet, ungreased

¾	cup	**butter**	
½	cup	**brown sugar**	Cream well.
½	cup	**sugar**	

2		**eggs**	
1½	tsp	**vanilla**	Mix well; add to above.
1½	Tbsp	**milk**	

1½	cups	**flour**	
1	tsp	**baking powder**	Combine; add; mix well.
½	tsp	**baking soda**	

1½	cups	**bran cereal**	
¼	cup	**raisins**	Mix together; stir into batter. Drop by rounded teaspoon onto cookie sheet. Bake.
½	cup	**walnuts,** chopped	
¼	cup	**candied fruit peel,** chopped	

Marion Wallin, Devon

Peanut Butter Cookies
(Sourdough)

Another sourdough delight

Yield: 4 doz
Bake: 350° 10-12 min
Pan: cookie sheets, greased

½	cup	vegetable shortening
1	cup	sugar

In a medium sized bowl, cream well.

1		egg
1	cup	sourdough I or II
1	cup	peanut butter

Add to above; mix well.

1	cup	flour
2	tsp	baking powder
¼	tsp	baking soda
½	tsp	salt

Sift together; add to above. Mix well then drop heaping teaspoons of batter onto cookie sheets. Flatten with fork. Bake.

Mary MacInnis, Fairfield

Crème de Menthe Brownies

"Very rich but so delicious"

Yield: 45
Bake: 350° 30 min
Pan: 13x9, greased

BROWNIE LAYER

½	cup	margarine
1	cup +	
	1Tbsp	sugar

Cream together well.

4		eggs
1	cup	flour
1	can	chocolate syrup (8oz)
1	tsp	vanilla

Add to above; beat until smooth.

1	cup	walnuts, chopped

Add to above; spread in prepared pan. Bake then cool.

CREME DE MENTHE LAYER

2	cups	confectioners' sugar
2	Tbsp	butter, melted
5	Tbsp	Crème de Menthe

Blend then beat until creamy; spread on cooled cake.

CHOCOLATE FROSTING

1½	cups	confectioners' sugar
6	Tbsp	margarine, melted
½	cup	chocolate syrup

Beat until smooth; spread over top, allow to set then cut into squares.

Carole Manjoney, Trumbull

Peanut Butter Krispies

"Super and the kids loved them"

Yield: 5 doz
Chill: 2-3 hr

½	cup	**butter,** softened	} Combine well.
2	cups	**peanut butter**	
3	cups	**crisp rice cereal**	} Add to above; mix well. Form into balls (1"); chill.
3½	cups	**confectioners' sugar**	
1	pkg	**semi-sweet chocolate morsels** (6oz), melted	Dip tops of cookies in chocolate to form cap.

Evelyn Fluegge, Trumbull

Tern Tide Bars

Peanut butter and chocolate bits

Yield: 39 (1x3)
Bake: 350° 20-25 min
Pan: 13x9

¾	cup	**butter**	} Cream well.
½	cup	**peanut butter**	
¾	cup	**sugar**	
¾	cup	**brown sugar**	
2	cups	**flour**	} Mix; add to above.
1	tsp	**baking soda**	
1	tsp	**vanilla**	} Add; cream well.
2		**eggs**	
¼	cup	**oatmeal,** quick	} Stir in. Bake until light brown, puffed. Do not overbake.
½	cup	**nuts,** chopped	
1	pkg	**semi-sweet chocolate morsels** (12oz)	

Louise Thoman, Trumbull

Chocolate Date Bars

Excellent!

Yield: 39
Bake: 350° 35 min
Pan: 13x9

1	cup	**dates,** chopped
1½	cups	**water,** boiling
1	tsp	**baking soda**

Combine; let stand a few minutes.

¾	cup	**vegetable oil**
1	cup	**sugar**

Cream together well.

2		**eggs**

Add; beat in well.

1¾	cups	**flour**
¾	tsp	**baking soda**
½	tsp	**salt**
		reserved date mixture

Add to above; mix well then pour into pan.

TOPPING

2	cups	**semi-sweet chocolate morsels** (12oz)
¼	cup	**sugar**
½	cup	**nuts,** chopped

Sprinkle over date mixture. Bake. Cut into bars (1x3).

Vivian Kral, Trumbull

"This Is It" Brownies

"Guaranteed most calories per mouthful"

Yield: 16 pcs (2x2)
Bake: 350° 18 min
Pan: 8x8, greased

2	sq	**unsweetened chocolate**
½	cup	**butter**

Melt together; set aside to cool.

2		**eggs**

Beat until frothy; stir into above.

½	cup	**flour,** sifted
1	cup	**sugar**
1	cup	**nuts,** chopped (optional)

Add to above; mix well. Bake then cool 1 hour.

¼	cup	**butter**
2	cups	**confectioners' sugar**
½	tsp	**vanilla**
¼	cup	**evaporated milk**

Blend in mixer until smooth; spread on brownies; chill at least 10 minutes.

3	sq	**bitter chocolate**
3	Tbsp	**butter**

Melt; blend well. Spread on brownies; chill at least 15 minutes. (If doubled, use 13x9.)

Kathy Miller, Easton

Choco-Chewy Upside-Down Brownies

"A moist fudgy brownie with chewy top"

Serves: 12
Bake: 30-40 min
Pan: 13x9, greased

| 1 | can | **Cherry Pie Filling** (21oz) | Spread over bottom of prepared pan. |

2¼	cups	**flour**	
1½	cups	**sugar**	Stir together to combine, in a bowl.
¾	cup	**cocoa**	
1½	tsp	**baking soda**	
¾	tsp	**salt**	

1½	cups	**water**	Combine; add to flour ALL AT ONCE. STIR just enough to moisten. Pour over filling. Bake: 350° (30-40min). Cool in pan (10min); invert and cool thoroughly.
½	cup	**vegetable oil**	
¼	cup	**vinegar**	
1½	tsp	**vanilla**	

Marjorie Dickey, Fairfield

Cake-like Brownies

Especially for dieters

Yield: 8 squares
Bake: 350° 15 min
Pan: 8x8, vegetable spray

2		**eggs**	
2	env	**Alba 77** (chocolate)	Beat together with electric mixer. Pour into prepared pan. Bake then cool and cut into squares. Best when doubled (11x7).
1	cup	**Cheerios** OR **Rice Krispies**	
1	sm	**banana**	
1	tsp	**cream of tartar**	
½	tsp	**baking soda**	
¼	tsp	**cinnamon**	

Judy Webster of Thin's Inn, Monroe

 To soften brown sugar, add a wedge of apple or half a slice of bread. It really works.

Snack Bars

A great way to get good nutrition into the kids

Yield: 30 bars
Bake: 350° 30-35 min
Pan: 13x9, greased

1½	cups	**flour,** unbleached	
1	cup	**whole wheat hot cereal,** uncooked	Mix together.
¾	cup	**dark brown sugar**	
¾	cup	**butter**	Cut in until particles resemble coarse meal; press half of mixture into pan.
2	cups	**apple butter**	Mix together; spread evenly over lined pan.
1	cup	**raisins**	
1	cup	**nuts,** chopped	Mix nuts with remaining crumb mixture; sprinkle over filling. Bake until golden brown. Cool; cut into bars.

Marguerite Weeks, Monroe

Apricot Nut Squares

Oatmeal makes it really nutritious

Yield: 24-36
Bake: 350° 30 min
Pan: 9x9, greased

½	cup	**margarine,** softened	Beat until fluffy.
½	cup	**brown sugar,** packed	
1	cup	**flour,** sifted	
¼	tsp	**baking soda**	Combine well; stir into above.
½	tsp	**salt**	
1½	cups	**oatmeal**	Add and blend thoroughly. Press ⅔ of mixture into pan.
1-1½	cups	**apricot preserves** (12oz)	Combine; spread over crumb mixture. Sprinkle remaining crumb mixture over and pat lightly. Bake until golden. Cut while slightly warm.
¼-½	cup	**nuts,** chopped	

Lynne Dawson, Salem, NH

 OATMEAL is made from hulled oats that are softened by steam and flattened by rollers. Quick oats are steamed longer.

Krispies Date Squares

Three layers of good taste

Yield: 24 bars
Simmer: 3 min
Bake: 375° 10-12 min
Pans: saucepan (2qt); 11x7 OR
9x9, ungreased

CRUST

1	cup	**flour**
½	cup	**brown sugar,** packed
½	cup	**butter,** softened

Combine; mix until crumbly then press into pan. Bake until golden.

FILLING

1	cup	**dates,** chopped
½	cup	**sugar**
½	cup	**butter**

Combine in saucepan; bring to a boil while stirring constantly. Simmer (3min).

1		**egg,** beaten

Blend ¼ cup hot mixture into egg; return to saucepan. Cook just until mixture bubbles while stirring constantly. Remove from heat.

2	cups	**crisp rice cereal**
1	cup	**nuts,** chopped
1	tsp	**vanilla**

Stir into date mixture; spread over baked crust then cool completely.

FROSTING

2	cups	**confectioners' sugar**
3	oz	**cream cheese,** softened
2-3	tsp	**milk**
½	tsp	**vanilla**

Beat together until smooth; spread over filling.

Chris Henschel, Fairfield

Lekvar Squares
(Hungarian)

Yield: 35-40 (3x3)
Bake: 375° 30-35 min
Pan: 15x10

2	cups	**flour**	Sift together.
1	tsp	**baking powder**	
¼	tsp	**salt**	
1	cup	**butter** OR **margarine**	Add; cut in well.
4		**egg yolks** (reserve whites)	Add to above; mix well then spread over bottom of pan.
1	cup	**sugar**	
1		**lemon**, juice of	
8	oz	**lekvar** OR **apricot** OR **raspberry jam**	Spread over dough in pan.
		reserved egg whites	Beat until stiff.
			Combine; fold into egg whites; spread over filling. Bake then cool and cut into squares. Can be topped with whipped cream or ice cream.
8	oz	**walnuts**, chopped	
3	Tbsp	**sugar**	

Ann Hawie, Stratford

Marcie's Favorite Pineapple-Cheese Bars

Great for a church social or shower

Yield: 36
Bake: see recipe
Pans: 13x9; saucepan (1½qt)

CRUST

2	cups	**flour**	
⅔	cup	**brown sugar** (lt), packed	Combine in bowl (med).
½	tsp	**salt**	

⅔	cup	**margarine**	Cut into above until crumbly.
1	cup	**walnuts**, chopped	Stir into above. (Reserve 1 cup of mixture.) Press remainder into pan. Bake 350° (15min) or until lt brown.

2	tsp	**flour**	
		reserved cup of mixture	Combine; set aside.

FILLING

½	cup	**sugar**	Combine in saucepan.
2	tsp	**cornstarch**	

2		**egg yolks**, lightly beaten	Stir in; cook (med heat) stirring until thickened. Remove from heat.
1	can	**pineapple**, crushed, undrained (8oz)	

1	cup	**coconut** (optional)	Add; stir well; spread over baked layer.

TOPPING

8	oz	**cream cheese**	Blend together well.
¼	cup	**sugar**	

1		**egg**	Add and beat well. Spread over pineapple. Sprinkle reserved crumb mixture over top. Bake: 350° (20-25min). Be careful not to overbake. Cool before cutting.
2	tsp	**milk**	
1	tsp	**orange juice**	
½	tsp	**vanilla**	

Lynne Dawson, Salem, NH

Cheesecake Bars

They are delicious

Yield: 16
Bake: see recipe
Pan: 8x8

⅓	cup	butter	} Cream together well.
⅓	cup	brown sugar, packed	

1	cup	flour	} Add to above; mix together to form crumb mixture (reserve 1 cup for topping). Press remainder into pan. Bake: 350° (12-15min) until lightly browned.
½	cup	walnuts, chopped fine	

FILLING

¼	cup	sugar	} Beat together until smooth.
8	oz	cream cheese, softened	

1		egg	} Add to cheese mixture; beat well. Spread over baked crumb crust; sprinkle with reserved crumb mixture. Bake: 350° (25min). Cool; cut into 2" squares.
2	Tbsp	milk	
1	Tbsp	lemon juice	
½	tsp	vanilla	

Edna May Hoad, Bridgeport

Luscious Lemon Cream Bars

A great chilled creamy dessert

Yield: 15
Bake: 350° 20 min
Pan: 13x9

1½	cups	flour	} Mix together; press into pan. Bake until lightly browned. Cool thoroughly.
¾	cup	margarine	
¾	cup	walnuts, chopped	

8	oz	cream cheese	} Beat together; spread over base.
1	cup	confectioners' sugar	
1½	cups	frozen whipped topping, thawed (reserve ½ cup) (16oz)	

2	pkg	lemon pudding, instant (3¾oz,ea)	} Beat together; spread over cheese mixture.
3	cups	milk	

	reserved whipped topping	Spread over top; refrigerate overnight for easier handling.

Ruth Gilchrist, Wenham, Ma

Canadian Tea Cakes

Yield: 64 (1" squares)
Bake: see recipe
Pan: 8x8, buttered

¼	cup	**confectioners' sugar**
1	cup	**flour**

} Combine.

½	cup	**butter**

Cut into above until texture of fine meal; pat into baking pan. Bake: 350° (10min) until golden.

2		**eggs**
1½	cups	**light brown sugar**
¼	tsp	**salt**
1	tsp	**vanilla**
1	cup	**coconut**
1	cup	**walnuts,** chopped
2	Tbsp	**flour**
½	tsp	**baking powder**

While above is baking, mix together. Remove base from oven when golden; spread mixture over base while still warm; return to oven. Bake: 350° (35min). Cut in squares; serve when cooled. Doubles well.

Emily Semonick, Trumbull

Peanut Butter Squares

Quick to make

Yield: 8 doz (1")
Pans: double boiler;
9x13, buttered

1	lb	**confectioners' sugar**
½	cup	**graham cracker crumbs**
1	cup	**peanut butter**
1	cup	**butter** OR **margarine,** melted

Mix by hand until well blended (will be very thick). Spread in dish smoothly; refrigerate (20min).

1	pkg	**chocolate morsels,** semi-sweet (12oz) OR **milk chocolate,** melted

Spread evenly over above; refrigerate until firm (1hr).

Joyce Harney, Stratford

399

409

411

412

corn pudding   pp 228

Our Special Blend a cookbook
226 Mill Hill Ave.
Bridgeport, Ct. 06610

Please send me _____ copies $13.95 ea $ _____
Add postage/handling $ 1.50 ea $ _____
Add gift wrap (if desired) $ 1.50 ea $ _____

                 Total Enclosed $ _____

NAME _____

ADDRESS _____

CITY _____

STATE _____ ZIP _____

Make checks payable to:
The Rehabilitation Center of Eastern Fairfield County
No COD's, foreign checks or currency accepted

FROM: Our Special Blend
226 Mill Hill Avenue
Bridgeport, Ct. 06610

TO:
NAME _____
ADDRESS _____
CITY _____
STATE _____ ZIP _____

Mailing Label – Please Print

Our Special Blend a cookbook
226 Mill Hill Ave.
Bridgeport, Ct. 06610

Please send me _____ copies $13.95 ea $ _____
Add postage/handling $ 1.50 ea $ _____
Add gift wrap (if desired) $ 1.50 ea $ _____

                 Total Enclosed $ _____

NAME _____

ADDRESS _____

CITY _____

STATE _____ ZIP _____

Make checks payable to:
The Rehabilitation Center of Eastern Fairfield County
No COD's, foreign check or currency accepted

FROM: Our Special Blend
226 Mill Hill Avenue
Bridgeport, Ct. 06610

TO:
NAME _____
ADDRESS _____
CITY _____
STATE _____ ZIP _____

Mailing Label – Please Print

Our Special Blend a cookbook
226 Mill Hill Ave.
Bridgeport, Ct. 06610

Please send me _____ copies $13.95 ea $ _____
Add postage/handling $ 1.50 ea $ _____
Add gift wrap (if desired) $ 1.50 ea $ _____

                 Total Enclosed $ _____

NAME _____

ADDRESS _____

CITY _____

STATE _____ ZIP _____

Make checks payable to:
The Rehabilitation Center of Eastern Fairfield County
No COD's, foreign check or currency accepted

FROM: Our Special Blend
226 Mill Hill Avenue
Bridgeport, Ct. 06610

TO:
NAME _____
ADDRESS _____
CITY _____
STATE _____ ZIP _____

Mailing Label – Please Print

Unless otherwise instructed, all books will be sent to the same address. Please enclose specific instructions and complete names and addresses if you wish any books sent as gifts.

Unless otherwise instructed, all books will be sent to the same address. Please enclose specific instructions and complete names and addresses if you wish any books sent as gifts.

Unless otherwise instructed, all books will be sent to the same address. Please enclose specific instructions and complete names and addresses if you wish any books sent as gifts.